CONTEMPORARY AMERICAN JUDAISM

Contemporary American Judaism

TRANSFORMATION AND RENEWAL

DANA EVAN KAPLAN

COLUMBIA UNIVERSITY PRESS   NEW YORK

COLUMBIA UNIVERSITY PRESS
Publishers Since 1893
NEW YORK   CHICHESTER, WEST SUSSEX

Copyright © 2009 Columbia University Press
Paperback edition, 2011

Library of Congress Cataloging-in-Publication Data
Kaplan, Dana Evan.
   Contemporary American Judaism: transformation and renewal / Dana Evan Kaplan.
     p.   cm.
   Includes bibliographical references and index.
   ISBN 978-0-231-13728-7 (cloth : alk. paper)—ISBN 978-0-231-13729-4 (pbk. : alk. paper)—
ISBN 978-0-231-51041-7 (ebook)
   1. Judaism—United States—History—20th century.   2. Judaism—21st century.   3. Spiritual
life—Judaism.   4. Jews—United States—Identity.   5. Jews—United States—Social conditions.
I. Title.
   BM205.K365 2009
   296′.0973—dc22

                                                                                    2008052006

To all who have kept the flame of
Judaism alive in Southwest Georgia

Be careful that you do not forget the Lord your God, failing to observe His commandments, His laws and decrees that I am giving you this day. Otherwise, when you eat and are satisfied, when you build fine houses and settle down, and when your herds and flocks grow large and your silver and gold increase and all you have is multiplied, then your heart will become proud and you will forget the Lord your God, who brought you out of Egypt, out of the land of slavery.

—Deuteronomy 8:11–14

Contents

Foreword

Rabbi David Ellenson

Contemporary American Judaism: Transformation and Renewal offers a much-needed and unique historical perspective on the modern American Jewish landscape. While works such as *American Judaism* by Jonathan Sarna and *Jews of the United States* by Hasia Diner provide valuable portraits that cover the panorama of Jewish history in the United States, Dana Kaplan offers a study that focuses on the contemporary state of American Jewish life. His narrative of present-day American Judaism is always placed in an informed historical context and his analysis of developments in American Judaism over the last sixty years is designed to engage the reader. Indeed, the very titles of so many of his chapters—"The Reengagement with Spirituality," "The Rise and Fall of American Jewish Denominationalism," "Facing the Collapse of the Intermarriage Stigma," "Inclusivity as a Social Value," "The Popularization of Jewish Mystical Outreach," and "Herculean Efforts at Synagogue Renewal"—reflect his comprehensive and pointed approach to the topic of his book.

Indeed, Kaplan is hardly a disinterested observer of the modern American Jewish scene, and his autobiography reflects many of the themes he presents in his work. Raised in a Reform temple, he attended the modern Orthodox Ramaz School in Manhattan throughout his elementary school years, and he ultimately received his rabbinical ordination at Hebrew Union College in Jerusalem and his doctorate in American Jewish history at Tel Aviv University under the direction of Lloyd Gartner. Kaplan has served congregations and taught at colleges throughout the United States, and his own commitments embody much of the boundary crossings and ferment he describes as taking place in American Judaism today. One of the great virtues of *Contemporary American Judaism* is that one sees the passion Kaplan has for his subject on virtually every page of his work. At the same time, he never allows those passions to compromise his academic integrity and his observations remain judicious and stimulating even as they are challenging and provocative.

As I read this book, I was impressed by its successful identification of the many sociological factors that have become seminal in shaping the contours of American Judaism as we know it today. Kaplan is well aware that after the 1960s the American Jewish community was no longer an immigrant community seeking to adjust to the United States. Old ethnic patterns that formerly preserved and divided the Jewish religious community into three distinct denominations were no longer present and the rivalry that had existed between American Jews of German and Eastern European descent was little more than a historical memory for most American Jews. While large numbers of Israeli, Russian, Iranian, and South African Jewish immigrants have come to the United States in recent years, they now enter—unlike the Eastern European Jews of the 1880s—into a well-established and fully organized American Jewish community that is composed largely of fourth, fifth, and sixth generation American Jews. The cultural overlap among the overwhelming majority of American Jews is highly pronounced. As a result, the attitudes and beliefs that had so sharply divided Reform from Conservative Jews in the first half of the twentieth century now have been blurred for many of these people, and a permeability has emerged that allows for crossover between the disparate movements as well as the emergence of new movements and new forces in American Jewish religious life.

Larger societal developments occurring in the wider American society in addition to internal communal changes have contributed to this crossover. While the rise in America during the 1960s of what came to be known as the "new ethnicity"—what Kaplan points to as "symbolic ethnicity"—has allowed present-day Jews to express ethnic allegiances in an unself-conscious and public way that would have been unthinkable for American Jews of the 1940s and 1950s, Kaplan understands quite well that this embrace of ethnicity does not represent a retreat from American life. Kaplan correctly emphasizes that these overarching trends in American life have led to religious revival and a renewed search for religious and spiritual meaning in modern-day America, and he points to the decisive impacts these trends have had in promoting and shaping American Jewish religious expressions through the last fifty years. These dynamics of the late 1960s and 1970s led to the appearance of the havurah movement and the appearance of what is today called Jewish Renewal owes its origins to those years. The impact of feminism on organized Jewish religious life was first evidenced with the appearance of the women's group Ezrat Nashim during these years as well as the ordination of Rabbi Sally Priesand by Hebrew Union College–Jewish Institute of Religion in 1972 and Rabbi Sandy Sasso at the Reconstructionist Rabbinical College shortly thereafter. Feminist religious thinkers and activists such as Judith Plaskow, Rachel Adler, Marcia Falk, Paula Hyman, and Blu Greenberg rose to maturity during these years, and Kaplan discusses their influences on present-day American Judaism with great sophistication.

Kaplan is also extremely aware that the past four decades have witnessed an attenuation of traditional Jewish associational and kinship patterns that previously promoted Jewish affiliation and commitment among large numbers of American Jews. As the election of Barack Obama as president indicates, older forms of prejudice and discrimination—while they have surely not disappeared—just as surely do not possess the power and influence they once did. American Jews have now been fully accepted in an unprecedented way into American life, and contemporary Jews of all stripes and ethnic backgrounds as well as sexual orientations are now full participants in the cultural, social, political, and economic spheres of the United States. As Jews have become fully accepted by gentiles as social equals and as traditional Jewish attitudes that opposed exogamy have weakened, intermarriage rates have soared, and traditional Jewish communal attitudes opposing exogamy have undergone revolutionary changes. Kaplan pays keen attention to all these trends and observes that younger American Jews do not feel the sting of social antisemitism that their forebears did, and this informs their attitudes to Israel and Jewish identity and commitment in ways that are different than their parents and grandparents. These changes have been felt among all American Jews across denominational lines and have propelled many Jews to seek out Jewish community and religion with an indifference to denomination that was unknown earlier in the century while promoting changes within and growth beyond the traditional Jewish religious movements.

Kaplan is at his challenging best as he develops this theme and explains why more and more American Jews are indifferent to denominational labels in their highly eclectic and idiosyncratic search for meaning and community. To employ Leo Baeck's felicitous phrase, Kaplan argues that more and more Jews are likely to move away from "an adjectival Judaism," meaning a Judaism where the adjective—whether it be *Reform, Conservative, Reconstructionist, Renewal,* or *Orthodox*—is more important than the noun *Judaism.* They will not hesitate to move among movements and individual rabbis and religious teachers as they engage in their own personal religious and communal quests. The distinctions in theology and ideology that are so crucial to the elite leaders of the different movements are increasingly irrelevant to these Jewish folk, and many of the debates that occupy the leaders of these movements are regarded by many of these Jews as needlessly divisive and extraneous to the larger task of creating a Judaism that is vital and vibrant in the face of the challenges that modern-day America presents to Jewish life and commitment.

Of course, denominations are in no immediate danger of extinction. Any elementary course on sociology can tell us that well-established and powerful institutions never disappear quickly. Furthermore, as Kaplan points out, many of these movements and their institutions are not blind to these trends, and they strive mightily to reinvent and adapt themselves to these forces of change. He recognizes that this has led to unprecedented institutional cooperation across denominational lines and that some of the most significant transdenominational programs for the renewal and reconfiguration of synagogue life have emerged within denominationally sponsored structure. However, none of this can hide the larger and more pervasive reality at play in American Judaism today: all surveys of the American Jewish community indicate that "unaffiliated" is the largest growing category among contemporary American Jews, even as many of these Jews seek spiritual meaning and renewal.

As we move into the twenty-first century, Kaplan demonstrates that the tasks confronting Jews in the modern American context—whatever the ideological distinctions and organizational commitments that mark and sometimes divide them—are essentially identical. The charge that confronts all of them is how to make Judaism relevant, compelling, joyous, meaningful, welcoming, comforting, and challenging to American Jews who, as "sovereign selves," have infinite options open before them. The challenge, beyond and within denominations, is whether Judaism can succeed in doing this for large numbers of people.

American Judaism today stands at a crossroads where trends of weakened Jewish commitment and attachment compete with pockets of intense Jewish revival and knowledge—and all this takes place across traditional denominational lines and institutional patterns. The task of all concerned and committed Jews will be to strengthen these pockets of revival and knowledge, and this task will compel us to recognize that such revival and knowledge must take place both within and beyond traditional Jewish denominational and institutional structures and affirmations. The future of Judaism in the United States depends upon the ability of all Jews to maintain and revitalize Jewish religious tradition in light of the conditions that confront our community today. *Contemporary American Judaism: Transformation and Renewal* helps us understand and appreciate those conditions in an insightful and complete way. We are indebted to Dana Kaplan for the illumination his work sheds on the contemporary American Jewish condition and for his optimism that American Judaism will succeed in adapting to the novel conditions of the contemporary setting.

Preface

This book is a popular overview of how American Judaism has changed since 1945, with the focus on the last couple of decades. It is not a work of original research, nor is it an attempt to argue a boldly innovative central thesis. Rather, it is a broad description of how American Judaism has been molded by Jews and other people in response to societal trends and attempts to highlight some of the most important changes. These changes have been significant, indeed so significant that I feel no hesitation in using the word *transformation* in the title. Not only have the style and substance of the activities that we associate with American Judaism changed, but so has the way that American Jews understand their religious identity. In this preface, I want to briefly explain what Judaism is. In the introduction that follows, I will provide the context for understanding how Judaism developed in contemporary America.

The title of this book is *Contemporary American Judaism*. It is difficult and perhaps impossible to separate America from Judaism in the words *American Judaism*. American Jews are products of American culture and society to the extent that their Judaism is inseparable from American values. As a consequence, the Judaism that American Jews create and observe is shaped and reshaped by their distinctive conceptions as Americans. Judaism in the United States deserves the adjective *American* not just because it is the Judaism practiced there but also because it is the form of contemporary Judaism molded by the American experience.

Social scientists have found that many American Jews see themselves in a fundamentally different way than they did just a generation ago. In the 1950s, American Jews saw themselves as Americans and as Jews but they made a clear distinction between these two identities. Today, they no longer see their Jewish selves separate from their American selves. Rather, they integrate or confuse—depending on one's perspective—ideas and categories that are drawn from different sources. Some American Jews see their Jewishness as primarily ethnic, while others emphasize that they are Jewish because of their Judaic religious belief. Virtually all are proud to be Americans, but they differ dramatically in the way that they mediate between their Jewish and American identities. This book is concerned with only one aspect of that struggle—how American Jews have continually been adjusting their conceptions of Judaism according to their evolving expectations drawn from their daily lives.

On account of the fact that this book deals with the topic of American Judaism, it is important to explain what I mean by the term *Judaism*. The suffix *ism* would appear to indicate that Judaism is an ideological system, similar to communism, Zionism, capitalism, and so forth. This impression, however, is misleading because there is no official Jewish religious creed that all Jews accept. Likewise, the prefix suggests that Judaism is the belief in Judah or, alternatively, the belief held by those of Judah. This too is problematic because while Judea was the sole surviving province after the destruction of the northern Kingdom of Israel by the Assyrians in 722 BCE, the Jewish people identify themselves as the community of Israel rather than as Judeans. The modern Hebrew word for Judaism is *Yahadut*, but the closest biblical term may be *daat*, which literally means "knowledge" but is usually translated as "religion." Neither word is a direct parallel of the English word *Judaism*. Therefore, there is no Hebrew word that is a literal equivalent of the word *Judaism* or a direct equivalent of the concept that it represents.

Many writers have had difficulty in defining the term *Judaism*. I have several shelves of books that promise to introduce the curious reader to Judaism. I looked through them in preparation for the writing of this preface in search of a good, simple definition for what Judaism was and is. Unfortu- nately, I had a great deal of trouble finding any definition, much less a rich and comprehensive one. Many of the authors dodged the question entirely, writing that Judaism was and is the religion practiced by the Jews. They then went on to discuss the basic beliefs, practices, holidays and life cycle of the Jewish community without ever returning to the question of what Judaism is. Others tried to define it, but seemed to get bogged down in either excessive details or vagueness. Virtually all of the more perceptive authors immediately launched into a discussion of the "difficulties" or "problems" involved in defining Judaism.

While there was no clearly delineated concept of Judaism in the Talmudic period, later Jewish thinkers found an interesting rabbinic story told of three potential converts that seemed to suggest how the sages understood what constituted the core of the Jewish religion. Even at such an early stage, it is apparent that conceptualizing a clear and comprehensive definition of the Jewish religion was not an easy task. The three potential converts approach first Shammai, and then Hillel, two of the early sages. Each prospective convert asks to be converted, but each has a very specific condition. One wants to be converted in order to become the kohen gadol, the high priest who officiated in the Temple. Another wants to convert on condition that he need only accept the written Torah and not the oral Torah. The third will convert on condition that the sage teach him the entire Torah while the perspective convert is standing on one foot. Shammai chases all of the three prospective converts away, but Hillel accepts each of them and then goes about figuring out the most effective technique to help them understand why their condition is inappropriate or unreasonable. In the case of the person who demanded to be taught the whole of the Torah while standing on one foot, Hillel says, "What is hateful unto you, you shall not do to others. The rest is commentary. Now go and study" (Shabbat 31a).

While Hillel's definition is extremely broad and perhaps overly vague, a number of modern thinkers embraced the idea of reducing the teachings of the Torah to a single concept. The Zionist essayist Ahad Ha-Am wrote that if the same person had come to him, demanding to be taught the whole of the Torah while standing on one foot, he would have responded with the biblical citation from the Torah: "Thou shall not make unto thee a graven image, nor any manner of likeness" (Exodus 20:4). British Masorti Rabbi Louis Jacobs explains that Ahad Ha-Am is saying that "the essence of Judaism consists in the elevation of the ideal above all material or physical forms or conceptions." If we could actually use this definition under all circumstances, then our problem would be settled, but life is seldom so simple. There is just too much variation to Judaism, certainly when one compares the Judaism that one finds in different societies over the course of hundreds of years of history. Jacobs himself admitted that, even though many Jewish thinkers had tried to define the essence of Judaism, "this is an extremely difficult—some would say impossible—task, since the differing civilizations, Egyptian, Canaanite, Babylonian, Persian, Greek, Roman, Christian, Muslim, with which Jews came into contact, have made their influence felt on Jews and through them on Judaism itself. It is precarious to think of Judaism in monolithic terms."[1]

The most satisfying definition of Judaism, for me, would be an essentialist one. An essentialist definition would ascribe an essence to the subject, which would usually be accompanied by a set of defining characteristics. Without this essence, it would no longer be that thing. If we define a clock as an object that tells time, anything that does not do that would not be a clock. Orthodox Jews to this day hold that Judaism is the religion followed by Jews who believe that God gave the Torah—both written and oral—to Moses at Mount Sinai. This revelation was passed down from generation to generation exactly as it had been received. Any one who does not adhere to these beliefs, they argue, is not practicing "Torah-true" Judaism. Leaving aside the misnomer of calling Talmudic Judaism "Torah-true," these Orthodox Jews are holding to an essentialist definition.

Those who do believe that there is an essence to Judaism believe that it is therefore possible to speak of "normative Judaism," which posits that there is one long unbroken chain of tradition that the heterodox (the non-Orthodox) have deviated from. Pirkei Avot (the Ethics of the Sages) begins with the Mishnah (the early part of the Talmudic literature) describing how the oral tradition was passed down from God to Moses, and then to a sequence of teachers and scholars. Orthodox Jews to this day believe that an unbroken tradition was indeed transmitted from generation to generation and that the Judaism that they believe in and practice today is virtually identical to that of not only a thousand years ago but also of two thousand and even three thousand years ago.

While an essentialist definition would be useful, it does not reflect the reality of Jewish religious diversity. Some of the new Jewish religious philosophies and approaches developed over the last two hundred years denied that the Jews were God's chosen people, rejected the obligatory nature of Jewish law, and in a few cases, abandoned the belief in God entirely. What seemed completely outlandish and unacceptable in one generation began to seem borderline in the next and routine in the third. To use an analogy from football, the goalposts seem to be moved every several years. Nothing is for certain and everything is possible. Gershom Scholem, the great scholar of Jewish mysticism, put it this way: "There is no way of telling *a priori* what beliefs are possible or impossible within the framework of Judaism." He argued that "the 'Jewishness' in the religiosity of any particular period is not measured by dogmatic criteria that are unrelated to actual historical circumstances, but solely by what sincere Jews do, in fact believe, or—at least—consider to be legitimate possibilities."[2]

Jacob Neusner has argued that many writers have confused the Jews as an ethnic group with Judaism as a religion. The study of Judaism, according to Neusner, has to be restricted to those who believe and practice the religion. He uses the term *Judaists* to refer to those Jews who are followers of Judaism, and argues that studying Judaism requires restricting one's focus to the Judaists rather than all Jews. "While the facts of sociology are relevant, they are hardly central and compelling." Neusner argues that if Judaism is to be studied as a religion, it "has to be studied as such—as a *religious* phenomenon, in and of itself—and not solely or primarily as a cultural or social force. And when we study about a religion, we study about those people who live—who view reality—within the religious world view, whose conceptual life is shaped by that world view."[3]

This is a challenging mandate. But even if it is not possible to follow Neusner's directive entirely, it is nevertheless important to differentiate between Judaism the religion and Jewishness the ethnicity. Alan Avery-Peck explains that "the bottom line is the distinction between the practice of Judaism as a religion and all the other aspects of the lives of Jews that are ancillary to Jewish practices and beliefs, aspects that, once upon a time, were controlled by Judaism." This is extremely difficult to do since the lives of Americans are not separated into neat categories. Avery-Peck acknowledges this. "The problem, which is a tough problem today, is figuring out where Judaism stops and the lives of Jews—unshaped by Judaism but still understood by them as somehow 'Jewish'—begin."[4]

This may be why many of the writers of introductions to Judaism fall back on the ethnic definition of Judaism: Judaism is what the Jews do. It is pretty easy to identify some of the things that Jews do. Jews like to eat bagels with cream cheese. Jews like to argue with each other. Jews like to listen to Bob Dylan. But this approach is likewise problematic. If Jewish religion is seen as being whatever ethnic Jews do, then the term *Judaism* loses all meaning. So let us say that a dozen Jews play volleyball at their local Jewish Community Center. The volleyball game could conceivably be considered a form of Jewish religiosity, especially if there is Hebrew music playing on a stereo somewhere in the background. Judaism would thus be equated with anything and everything that Jews do, thereby reducing the term to something completely devoid of any religious meaning. This is why I assert that an essentialist definition would be the most satisfying. Unfortunately, I do not see how we can develop an acceptable essentialist definition. Therefore, we will have to look elsewhere for some solution to our quandary.

If an essentialist definition is not practical, and an ethnic definition is too broad, then what other options do we have? Jonathan Z. Smith has suggested that a polythetic definition of early Judaism would be preferable to an essentialist one. The word *polythetic* is actually taken from the biological or medical world. It denotes a taxonomic group classified on the basis of several characteristics, as opposed to a monothetic group.[5] Applying such a definition to a religion generally, or Judaism specifically, would require focusing on sets of overlapping characteristics rather than searching for a single core essence. This would allow for more flexibility even as it would require a sharper sense of judgment. Michael L. Satlow has recently undertaken such an attempt in his *Creating Judaism: History, Tradition, Practice*, also published by Columbia University Press.[6]

Let me return to the task at hand—providing the reader with a usable definition of Judaism. As a working description, we could start with the following: Judaism is the religion of the Jewish people, based on ideas and concepts embodied in the Hebrew Bible and the Rabbinic writings. According to Jewish tradition, the covenant between God and Abraham marks the beginning of a special relationship between God and the Jewish people. While the very earliest biblical sources may show faint residues of henotheistic beliefs, Judaism has definitively rejected polytheism. Judaism is the mother religion of the Abrahamic faiths, the main monotheistic religions. In contrast to many other faiths, its central authority is vested in sacred texts and traditions rather than an authoritative religious leader or a clerical chief. In the ancient world, the high priest in the Temple served as a central ritual leader, but the destruction of the Temple forced the sages to radically redesign the architecture of Jewish practice.

Since the early centuries of the common era, the Talmudic sages have been acknowledged as the wise teachers and authoritative transmitters of Jewish religiosity. In modern times, a number of divergent views have developed, dividing the Jewish people on the basis of both religious belief and practice. In an article on defining Judaism that he published in the *Journal of the American Academy of Religion*, Satlow explains that Judaism "is best seen as a family of communities that generally share a common sense of identity, a discourse transmitted through a more or less bounded set of authoritative texts and traditional practices."[7] This polythetic understanding balances the ethnic and religious aspects of Jewish identity.

I will leave it to others to theorize about the nature of the Jewish religion, and the exact relationship between Judaism and Jewishness. My goal in this book is much more modest: to show the uninitiated reader just how much the Jewish religion, as practiced by American Jews, has changed over the past fifty or sixty years, and especially over the past twenty or thirty. However, I do not regard anything and everything that Jews do or may do as Judaism. The key challenge is where to draw the line. Substantial numbers of American Jews today do things that not only violate Jewish law, but would have been seen in previous generations as undermining the basis of Jewish communal life. Because of their sometimes contradictory commitments to individualism and spiritual development, many American Jews are doing things that could be seen as self-contradictory. Whether it is a Jew planning for a traditional Jewish memorial service after their body has been cremated, picking out a Hebrew design for a tattoo, or even planning a "bark mitzvah" for their dog, American Jews are violating long-held standards of religious behavior in their search for spiritual meaning.

Let me state as clearly as I can what criteria I am using for determining whether material might warrant inclusion in this book. The belief or behavior needs to be expressed or performed by Jews and/or in the name of Judaism. Their actions need to have a religious motivation, which I understand to include the belief in God, in whichever ways God is understood. Secular humanists will disagree with me, but I find it hard to understand how one could be religious without God. I therefore do not discuss, at least not at length, those Jewish groups that claim to be religious as well as atheist or agnostic.

Also, they need to accept, at least symbolically, the holy books and "religious conversations" deriving from Judaic texts that have been accepted as central works of the Jewish tradition. This book will therefore not include anything on the Karaites, for example, who accept the written Torah but reject the oral law, which was written down as the Talmud. Neusner refers to the written and oral Torahs with the term *Dual Torah*, which is less awkward than talking repeatedly about the written and oral Torahs or the two Torahs. Regardless of terminology, modern Jews (or at least modern Jewish scholars) accept the rabbinic corpus of interpretation as an important, and, indeed, central, part of their understanding of religion. I will be flexible on this because it is an example where "book Judaism" may bear little in common with "lived Judaism." Nevertheless, the followers of Judaism discussed in this book have not rejected the religious authority or at least the historical importance of the classical rabbinic tradition.

Finally, I do not include any group that has broken through boundary definitions. As has been commented upon by many observers over the years, American Jews may not know what their religion stands for, but they know that they reject any type of belief in Jesus as the Messiah (Christ in Greek) and/or as the Son of God. Therefore, this book does not include any protracted discussion of the so-called messianic Jewish movements, which include Jews for Jesus and numerous other Judeo-Christian subgroups. It does, however, include material on Jewish Buddhists, for reasons that will be explained in the text itself.

In terms of any of my decisions on what to include or exclude, I do not mean to imply that I am making an essentialist-based decision on what counts for authentic Judaism. Both because of space limitations as well as the need to keep the book focused, I have had to leave out a great many things. The decisions on what to include and what to leave out were painful, particularly in cases where I had a personal connection to the subject. The art of writing a book is never neat or tidy.

Many decades ago, Martin Buber explained that, for a Jew, "the past of his people is his personal memory, the future of his people his personal task. The way of his people teaches him to understand himself and to will himself."[8] This profound thought may have been sage in Buber's time, but it is not likely to be the guiding wisdom for the future of American Judaism.

Acknowledgments

I first became interested in the topic of contemporary American Judaism as a boy growing up in Manhattan. My parents, Norman and Meriel, had been active in the Stephen Wise Free Synagogue and later Rodef Shalom, both on the Upper West Side. They sent me to the most religiously liberal Jewish day school they could find, Ramaz School on East 85th Street. Ramaz was Modern Orthodox, as they called it then. By the second or third grade, I was already trying to figure out why our synagogue and my school seemed to present Judaism so differently. This is a question that has followed me all of my life. I left Ramaz after the sixth grade, but I chose to have my bar mitzvah at the Jewish Center, a large Orthodox synagogue on West 86th Street. After my mother was diagnosed with breast cancer, my sister and I moved to Waterbury, Connecticut where we lived with my aunt and uncle, Ruth and Herman. I spent many hours discussing the state of the Jewish community in Waterbury with my Aunt Ruth, and although the ideas presented in this book differ radically from what I was arguing at the time, I owe much to her enthusiastic debating.

In the late 1970s, Waterbury had about twenty-five hundred Jews who were divided into three congregations: Conservative, Reform, and Orthodox. It was an active community and all of the congregations seemed stable. They each had rabbis who had been serving the community for a long time and a number of lay leaders who were well-known local businessmen and professionals. I was deeply concerned, however, by what I, in my youthful idealistic phase, saw as a lack of deeply felt commitment. Yet, even in my worse case scenario, I never imagined that just twenty-five years later all three congregations would essentially be gone. Waterbury was a factory town. Children grew up and went away to college, never to return. This created a demographic crisis much sooner than I would have predicted. It was also more extreme.

The large Conservative synagogue, Congregation Beth El, could no longer afford to maintain their aging building and tried to merge with another Conservative congregation in Meriden. When the proposed merger failed, they temporarily rented a storefront and are currently in flux. The Reform Temple Israel hemorrhaged members and eventually was absorbed into a new congregation that was in the process of being created in Southbury. The Orthodox B'nai Shalom lost most of its nonobservant Orthodox members, but was saved from financial ruin by a successful bingo game. I remember walking by the synagogue with my uncle one evening and seeing their parking lot entirely filled up with cars. The street in front of the shul was also completely filled on both sides. I looked at my uncle in amazement: what kind of program could they be having that would attract so many people? I was quite surprised and more than a little disappointed when he told me. The future looked dim indeed.

But then something amazing happened. Rabbi Ahron Kaufman approached the city of Waterbury with a proposal to create a new yeshiva community. He promised to bring in a hundred yeshiva families over several years in exchange for a lease on the old campus of the University of Connecticut, Waterbury branch. The mayor and the city council jumped at the opportunity. The yeshiva bought the Conservative synagogue building, a distinctive edifice with a large, round yellow dome right across the street from Fulton Park, where I used to go sledding and skiing with my Uncle Herman. About thirty Haredi (devoutly Orthodox) families moved into Waterbury to study in the kollel (advanced Talmudical program), and others followed once there was a viable Orthodox presence. Today there are a number of kosher food outlets, a Jewish bookstore, a mikveh (ritual bath), and even a local branch of Hatzolah, the volunteer Orthodox Jewish ambulance service.

Dr. Robert Glassman, a friend whom I have known since we worked together as co-counselors at Camp Laurelwood in 1978, e-mailed me recently to let me know that the *New York Times* had a feature article on the Orthodox influx into Waterbury. Journalist Jennifer Medina reported how the 7-Eleven on Cooke Street—which was less than half a block from my Uncle Herman's former house—now offered kosher Slurpees. The Orthodox influx has already begun to have a positive impact on the neighborhood. She described how a glatt kosher (a stricter form of kosher meat) deli that offered Shabbat specialties like cholent and kishke "sat on a blighted street where police block off vandalized homes." The new Orthodox residents of Waterbury are thrilled. Rabbi Kaufman told Medina that when he was growing up in New York he had "never even heard of Waterbury, and Connecticut—what was that?" Now he talks about Waterbury in glowing terms, which would have amazed the Jewish kids that I grew up with there, virtually all of whom desperately wanted to leave. "This is the best of every world; a city, the suburbs, the bungalows, and the Catskills, all wrapped into one."[1]

Meanwhile, there are a number of new congregations in distant suburbs (everything in Connecticut is a suburb of somewhere else) that are socially liberal and are finding success of another type, experimenting with innovative approaches to Jewish religious life. The new Reform congregation in Southbury swallowed up Temple Israel of Waterbury, but the congregation has a very different composition. Whereas the original temple was founded in the late nineteenth century by German Jews and retained much of its Central European feel, the new congregation was primarily fourth and fifth generation descendants of Eastern Europeans married to non-Jewish spouses who had not converted. "I have heard that as many as 90 percent of them are intermarried," my uncle's neighbor and close friend Jackie Marshak told me. This is not a book about Waterbury, Connecticut, but I think I have made my point—American Judaism has changed radically over the past twenty or thirty years. I could not have asked for a better example to illustrate the socioreligious changes that I describe in this volume.

I wrote this book while working as a pulpit rabbi in Georgia. This gave me a certain perspective, which can be clearly seen and felt throughout the book, for better and worse. I would like to thank my congregation, Temple B'nai Israel of Albany, Georgia for their warmth and support. Many of the ideas discussed in this manuscript were developed in response to what I saw and experienced in my congregation. In particular, I would like to thank temple president David Prisant and immediate past president David Maschke for their encouragement and support. Peggy Posnick, who was without a doubt the person who attracted me to move to Albany because of her tremendous devotion to the temple, would spend her Saturday afternoons after Torah study going through some of the ideas presented here. Gail Greenfield has helped me to transform our congregational offerings, bringing many new programs and much greater variety. I am grateful that both Peggy and Gail were willing to share their personal spiritual journeys with me. Despite our geographical location, far away from the innovative pioneers of New York or Los Angeles, we have seen many of the same changes happening right here in southwest Georgia. I try my best to present different perspectives, but I do not claim to be a neutral observer. I am deeply connected with the Reform movement, and this determines to a large degree what I see and how I interpret it.

I want to thank Wendy Lochner, my editor at Columbia University Press, for her encouragement of this project from conception through final manuscript. I would also like to thank Susan Pensak, senior manuscript editor, assistant editor Christine Mortlock, and the entire staff of Columbia University Press who helped make this book a reality. I would like to thank Rabbi David Ellenson for writing the foreword and Rabbi Zalman Schachter-Shalomi for writing the afterword. In addition, I would like to thank Alan Segal, religion adviser to Columbia University Press, for his enthusiastic endorsement of the project. Especially, I need to thank the anonymous readers for their many helpful suggestions for focusing the concept and improving the manuscript. I would like to thank Daniel J. Wood, Daniel Buckner, Mihana Mucci, Robert Griffin, Jessica Cates, Lisha Parish, Joey Trull, Mattie Blanton, and Angelica Albritton for working with me on the manuscript. I would also like to thank Holly Kosiewicz, Camila Pedraza, and Lina Vargas, who helped in the final editing of the manuscript in Bogotá, Colombia.

I would also like to thank the following people for technical assistance relating to the preparation of the manuscript or the digital formatting of the photos: Rabbi Gary Zola, Kevin Profitt, Fred Krome, Camille Servizzi, and Phillip Reekers of the American Jewish Archives (AJA) were helpful as always. Ever since my first contact with the AJA in the early 1990s, they have always gone out of their way to be of help. Michael Feldberg and the staff of the American Jewish Historical Society assisted me via e-mail and phone. I want to thank the following people for helping with photographs: Susan Saxe of ALEPH, Deena Schwimmer of Yeshiva University, Rabbi Ayla Grafstein, Dovid Zaklikowsky of Chabad.org, Carolyn McGoldrick and Regalle Ascuncion of AP Photographs, Sarah Sokolic of Storahtelling, Kyla Cromer of STAR, Ron Gompertz of Chrismukkah, Peter Pitzele of Bibliodrama. com, Rabbi Steve Greenberg, Mark Heutlinger of Temple Emanu-el in New York City, Rabbi David Ingber and Simon Abramson of Kehilat Romemu, Heather Wolfson of MAZON, Emily Grotta of the URJ, Dena Ratner of the Orthodox Union, Ann Silver and Mara Cohen Ioannides of Missouri State University, and many others.

I have tried to make the book as exciting to read as possible. To do so, I have sometimes used provocative language. These words, and the general tone conveyed in specific passages, do not necessarily reflect my personal views, as the careful reader will be able to ascertain. Despite the risk that some readers may misunderstand what I am trying to say, I have elected to keep some of the more expressive and evocative language. This language bias is particularly apparent when I discuss the failures of the mainstream Jewish leadership. The "Jewish establishment" is criticized both implicitly and explicitly in this volume, while their accomplishments are seldom noted and never dwelt upon. The reason for this is simple—the emphasis in this volume is on how the Jewish denominations, the Jewish federations, the Jewish mainstream organizations, the Jewish Community Centers, and so forth did not meet all of the religious needs of the American Jewish population. What they have done well—and they have done many things well—is a subject for a different book.

I would like to thank my intellectual rights attorney Bob Stein of Pryor Cashman LLP for his legal advice as well as my late father's attorneys Alan Laufer and Richard Kay of the same firm. I would also like to thank Alan for making useful suggestions on chapters 2 and 3. I reedited chapter 7 toward the end of the editing process because of a six-page letter I received from Peter E. Nussbaum, an attorney at Wolff and Samson. On behalf of his client, Kabbalah Centre International, Inc., Mr. Nussbaum objected to a large number of statements in the draft that I had sent to the Kabbalah Centre seeking guidance. This letter created a great deal of consternation on my part, as the reader can imagine. The details of this crisis can be read in that chapter.

I would like to thank the following people who read and commented on specific chapters in the book or helped by providing important information.

Many of those listed spent many hours going through material completely unrelated to anything that they were personally involved in. I was truly amazed at how helpful so many people were, including substantial numbers who did not know me at all: Richard Abrams of the University of California at Berkeley; Rabbi Yitzchok Adlerstein of Loyola Law School; Patrick Allitt of Emory University; Rebecca Alpert of Temple University; Rabbi Victor S. Appell of the Union for Reform Judaism; Alan J. Avery-Peck of Holy Cross College; Yaakov Ariel of the University of North Carolina at Chapel Hill; Rabbi Aaron Bisno of Rodef Shalom Congregation; Rabbi Alan Brill of the Kavvanah Center; Menachem Butler of Yeshiva University; Edmund C. Case of InterfaithFamily.com; Rabbi Bob Carroll of Jerusalem; Rabbi Mitchell Chefitz of Temple Israel in Miami; Steven Cohen of Hebrew Union College-Jewish Institute of Religion; Rabbi David Eliezrie of Chabad; Rabbi Irwin H. Fishbein of the Rabbinic Center for Research and Counseling; Luke Ford of lukeford.net; Rabbi George Gittleman of Congregation Shomrei Torah; Robert H. Glassman of Short Hills, NJ; Nathan Glazer of Harvard University; Stuart Goldsmith of Albany, Georgia; Lou Gordon of Los Angeles; Rabbi Irving "Yitz" Greenberg of the Jewish Life Network; Stanley and Gail Greenfield; Fred Greenspahn of Florida Atlantic University; Rabbi David Greenstein of the Academy for Jewish Religion; Lawrence Grossman of the American Jewish Committee; Peter Haas of Carnegie Mellon University; Carol Harris-Shapiro of Gratz College; Samuel Heilman of Queens College; Susannah Heschel of Dartmouth College; Rabbi Richard Hirsh of the Reconstructionist Rabbinical Association; Rabbi Lawrence Hoffman of Hebrew Union College–Jewish Institute of Religion; Stanley Hordes of New Mexico; Boaz Huss of Ben Gurion University; Rebbetzin Esther Jungreis of Hineni; Rabbi Elie Kaufner of Hadar; Debra Kaufman of Northeastern University; Rabbi Jan Kaufman of the Rabbinical Assembly; Stuart Knee of the College of Charleston; Matthew Kraus of Wright State University; Rabbi Norman Lamm of Yeshiva University; Rabbi Michael Lerner of *Tikkun*; Rabbi Joel Levine of Temple Judea of West Palm Beach, Florida; Jay Levinson of Jerusalem; Rabbi Richard Levy of the Hebrew Union Collge-Jewish Institute of Religion; Rabbi Cliff Librach of the United Jewish Center in Danbury, Connecticut; Rabbi Mordechai Liebling of the Jewish Funds for Justice; Shaul Magid of Indiana University; Rabbi Beverly Magidson of United Jewish Federation of Northeastern New York; Shawn Landres of Synagogue 3000; Jackie and Evelyn Marshak of Waterbury, Connecticut; David Maschke of Maschke Associates; Rabbi Paul Menitoff of the Central Conference of American Rabbis; Michael A. Meyer of the Hebrew Union College–Jewish Institute of Religion; Rabbi Joel Meyers of the Rabbinical Assembly; Rabbi Adam Mintz of Queens College; Sharon Liberman Mintz; Rabbi Evan Moffie of Chicago Sinai Congregation; Rabbi Leon Morris of the Skirball Center; Jacob Neusner of Bard College; Rabbi Stacy Offner of Congregation Shir Tikvah; Rabbi Stephen Pearce of Congregation Emanu-El; Judith Plaskow of Manhattanville College; Rabbi Ron Price of the Union for Traditional Judaism; Peggy Posnick of Albany, Georgia; Marc Lee Raphael of the College of William and Mary; Simcha Raphael of La Salle University; Rabbi Michael M. Remson of Synagogue Church Consulting; Mary Rosenbaum of the Dovetail Institute; Rabbi Yitzchak Rosenbaum of the National Jewish Outreach Program; Jonathan Sarna of Brandeis University; Susan Saxe of ALEPH; Marvin Schick of the Rabbi Jacob Joseph School; Rabbi Immanuel Schochet of Chabad; Rabbi Sidney Schwarz of the Washington Institute for Jewish Leadership and Values; Robert Seltzer of Hunter College; Rabbi Avi Shafran of Agudath Israel; Rabbi Misha Tillman of Chicago; Hava Tirosh-Samuelson of Arizona State University; Rabbi Yakov Travis of the Tiferet Institute; Rabbi Stanley Wagner of Jerusalem; Rabbi Arthur Waskow of ALEPH; Chaim Waxman of the Jewish People Policy Planning Institute; Rob Weinberg of the Experiment in Congregational Education (ECE); Stephen M. Weitzman of Long Island; Jack Wertheimer of the Jewish Theological Seminary; Alan Wolfe of Boston College; Ron Wolfson of Synagogue 3000; Rabbi David Wolpe of Sinai Temple; Jonathan Woocher of JESNA; Zion Zohar of Florida International University; and all others who helped me in any way.

I would like to take this opportunity to remember my father, Norman Kaplan, and my uncle, Herman Moskowitz, who both passed away this past year. Both were strong influences on my development and I love them both very much. May their memories be for a blessing. I would also like to remember my grandparents, Max and Flora Moskowitz and Morris and Dora Kaplan, my uncle, Bernard Moskowitz, and my aunt, Ruth Moskowitz. I hope that this work will be a small part of the contribution that our family has made to our community and to our country.

This book is dedicated in memory of Karl Faschingbauer, Dr. Harry Weiser's beloved grandfather and mentor; Wallace N. Moses's parents, Carolyn and Jack; Joan and Alex Dimant's relatives who died in the Holocaust;

Bell and Irving Moskowitz, who brought happiness and love to all those they touched; Carol LaSchober's loved ones; Ed Fink; and Frances Kaplan. This book is in honor of Florence Prisant's grandchildren Lisa, Marci, Kevin, and Rachel; Thomas L. Shanks, with many fond memories of the temple's gardens in honor of Peggy Kobley; and Holli and Brian Bruck's children Ethan and Dara, who will carry the torch of Judaism into the next generation.

Chronology of Events

1945   World War II comes to an end; Nuremberg Trials begin.

1945   *Commentary* magazine founded by the American Jewish Committee

1945   The Union of Orthodox Rabbis of the United States and Canada issues a herem at the Hotel McAlpin against Rabbi Mordecai M. Kaplan because of alleged heresies in his *Sabbath Prayer Book*.

1946   Rabbi Joshua Loth Leibman publishes *Peace of Mind*, which becomes a best-seller.

1947   Jacob Rader Marcus founds the American Jewish Archives on the campus of Hebrew Union College in Cincinnati.

1948   *The Publications of the American Jewish Historical Society* is transformed from an annual to a quarterly. Its name is later changed to the *American Jewish Historical Quarterly* and then to *American Jewish History*.

1948   The State of Israel becomes an independent country.

1949   David Ben Gurion becomes Israel's first prime minister and Chaim Weizmann is elected Israel's first president.

1950   Paula Ackerman, widow of Rabbi William Ackerman, begins serving Temple Beth Israel of Meridian, Mississippi as its unofficial rabbi.

1950   Rabbi Joseph Schneerson passes away. His son-in-law, Rabbi Menachem Mendel Schneerson, becomes the seventh Rebbe, assuming leadership of the worldwide Chabad-Lubavitch movement.

1952   The Central Rabbinical Congress (CRC) of the U.S.A. and Canada was established in order to represent "True Torah Jews" against Zionism.

1953   Frank Lloyd Wright designs the Beth Sholom Synagogue in Elkins Park, Pennsylvania.

1954   Stern College for Women, the first degree-granting college of liberal arts and sciences for women under Jewish auspices, is established as part of Yeshiva University in New York.

1955   Will Herberg publishes *Protestant Catholic Jew: An Essay in American Religious Sociology*, in which he describes the United States as being a "three-religion country."

1956   Hank Greenberg of the Detroit Tigers is inducted into the Baseball Hall of Fame.

1958   Leon Uris writes *Exodus*, which is made into a film by Otto Preminger in 1960.

1960   Elie Wiesel publishes *Night*, a memoir describing his experiences in Auschwitz.

1963   Followers of Rabbi Mordecai M. Kaplan begin concrete plans to create the Reconstructionist movement as a fourth denomination in American Judaism.

1965   Abraham Joshua Heschel marches for civil rights with Martin Luther King Jr. in Selma, Alabama.

1966   Elie Wiesel publishes *The Jews of Silence*, a description of the plight facing the Jews in the Soviet Union.

1967   Facing Arab threats to annihilate her, the State of Israel launches a preemptive attack, conquering the West Bank and Gaza Strip in the Six-Day War.

1968   Havurat Shalom is founded in Somerville, Massachusetts, and serves as a model community for the Jewish counterculture.

1968   The Reconstructionist Rabbinical College is founded by Rabbi Ira Eisenstein in the Philadelphia area.

1969   The Association for Jewish Studies, a learned society and professional organization that seeks to promote Judaic Studies on the university level, is founded in Boston.

1972   Rabbi Sally J. Priesand is ordained by Hebrew Union College–Jewish Institute of Religion.

1972   Gerson D. Cohen succeeds Louis Finkelstein as chancellor of the Jewish Theological Seminary.

1973   *The Jewish Catalog: A Do-It-Yourself Kit* is published, helping to promote the idea that young countercultural Jews could perform their own Jewish ritual, without relying on rabbis or synagogues.

1973   The Committee on Jewish Law and Standards of the Conservative movement passes a response permitting women to count in a minyan, leaving the decision on whether to be egalitarian to individual congregations.

1976   The Central Conference of American Rabbis adopts "Reform Judaism: A Centenary Perspective" in San Francisco.

1983   The Reform movement accepts patrilineal as well as matrilineal descent as determining the Jewish status of offspring born to intermarried couples.

1984   *The Complete ArtScroll Siddur*, edited by Nosson Scherman, is published and quickly becomes the standard Orthodox prayer book.

1985   The Jewish Theological Seminary votes to admit women to the rabbinical school.

1985   President Ronald Reagan visits the German military cemetery at Bitburg containing the graves of forty-seven members of the Waffen S.S.

1985   Rabbi Joseph B. Soloveitchik ordains the two thousandth Orthodox rabbi at the Rabbi Isaac Elchanan Theological Seminary of Yeshiva University.

1985   The right-wing of the Conservative movement secedes to form the Union for Traditional Conservative Judaism, later dropping the word *Conservative* from their name.

1986   Ismar Schorsch becomes chancellor of the Jewish Theological Seminary.

1986   Elie Wiesel is awarded the Nobel Peace Prize.

1988   The leadership council of Conservative Judaism issues an official statement of belief, titled "Emet Ve-Emunah: Statement of Principles of Conservative Judaism."

1994   The Synagogue Council of America, an organization of American Jewish Synagogue Associations, founded in 1926, dissolves.

1994   The seventh Lubavitcher Rebbe, Menachem Mendel Schneerson, is buried in Queens, NY, but no successor is appointed.

1997   On the occasion of the centenary of the first World Zionist Congress, the Central Conference of American Rabbis adopts the Miami Platform, dedicated to strengthening the relationship between Reform Judaism and Zionism.

1999   The Central Conference of American Rabbis passes a new Pittsburgh Platform, the "Statement of Principles for Reform Judaism," which calls for greater ritual observance.

2001   David Ellenson becomes president of the Hebrew Union College–Jewish Institute of Religion.

2003   Richard Joel replaces Norman Lamm as president of Yeshiva University.

2003   The Union of American Hebrew Congregations changes their name to the Union for Reform Judaism to better reflect their actual mission.

2004   The American Jewish community celebrates 350 years of American Jewish life.

2006   Arnold Eisen of Stanford University is appointed the new chancellor of the Jewish Theological Seminary.

2007   A new Reform prayer book, *Mishkan T'filah*, is published by the Central Conference of American Rabbis.

The Ben Gamla Charter School, the first Hebrew language charter school in the United States, opens in Hollywood, Florida.

The Torah: A Women's Commentary is published by the Union for Reform Judaism.

2008   Congregation Sha'ar Zahav, a San Francisco synagogue with an emphasis on outreach to the LGBT community, publishes their own prayerbook, *Siddur Sha'ar Zahav*.

United States Immigration and Customs Enforcement raids Agriprocessors, a Kosher slaughterhouse in Postville, Iowa.

Hebrew College in Boston ordains its first class of eleven trans-denominational rabbis.

The Conservative movement publishes guidelines for a Hekhsher Tzedek kashrut certification, outlining ethical requirements that needed to be met, in addition to the traditional ritual requirements, for a food product to be certified by them as kosher.

2009   Jewish organizations of all kinds begin to feel the effects of the October 2008 stock market crash as well as a number of Ponzi schemes that disproportionately affected the Jewish community.

2010   The Conservative movement publishes a new High Holy Day machzor, Lev Shalem, which means "whole heart" in Hebrew.

Introduction

American Judaism has changed dramatically since 1945. Until the end of World War II, religion was generally seen as an ascribed part of identity rather than an achieved status. It was ascribed because, like one's race, it was held to be immutable. A 1955 Gallup poll found that only one in twenty-five Americans had switched from the religion in which they had been raised. This was a negligible number and therefore, for all practical purposes, an American was no more likely to switch his religion than he was to switch his race. But, by the mid-1980s, the Gallup organization found that the situation was entirely different. One out of three Americans was no longer practicing the religion in which they had been raised. Even the two-thirds who said that they still affiliated with the same denomination as their parents were not necessarily practicing their religion in the same way. There were many reasons suggested for this dramatic shift, including intermarriage, geographic mobility, changing social mores, and others.

The United States was and remains a highly religious country, with polls consistently showing that a very high percentage of Americans believe in

God and feel that they should act on that belief. Indeed, some polls put the number of believers at over 90 percent. And yet, it has become clear that there has been an immense shift in how they view God. As people began to embrace "cultural egalitarianism" as a creed, they were more prone to question all types of hierarchy and authority. For the majority, God is no longer an omnipotent and transcendent deity, but is instead, or at least primarily, a comforting presence. Rather than shaping events directly through history, God has become a source of psychological guidance and emotional support.

Many Americans have shifted from believing in a religion that has an established church and set rituals to a privatized spirituality. Rather than trying to placate a demanding deity, they are looking to find ways to realize their human potential. Individual seekers are looking for transcendent meaning in a universe where no single person or institution has the ultimate religious authority or absolute knowledge of religious truth. Divinity is a treasured, if elusive, quality, providing a sense of peace and self-empowerment. Each person needs to embark on her own spiritual journey in order to find her own personal path to the sacred.

This spiritual search is not based on the acceptance of any specific dogma, theological belief, or ideology. The "sovereign self" yearns for spiritual nourishment but is repelled by strict behavioral codes. There is little interest in reading ancient religious texts that were believed to have the authority to require specific ritual practices. Rather, Americans want to experience God in their own way and will therefore reject anything that does not seem consistent with the perception of authenticity. Ceremony becomes a tool for nurturing individual spirituality rather than a way of responding to divine command. Many feel an absolute obligation to search for their true inner voice. As a result, the rejection of the old fashioned religious teachings is not just an option, but a moral imperative.

Americans have a declining respect for authority of all types with a corresponding increasing emphasis on democratic participation. They are no longer content to follow the priest, minister, or rabbi, wanting, at least, to be a part of the decision-making process and preferring to share leadership. As George Gallup Jr. put it, "Americans do not see their role, as it once was, to 'pay, pray and obey.' They see their role as taking part fully in church life; the church, they believe, serves them, not the other way around."[1] They want to be directly involved in order to ensure that what is transpiring will be meaningful. In the shift from central authority to individual autonomy, established religious groups can no longer count on traditional allegiance. Community is a "second language," still of interest but in need of redefinition in order to find a place in the new hierarchy of values.

The rise of the sovereign self was exemplified by Sheila Larson, the pseudonym for a young nurse who was interviewed by Robert N. Bellah and his coauthors in the 1985 book *Habits of the Heart*. Having been through a great deal of psychotherapy, she described her religious faith as sincere and serious, but intensely personal. "I believe in God, [but] I am not a religious fanatic. I can't remember the last time I went to church. My faith has carried me a long way. It's Sheilaism. Just my own little voice." Sheila explained that her faith was relatively simple and emphasized a personal relationship with God rather than a complex theological system. Bellah commented dryly that Sheila's faith had some tenets beyond belief in God, "though not many." She explained: "It's just try [sic] to love yourself and be gentle with yourself. You know, I guess, take care of each other. I think He would want us to take care of each other."[2]

An individualistic spirituality emphasizes that religion can inspire and enlighten, but has no obligatory claim upon the individual. Sheila and the many Americans like her believe that religion is essentially a private matter, one that might be called religious privatization. Her belief in "Sheilaism" is, according to Bellah, "rooted in the effort to transform external authority into internal meaning."[3] A Gallup poll conducted in the early 1980s indicated that fully 80 percent of Americans agreed with the statement that "an individual should arrive at his or her own religious beliefs independent of any churches or synagogues." Americans felt a strong visceral sense that belief should be a purely personal thing.

For those who follow traditional approaches to religion, the new stress on personalism and voluntarism generates a great deal of cognitive dissidence. The increasing emphasis on individualism makes it harder for nonfundamentalist religious organizations to make any types of demands—whether ritualistic or communal—on their followers. People want to choose which ceremonies, if any, they will observe and how they will observe them. Any hint that they are being told what to do or how to do it might upset them, because that would be a breach of their independence, a violation of their right to make their own decisions, free of meddling outside influences.

Americans who have now been liberated from their inherited identities are taking full advantage of their newly acquired autonomy. They may reject the religion of their parents completely or they may seek to adapt it, remolding parts to fit their wants or needs. They may go "shopping" in the religious marketplace for a faith that suits them better, whether an ancient religion with all sorts of venerable institutions or one of the newer religious movements. Nevertheless, breaking ties with their inherited identity is not as simple or neat as it may sound. Some can do it and never look back; others may feel varying degrees of conflicted emotions and even considerable guilt.

Jews, like most Americans, feel compelled to go beyond the basic necessities of food, shelter, and sex and up the hierarchy of needs to the apex of self-actualization. In an affluent country where one's material needs are fairly easily satisfied, even during an extended period of economic difficulties, Americans have a great deal of time and energy to devote to postmaterialistic values. They experience less authoritative direction, but enjoy diverse options for guidance. Because of the pluralistic nature of modern society, Americans have the flexibility to make almost any type of religious choice or choices: they have become known for being religious switchers. This can send American Jews in all sorts of unlikely directions. One becomes interested in Buddhism, only to discover Orthodox Judaism in India and end up a Bratslaver Hasid living in the Old City of Jerusalem. Another is raised Orthodox, only to rebel and marry a Christian minister, but then embrace Jewish Renewal. A third is raised in a culturally Jewish but secular home and later becomes a so-called messianic Jew. The possible permutations are endless.

While much of this religious switching is self-motivated, the different religious groups have become much more conscious of the need to recruit. The United Methodist Church, for example, recently launched a multimillion-dollar television advertising campaign portraying their church as a warm, open-minded community that can help people get through emotional difficulties. In such a competitive religious marketplace even ethnically based religious groups have to get out and be proactive to both hold their existing members and attract new followers. As the *New York Times* reported, "Jewish religious leaders, driven by fears about shrinking numbers, are becoming increasingly sophisticated and aggressive about marketing Judaism, turning to the same kinds of outreach techniques that evangelical Christians rode to mega-church success." The newspaper quoted Jack Wertheimer, who explained that "I think what's going on is a product of the consumer-driven nature of this culture and the need to compete for people's time and attention. Christians do it from the imperative of evangelizing. Jews are doing it far more because they see their community shrinking."[4] As I have argued in earlier books, the problem with this approach is that there needs to be a compelling theological reason to continue bothering with all the demands of a religious practice. Otherwise, there is insufficient reason to put in the effort—certainly over the long haul.[5]

Judaism in America is an integral part of the American religious landscape, but it has a number of special characteristics. To an extent unknown in most other religions, Judaism focuses on the Jews as a people. The ancient Israelites identified themselves as part of a nation and not just followers of a religion. God makes a covenant between Himself and the Jewish people. Moses is privileged to receive the revelation from God on Mount Sinai because he is the recognized leader of the Israelites, a people. This is not always understood clearly. Over the last two centuries, many Jews have wanted to stress that their identity was purely religious in order to better fit into their host society. Some of the early leaders of the Reform movement in both Central Europe and the United States made a point of identifying themselves as "Germans of the Jewish faith" or "Americans of the Israelite belief" in order to indicate to others that being Jewish was solely a religion. Yet few believed them, and it seems clear that many of those making the argument did not even believe it themselves. As a result of this discrepancy, professional scholars and even many Jews themselves are confused about the real nature of Jewish identity.

American Jews have been trying to reconcile individualism with commitment. They have been thrust into a position without precedent, and traditionalists fear much of the religious wisdom that is precious to them may be lost forever. Given the same latitude as other Americans to choose whether or not to undertake different types of commitments, they carry the heavy burden of a profound but deeply troubled history. Their ancestors long carried the flag of monotheism and a unique religious vision that emerged out of a distinctive worldview. Whether or not they regard themselves as religious, they remember the centuries of persecution culminating in the murder of six million Jews by the Nazis during the Second World War. They feel a sense of responsibility to carry on the legacy of the many martyrs who suffered and died for their faith over the past two millennia. But, despite the gnawing sense of obligation to their forebears, Jews in contemporary America are exploring virgin territory and have no idea where it may lead.

1 A Historical Overview from 1945

Bess Myerson was crowned Miss America on September 8, 1945, four months to the day after the surrender of Nazi Germany. American Jews beamed with pride. Many felt that her crowning symbolized a new level of social acceptance that they had long craved but had seemed elusive. When Myerson went to Atlantic City, New Jersey to compete in the pageant, a Holocaust survivor with concentration camp numbers tattooed on her arm asked her in Yiddish if she was Jewish. When Myerson said that she was, the woman hugged her. "If America chooses a Jewish girl to be Miss America, I will know that I've come to a safe country."[1]

In the years following 1945, Americans were astonished at the incredible prosperity they were beginning to enjoy. This prosperity spawned a new world of consumerism that offered them unimaginable choices. For a nation that had been deprived of luxury goods since the Great Depression of 1929, the plethora of available new commercial products was staggering. People rushed out to buy everything from Frigidaire refrigerators to Chevrolet automobiles, reveling in the economic boom that almost no one

FIGURE 1.1. Bess Myerson, in a later photo, became the first Jewish woman to win the Miss America Pageant in 1945. On a Victory Bond Tour, she became the target of anti-semitism. Myerson then launched a school tour with the motto "You can't be beautiful and hate." *Courtesy of the Jacob Rader Marcus Center of the American Jewish Archives*

expected. Between 1945 and 1960, highways were built to connect downtown centers with faraway marshlands now called suburbs. Postwar growth on the "crabgrass frontier" was stimulated by veteran's benefits, principally those provided through the Servicemen's Readjustment Act of 1944, commonly known as the GI Bill; 7.8 million World War II veterans took advantage of the GI Bill to study in a university or training center. Most important, huge numbers of Americans were able to buy their first homes, frequently without even having to make a down payment. The Federal Housing Authority (FHA) offered mortgages of up to 90 percent of a home's value and the Veteran's Administration (VA) offered additional incentives.

The Jews in the United States shared in this sense of limitless possibility, but they were also acutely aware of the Nazi extermination of the vast majority of European Jewry. When World War II ended, American Jews slowly began to realize the enormity of the tragedy that had occurred in Europe. The Nazis not only murdered six million Jews, but wiped out the center of Jewish religious life. The American Jewish community suddenly became the largest and most important Jewish community in the world. As Salo Wittmayer Baron explained: "If during the first World War American Jewry came to maturity, the Second War has placed in its hands undisputed leadership of world Jewry, with all the challenges and responsibilities which it entails."[2] American Jews, however, were ill equipped to take on such weighty responsibility. Although there had been Jews in America since 1654 or even a bit earlier, American Jewish institutions were still relatively young and developing.

In 1945, most American Jews were the children of immigrants from Eastern Europe. There was a succession of immigration waves, beginning with the Sephardim in the colonial period and then the "German" Jewish immigration burst after 1820. Contrary to the original historiographical account, Ashkenazim began arriving much earlier than had been previously thought, comprising a majority of the Spanish and Portuguese Congregation Shearith Israel as early as 1740.[3] The Eastern European immigration starting in 1881 was much greater than these earlier waves. Most Eastern European immigrants were traditional, although out of necessity many quickly dropped their Sabbath observance. Before 1933, strictly Orthodox Jews were less likely to have emigrated. The Chofetz Chaim, a prominent Eastern European rabbinic authority, had stated that "whoever wishes to live properly before God must not settle in that country." Orthodox rabbis referred to the United States as the *trefe medinah*, the nonkosher country, because it was believed that it was nearly impossible to remain Orthodox in a country where everything was so economically competitive. But, after the rise of the Nazis, growing numbers of Orthodox Jews found themselves (fortunately) in the United States as a consequence of political events beyond their control. They did not come to the United States in search of wealth or even freedom, but ended up in the New World to avoid being murdered in the old country.

Virulent antisemitism was virtually unknown in the United States, but there was substantial prejudice against Jews, much of which was quite nasty. That dislike diminished greatly in the immediate aftermath of the war, and there was a warm feeling toward all Americans who had contributed to the great victory. People felt a sense of solidarity with each other that transcended residual ethnic differences and classic religious doctrines. Furthermore, non-Jews were shocked by the atrocities committed by the Nazis and any public expression of antisemitism, no matter how mild, became associated with German barbarism. Nevertheless, a "polite" form of antisemitism remained, constituting a threat to social and economic advancement, and most American Jews tried as best they could to keep a low profile.

When the Eastern European immigrants began arriving in large numbers in 1881, they—along with the other ethnic immigrants—understood that they were being asked to give up their specific national heritage and assimilate into white, Anglo-Saxon Protestant (WASP) society. This proved to be impossible, and the concept of American society as a "melting pot" emerged, in which a new type of American would be created through the intermingling of people from different ethnic and religious (although probably not racial) backgrounds. But this proved to be impractical as well. As Nathan Glazer and Daniel Patrick Moynihan wrote in their 1963 *Beyond the Melting Pot*, "the point about the melting pot is that it did not happen." They explained that the reason for this was because of "some central tendency in the national ethos which structures people, whether those coming afresh or the descendents of those who have been here for generations, into groups of different status and character."[4] While the book gave the impression that substantial assimilation was occurring among European American groups, it was clear that most ethnic groups—including the Jews—were not going to disappear anytime soon. By the late 1940s or early 1950s, the idea of cultural pluralism was being promoted more prominently as an alternative. The theory was developed in the World War I period, most notably in Horace M. Kallen's 1915 *Nation* essay, "Democracy Versus the Melting Pot." People could be good, loyal Americans while at the same time preserving and even emphasizing their distinctive ethnic heritage. This worked well for most American

Jews, who wanted to acculturate; they wanted to accommodate themselves to the larger society without totally losing their traditional cultural identity. Most did not want to assimilate, where they or their descendants would completely disappear as distinctive ethnic types. Even if they had wanted to assimilate, social barriers prevented or at least inhibited that ambition.

Open expressions of ethnicity were still looked down upon in many circles. What was regarded as a positive American virtue was religiosity. Americans saw religion as a way of reinforcing family stability. "The family that prays together stays together" was a popular expression. The anti-Communism of the cold war years was based in part on distinguishing Western values from godless Communism. The specter of nuclear catastrophe worried every American, including children who had to practice evacuating their schools in the event of a possible nuclear attack. On Flag Day in 1954, President Dwight Eisenhower urged Americans to be good citizens by believing in God. "Our government makes no sense unless it is founded in a deeply felt religious faith—and I don't care what it is."[5] After a campaign organized by the Knights of Columbus, the Congress added the words "under God" to the Pledge of Allegiance that same year. In 1955, Congress added the phrase "In God We Trust" to all American currency, and in 1956 it became the nation's official motto, replacing "E Pluribus Unum." While most Americans were Protestant, the president deliberately avoided using language that would exclude people of other faiths. The important thing was to be committed to the American civil religion, which was good for the individual American, American families, American communities, and the United States as a whole. The idea of civil religion was derived from Jean-Jacques Rousseau, who wrote that there were certain basic dogmas that formed the foundation of secular society. These dogmas included the existence of God, the world to come, the reward of virtue and the punishment of vice, and religious tolerance. Other religious beliefs could be embraced by individual citizens if they so chose. American thinkers adapted the concept of civil religion to the needs of American society, resulting in something very different than what Rousseau envisioned. As Nathan Glazer explained, "yes, he wanted a civil religion too, but I think it was much less religious in traditional terms than American civil religion, more state oriented, with less ground for religious difference or difference of any kind."[6]

Sociologists explained that by the mid-1950s, America expected immigrants to fully adopt American ways. One of the most popular interpreters of contemporary religion was Will Herberg, who set out to explain why religious identification in the United States was so pervasive. "Almost everybody in the United States today," he wrote, "locates himself in one or another of the three great religious communities."[7] Herberg argued that the reason was that while overt expressions of ethnicity was looked down upon, religious identification was strongly encouraged. Tracing the roots of this process, he described the ways in which immigrants were expected to assimilate: "The newcomer is expected to change many things about him as he becomes an American—nationality, language, culture." The perpetuation of "ethnic differences in any serious way" is not consistent with "the logic of American reality." But, Herberg explained, there was one thing that the immigrant was not expected to change—his religion. As a result, religion "has become the differentiating element and the context of self-identification and social location."[8] While Herberg's interpretation was and remains controversial, it was enormously influential.

Herberg described the United States in 1955 as being a "three-religion country" consisting of Protestants, Catholics, and Jews. There were three "communions" which were seen as "diverse, but equally legitimate, equally American, expressions of an over-all American religion, standing for essentially the same 'moral ideals' and 'spiritual values.'" Herberg hastened to add that he was not suggesting that this idea was necessarily theologically sound, but only that it was a conception held, "though hardly in explicit form," by many Americans. Jews were a tiny percentage of the American population, but Herberg's formulation implied that they represented a full third. Whatever their number, their religion was one of the three primary American faiths. Citing Ruby Jo Reeves Kennedy's research on intermarriage trends in New Haven, Connecticut from 1870–1940, Herberg agreed that the idea of a single melting pot must be replaced by the triple melting pot theory of American assimilation in which the different national groups are merging into "three religious compartments rather than indiscriminately."[9] All three American faiths believed in American values, including political democracy, economic free enterprise, and social egalitarianism.

Herberg argued that Americans had made religion important for social, rather than theological, reasons. Bluntly put, they wanted to be accepted and felt that they had to belong to one of the three major faiths to fit in. The result was that many who were joining churches and synagogues in the 1950s were not really searching for God. They were willing to make an outward concession in order to achieve respectability, but the religious message was not being taken to heart. Many suburbanites practiced "religiousness without religion, a religiousness with almost any kind of content or none, a way of sociability or 'belonging' rather than a way of reorienting life to God. It is thus frequently a religiousness without serious commitment, without real inner conviction, without genuine existential decision."[10]

Jewish Theology and Religious Thought in the Postwar Period

Literally referring to discourse about God, theology has come to encompass the study of dogma and doctrine in all its forms. Even though the statement that religion prospered while theology went bankrupt was largely true, the postwar period saw a flurry of theological activity as well as a flowering of Judaic scholarship in general. Much of Jewish thought did not fit into the narrower limitations of what was considered theology because, rather than dealing directly with God, it focused on other issues arising from the challenges of modernity including ritual and ceremony, liturgy, the meaning of community, and even political issues. American Jews were more likely to respond to religious thinkers who could tie thoughts about God to pragmatic concerns since they generally understood Judaism as a religion that focused on practice rather than dogma. American Jewish intellectuals enjoyed unprecedented respect as communal leaders saw the need for educated spokespersons who could articulate the beliefs and values of Judaism for the general public. These intellectuals were part of what has been called the "elite religion" of American Jewry, which was the understanding of Judaism held by the most educated and involved members of the community. While the elite tended to look down on "folk religion," the community as a whole relied upon these intellectuals to justify what they were doing.

In the latter half of the nineteenth and the first half of the twentieth century, most Jewish theologians emerged out of one of the Jewish denominations. The United States was the only country in the world where the non-Orthodox movements dominated the Jewish community. Elsewhere, most Jews belonged to Orthodox synagogues. They did not necessarily observe Jewish rituals consistently, but they accepted the authority of Orthodox Judaism over Jewish communal life. "America was different," as a popular expression put it. Denominationalism prevailed on the religious landscape and occupied the attention of most Jewish theologians. American Jewish theology before World War II focused primarily on intradenominational and interdenominational thinking.[11] This would change after World War II.

One of the main theological issues that preoccupied American Jewish thinkers before the war was the nature of divine revelation and its consequences for religious authority. Orthodox Jews believed in *Torah min ha-shamayim*, a theological doctrine holding that God gave the Torah—both written and oral—to Moses on Mount Sinai. Conservative theologians followed Solomon Schechter in arguing that revelation was a dialogue between God and man (gender neutral language was not yet used). Therefore the Jewish people were the final authority in determining both the nature of Judaism and the proper way to practice the Jewish religion. Reform theologians accepted the doctrine of progressive revelation, which held that people move to a higher perception of truth through the course of history and are therefore in a better position to ascertain the nature and will of God. All of the movements declared their commitment to Klal Yisrael, the importance of the community of Israel, and the loyalty each Jew should have for all other members of the nation. They interpreted this concept differently, with Reform thinkers such as Rabbi Kaufmann Kohler defining Judaism primarily as a "religion" rather than as an ethnoreligious community. Nevertheless, even the most radical classical Reformer displayed certain indications of group loyalty that went beyond simple religious abstractions.

After the war, new thinkers began publicizing new approaches to Jewish theology. The range of Jewish thinking broadened considerably, with many thinkers deliberately avoiding the rigid categories that had dominated theology before the war. Diverse thinkers including Will Herberg and Abraham Joshua Heschel demonstrated what could be termed an existentialist approach to Jewish thought. Rather than trying to state what their denomination believed or should believe, these existentialist theologians tried to describe what the classical rabbinic tradition had to teach about Jewish belief and practice and how it was relevant in the contemporary world. Perhaps sensing that Americans of all backgrounds were increasingly open to religious wisdom from new sources, these theologians argued that Judaism could answer many of the most pressing personal questions that people had started asking. The existentialists put an emphasis on the recognition of human frailty and the need to submit to God rather than to understand Him. Some found this approach to Judaism to be fresh and exciting, while others criticized it as irrational, overly romantic, and even dehumanizing.

Many Americans began to look to a softer, gentler form of religion to help them cope with the difficulties of life. Already in 1946, Boston Reform rabbi Joshua Loth Liebman published *Peace of Mind*, which today might be called a self-help book. It became a runaway best-seller. Liebman argued that a psychotherapeutic approach to religion could provide Americans with the personal spiritual tranquillity necessary to feel less troubled at a time of tremendous social change. "It may seem strange for a man to write a book about peace of mind in this age of fierce turmoil and harrowing doubts. I have written this book in the conviction that social peace can never be permanently achieved so long as individuals engage in civil war with themselves." He proposed a methodology for achieving peace of mind. "Every person who wishes to attain peace of mind must learn the art of renouncing many things in order to possess other things more securely and fully. This is a most important and difficult step . . . Yet as we grow older we learn that every stage of human development calls upon us to weigh differing goods in the scales and to sacrifice some for the sake of others."[12]

An intellectual elite built a vibrant subculture discussing and debating Jewish theology and related concerns. Some published serious monographs on topics dealing with Judaism that were carefully read by an impressive following. Academic and semi-academic journals were either founded or expanded in order to provide outlets for not only famous theologians, such as Abraham Joshua Heschel and Mordecai Menahem Kaplan, but also a much larger group of serious, if obscure, pulpit rabbis, academics, and even lay people. The goal was to stimulate new approaches to Jewish thought, as well as to promote discussion and analysis of philosophies and methodologies that had already been developed. A group of thinkers pronounced the need for a "new Jewish theology," an approach to Jewish thought on its own terms, rather than based on categories imposed from the outside.

A number of influential journals and magazines were founded in the years after World War II. *Commentary* and *Conservative Judaism* began publishing in 1945, the *CCAR Journal* in 1953, *Midstream* in 1955, and *Tradition* in 1958. *Judaism: A Quarterly Journal of Jewish Life and Thought*, founded in 1950, quickly became one of the broadest and most popular. Rabbi Robert Gordis, the founding editor, wrote that "we are committed to the proposition that Judaism has positive value today for Jews and for the world. . . . At the same time, we disassociate ourselves from the dangerous tendency toward the hardening of party lines on the contemporary Jewish scene. . . ." Gordis proudly told his readers that "the members of the Board of Editors belong to every school of Jewish life or to none. The trends popularly referred to as Orthodox, Conservatism, Reform, Reconstructionism, as well as others that as yet have no specific names, have their advocates among us, though no institution or movement is officially represented. . . ." He readily agreed that "our differences will find expression in these pages, but we shall be at one in opposing the dogmatism which takes for granted that one's own particular standpoint has a monopoly on truth and the authoritarianism which would suppress any contrary point of view."[13]

Many of the book-length monographs focused on the theme of the search for God. The concern was not primarily "how can one believe in God after the Holocaust?" but rather, "how can people in the suburbs find religious meaning?" Will Herberg, later to become known as the author of *Protestant, Catholic, Jew*, wrote *Judaism and Modern Man* in 1951. Abraham Joshua Heschel published *Man Is Not Alone* the very same year and then, in 1955, *God in Search of Man*, declaring, "It is customary to blame secular science and antireligious philosophy for the eclipse of religion in modern society. It would be more honest to blame religion for its own defeats. Religion declined not because it was refuted, but because it became irrelevant, dull, oppressive, insipid." Heschel argued that "when faith is completely replaced by creed, worship by discipline, love by habit; when the crisis of today is ignored because of the splendor of the past; when faith becomes an heirloom rather than a living fountain; when religion speaks only in the name of authority rather than with the voice of compassion—its message becomes meaningless."[14]

Heschel was one of many Jewish theologians who became active in ecumenical activities. Americans felt that it was important for people of all faiths to get along with one another and so it was considered important for religious leaders to dialogue. In the case of Jewish-Christian relations, there was a two-thousand-year history of antagonism and persecution that had to be acknowledged and repudiated. The Catholic Church was intensely interested in finding a way to reconcile with the Jewish people, and Augustin Cardinal Bea held discussions with Heschel in Rome in 1961. The rabbi urged the Vatican to reject the idea that the Jews as a people were responsible for the crucifixion of Jesus. Judaism had an integrity and legitimacy in its own right and not just as a precursor to Christianity. The Church could promote better relations by participating with Jews in a wide range of communal as well as scholarly projects. Some of Heschel's recommendations were later included in *Nostra Aetate*, part of the "Declaration on the Relationship of the Church to Non-Christian Religions," a document issued as part of Vatican II.

Intellectuals began reacquainting themselves with what later became known as Jewish spirituality, studying texts that had been deliberately ignored for many decades. The prevailing ethos up to this point favored highly logical scholarly study that looked down upon anything mystical. Scholars followed the rationalism of Wissenschaft des Judentums, the pedantic Germanic historical approach developed in the nineteenth century. Wissenschaft used scientific methods of investigation to trace the origin and development of Jewish traditions and place them in the wider context of world history and culture. American Jewish students of Judaism began to slowly expand their horizons, not being as quick to reject anything just because it approached the subject from a more personal, mystical, or subjective perspective. Martin Buber's books played a key role in this process. Buber, whose concept of the I-Thou relationship became a central pillar in certain psychological theories, was a highly trained German scholar who emphasized, at the same time, the importance of the nonrational and particularly Hasidic culture.

If Buber helped to rehabilitate the reputation of the Hasid, then Gershom Scholem restored single-handed the image of the Jewish mystic as a legitimate religious figure. Scholem is credited with creating the academic study of Jewish mysticism, including Lurianic Kabbalah, and his works opened up an entirely new approach to the study of Jewish religion. All scholars and popular writers publishing on the Kabbalah today owe much to his pioneering studies. Franz Rosenzweig was yet another German Jew whose writings became increasingly influential in the United States. Rosenzweig's *The Star of Redemption* portrays the relationships between God, humanity, and the world as they are connected by creation, revelation, and redemption. While not Orthodox by most criteria, he urged fellow Jews to consider taking upon themselves more traditional observances. Although he died in 1929, his thought was carried over to a wide audience by Brandeis University professor Nahum Glatzer.[15]

During the Eisenhower years, Americans of all backgrounds embraced their common "Judeo-Christian heritage." Later commentators would point out the absurdity of referring to such a common religious background when in actual fact the two religions had a long history of antagonism based on both theological differences and historical factors. But, for second-generation American Jews trying to build a peaceful and happy life, the post-WWII emphasis on "brotherhood" was warmly welcomed. The atmosphere of acceptance made it easier for Jewish theologians to write about the ways in which Judaism was distinctive. Abba Hillel Silver published *Where Judaism Differed* in 1957 and Leo Baeck wrote *Judaism and Christianity* in 1958. Both tried to explain how Judaism differed not only from Christianity, but also from the surrounding American civil religion. Silver's manuscript had originally been titled *Where Judaism Differs*, but his editors at Macmillan insisted that he put the title in the past tense. As his son explained, much later, "the book appeared during the comfortable Eisenhower era, when many people believed, or at least wanted to believe, that the hates and wars of the past could be left behind and that one way to hasten this happy event was to bury, once and for all, old controversies and prejudices."[16]

Jewish Religious Practices in the Postwar Period

In his 1957 *American Judaism*, Nathan Glazer suggested that "American Jews, if they believe in anything, believe in the instrumental efficacy of religion."[17] Synagogues were useful for keeping the Jewish people unified and providing a framework for the maintenance of Jewish ritual, but what was more important to most of the new suburbanites was the opportunity they offered to meet new friends and neighbors and provide valuable extracurricular activities for the kids. What many Jews did not see was that the primary role of religion, in theory, was to embody universal truths that could help people build a closer relationship with God and live more ethical lives.

Most suburban Jews were not "religious" in the classical understanding of this term. While it is always dangerous to generalize, many were trying to express an essentially secular Jewish identity in a religious framework where it did not comfortably fit. Herbert J. Gans later spoke of symbolic ethnicity where ethnic Americans showed interest in selected cultural aspects of their roots, but did not feel that these interests needed to be supported by a long-term commitment to any specific belief or set of practices. This can help us understand the sporadic and inconsistent ceremonial observances that characterized the behavior of most American Jews. Marshall Sklare outlined five criteria that promoted certain types of Jewish ritual practice over others "on the suburban frontier." A ritual was most likely to be retained when it "is capable of effective redefinition in modern terms."[18] It does not "demand social isolation or the adoption of a unique life style" and it "accords with the religious culture of the larger community," providing a Jewish alternative to a Christian celebration or holiday when such an alternative is felt to be needed. The ritual is most likely to be retained if it is centered on the child, since much of what the adults do is for the children's sake. Finally, the ritual is more likely to be observed if it is performed once a year or, at the very least, infrequently.

Whatever their parents' degree of observance, Jewish children knew from an early age that they were a minority. This sense was sharpest at Christmas time, when it seemed that the entire country was celebrating a holiday that they were not a part of. Some Jewish families gave in to the pressure, putting up trees in their living rooms that they sometimes called Hanukkah bushes. Others eagerly embraced Christmas practices, believing that it made them more American and helped them integrate into society. Nevertheless, the majority did not want to celebrate a Christian holiday and so began placing greater emphasis on Hanukkah, a relatively minor celebration that had never been seen as a central Jewish holiday. The story of Hanukkah commemorated the victory of Judah Maccabee and his brothers over the Greek Syrians who had desecrated the Temple and ordered the Jews to violate the commandments. The story was based on a historical event, but the actual rebellion was not only a war against the Greek Syrians but also a civil war between Hellenizing and anti-Hellenizing Jews, a point that was sometimes deliberately ignored. American Jews did not want to delve into the historical details, preferring to see it as a "celebration of light" or a "festival of freedom." Electric Hanukkah menorahs were introduced in the late 1940s and early 1950s, which fit into the "no muss, no fuss" sensibility of the times.[19]

Most Jews let the Sabbath become a vague presence in their homes. Strict Sabbath observance imposed a heavy economic burden on many retailers, who usually relied on Saturday for a disproportionate percentage of their weekly sales. The monetary loss suffered by those who insisted on closing on Saturdays was much worse in states where blue laws restricted Sunday commerce. Sabbath-observing Jews who were not allowed to open their stores on Sunday instead of Saturday brought a number of lawsuits to try to remedy this inequality. In 1961, the Supreme Court ruled against furniture store owner Abraham Braunfeld, who argued that the Pennsylvania Sunday Closing Law compromised the free exercise clause of the First Amendment. The Supreme Court disagreed, stating that the law was not primarily religious in nature and that a genuine public interest was being served. Despite this setback, traditional Jews were increasingly likely to be able to open their stores on Sunday, provided that they closed on Shabbat. In time, under pressure from large chain stores, many states repealed their blue laws altogether.

Life cycle events played an important role in reinforcing bonds within the Jewish community as well as creating lifelong Jewish memories. Virtually all Jewish baby boys were circumcised, but fewer had a brit milah ceremony, which symbolized the bringing of the child into the covenant. More traditional families had a mohel, a ritual functionary who specialized in circumcision, perform the ceremony in their house or at the synagogue on the eighth day. Others preferred to have a doctor do the surgery in the hospital and then have a religious ceremony at home. There was no parallel ritual for girls until the 1960s or 1970s, when baby-naming ceremonies for baby girls began to become popular.

But while the birth of a child was celebrated, it was the coming-of-age ceremony that became paramount. The bar mitzvah gradually became the hallmark of all Jewish life cycle events. While it had traditionally marked the day that the Jewish male accepted the yoke of the commandments, in postwar America it was more likely to mark the end of all serious study and practice. Synagogues tried to develop different types of formal and informal programs to keep post–bar mitzvah teenagers involved in congregational activities, but they were competing with many other extracurricular activities. Rabbi Mordecai M. Kaplan introduced a parallel ceremony for girls called a bat mitzvah, starting with his own daughter Judith in 1922. The bat mitzvah began to become popular in the 1950s, when newly affluent suburban Jews were looking for ways to mark their newfound economic and social status.

Whereas traditional Judaism had required each and every Jew to keep kosher, many suburban Jews placed the emphasis on keeping their homes kosher, as if it was the house that needed to observe the religious obligation. The majority of Jews moving to the suburbs were coming from backgrounds where the kosher laws had been observed or they were at least cognizant of the fact that many of their friends, neighbors, and relatives observed kashrut. Many of those who leaned towards the more traditional side kept "Conservative kosher," at least at home. They avoided pork and shellfish but had only one set of plates—usually made out of glass—and silverware. Rabbis liked to joke that the plates of their congregants were sure to go to heaven. Kosher restaurants that served Eastern European Jewish cooking became popular. The meat was generally purchased from a kosher slaughterhouse, but the more detailed rules of kashrut were not always adhered to and the restaurants remained open on Saturday. Therefore, no *mashgiach* (kosher supervisor) would give them a *hechsher*, a certificate that the restaurant was indeed strictly kosher. This made no difference to most of their customers. Suburban Jews loved "kosher" and "kosher-style" eating as long as it reinforced their sense of ethnicity without limiting their choice. Elizabeth Ehrlich, reminiscing about her Jewish childhood in the Detroit area, stated, "In mid century America, that's what the good life was all about—choice."[20]

Building Synagogues in the Suburbs

Between the end of the war and the inauguration of President John F. Kennedy, many Jewish families joined a synagogue for the first time. Whereas in 1930 only about 20 percent of American Jews were members of a synagogue, by 1960 almost 60 percent were. This threefold increase in only thirty years was not because Jews were necessarily becoming more devout. As Herberg explained it, joining a suburban synagogue was "a way of sociability or 'belonging' rather than a way of orientating life to God."[21]

The synagogue became by far the most important, and certainly most visible, Jewish institution in most communities. The increasing rate of synagogue membership was directly tied to the massive move to suburbia. Entire new communities were created as developers bought up huge tracts of land and built tens of thousands of new single-family homes. Many Jews were moving from heavily Jewish urban neighborhoods where they had practiced very little Jewish ritual. While they were still living in the Jewish ghetto, they were part of the Jewish community, if only through osmosis. Once they relocated, however, many let residual connections with Judaism die. Others reevaluated their Jewish identity and perceived the need for a new approach. As they began moving into their new suburban homes, they saw their Christian neighbors building new churches. When Barbara Ward wrote her "Report to Europe on America" in 1954, she explained that "we did not need the evidence of polls or church attendance to confirm what we could so easily observe-the walls of new churches rising in town and countryside wherever we went."[22] Jewish suburbanites felt that they too needed to organize for religious purposes and began a huge synagogue building boom that lasted from the late 1940s through the 1960s and even into the 1970s. Some joked that the American Jewish community had an "edifice complex," the obsession with building for its own sake. Not surprisingly, each room, hall, and office had a separate plaque dedicated in honor of a distinguished donor or in loving memory of one of the donor's deceased relatives.

The growth of new synagogues was truly exponential. Between 1945 and 1960, many hundreds of synagogue buildings were built in the suburbs. Most were relatively large and required substantial-sized congregations in order to support them. The buildings alone required the expenditure of huge sums. The congregations were able to raise these moneys because of the constant flow of people into the suburbs. The central challenge was how to design a synagogue building that would be intimate enough for the sparse numbers

FIGURE I.2. Artistic rendition of North Shore Congregation Israel of Glencoe, Illinois in the early 1960s, one of two synagogue buildings designed by Minoru Yamasaki, the architect of the twin towers of the World Trade Center. The sanctuary rises 55 feet and covers more than 10,000 square feet of area. During the High Holy Days, more than 1,650 worshippers can be accommodated in the sanctuary and the Frank Memorial Hall, which adds an additional 5,000 square feet of space. *Courtesy of the Jacob Rader Marcus Center of the American Jewish Archives*

who came weekly but expandable to accommodate the overflow crowds on the High Holy Days. Most had a sanctuary that could seat two or three hundred with a removable partition separating it from the social hall. On Rosh Hashanah and Yom Kippur, the partition was opened, providing seating for several hundred additional congregants. Some congregations held overflow services or scheduled early and late High Holy Day services so that everyone could be accommodated.

With so much emphasis being placed on the buildings themselves, religious programming lagged behind. Rabbis and program directors did their best to try to draw in congregants and visitors, but found the demand for serious study to be quite limited. There were all sorts of social activities, many of them sponsored by sisterhoods and brotherhoods, but the central focus was on the weekly Shabbat services. Orthodox congregations had services that were almost entirely in Hebrew, with men and women sitting separately. Conservative synagogues maintained most of the traditional prayers, but introduced a number of innovations designed to appeal to the suburban crowd. Reform congregations in the suburbs included more Hebrew in their worship services than the classical Reform temples in the cities, but still used much more English than the more traditional congregations.

In the postwar era, American Judaism was denominationally structured. While many American Jews did not have a clear theology, they were nevertheless expected to pick one of the three American denominations: Reform, Conservative, or Orthodox. Eventually, the Reconstructionist movement would be included as well,. The word *denomination* had been borrowed from the Protestants, and the Jewish streams, wings, or movements were a bit uncomfortable with the use of this term. Critics felt that it sounded too Christian and did not express the reality of Jewish religious life. Indeed, many of the leaders within each of the movements were only slowly adjusting to the reality that their particular denomination represented a segment of the American Jewish population rather than the entire community. But, in the suburbs, each congregation was a world unto itself. While many synagogues emphasized their denominational affiliation when possible, most of their members remained uninterested in the details of what that meant.

In the decades immediately following the end of World War II, the Conservative movement dominated the American Jewish religious landscape. Conservative Judaism stood for a moderate centrist perspective, stressing the importance of tradition as well as the need for change. That change had to be within the acceptable parameters of the halacha, and it had to be gradual. Movement leaders had every reason to be optimistic. The number of synagogues affiliated with the United Synagogue of America increased from around 350 in 1945 to about 800 just twenty years later. Most of these congregations were growing in size, with their religious schools attracting more students every year and new families signing up all the time. Despite an obvious gap between what the movement was preaching and what the congregants were doing, there was a lot of activity going on in these suburban congregations. The centrist orientation of the Conservative synagogue was a perfect fit for the mentality of the postwar years.

For much of this time period, the Conservative and Orthodox movements were similar to each other. While Orthodox leaders certainly understood the basic theological differences and tried to impress the importance of those differences on their laity, many Orthodox-trained rabbis served Conservative congregations, and there was a great deal of interaction between the two movements on all levels. Many rabbinical students at the Jewish Theological Seminary came from Orthodox homes and many Conservative rabbis had attended Yeshiva University as undergraduates and even as rabbinical students. It was not uncommon to have a large Conservative synagogue led by an Orthodox rabbi who continued to identify as Orthodox. If asked, he might readily admit that he had taken the position not because of his religious beliefs or approach to halacha but rather in order to make a (better) living. The Conservative movement relied on Orthodoxy for mohels, ritual functionaries who performed circumcisions, sofers, scribes who carefully copied Torah scrolls, as well as for the use of mikvehs, ritual baths that were used by women after the end of their menstrual period and for other purposes, including the ceremony for Jewish conversion.

Since relatively few Conservative women actually followed the laws of niddah, the mikveh was used infrequently, with few Conservative synagogues bothering to build one. This created a conundrum for Conservative rabbis, particularly those from traditional backgrounds. They could use any body of running water, but rivers and streams were generally too cold and too public. Swimming pools would have been ideal, but most halachic authorities did not regard them as being kosher. The mikvehs built within Orthodox synagogues were generally the preferred solution, but by the 1950s, some were beginning to ban the use of their mikvehs for non-Orthodox conversions. The rationale was that Orthodox synagogues should not collude with Conservative rabbis in the making of Conservative conversions, which they did not deem to be authentic. Rabbi Joseph B. Soloveitchik, the rosh yeshiva of YU, favored a permissive position, and his influence swayed some. Nevertheless, the trend was toward greater restrictions.

Many congregations occupied a position midway between Orthodoxy and Conservatism. The issue of mixed seating became the decisive decision that determined which direction they would head. During the 1950s, there were a series of court cases dealing with mixed seating in synagogues that forced congregations—with increasingly rare exceptions—to choose between strict Orthodox practice or mixed seating. The legal cases differed in their specifics, but all dealt with the question: could a congregation vote to allow mixed seating even if they had a constitution that required them to practice traditional Judaism? The courts generally refused to get involved in the religious issues themselves and in most cases threw the decision back to the congregation. Since each individual congregation owned their synagogue building, there was no reason to involve any national religious body. The bottom line was that the majority could make whatever changes they wanted, based on the religious and social needs of the congregation.

Although the legal rulings went against the Orthodox minority in several specific cases, it reinforced the Orthodox contention that separate seating with a *mechitza* (a physical barrier) was a requirement for any Orthodox prayer service. Congregations found it increasingly untenable to offer services that broke with the halacha while at the same time claiming to be Orthodox. Yeshiva University continued to acquiesce when its rabbinic graduates accepted pulpits without *mechitzas*, but insisted that the rabbi work quickly to rectify the halachic violation or else leave the congregation. Synagogues in the South or Midwest that continued to prefer the middle ground began to call themselves traditional rather than Orthodox. They generally remained independent, not joining any congregational organization.

Another issue that helped to differentiate the Conservative synagogue from the Orthodox shul was the use of electronic microphone systems. Orthodox synagogues would not allow the use of any electric mechanism on Shabbat. This meant that rabbis and cantors had to project well without the use of artificial amplification. This obviously made it hard for congregants to hear, especially in large congregations with huge sanctuaries. The Rabbinical Council of America (RCA) came under increasing pressure and actually condoned the use of certain types of amplification in 1948, a ruling that was reversed in 1954.[23] Many Conservative congregations, on the other hand, allowed for the use of not only a microphone but other electric devices as well, including an organ. While some Conservative congregations, including many in the more densely populated Jewish areas with large Orthodox communities, remained traditional, others began to resemble Reform temples. The religious needs of the suburban congregations were difficult to define and therefore nearly impossible to meet. Weekly services were generally sparsely attended, although some congregations attracted large crowds of music lovers if they had a cantor with a spectacular voice. For this same reason, many congregations would make strenuous efforts to find specially trained choirs that could perform on the High Holy Days. Worship continued to become more formalized, with congregants becoming passive observers rather than participants. Infrequent visitors might mistakenly refer to the congregation as the "audience," a subconscious recognition that the worshipers were not actually praying but rather watching a performance.

Despite the many problems, suburban Jews were proud of the communities they had built. The synagogue building symbolized both success and acceptance. A number of architects became known for their synagogue designs. Frank Lloyd Wright's 1953 Beth Sholom Synagogue in Elkins Park

FIGURE 1.3. Frank Lloyd Wright's Beth Sholom Synagogue in Elkins Park, Pennsylvania, designed in the Mayan Revival architecture style in 1953–1954 and dedicated in 1959. The design is notable for its steeply inclined walls of translucent wire glass and plastic projecting skyward like a "luminous Mount Sinai." Designated a National Historic Landmark in the Spring of 2007, it was the only synagogue that Wright ever designed and the last project that he completed before his death. Photo Phil Carrizzi. *Courtesy of Phil Carrizzi*

Pennsylvania was probably the most famous synagogue built in the postwar years because of the prominence of the architect. There was plenty of work to keep architects busy. Percival Goodman, Erich Mendelsohn, and a number of other mostly Jewish architects designed about one thousand new synagogue buildings in the 1950s and 1960s.[24] Abstract expressionist artists including sculptors such as Herbert Ferber, Ibram Lassaw, David Hare, and Seymour Lipton and painters such as Robert Motherwell and Adolph Gottlieb collaborated with the architects to decorate synagogues in a way that would define the public image of Judaism in America. Goodman argued that building physical communal structures gave American Jews a way to express their increasing sense of group consciousness. "Suddenly there occurred the fact that six million Jews were slaughtered in three or four years, just because they were Jews. We do not know in what ways other groups would react to such a happening, but among the Jews it seemed to have the following effect: they became aware of themselves as a physical community, a congregation."[25]

Already, in the prewar years, many Conservative congregations had begun building "synagogue centers" which were designed to serve a multiplicity of community functions and not just be a place to pray. While the sanctuary was still of great importance, the synagogue center had large kitchens that could accommodate not just one or two chefs but an entire sisterhood. There were meeting halls of all different types and tons of classroom space. Ideally, they would also include a gym and a pool, although this did not happen as often as the building committees would have liked. Expenses were one reason, as was the desire not to compete with the local Jewish Community Center (JCC).

The school wing was usually the largest part of the synagogue building, with many classrooms designed for the afternoon Hebrew school and the Sunday morning religious school. Whereas, before the war, Jewish communities ran community Talmud Torahs, most congregations now opened their own religious schools. Synagogues used these schools to attract families who might become members, and so the development of a well-regarded school was a requirement for congregational growth. Conservative afternoon schools met twice or even three times a week, while Reform temples usually sufficed with two or three hours every Sunday morning. The pattern here was clear—many were becoming more involved in individual congregations at the expense of communal institutions.

Before the mass exodus to the suburbs, Jewish education had been in an embryonic stage of development. While there were innovative Jewish educators working hard to transform the field, most heder teachers in the 1920s and 1930s were elderly Eastern European refugees who took the job as a matter of last resort. They knew nothing about pedagogy and not too much more about the actual subject matter. My uncle Bernard Moskowitz told me how his heder teacher in Waterbury, Connecticut in the 1930s would yell at the students and would actually rap the students over the knuckles with a ruler if they were too slow in responding to a question. With the partial exception of the Orthodox, no one sent their children to Jewish day schools. Creating Jewish parochial schools was regarded as "ghettoizing" their children—something that the immigrants and children of immigrants wanted to avoid at all costs.

Even though the afternoon religious schools improved after World War II, they were still not terribly successful at teaching the students about Judaism. This sense of failure was felt by Sunday school educators in every religion and denomination. Public school was becoming more rigorous and taking up more time. Kindergartens had been established in most schools by the 1950s; many were even attending nursery schools. At the same time, elementary schools began working off of a nine-month rather than an eight-month calendar. Religious schools were caught in a lose-lose situation. If they tried to replicate the academic experience of the public elementary school, the children would resent the vigor. If they tried to make the Sunday school more relaxing, the children might find the experience superficial. The purpose of the afternoon school was primarily utilitarian: to teach the children enough Hebrew so that they could get through their bar and bat mitzvah ceremony. Hebrew School, cynics remarked, was the place where students failed to learn Hebrew.

Most suburban Jews attended synagogue sporadically, if at all. They did participate in Jewish rituals on specific holidays, particularly those that emphasized home and family. They attended a Passover seder at which they ate matzah with bitter herbs and they lit Hannukah menorahs, eating latkes with apple sauce. Many young people would carry the memories of these home observances with them and would feel a strong emotional need to celebrate those same rituals as a way of remembering their departed parents and grandparents.

Problems and Challenges in the 1960s

The social revolution of the 1960s emphasized the importance of free choice, and this accelerated the already extensive experimentation going on in the American religious world. The ten years between the assassination of President John F. Kennedy in 1963 through the Watergate scandal and subsequent resignation of President Richard M. Nixon in 1973 was a turbulent if exciting time. Assumptions that had proven themselves to be reasonable over a fairly long period were suddenly questioned and, in many cases, overthrown. This was true for the many veterans who believed serving their country was a great honor and privilege and that service was for a great cause and it was true for the mother who believed that her daughter's future was dependent in large part on remaining chaste until marriage. A "generation gap" made it difficult for parents to talk with children. It was as if they inhabited different universes.

By the early to mid-1960s, the religious revival of the post–World War II period was coming to an end. Membership in religious communities of all sorts stopped expanding. By 1965, membership was declining in many denominations and continued to decline until at least 1975, when it partially stabilized. All the American Jewish denominations felt the pressure, but the end of this revival period was particularly hard on the Conservative movement. The Conservative movement was incredibly diverse, held together primarily by the pull toward the center that was a feature of this time period. As the years went by, many of those affiliated with a Conservative congregation found they did not really feel they belonged there.

But the problems were not restricted to the Conservative movement. There were early signs that the Jewish community as a whole might have difficulty perpetuating itself. In 1964, the original *Look* magazine published a cover story written by Thomas B. Morgan on "The Vanishing American Jew." The magazine cited what was to become the usual litany of sociological problems: Jews were not particularly devout, increasing numbers were intermarrying, fertility rates were low, and so forth. While cynics would later point out that *Look* magazine itself disappeared not once but twice while the Jews remained, Morgan's article remains eerily clairvoyant.

If the 1950s was a decade of religious resurgence, the 1960s was one in which religious institutions struggled. Young people in particular were disillusioned with society as a whole, and that included religious institutions of all types. Like many Protestant ministers and Catholic priests, rabbis started

FIGURE 1.4. Rabbi Maurice Eisendrath, president of the Union of American Hebrew Congregations, presents President John F. Kennedy with a Torah scroll at the dedication of the Religious Action Center of Reform Judaism in 1961. The Torah had belonged to Rabbi Isaac Mayer Wise, the founder of American Reform Judaism. *Courtesy of the Union for Reform Judaism*

to feel that Judaism as a religious faith was neither addressing people's central existential questions nor comforting them in their times of need. Large numbers of Jewish youth rejected any connection with the organized Jewish community. They were in revolt against religion generally and particularly upset by what they saw as the superficiality and hypocrisy of American Jewish life. Although most felt their parents' lifestyle did not merit extended analysis, they instinctually sensed that their parents did not believe in many of the values that they claimed to treasure. In simple words, their parents were pretending to be religious, but were not.

The need to mask ethnicity, or at least put a religious veneer over it, continued into the 1960s. Eugene Borowitz said that "if the American Jew were truly religious, he would create a living American Jewish community, but though he organizes his community along religious lines, his life shows little religious belief and practice." Shockingly, he argued that what most American Jews seemed to want was "secular Judaism." However, few would be willing to buck the American religious consensus, and so most chose to affiliate with a "religious" denomination. This actually hid the inner emotional reality that most people experienced. Borowitz described this as "the mask Jews wear."[26] American Jews were a "species of Marrano in reverse," meaning that while the Spanish Jews during the Inquisition period had pretended to be Christian while secretly holding onto their Jewish faith, American Jews pretended to believe in Judaism, while having no inner Judaic convictions. "God lurks behind the chopped liver," Borowitz deadpanned.

Andrew Greeley found that, between 1952 and 1965, Jews showed the greatest percentage increase in "church membership." The emphasis was, however, on affiliation rather than participation or theological commitment. Less people were going to synagogue services on a weekly basis, although more were putting in an appearance on the High Holy Days. During the same years, the percentage of Jews who said that they believed in God actually declined by 21 percent, in prayer 19 percent, in life after death 18 percent, and in heaven 15 percent. Less inhibited by the conformity expected in the cultural environment of the 1950s, more Jews were admitting what had probably long been true: that they had no heartfelt religious faith. Much of American Jewish identity was expressed culturally, although there was a significant and perhaps even central component that remained religious. What baffled Greeley was that in the interval of these thirteen years in which Jewish religious belief supposedly eroded so substantially, "active church membership among American Jews has gone up some twelve percentage points."[27]

American Jews were finding additional ways to express their ethnic identity. Jewish-themed theatrical and cinema productions became quite popular in the 1960s, including *The Tenth Man, Milk and Honey, Judgment at Nuremburg, The Pawnbroker, The Fixer, Goodbye Columbus, I Can Get It for You Wholesale, The Deputy, After the Fall, Incident at Vichy*, and *Fiddler on the Roof. Fiddler on the Roof* introduced a series of songs that became American Jewish classics, played and replayed at weddings, bar mitzvahs, and even funerals. "Tradition, Tradition" became an anthem recalling the nostalgic Judaism of one's grandparents, while "Sunrise, Sunset" was a sentimental ballad recounting the various stages of life. American Jews saw *Fiddler* as their story, a musical that described the challenges they faced and the struggles they overcame.

Eli Lederhendler has argued that "*Fiddler* was a parable of self-validation *at the expense of the past*."[28] The play and movie reinterpreted the Sholem

Aleichem original to emphasize the American experience of the theatergoers rather than the shtetl experience of the historical types that the characters represented. Tevye grapples with the idea of romantic love, first denying that such a concept could exist and then eventually coming to terms with what it meant for his own relationships. Likewise, he originally expects his daughters to follow a predetermined path, but eventually comes to accept, albeit reluctantly, that they need to have the freedom to make their own life decisions. This foreshadows the dilemmas of freedom and autonomy that American Jews would face in the coming years.

American society was soon hit with a number of blows: the assassinations of President John F. Kennedy, Reverend Martin Luther King Jr., and Robert F. Kennedy, riots in large urban ghettos from New York to Los Angeles, an unpopular war in far-off Southeast Asia, and a number of other crises that shook public confidence and security. The religious consensus of the 1950s seemed like it had been a thousand years ago. Some Protestant theologians were declaring the "death of God," a sentiment that would have been unimaginable just ten years earlier. Richard Rubenstein became the main Jewish advocate for a type of "death of God" theology with the publication of his *After Auschwitz* in 1966. Rubenstein was not a Holocaust survivor, but he had lost his infant son on the morning before Yom Kippur and the Holocaust represented for him the concept of purposeless catastrophe.

Many young Jewish people joined the counterculture in the middle and late 1960s. They listened to rock and roll, experimented with drugs, and joined in "free love." Hippies, flower children, runaways, cult followers, and groupies all searched for love, peace, and understanding. Full of youthful enthusiasm, Jewish activists joined other young Americans in trying to overturn the status quo. Many became enamored with left-wing ideas and causes. They looked to Chinese and Cuban communism as models of social justice, just as the parents of the "red diaper babies" had idealized the Bolsheviks. They hung posters of Che Guevara in their dorm rooms and, after the Vietnam War began, threatened to burn their draft cards.

Jewish liberals marched in favor of civil rights in various Southern cities, joined urban Peace Corps projects such as VISTA, helped out in voter registration drives, and participated in the ubiquitous protests against the Vietnam War. The Jewish religious denominations responded with a mixture of fear and enthusiasm. Religious leaders certainly wanted Judaism to speak to the issues of the day, but they were also worried that the youth wanted to destroy all established institutions, including theirs. In this radical environ-ment, it was hard to build enthusiasm for the standard synagogue Judaism. Many of those in the suburbs were relatively unaffected by the social trans-formation of the sixties, and they continued doing the very same things they had been doing up till then. But those involved in social and political causes could not help but feel that the times required a new approach to Jewish religious activism.

Many American Jews devoted themselves to the civil rights movement. Jews who had been raised with the belief that Judaism stood for prophetic justice found a cause that they could embrace with a full heart. Many were strong supporters of Martin Luther King Jr., who advocated passive resis-tance rather than confrontation and violence. Those Jews devoted to social justice believed that they were fulfilling their Jewish religious obligation by supporting the civil rights movement and other liberal causes. Feminism be-came an important issue for many Jewish women, who felt that their distinc-tive vantage point gave them a unique perspective on gender roles in society. Women such as Betty Friedan and Gloria Steinem (whose father was Jewish) played crucial roles in the building of the American feminist movement (see chapter 5). Liberalism in all its forms became the new orthodoxy. Many rab-bis, particularly the more traditional ones, tried repeatedly to emphasize that Judaism was more than just liberal politics.

Rabbi Abraham Joshua Heschel became known for his enthusiastic in-volvement in the Civil Rights Movement and his belief that this involvement was a direct outgrowth of his Jewish religious commitment. He delivered the keynote address to the National Conference on Religion and Race on January 14, 1963, where he linked the struggle for Negro equality with that of the ancient Israelites in Egypt. At the conference, Heschel met Martin Luther King Jr., and the two became allies and friends. King pioneered a suc-cessful strategy for promoting social change in the late 1950s and early 1960s and was awarded the Nobel Peace Prize in 1964 for his contributions to har-monious and equal relations between the races. On March 21, 1965, Heschel walked with King across the Pettus Bridge in the march for civil rights from Selma to Montgomery, Alabama, a distance of about fifty miles. Heschel's daughter Susannah later wrote: "my father had lived in Nazi Germany, es-caping at the last minute, and his mother and sisters were murdered by the Nazis. For him, those experiences meant both a deepened commitment to his faith and his people, and also a heightened sensitivity to the suffering of

FIGURE 1.5. Rabbi Abraham Joshua Heschel in an antiwar protest alongside the Rev. Dr. Martin Luther King Jr. in 1968. On March 21, 1965, Heschel accompanied King in the historic civil rights march from Selma to Montgomery. After the march, Heschel wrote, "I felt my legs were praying." *Courtesy of the Jacob Rader Marcus Center of the American Jewish Archives*

all people." She explained that, for her father, "Nazism began with a debased view of human beings, which, in turn, was rooted in contempt for God. 'You cannot worship God,' he would say, 'and then look at a human being, created by God in God's own image, as if he or she were an animal.'"[29]

Many American Jews believed that political liberalism was the best vehicle for showing their ethical concern for humanity. They were particularly upset by the social inequality that was so apparent in the country and they were determined to try to rectify it. At first, their involvement in the civil rights movement was welcomed, but, over the course of time, many African American leaders began to resent white and particularly Jewish involvement in what they saw as their cause. Already in 1964 and 1965, there was a debate within the Student Nonviolent Coordinating Committee (SNCC) over how the civil rights movement could best achieve its goals, with some of the more extreme elements calling for "Black Power." Stokely Carmichael and other radical leaders made it plain and clear that they were not willing to play by the rules that the white establishment had made.

While they were probably most concerned with preventing Martin Luther King Jr. from taking credit for the SNCC's successful fieldwork, they were also determined to keep white liberals (most of whom were Jews) from dominating the civil rights movement. In 1966, a group calling themselves the National Committee of Negro Churchmen wrote the "Black Power Statement," which took a more aggressive position on how American blacks should fight for greater rights in American society. They argued that depending on the transforming power of Christian love was passive and unhealthy and that what was needed was not so much love as it was justice. As the black power movement grew in 1965 and 1966, Jews were pushed out of the civil rights hierarchy. Many remained involved, but the seeds of mutual antagonism between the African American and Jewish communities had been planted. The split widened in the weeks leading up to the Six-Day War in 1967. Many Jews felt betrayed by their black civil rights colleagues, many of whom expressed sympathy for the Palestinians and overt hostility toward Israel.

The concept of black power did provide all American ethnic groups, including Jews, with a new model for how they could redefine themselves. The "invisible ethnics" no longer had to be content with the melting pot model, but could now assert their ethnic pride and argue that they were making a valuable contribution to the United States as an ethnic group and not strictly as individuals. The Americanness of American Jews was no longer in question, reasserting their Jewishness an asset rather than a liability.

By the late 1960s, the sociopolitical atmosphere had changed so dramatically that it was hard to understand how American Jews had been politically timid during the Holocaust years. Brooklyn-born rabbi Meir Kahane attracted eager crowds of young lower-middle-class urban youth by mocking the apathy and impotence of the World War II–era Jewish establishment. He went on numerous speaking tours, saying that the Jewish organizations should have organized a protest, with the participants chaining themselves to the White House fence. This argument conveniently ignored the fact that this type of civil disobedience was only pioneered by Martin Luther King Jr. years after the Holocaust ended.

In 1968, Kahane founded the Jewish Defense League (JDL) to fight antisemitism and promote Jewish pride. Jews should worry about themselves because nobody else in the world worried about them. They should embrace their religion in the traditional form because the non-Orthodox had watered it down, making Judaism less vital and inspirational. They should band together for protection and solidarity and eventually move to Israel, the only place they could really be themselves. Kahane's motto was "Never Again!" a solemn pledge that he and his followers would never allow themselves to be persecuted without fighting back. He advocated helping Soviet Jewry long before the persecution of Russian Jews became an international issue. Although communal leaders worried about his extremism, Kahane was an inspiration to many youth looking for an activist Jewish political identity and, in many cases, an Orthodox religious commitment.

In the years after World War II, it gradually became known that the Jews in the Soviet Union were being singled out for systematic harassment. The Soviet Union was officially atheistic and the government took stern measures to discourage religious belief and practice of any sort. While all religions were considered enemies of the state, Judaism was regarded as a particular threat since Jews were seen as a people whose loyalties were only to their own and not to the Communist cause. Refusenik leaders such as Anatoly (later Natan) Sharansky, a computer scientist who was sent to prison for daring to teach Hebrew, became heroes in the American Jewish community. In July 1978, I remember pasting the *New York Times* article that conveyed the news that he had been convicted by a Soviet court on charges of treason and spying for the United States, and sentenced to thirteen years of forced labor, on the wall of my summer camp cabin. The Soviets came under increasingly heavy pressure to allow Jews and other ethnic minorities to emigrate, and, by the late 1970s, substantial numbers were indeed being allowed to leave. The success of this American Jewish activist initiative contrasted starkly with the failure to help their fellow Jews during World War II. Unfortunately, many of these same American Jewish activists were disappointed when they began receiving Soviet Jews, who were more materialistic than the activists had expected and, in many cases, were barely interested in preserving their Jewish identity.

For most American Jews, being Jewish meant feeling a part of the Jewish people. In *Sacred Survival*, Jonathan Woocher described what he called "civil Judaism," the civil religion of American Jews. This was based on Robert Bellah's 1967 essay, "Civil Religion in America," which argued that, in addition to various forms of denominational religion, Americans also embraced a common set of supplementary beliefs and values. Woocher argued that while American Jews paid lip service to their supposed denominational commitments, what really made American Jews passionate was their concern for the survival of the Jewish people. This commitment to "sacred survival" gave meaning to their identity as Jews by connecting them to the recent historical dramas of destruction and rebirth. This included, first and foremost, support for the State of Israel, particularly after the Six-Day War of 1967. American Jews became deeply engaged in the struggle to free Soviet Jewry and later extended this effort to other oppressed Jewries around the world. They emphasized the Jewish value of *tzedakah,* frequently translated as charity, but now extended to include all types of philanthropy. What really mattered was remembering the past and being willing to publicly identify themselves with the Jewish people.

The emphasis on helping Jews throughout the world grew tangible as Jewish immigrants began arriving from all corners of the globe. This was a consequence of the relaxation of the strict immigration laws that had been in effect since 1924. The McCarran-Walter Act of 1952 ended the prohibition against immigration from Asia and the Immigration and Nationality Act of 1965 ended quotas based on national origin. These immigration laws radically changed the ethnic composition of the United States. The new immigrants included Hindus and Buddhists from Asia, Muslims from Arab and African countries, and Catholics from Latin America. Whereas the bulk of the American Jewish community arrived before 1924, there were spurts of Jewish immigration after World War II. In addition to Holocaust survivors, Jews came from various Arab countries in the years following the creation of the State of Israel in 1948, Hungary after the failed revolution in 1956, Cuba after the Castro revolution in 1959, the Soviet Union after the Six-Day War in 1967, Iran after the fall of the shah in 1979, and so forth.

Many of these Jewish ethnic groups settled in particular cities or regions: Cuban Jews in Miami, Persian (Iranian) Jews in Los Angeles, Syrian Jews in Brooklyn and New Jersey, Bukharin Jews in Queens, New York, Mexican Jews in Texas and Southern California, South African Jews in Atlanta and San Diego, Babylonian (Iraqi) Jews on Long Island, and so forth. There were also Israelis moving to the United States, many of whom settled here permanently. The American Jewish community had some difficulty integrating these Israelis, most of whom were either resolutely secular or fervently Orthodox.

FIGURE 1.6. Youth from Congregation Bene Naharayim of Jamaica Estates and the Babylonian Jewish Center of Great Neck marching in the 2006 Israel Day Parade with the Northeast Queens Jewish Community Council. There are about fifteen thousand Iraqi Jews in the United States, concentrated in New York and Los Angeles. Photo Joseph Levine. *Courtesy of Joseph Levine of the Northeast Queens Jewish Community Council*

The Rediscovery of the Holocaust

In his memoirs, Rabbi Arthur Hertzberg described how the Holocaust suddenly became a central part of American Jewish memory. "In the immediate aftermath of the Second World War, American Jews did not want the mass murders in Europe to be much mentioned in public, although privately the trauma was often discussed." He remembered inviting the then struggling Elie Wiesel to give a talk in 1961, but found that virtually no one in his congregation wanted to come hear the writer speak. By the mid-1970s, however, he saw a radical reversal take place. "I was astonished." Hertzberg wrote that at first he did not understand why his congregants were suddenly willing to talk about the Holocaust, but he soon figured it out. "American Jews were very worried about their children. They had bet the future on pride in Israel. Their children and their children's children would be glad to continue this glorious identity—but by the 1970s, a generation after the State of Israel had been founded, American Jews were becoming very nervous."[30] Concerned that pride in Israel might not be enough to perpetuate a strong Jewish identity, American Jews began to look to the Holocaust as an additional reason why Jews in general and their children in particular should feel obligated to remaining Jewish. The Jewish communal agenda slowly began shifting its focus from universalistic issues such as civil rights and the Vietnam War to more specifically Jewish concerns, including in particular the Holocaust.

The specific impetus was the Adolf Eichmann trial, held in 1961–1962. Eichmann had been the Gestapo bureaucrat responsible for overseeing the implementation of the "Final Solution," the murder of six million Jews. Prime Minister David Ben Gurion announced on May 23, 1960, that Israeli secret agents had found him in Argentina and brought him to Jerusalem, where he would stand trial for crimes against humanity and the Jewish people. Up until this point, American Jews had generally tried to downplay the Nazi "war against the Jews." When Nathan Glazer wrote his *American Judaism* in 1957, he explained that "the murder of six million Jews by Hitler had remarkably slight effects on the inner life of American Jewry."[31] This was the consensus at the time. In recent years, scholars have begun paying more attention to the many commemorative efforts that were made in the early years, but, even now, it seems startling how much more emphasis was placed on the Holocaust after the Eichmann trial.

Much of the initial publicity was due not only to the trial but also to the controversial reporting done by Hannah Arendt. In February and March of 1962, Arendt wrote a series of five articles for the *New Yorker* on the trial, which became the basis for her book *Eichmann in Jerusalem: A Report on the Banality of Evil* . She was attacked because of her comment that "the essence of totalitarian government, and perhaps the nature of every bureaucracy, is to make functionaries and mere cogs . . . out of men, and thus to dehumanize them." Some thought that she was holding the system solely responsible for the terrible crimes that had been committed, thereby excusing the acts perpetuated by individual Nazis including Eichmann.

Even more upsetting was Arendt's approach to Jewish victimhood. She wrote that the Jews of Europe had been socially myopic and their political inaction had been one of the main factors leading to their destruction. While she certainly did not blame the Jews for their own murders, she did write that the Jews were targeted by the Nazis for "logical" reasons. The Nazis were rebelling against a political and social system the Jews helped to build and had a vested interest in maintaining. By refusing to use their potential political power as a group, they were making themselves vulnerable to attack, and the Nazis took advantage of this weakness. Her critique was a broadside against the cosmopolitan Jewish consensus, which held that while Jews might be involved as individuals in political life, they should not seek to work together. There was therefore no such thing as, for example, "the Jewish vote." Arendt cast doubt on the wisdom of this approach. Whatever one thought of her controversial views, Arendt's essays and the responses to them drew a great deal of attention to the murder of European Jewry.

The term *Holocaust* was first used by American journalist Paul Jacobs. In one of the reports that he sent back from the Eichmann trial, he wrote of "the Holocaust, as the Nazi annihilation of European Jewry is called in Israel."[32] The Israelis actually used the Hebrew word *shoah*, meaning catastrophic upheaval, or *hurban*, meaning total destruction. Both words had very different implications than the English word *Holocaust*, which could be understood as implying that those who died did so as a noble religious sacrifice paralleling the ritual sacrifice of animals in the Jerusalem Temple. Despite the potential theological problems with the term, Elie Wiesel popularized it throughout the 1960s, making the word *Holocaust* synonymous with the Nazi murder of the Jews. Wiesel had written *Night*, a short book dealing with his experience in Auschwitz. First published in English in 1960, the memoir described a teenage boy deported from his Orthodox home in Hungary along with his family. He was shocked to realize that God could betray His own people, but is even more upset by the way he behaved toward his dying father. The book became a publishing sensation because the language was graphic and yet mythic, its events both set in a specific historical context yet seemingly timeless. In 1986, Wiesel was awarded the Nobel Peace Prize, an award that was widely viewed as acknowledging the importance of the Holocaust and the suffering of the Jewish people.

The Eichmann trial marked a turning point for how Holocaust survivors were perceived. Up until this point they had kept a low profile. Believing that nobody wanted to hear their stories, they tried to rebuild their lives and avoid looking back. But the Eichmann trial changed the way they were perceived by others as well as the way they saw themselves. Holocaust survivors played a key role at the Eichmann trial, providing testimony concerning all aspects of the Final Solution as planned and implemented by Eichmann and other Nazis. Now these Holocaust survivors began receiving requests to speak, not only at synagogues, but schools and churches and the gamut of other venues. Their status as survivors gave them an authenticity and legitimacy that was irreplaceable.

In the years following the Eichmann trial, both fiction and nonfiction works on the Holocaust became international best-sellers. American Jews as well as many others became interested in the Holocaust and wanted to understand it in historic as well as religious terms. Jewish theologians tried to grapple with the enormity of the question: How could God allow such a terrible thing to happen? Several important nonfiction books were written, detailing exactly what the Nazis had done and how they had done it. Even more influential were those writers capable of placing mass murder in a personal perspective.

The first and most important first-person account was that written by a young German-born Jewish girl named Anne Frank who had fled with her family to the Netherlands where they had unsuccessfully tried to hide from the Nazis. After being betrayed by a neighbor, her family was sent to concentration camps, where she died in the closing weeks of the Nazi reign of terror. Her book, *The Annex*, was first released in Dutch in 1952 and came out that same year in an English translation published in the United States by Doubleday under the title *The Diary of Anne Frank*. A play based on her diary was first performed in 1955 and won the Pulitzer Prize, the New York Critics Circle Award, and the Tony Award for best play. It was made into a movie in 1959. Readers responded with grief because they knew that the author of the diary had not survived, but they were inspired by her irrepressible spirit and boundless optimism, sentiments that fit well with the upbeat outlook of the times.

The question that was often thought but seldom spoken out loud was how could God, who is described in the Torah as loving and merciful, have stood by while six million Jews and millions of others were gassed to death and murdered by other means by the Nazis? Religious thinkers tried to answer this question, positing various theological theories. Some argued that no new theological response was needed because the Holocaust was like numerous other tragedies that had befallen the Jewish people throughout history. Others believed that God will not interfere with history because if God did so, that would negate the free will that humans absolutely must have. Some wrote that the Holocaust is a mystery beyond human comprehension. God may have reasons for allowing terrible things to happen, but human beings are not capable of understanding God's ways. Some, mostly Orthodox thinkers, argued that the Holocaust was punishment for sins that were committed by German Jews before the war. Despite a tremendous amount of thinking and writing, none of the theologians could satisfactorily answer such a question.

While no one could understand the ways of God, many began to question the policies of the American government during World War II. In 1967, Arthur Morse published *While Six Million Died*, which charged that the Roosevelt administration sat by while the Nazis were exterminating millions of Jews. The book focused on President Franklin Delano Roosevelt's apparent apathy, but it also raised the question whether the American Jewish community had done enough to save European Jewry. The delayed evocation of the terrible events of the Nazi years was an inevitable, if painful, catharsis. American Jews had felt that they needed to repress the memory of the Holocaust. They had been worried about their acceptance in American society and preoccupied with earning a living and improving their social status. They also felt a degree of guilt. The American Jewish community had done very little to try to rescue the millions who had eventually been killed. The political and social circumstances of the war years were certainly difficult, but some felt that American Jewish organizations could at least have tried to do more. A handful of small Orthodox groups had had remarkable success, and the unspoken sense was that American Jews had let their brethren down.

By the 1970s, the inhibitions that had encouraged repression of such discussion lifted. Many books were being written about the Holocaust itself as well as the passive role that the American government played in allowing mass murder to take place. The Jewish community became obsessed with the subject. Not only was it important to teach the history of the persecution and destruction, it was also important to convey what was generally acknowledged to be the central lesson: Jews had an obligation to perpetuate Jewishness so as not to let the Nazis retroactively "win the war." Philosopher and Reform rabbi Emil Fackenheim spoke of a 614th commandment. Every Jew living after the Holocaust should know that he or she was, in a sense, a survivor, part of "an accidental remnant."[33] Fackenheim said that "the authentic Jew of today is forbidden to hand Hitler yet another, posthumous victory" by failing to survive as a Jew.[34]

Fackenheim's understanding was based on the fact that "a Jew today is one who, except for an historical accident—Hitler's loss of the war—would have either been murdered or never been born."[35] As a consequence of this horrible reality, religious faith cannot continue as it was before the Holocaust because faith in the covenant presupposes "an unbroken historical con-

FIGURE 1.7. David Ben Gurion and Abba Eban presenting a menorah to President Truman on May 8, 1951, in appreciation for his timely recognition of the State of Israel three years earlier. On May 14, 1948, Truman had recognized the provisional Jewish government as de facto authority eleven minutes after the provisional government of Israel proclaimed the new State of Israel. In so doing, Truman went against the advice of Secretary of State George Marshall and most of the cabinet. Truman's wife Margaret said it was the most difficult decision he had ever faced as president. Photo Abbie Rowe of the National Park Service. *Courtesy of the Harry S. Truman Library and Museum*

tinuity from past to present." That continuity was traumatically ruptured by the murder of six million Jews. Fackenheim was of course aware that many might see this as proof that the omnipotent God of the Torah could not possibly exist, but that was not his message. Rather, he felt that Jews should devote themselves to making sure that the Jewish people survive as a religious as well as political response to the Nazis' attempt at genocide.

According to Fackenheim, the Zionists who created the State of Israel were responding to this challenge. Even though most were secular, Fackenheim sees their behavior as religious. Their accomplishment was proof of their commitment to what he called "secular holiness." Other American Jewish philosophers picked up on this same theme. Modern Orthodox Rabbi Irving Greenberg referred to a similar concept, which he called "holy secularity," arguing that this commitment to the common Jewish good was the religious framework for contemporary Jewish life. What had previously been an obligatory covenant had now become voluntary. This new covenant called Jews to be witnesses to the "divine presence in history," a phrase used by several thinkers. Greenberg wrote that the covenant "was broken but the Jewish people, released from its obligations, chose voluntarily to take it on again."[36]

One of the possible implications of this idea was that all interpretations of Judaism were now valid, because Judaic religious authority had been destroyed by the barbaric acts of the Nazis. Therefore all forms of Judaism, with the exception of so-called messianic Judaism (which was regarded as a form of Christianity), were now legitimate religious responses. The concept of pluralism, religious and otherwise, thus became a central value in the Jewish civil religion. Jews had suffered so much; they needed to devote themselves to preserving the Jewish people. While they might believe different things and practice Judaism to varying degrees (if at all), what was important was Jewish solidarity.

The Importance of Israel for American Jewish Identity

The two core historical events of the twentieth century for American Jews were the Holocaust and the creation of the State of Israel. Much of the Jewish civil religion was based upon a sense of guilt that American Jews had not done more to initiate rescue attempts during the Holocaust. This was coupled with a sense of pride in the accomplishments of the young and struggling Jewish state, which had been created with a tremendous amount of help from America's Jews. This commitment to the State of Israel intensified in the weeks leading up to the Six-Day War in June 1967. Egypt under Arab nationalist leader Gamal Abdel Nasser promised to obliterate Israel and drive the Jews into the sea. Abraham Joshua Heschel later recalled the sentiments many had at that time: terror and dread fell upon Jews everywhere. "Will God permit our people to perish? Will there be another Auschwitz, another Dachau, another Treblinka?"[37] Heschel did not need to remind American Jews that the establishment of the State of Israel had been the "one gleam of light" in "the midst of that thick darkness."

After three weeks of fearing attack, the Israelis launched a preemptive strike and defeated several Arab countries in just six days, paralleling the six days that God took to create the world in the Book of Genesis. Jews flocked to synagogues throughout the world to express their relief and many shared an emotional connection with the Jewish state they had never before felt. Arthur Hertzberg commented in August of that same year that "the mood of the American Jewish community underwent an abrupt, radical, and possibly permanent change [following the war]. . . . The immediate reaction of the American Jewry to the crisis [preceding Israel's preemptive strike] was far more tense and widespread than anyone could have foreseen."[38] In the face of the Israeli victory, American Jews felt a sense of the miraculous. No longer perpetual victims of persecution, their country had vanquished the entire Arab world.

Support for Israel now became a central pillar of the American Jewish civil religion. Jack Wertheimer summarized the change: "Whereas American Jews had demonstrated sympathy in the past, Israel is now incorporated into the very structure of American Jewish identity."[39] Giving money was not just an act of charity but a way to participate in Israel's struggle for survival and help build a modern and prosperous Western country where most still believed that there had been just sand. Many wealthy American Jews gave huge sums to various charities in Israel. In some cases, people donated millions of dollars to institutions that they had never even seen; they were supporting a romantic ideal more than an actual country. The destruction of European Jewry and the creation of the third Jewish commonwealth began to blend together as a single narrative, a narrative that had a great deal of religious meaning. The Holocaust was such a shattering event that it seemed impossible to explain it. But now, with the stunning Israeli victory in the Six-Day War, many began to see the Holocaust as a catastrophic event that was destined to lead up to miraculous victories. Jacob Neusner explained that the Six-Day War transformed political and military events into a sacred story with not only tragedy but also a miraculous conclusion. This "Judaism of Holocaust and Redemption" provided American Jews with a compelling contemporary religious history.[40]

The State of Israel has played a central role in defining the nature of Jewish identity. While there is no Jewish equivalent to the pope, the State of Israel is the only Jewish country in the world and therefore in a unique position to determine "Who is a Jew?" The traditional definition was clear enough: a Jew was someone born of a Jewish mother or a person who had converted to Judaism. The Law of Return, which was passed by the Israeli Knesset in

1950, established that "every Jew has the right to come into Israel as an immigrant." The rationale behind this was obvious: the Nazi persecution had shown that all Jews shared a common fate, and the purpose of Zionism was to provide a Jewish homeland for every member of the Jewish people. Classical Zionism held that all Jews should move to the Jewish state, something that most American Zionists rejected. Indeed, Zionism became a respectable American Jewish ideology only after soon to be Supreme Court Justice Louis D. Brandeis became president of the Federation of American Zionists in 1914, helping to redefine American Zionism as support for the creation of a Jewish state rather than the commitment to move to a Jewish homeland. For the American Zionist, the Jewish State became the authoritative symbol of everything Jewish. During the course of the 1970s and 1980s, Orthodox political parties in Israel made several attempts to amend the Law of Return to add the words "converted according to halacha" in order to exclude those who had converted through the non-Orthodox denominations . The Reform and Reconstructionist movements did not claim to be following halacha, and, although the Conservative movement did, the Orthodox political parties did not regard Conservative practices as truly halachic. In practice, a change to the Israeli law would have excluded all converts except for a small number of strictly Orthodox ones. The number of converts moving to Israel in any given year was relatively small, and so the purpose of the law was primarily to reinforce the authority of the Orthodox rabbinate rather than discriminate against a few hapless souls. These attempts failed after American Jewish leaders told the Israelis that such a change would have a devastating impact on relations between Israel and the American Diaspora.

The American Jewish civil religion had one central principle: Jews had a responsibility to take care of each other. This meant not only giving charity to help underprivileged individuals, but, even more important, doing whatever was necessary to help ensure the survival of the Jewish State. American Jews should lobby their political representatives to support the State of Israel, encouraging them to vote for positions recommended by Israeli political leaders of the time. They could offer advice to the Israeli leaders privately and discreetly, but they should never, ever publicly criticize Israel, her leaders, or her policies. This arrangement seemed satisfactory to the vast majority of American Jews for a couple of decades. But, by the 1980s, more American Jews were expressing dissatisfaction with specific Israeli actions and, in some cases, opposition to Israeli government policies. It became harder for the leaders of the American Jewish establishment to keep the dissidents quiet.

There are a number of reasons why many American Jews changed their political viewpoint on the State of Israel, and changed how they felt about expressing their political opinions. The election of Menachem Begin as Israeli prime minister in 1977, the 1982 invasion of Lebanon, the 1985 Jonathan Pollard spy affair, the Palestinian Intifada that began in December of 1987, the breakdown of the Oslo Accords, the assassination of Prime Minister Yitzchak Rabin, the election of Prime Minister Benjamin Netanyahu, the second Palestinian Intifada, the election of Prime Minister Ariel Sharon, and other political events loosened inhibitions and made it increasingly acceptable to be selectively critical.[41] While many American Jews remained deeply committed to supporting the Israeli government without airing any criticism, increasing numbers began to believe they had the right and even the obligation to hold Israel to the highest of standards, even if that meant speaking or writing against a specific Israeli government policy. This was virtually unprecedented. In the mid-1970s, a group of left-wing American Jews formed Breira, an organization devoted to publicly presenting an alternative vision of how the State of Israel should behave. Almost every mainstream Jewish organization condemned their breaking of ranks.[42] Twenty years later, their criticisms seem mild and not threatening in the least. At the time, however, they were considered radicals and even traitors.

The State of Israel has clearly played an enormous role in American Jewish identity. Yet, many American Jews are deeply ambivalent about her for a number of different reasons. While many Orthodox Jews have extensive social, religious, educational, and even business connections, the vast majority of American Jewry have little direct contact. In recent years, many American Jews have been struck by the contrasting and conflicting images that the State of Israel conveys. As Paul Wilkes put it, "Israel, to Jews around the world, is both holy object and graven image. It is a loving father and an incorrigible brother; a beam of religious integrity and the harsh light of hate and retribution; a precursor of universal Judaic observance and a bellwether of blatant secularity; a holy land of milk, honey, and bloodshed."[43]

New Approaches to Religious Identity in Recent Decades

Novelist Tom Wolfe was the first to put a label on the narcissistic attitude that came of age in the aftermath of the 1960s. Writing in *New York* magazine, he called the 1970s the "me decade." Wolfe noted that the dominant concern had shifted from social and political justice to a selfish focus on individual well-being. There was a new American preoccupation with self-awareness and a collective retreat from human reciprocity and community. Not everyone saw the change in this light, but it was clear that there had been a major social reorientation. This shift was not restricted to religion or religious concerns, but obviously it had a tremendous impact on how Americans looked at religion and what they expected from religious institutions. Compared to the supposedly idealistic 1960s, from the 1970s onward, Americans seemed incredibly self-absorbed. Interest shifted from street theater designed to protest unjust political policies to psychotherapy designed to help the affluent deal with self-imposed psychological frustrations. What now counted was the well-being of the individual.

The increased focus on individualism prompted many young American Jews to look for a new type of Jewish religious experience. For those looking for "cutting edge" Judaism, there were a number of innovative approaches that emerged out of the 1960s experience. The havurah movement, for example, consisted of small spiritually-oriented communities that integrated creative religious readings and joyous musical expression. Like-minded intellectuals in places like Cambridge, Massachusetts and Berkeley, California were searching for opportunities to develop their spirituality in a personal way that would avoid the passivity and materialism that they had experienced in their parents' congregations growing up.

They founded their havurahs in living rooms or dens and pretty much did whatever participants felt like doing. The emphasis was on trying to do things themselves rather than relying on a rabbi or cantor to "do" Judaism for them. From the moment it was published in October 1973, *The Jewish Catalog* became a "bible" for havurah-oriented people. Later renamed *The First Jewish Catalog*, after two more volumes were published, the subtitle appropriately read "A Do-It Yourself Kit!"[44] As lead editor Michael Strassfeld put it: "We don't need rabbis. We should just do it ourselves and rabbis get in the way."[45] Ironically, Strassfeld later became a rabbi himself. Even though the tone of the handbook was anti-establishment, many Jewish professionals were pleased, citing the *Catalog* as one indication that alienated youths were returning to Judaism. As Rabbi Yitz and Blu Greenberg saw it: "one of the most heartening phenomena on the North American scene during the past few years has been the resurgence of interest by Jews in living Jewishly."

While most enthusiastically endorsed the *Catalog*, Marshall Sklare expressed concern with the uncritical reception: "I am both mystified and distressed by the sacralization of the *Catalog*," pointing out that the editors seemed to be "not merely indebted to the youth culture in its interpretations of Judaism but subordinate to it."[46] Sklare was offended by the seeming incorporation of modern, secular, liberal values into Judaism at the expense of the ethical and ritual demands of what he saw as authentic Judaism. Many years later, Conservative Rabbi Leonard Gordon argued that, rather than surrendering to secular culture, havurah Judaism was developing a new theological model. "The move from an architecture in which the rabbi is up on a bimah and the congregation below, to one in which the Torah is at the center of a circle, implies a whole new theology. In the old model, the rabbi is a professional holy man, living an exemplary Jewish life on our behalf. In the havurah model, there's a bit of God in each of us, and the Torah is at the center."[47]

The havurah movement eventually developed into what became known as the Jewish Renewal movement, and then the two separated again. Former 1960s activist Arthur Waskow gave the movement its name in a 1978 article in his journal *New Menorah*. Originally postdenominational, the Jewish Renewal movement slowly evolved into what many regard as a new denomination. Rabbi Zalman Schachter-Shalomi became the most prominent Jewish Renewal religious leader. Schachter-Shalomi was originally a Lubavitcher Hasid who was sent out as an emissary for the Rebbe. He advocated what he called Davenology, the art of enhancing Jewish worship through meditative practices.

Other young American Jews were looking to embrace traditional Judaism. Growing up in nonobservant homes, they hoped to find a Judaism that would be more authoritative and substantive. A new word describing a born-again Jew entered the American Jewish vocabulary: a *baal teshuva* was a person who embraced Orthodox Judaism, sometimes after an extensive spiritual search for religious meaning. There seemed to suddenly be a large number of such young American Jews, proudly wearing yarmulkes and tzitzit for the first time in their lives. The baal teshuva movement hit the mainstream when *Rolling Stone* journalist Ellen Willis wrote a long personal account of her visit to her brother Chaim, a baal teshuva who was studying at Aish HaTorah in the Old City in Jerusalem. Willis wrote how she was initially shocked that her beloved brother could embrace such an alien ideology, but during her visit she began to understand his attraction to Orthodoxy. In fact, she was so moved by his transformation that she briefly considered leaving everything behind and staying in Jerusalem herself.

A new generation was looking for religious answers that could help them understand why life was so hard and sometimes seemed so unfair. In 1981, Conservative Rabbi Harold S. Kushner published *When Bad Things Happen to Good People* to help him deal with the death of his young son. Aaron Kushner had been born with a debilitating and eventually fatal disease, and the family had struggled to nurture him until his death at age thirteen. Kushner wanted to write a personal book that could help him explain his "deep, aching sense of unfairness." As a rabbi, he was committed to believing in God's existence. But if God really existed, "how could He do this to me?"[48] Perhaps Kushner had egregiously sinned, but what could his infant son possibly have done to deserve such a terrible disease? This question haunted Kushner and compelled him to document what he saw as the most important spiritual lessons he had learned during his years of emotional turmoil. He wanted to encourage people to believe in God in spite of life's difficulties. God was responsible for what was good in the world, but could not be held responsible for many of the random tragedies that might befall us. Even though many theologians were less than impressed with Kushner's spiritual revelations, millions of Americans of all faiths found comfort in his words.[49]

Despite the many accomplishments of individual congregations, the synagogue world was slow to react to the changing cultural environment. Mainstream congregations appealed primarily to the middle-aged and the elderly, and young people found little within them of interest. Most Jewish children attended afternoon religious schools, which, because of extremely limited time and a host of other factors, could teach only the basic facts about Judaism. Many congregations had become quite large but this did not mean that the quality of the education that they offered had improved. Partially as a result of their tedious educational experience, young people prepared for their bar and bat mitzvahs and then dropped out of Jewish life. While many later found their way back into the synagogue, others remained alienated from Jewish life throughout their adult life. Some even joined one of the new religious movements, popularly referred to as "cults," an act of repudiation that traumatized most of their parents. These new religious movements included the Unification Church, the Church of Scientology, the Family, and the Church Universal and Triumphant. Eastern philosophies also attracted many followers, including the Hare Krishna Society, the Healthy-Happy-Holy Organization, the Meher Baba movement, Transcendental Meditation (TM), and various types of yoga groups. Many Jewish participants later brought their interest in Eastern spirituality with them if and when they returned to Judaism. Most of the new religious movements had significant numbers of Jewish members, usually far more than their percentage in the general population. Experts pointed out that many of these Jewish youth had received little religious direction growing up. Most of their families had performed Jewish ritual only sporadically, and religious school had usually been a negative experience. As a result, they looked elsewhere for deep-felt spirituality. Syncretist permutations became common.

Much of the spiritual innovation emanated from the West Coast, putting stress on movements and coalitions that tried to span a broad spectrum of beliefs and positions. Affectionately referred to as the "left coast," the West Coast was and is an incubator of new religious approaches. All of the movements have institutional branches in Los Angeles, and their activities in California tend to be on the cutting edge. The Conservative movement, for example, is dealing with a number of controversial issues, most recently the question of same-sex commitment ceremonies and the ordination of gays and lesbians. A great deal of the pressure to reevaluate their position on this issue came from rabbis and lay leaders on the West Coast. The Committee on Jewish Law and Standards sanctioned the idea of gay or lesbian clergy in December 2006 and the Ziegler School of Rabbinic Studies at the University of Judaism in Los Angeles announced that it accepted its first openly gay students by the beginning of March. Meanwhile, JTS in New York was still considering how to proceed. Each successive innovation opened the gap between the right and the left just a little bit wider, as those in the middle came under pressure to choose which way they would go.

The last two or three decades have seen a polarized American Jewish community. American Jews were increasingly split in a number of different divisions, but most fundamentally between those who still cared about Judaism and those who did not. In turn, those who cared were divided between the haredim (the fervently Orthodox) and the liberal non-Orthodox, with the Modern Orthodox caught in the middle. *Haredim*, meaning "God fearers," became the accepted term for referring to all Orthodox Jews on the right. It was a term that was borrowed from Israel in the early 1980s, where the haredim had already been using the word to differentiate themselves from the Mizrachi, the Orthodox Zionists. The haredim had many children and appeared to be growing rapidly, in dramatic contrast to the rest of the Jewish

FIGURE 1.8. Orthodox students recite the prayer over the four species during the holiday of Sukkoth as part of their participation in the Orthodox Union's Jewish Learning Initiative on Campus (JLIC). The JLIC provides study and worship opportunities, mentoring, and counseling to Orthodox students and others on university campuses throughout North America. *Courtesy of the Orthodox Union*

community. Calvin Goldscheider put it bluntly: the question about how to be Jewish in America "has tended to become an either/or choice—with a range within both extremes and with fewer options to remain within the middle."[50] Jack Wertheimer explained that "in the religious sphere, a bipolar model is emerging, with a large population of Jews moving toward religious minimalism and a minority gravitating toward greater participation and deepened concern with religion."[51] Samuel Heilman agreed, pronouncing that "the story of the Jews of America during the years that would follow [after 1975] would become more and more an account of only two types: those Jews for whom a passive, minimalistic Jewish-American heritage that was symbolic or latent was enough and those for whom being distinctly Jewish was an engaging, salient, and active component of who and what they were."[52]

Despite the awareness that polarization was increasing, the 1990 National Jewish Population Survey (NJPS) nevertheless shocked many American Jewish leaders. The key finding was that 52 percent of American Jews who had married in the previous five years had chosen someone who was not Jewish and had not converted before marriage. While the exact percentage soon became a hotly contested issue, the basic fact that American Jews were successfully integrating into the broader society was without doubt. This was a positive development because it allowed American Jews to study, work, live, and entertain themselves in almost any way they wanted, but it did have repercussions for the future of Jewish life in the United States. American Jewish organizations, as well as private family foundations, soon began diverting funds toward the new obsession—the struggle for Jewish continuity. A number of programs were developed for synagogue renewal, including Synagogue 2000 (later renamed Synagogue 3000) and Synagogues: Transformation and Renewal (STAR).

The various Jewish religious denominations launched efforts to revitalize their congregations, as well as modernize their theology and ritual policies. The Reform rabbinate voted to endorse a new platform at their Pittsburgh conference in 1999, returning to the same synagogue where the 1885 Pittsburgh Platform had been debated and accepted. The new platform was a sharp rejection of classical Reform theology and practice. Even though it was watered down by those who opposed its strident neotraditionalism, it retained enough of its original emphasis to please those who had been raised in more traditional homes or who had come to find meaning in traditional practices. The Conservative movement moved toward many of the more liberal social positions that had long characterized the Reform movement, first accepting women rabbis and later gay and lesbian commitment ceremonies and rabbinic ordination and the investiture of cantors. This led many to wonder whether they would also endorse patrilineal descent, a key element in the strategy to recruit interfaith families, many of whom had Jewish fathers and non-Jewish mothers.

American Jews became successful in almost every field of endeavor. While many prominent Jews had little or no interest in Judaism, others were deeply involved and eager to share the details of their participation with the public. When Democratic presidential candidate Al Gore announced that he had chosen Connecticut senator Joseph Lieberman as his running mate in the 2000 election, he was hoping to make a dramatic statement. Americans who had previously known little about Judaism were given a crash course, since Lieberman's religion now had tremendous potential significance. Many commentators pointed out that it was probably not an accident that the first Jew chosen for a national ticket was not a typical "Federation Jew" with little religious sentiment, but rather a man committed to Modern Orthodoxy. Fundamentalist Christians in particular loved his fervent dedication to religion, even if it was a different one.

His Sabbath observance became the most publicized aspect of his religious practice during the campaign. Many Americans learned for the first time that Jewish days start at sundown on one day and continue to sundown on the next. They also became aware that observant Jews abstain from all "work" on the Sabbath and therefore do not use electricity, write, travel in cars, or talk on the telephone. Lieberman tried to observe his religion as best he could while meeting the rigorous demands of his position as senator as well as vice presidential candidate. One reporter found that he had been drinking water on a minor fast day and attending a political rally with live music, both violations of the halacha. Despite these apparent lapses, Orthodox leaders were generally understanding of Lieberman's compromises. Rabbi Avi Shafran, director of public affairs for Agudath Israel of America, quipped that "he's running for vice president, not chief rabbi. Therefore, there might be some things we would consider not thought out from a religious perspective, but we're not here to critique his religious life."[53] The Gore-Lieberman ticket lost, but Lieberman was credited with helping to attract votes.

Like other Americans, Jews flocked to synagogues in the days and weeks after the September 11 attacks in 2001. While many rabbis hoped the spike in attendance would become permanent, this turned out not to be the case. Synagogues tightened security after a number of attacks on Jewish communal institutions, perpetuated not only by Muslim extremists but by white supremacists as well. Despite these threats, American Jewish life continued to be relatively idyllic. The biggest question remained whether the American Jewish community could sustain itself. Several demographic studies showed a drastic decline in the number of Jews in the United States, due to intermarriage and a low fertility rate, but other sociological studies seemed to suggest the opposite. Some felt that each study revealed more about the researcher than it did about the Jewish community. The arguments made by the various sociologists hinged in large part on how the measure of success or failure is defined, with the social scientists mixing academic research with a healthy dose of ideological posturing. The debate over the basic demographic facts and especially how to interpret them has become quite bitter, pitting optimists against pessimists, advocates of "Inreach" versus advocates of "Outreach." Many have tired of the constant quantitative studies, comparing it to the taking of a sick patient's temperature every three minutes. Beyond the question of survival, American Jews are increasingly asking themselves how their Judaism can help them explore their spirituality. They yearn for a Judaism that can address their deepest emotional needs and help them to expand their notion of God and how religion can enrich their lives.

2 The Reengagement with Spirituality

Americans see themselves on spiritual journeys. These journeys are fluid and changing, and their spiritual experiences will unfold gradually, leading in all sorts of directions. Journeys have a definitive starting point, and they will eventually have an ending point, but in the decades in between there is the possibility for all sorts of surprises, as individuals explore their spirituality in the context of what is happening in their work and home lives and in their community, the country, and the world. Speaking of the spiritual quest as a journey emphasizes the dynamic aspect of the process. There are many different possible conceptions of God and the world, and those conceptions may be more or less meaningful depending on an individual's particular point in the journey. Describing the spiritual journey is a way of accounting for who we are and what we do and will also help individuals to understand the people in their lives as well as themselves and connect their being to the cosmos.

Spirituality has no absolute definition. Each of the Jewish teachers of spirituality have their own way of phrasing what spirituality is and how it can be defined—if it can be defined. In a narrow sense, spirituality is anything that concerns itself with matters of the spirit. Rabbi Lawrence Kushner defines it succinctly as "the immediacy of God's presence." The spiritual involves eternal truths regarding the ultimate nature of God and human beings and is seen as being in contrast with the material world, that which we can see, touch, or smell. Spirituality may involve perceiving life as involving or aspiring to higher lofty goals beyond the practical daily material needs.

Rabbi Arthur Green sees it as the "striving for life in the presence of God and the fashioning of a life of holiness appropriate to such striving." He explains that spirituality is a way of looking at religion that "sees its primary task as cultivating and nourishing the human soul or spirit." Each person, according to his view, "has an inner life that he or she may choose to develop; this 'inwardness' goes deeper than the usual object of psychological investigation and cannot fairly be explained in Freudian or other psychological terms."Ultimately, he writes, "it is 'transpersonal,' reaching beyond the individual and linking him/her to all other selves and to the single Spirit or Self of the universe we call God. God is experientially accessible through the cultivation of this inner life."[1] There is no biblical Hebrew word for spirituality. The Modern Hebrew word for this concept, *ruchaniut*, was originally meant to refer to that which contained the presence of God. The root, *ruach*, is from the second verse of the book of Genesis, where it is written that the spirit of God hovered over the face of the waters. In rabbinic thought, *Ruchaniut* was contrasted with its companion word, *gashmiut*, corporeality. The sages urged Jews to devote their lives to ruchaniut, spiritual activities such as study, prayer, and good deeds, as opposed to gashmiut, materialism and hedonistic pleasures.

Rabbi Rachel B. Cowan explains that "in spiritual life there are many types whose needs are different—some are contemplative, some are intellectual and scholarly, some are activists, and all are valid paths." But in the post–World War II period, the spiritual options offered through the synagogue narrowed. "In the 1950s and '60s Judaism became reduced to liturgy, and what usually brought you to synagogue then was not a spiritual quest."[2] Few were even aware that the concept of spirituality, as distinct from religion, existed. Rabbi Lawrence A. Hoffman remembers speaking at the University of Notre Dame on the rituals of Passover in 1975 when a woman in the audience asked him, "What is the spirituality of the seder? You have talked for a week, covering every conceivable aspect of the Passover experience, but not once have you addressed anything spiritual. Isn't there such a thing as Jew-

FIGURE 2.1. Sounding the shofar at Saguaro Lake, Arizona. Many American Jews have begun looking for spiritual experiences that can reawaken their sense of the holy. Photo Barry Bisman. *Courtesy of Rabbi Ayla Grafstein*

ish spirituality?" Remembering the occasion much later, Hoffman remarked that "unbelievable as it may seem a quarter of a century later, I was at the time completely stumped: I had no idea what to say."[3]

The lack of spirituality bothered the new generation, which responded by various means. Some explored New Age philosophies, joined new religious movements, or tried alternative spiritual paths. While there were those who dismissed these approaches as nutty or wacky, Nathan Katz cautioned that it was important not to marginalize the attraction of Eastern religions and other non-Western spiritualities. "To label these things as cults is not to take them seriously and to misunderstand their real appeal to people and also what we lack. Many Jews have real spiritual questions and they're not finding them addressed in mainstream Judaism."[4] Our focus in this chapter is on those who experimented with approaches to Judaism that differed radically from what they had experienced in their parents' suburban synagogues. They wanted something more, even if they did not know exactly what they were looking for.

Many were drawn to experimental spirituality rather than institutional religiosity. Like so many other cultural trends in contemporary America, the current interest in spirituality has its most immediate roots in the 1960s. According to Wade Clark Roof, this experimental spirituality places "primacy not on reason, not even on belief systems, but rather on a mystical experiential stance."[5] Roof found that the baby boom generation had similar levels of religious involvement as the previous generation during their childhood and teen years, but by their early twenties, only about one in four was still involved in organized religion. Rather than interpreting this as a widespread disillusionment with God, most social scientists believed that the younger generation was simply expressing their spirituality in more individualistic ways. Meditating by themselves at a time of their choosing might be more spiritual to them than worshipping with others in a church or synagogue at a set time. If they did seek out an organized approach, it was more likely to be nontraditional and nonconformist.

There was a great deal of excitement about a broad array of innovative spiritual pursuits collectively called New Age. New Age religion was diverse, but could include astrology, spiritualism, alchemy, tarot cards, psychic phenomena, goddess worship, neopaganism, Wicca, out-of-body experiences, near-death experiences, reincarnation, angelology, Satanism, the occult, spiritual energy, faith healing, yoga, transcendental meditation and other meditation techniques, holistic health, therapeutic techniques, healing crystals, karate, tai chi, Sufi dancing, vision questing, the twelve steps, the Gurdjieff work, and other practices. Most Jews saw these interests as relatively harmless, but rabbis across the denominational spectrum tended to take a harder line.

Rabbi Jeffrey Salkin writes that "everywhere you go . . . the word on people's lips is 'spirituality.' It is the religious buzzword of our age." He believes that it has greatly enriched American Judaism, and particularly the Reform movement, which was once overly intellectual, rational, and formal. But, he warns, "as with any swing of the pendulum, the rush toward an ill-defined spirituality poses a potential threat." New Age practices can be "instant karma" or, even worse, "microwave religion." Judaism stands in fundamental opposition to the pantheism that he believes is characteristic of New Age teaching. "If God is in everything, then everything is holy and nothing is profane. New Age speaks of 'getting in touch with one's inner voice' or 'following your bliss,' but 'following your bliss' is the antithesis of living in covenant."[6]

Despite Salkin's criticism, many American Jews found New Age enticing. They were particularly interested in the self-help movement. During the 1990s, a number of guides attracted huge followings by blending health advice with spiritual wisdom. Andrew Weill, Jon Kabat-Zinn, Deepak Chopra, Tony Robbins, James Redfield, Marianne Williamson, John Bradshaw, and Robert Bly, among others, taught that the American stress on career at the expense of a balanced lifestyle could damage people's health and lead to illness and premature death. They explained the mysteries of the universe and how each person can harness their personal spiritual power to get onto the path toward enlightenment. Many of these teachers had legitimate spiritual wisdom and were sincerely trying to help their listeners and readers get more out of life.

Nevertheless, they had their critics, who felt that they were modern versions of the snake oil salesmen. Wendy Kaminer, a commentator on National Public Radio, was one of the skeptics who tried to explain "why we love gurus." "They seduce us by telling us what we want to hear: we're wonderful and we'll live forever. What's wrong with that? Plenty."[7] Kaminer compared buying into their vague philosophies of enlightenment to "a steady diet of happy pills." They are charismatic authority figures who malign rationalism and exhort their followers to abandon critical thinking in order to achieve spiritual growth. These "pop gurus" prey on the existential anxieties Americans have developed and they thrive when peoples' fear of being alone and mortal in an indifferent world overpowers their sound judgment. Despite such criticism, huge numbers of Americans continued to flock to these self-help teachers, preferring their commonsense spiritual wisdom to the dogmatic religion they might have grown up with.

Many Americans now identify themselves as "spiritual but not religious." Some find the phrase confusing because they consider the words *spiritual* and *religious* to be synonymous, since both indicate a belief in some type of divine power and an interest in building a personal relationship with this power. But the two words mean different things. The word *spiritual* is associated with the private realm of experience, while the word *religious* is linked to the public affiliation with an institution or institutions. Those who see themselves as spiritual may experiment with unorthodox beliefs and practices, including, in many cases, mysticism, whereas those who identify themselves as religious usually have ongoing relationships with members of the clergy and attend a formal house of worship on a regular basis.

There are many ways to explain the difference between religion and spirituality. One parable describes a man who traveled through a wild country full of dense brush, when he came to a small stream flowing between tall pine trees that created a magical ambience. The water was clear and translucent, sparkling, gleaming, and shimmering in the sunlight as it flowed downstream. It was like no other water he had seen in his life. He asked his guide, "Is this the water of life, the elixir of youth?" The guide, as astounded as the man, remained silent. Fascinated with his discovery, the man was determined to bring some of the beautiful water home with him. He filled up his canteen—which was the only vessel that he had with him—and carried it back with him to his home, being careful not to drink of the magical liquid. On his return home, he told his friends about the mesmerizing water and showed them the canteen with its sparkling contents. They all marveled at his discovery.

As the days went by, more people came to see the water and marvel at its beauty. Many of them told him how moved they were by the experience of just looking at the water in the canteen. He felt that the old canteen was not appropriate for displaying such an awe-inspiring liquid and so he first poured the water into a silver mug and then into a magnificent jeweled bowl. But when people came to see the water, they began to marvel at the magnificent bowl rather than the shimmering, sparkling water. They were more interested in the container than its contents. Unintentionally, the focus was shifted. The way I interpret the story is as follows: the container is religion with its rituals and particular forms of worship. The contents of the container are spirituality. Spirituality needs the container to give it form Religion is meaningless without spirituality and spirituality is structureless without religion.

Having a precious spiritual tradition and a ritualized structure for it is not enough. There needs to be a community that can maintain not only the external structure but also the internal contents. Jonathan Omer-Man, a longtime meditation teacher on the West Coast, tries to reconcile the privatizing tendency of much of contemporary spiritual endeavors with the strong communal focus of traditional Judaism. "There is a tendency today to see 'spirituality' as a private matter, flowing from an individual's unique psyche or natural intuitive powers. According to this view, there is really nothing to learn, either from tradition or from other people. If, however, we see spirituality as a journey that others have taken and about which they have communicated their discoveries and difficulties, their insights and warnings, our own lives can be enriched."[8]

As Omer-Man suggests, while personalized forms of spirituality can provide intense satisfaction, they also have a considerable downside. Religious leaders who are skeptical of "personal spirituality" compare it to a person walking around the city listening to her iPod playing. People can choose any one of hundreds of different recordings of music or books or anything that interests them at that moment, but only they can hear whatever it is that they are listening to. That is the whole point of having an iPod with headphones—they can make their own personal selection without infringing upon anyone else. But the same privacy that allows them to enjoy a huge range of choice also limits their impact on those around them. They do not have to convince anyone else that something is worth listening to, because the other people are not going to have to hear it. Taken to its logical conclusion, the United States could end up with three hundred million different spiritualities.

If every American Jew went on their own spiritual search without regard to ancestral tradition or community influence, that would mark the end of organized Jewish religion in the United States. But that has not happened. On the other hand, American Jews are much less likely to simply accept the traditions that they were taught by their parents. Rather, they want to experience intense spirituality and will undertake a serious search for it if they do not feel that it exists in their present religious environment. Some of those dissatisfied with what they believe to be the lack of spirituality in Judaism may switch religions entirely but many others may seek to find alternative sources of spiritual wisdom that they can bring back with them to the synagogue. Gail Greenfield's spiritual path is a perfect example of this. She grew up in a traditional Jewish household in Jacksonville, Florida where they celebrated all the holidays, kept kosher, and observed Shabbat. "There was little mention of God, and somehow I felt that there was something absent from my life." During confirmation class at her Conservative synagogue, she asked the rabbi about God and he answered, "We don't ask those questions." Greenfield suppressed her spiritual yearnings for many years. "We were very involved with a synagogue when our children were young, and one day I got up the nerve to ask the rebbetzin, who was a friend of mine, about her beliefs in God. 'How can you believe in God after the Holocaust?' she responded.

FIGURE 2.2. Gail Greenfield lighting Shabbat candles in front of the Ark at Temple B'nai Israel, Albany, Georgia. Photo Dana Evan Kaplan. *Courtesy of the author*

'I just believe in the Jewish people.'"[9] Greenfield did not find this answer satisfactory, but she wasn't aware of any alternative until she moved with her family to Maryland in the 1980s. A friend gave her a copy of *The Nature of Personal Reality* by Jane Roberts, which was supposed to be metaphysical knowledge channeled through the author. "This catapulted me into involvement with New Age interests because it answered a lot of the questions I had been looking for about the universe and how it works." Greenfield found that she was finally learning about the questions that had long consumed her, such as "what is the purpose of our life?" and "why are we here?"

"Fortunately, I was not motivated by a tragedy. So many times people are motivated by tragedy. I was just motivated by my own emotional needs—my own yearnings to find metaphysical answers. It was sort of like a search to find God, in a way, but it has just gone in many different directions." A registered nurse, she became interested in healing and did a weeklong training session with Louise L. Hay, the author of *You Can Heal Your Life*. "She talked about how we harbor resentment and anger and how it affects our bodies. Frustration can actually lead to disease. That's when I got involved in Reiki, which is a healing modality. You learn how to transmit healing energy through your hands." The next step in her spiritual evolution was to begin a Buddhist meditation practice. She began doing Vipassana meditation, which is a simple technique consisting of the experiential observation of mind and matter in their aspects of impermanence, unsatisfactoriness, and devoidness of self. "You really get to learn the workings of your mind and how your thoughts cause many of the problems that you have. Eventually I learned to stop most of my negative thinking."

Throughout this time, Greenfield still felt a connection to the Jewish religion. "I continued to do my Judaism, but on my own terms. I began developing my own rituals. I put together a Tu B'Shevat seder which was meaningful and spiritual. I wrote a Purim play and even edited a Rosh Hashanah and Yom Kippur service." Greenfield brought together a group of like-minded friends who also belonged to a synagogue, but were not interested in attending on a regular basis because they found it boring and repetitive. They were looking for a connection with God and a way to express their spirituality through Judaism. "I love the idea expressed by Rabbi Nachman of Bratslav, which I included in my Tu B'Shevat seder: 'Master of the Universe, grant me the ability to be alone; may it be my custom to go outdoors each day among the trees and grass, among all growing things, and there may I be alone, and enter into prayer, to talk to the One that I belong to.'"

The Decline of "Historical Familism"

Jews have different ways of identifying themselves. Some see their Jewish identity as primarily or exclusively ethnic, similar to how an Italian American, Irish American, or Asian American sees him or herself. Others see their Judaism as a religion and minimize or ignore the tribal element. If they are a convert to Judaism and they do not have a Jewish-born spouse, then they do not have any direct "blood" or genetic connection to the Jewish people, and it would make sense for them to define their identity in primarily religious terms. But for most American Jews of Eastern European origin, Jewishness was much broader than just religion. Indeed, the categories of ethnicity and religion were separate in their minds, at least until the mass movement into the suburbs. As Arthur A. Goren explains, "It is important to remember that, for American Jews, Judaism and Jewishness became identical only during the decade beginning in 1945." Eastern European immigrants had "created an ethnic and secular reality that overran without obliterating the purely religious formulation of Jewishness."[10]

Like other ethnic groups, Jews see themselves as part of an extended family, a term that Charles S. Liebman and Steven M. Cohen named "historical familism."[11] Liebman and Cohen explained that there are two elements to familism among American Jews that are particularly important. One is ascription, the idea that a person is born into and remains a part of the family regardless of what he does. The second element is a sense of mutual responsibility, which obligates all members of the family to care about and help each other for all time.[12] Familism in its original context refers to a social pattern in which the family assumes a position of ascendance over personal interests. Regardless of what a parent, child, aunt, or uncle may want for themselves, they have to subordinate their own wants and needs in the interests of what is good for the family as a whole. This was particularly important in poor countries or in poor communities where the family needed to work together in order to survive. As a society becomes more affluent, it becomes harder to pass on familial values because the younger generation will not see a pressing need to subordinate their interests to that of the family's.

Like those born into a particular family, those raised with an ethnicity feel that they carry that identity with them throughout their lives. They may proudly trace their origins or they may attempt to hide their tribal connection, but, either way, it is seen by others (and usually by themselves) as an undeniable fact. For example, Helen Fremont was raised a Catholic in a

Detroit suburb. Many years later, she and her sister Lara somehow sensed that their parents were (perhaps subconsciously) hiding the family's Jewish identity. They investigated and found that their mother indeed escaped from Nazi-occupied Poland and her Hungarian father was sent to a Siberian gulag. The parents survived by developing an elaborate cover story that they were Catholic, and, for psychological and social reasons that are difficult to fully understand, they kept up the cover story even after the defeat of the Nazis and their immigration to the United States. Fremont "discovers her parents were Jewish," even though they were supposedly devout Catholics and the two daughters were raised in the Church.[13] This idea that a Jew always remains a Jew was codified in the halacha. The Talmud recorded the view of the third-century sage Abba ben Zavda, who said, "A Jew, even though he sins, is still a Jew," and the *Shulchan Aruch*, the authoritative sixteenth-century code of Jewish law, repeated the comment as legally binding even if the person had converted to another religion.[14]

The Fremont daughters saw great significance in their parents' Jewish origin and, once they found out, embraced their Jewish ethnic heritage. Others, however, find no existential meaning in their familial origins and are perfectly happy assimilating. Sarah Bershtel and Allen Graubard interviewed a man they called "Sam Silverman" for their book *Saving Remnants: Feeling Jewish in America*. Silverman was born and raised in Philadelphia in the early 1940s and then served in the military in Japan, where he met and married a Japanese woman. While he never converted to another religion, he dropped any pretense of being actively Jewish. He explained why he was able to "let it go." "The farmers all moved to the city. Why is that? Because they didn't want to be on the farm anymore. They hated being on the goddamn farm. 'Oh, the old family farm.' Let it go. If there's no need for it, let it go. Sure, I love those old houses with the verandah, the swing on the back porch, grandpa, grandma, the picnic table out in front. 'Won't you have some fried chicken?'"[15] Silverman says that he does feel a pang in his gut that he's losing something, but "everything changes." That is just a fact. "Nothing stays the way it is. So? What's the big deal? Why is that a terrible thing? What's so terrible about that? If Jewishness disappeared completely off the face of the earth, what would be lost? Jewish folk songs? People who wanted to could still listen to them. Jewish literature? It would still be there for those interested in reading it." People could "still keep talking about the Haggadah and Queen Esther. It's mythology, just like the Roman and Greek myths, and they're still part of our culture even though we don't believe in Apollo.

The Jewish Law? Nobody would follow the Law? Nobody would be kosher? Oh, my God, where would we get a good pastrami sandwich? Well, that's how it is."

Silverman understands Jewishness in strictly ethnic terms and does not see any convincing reason to bother perpetuating that ethnic identity. He shows little hunger to connect to anything Jewish. He says that he feels regret but that he does not feel any guilt about his decisions. What made his statement so memorable when I first read *Saving Remnants* in 1992 was his concluding thought: "Look, if the whooping crane ain't gonna make it, the whooping crane ain't gonna make it. No hatcheries are going to do it. That's what these rabbis are trying to do, make hatcheries for whooping cranes."

Many American Jews see this familism in strictly tribal terms. What is important (or not important) is the connection with other Jews. But others take the concept of familism a step further. They see themselves as part of a larger family, but not just because of historical kinship. They believe that being Jewish means that they are part of a people who were chosen by God to be given a divine revelation. Israel is the holy people whom God has called into being through Abraham and Sarah, Isaac and Rebecca, Jacob and Rachel and Leah. God brings the children of Israel to Sinai, where He renews the covenant that had first been made between Him and Abraham.

The children of Israel agree to follow God's law, and in return God promises to make Israel a great nation. As a consequence, being part of the Jewish people is not just an eccentricity but has well-thought-out religious meaning. Parents who understood enough about Judaism as a religion could theoretically explain their ethnic particularism by appealing to theological justifications. This was, however, unlikely to be terribly effective. Either their children felt Jewish and it mattered to them on an emotional level, or they did not. Religious justifications might be useful for explaining Jewish ethnicity to outsiders, but it was unlikely to be the central feature of Jewish identity for Jews themselves. They had to want to be part of the Jewish community, to feel that there was some emotional benefit in connecting with the tribe.

Jewish spirituality is deeply embedded in the concept of community. As Rabbi Lawrence Kushner put it, Jews "simply cannot do it alone. Hermits and monasteries are noticeably absent from Jewish history; we are a hopelessly communal people."[16] This communal tendency continued even after the religious basis for it had disappeared. The refocusing on spirituality is helping to make it clearer why people should want to be Jewish. Encountering the divine by addressing God in their own words and seeking a direct reply allows contemporary individuals to experience revelation. When God becomes manifest to people, they have a compelling desire to perpetuate the relationship, which is a source of inspiration and spiritual renewal for them. That spirituality is possible on a long-term basis only through community. Rabbi Lawrence A. Hoffman speaks of sacred community as beginning "with a modest but firm commitment to the project of our generation: to transcend ethnicity and seek out the holy in such things as the ways we think, the blessings we say, the truths we discover, and the homes we have or seek to find. Jewish spirituality is not just real. It is reasonable and it is deep. And it beckons us now more than ever to return home to find it."[17]

The Reengagement with Jewish Ceremonial Practice in the Search for Spiritual Enlightenment

Wade Clark Roof has argued the need for "new maps" when the "old ways of describing religion fail to capture what is happening in our everyday lives." As society changes, the way we look at religion also changes. Americans of all backgrounds and beliefs are behaving differently and it is not just popular religious beliefs and practices that are changing. According to Roof, religious institutions as well are undergoing "transformations in form and style, encouraged by a democratic, highly individualistic ethos and rapid social and cultural change." As a consequence, "boundaries separating one faith tradition from another that once seemed fixed are now often blurred; religious identities are malleable and multifaceted, often overlapping several traditions."[18] As American Jews embrace a variety of spiritual acts that they find religiously meaningful, there is inevitably going to be a blurring of boundaries and a violation of traditional norms.

Before the Emancipation and the Enlightenment, virtually all Jews followed halacha, the system of Jewish law that governed all aspects of life. According to traditional belief, God had given the Torah to Moses at Mount Sinai and that Torah was therefore divinely revealed. The Torah included both a written law and an oral law, the latter interpreting the former. Jews were obligated to observe the system in its entirety, which meant that it was important to refer to the oral law in order to understand commandments mentioned, but not necessarily described, in the written law. Spirituality followed observance. For example, it was required to say the Shema every morning and every evening. The halacha did not include an exemption for a person who did not feel spiritually prepared to say what is probably the most important prayer in Judaism. Every Jew was obligated to do it. Even if the person found no spiritual meaning in a particular ritual, they were still obligated to perform it.

This approach has a sound logic to it but it is based on the assumption that Jews will commit themselves to follow the halacha in its entirety. Most American Jews, however, had long ago abandoned any pretense of following the halacha. Rather, they were motivated to observe selected ceremonies for more personal and, some would say, idiosyncratic reasons. Since much of Jewish ceremonial practice in the post–World War II period was a way of expressing Jewish ethnic particularism, the level of ritual activity declined as Jewish ethnicity decreased. This was particularly problematic in the realm of Jewish prayer. In order for prayer to be meaningful, it has to be repeated frequently. The worshipper has to feel an emotional connection with the words, as well as with the religious concepts. They need to feel so familiar with the liturgy that it seems like it was fed to them along with their mother's milk. Occasionally attending a service that they had only the most superficial familiarity with was a sure recipe for boredom and alienation. Even relatively committed Jews were increasingly likely to see the religious service as a formal performance that they had to suffer through rather than a spiritually vibrant event which could help them to come face to face with God. Synagogue services were likely to stifle rather than stimulate the emotions necessary for an intense religious experience.

Rabbi Zalman Schachter-Shalomi, the founder of the Jewish Renewal movement (discussed in chapter 6), explained the problem clearly: "We have learned to think of prayer as something that happens in houses of worship, and what happens in our synagogues—the responsive readings, the cantor, the choir—rarely touches that feeling space inside us. The hushed reverence that synagogues try to preserve unfortunately inhibits any spontaneous expression of wonder or joy."[19] But, over the past ten years or so, something very interesting has happened. Many American Jews have been reengaging in Jewish ceremonial behavior, but now as part of their search for spiritual fulfillment. They are less focused on Jewish folkways that reinforce their sense of historical familism, but they are enthused by the possibility that a given Jewish ceremony can help them in their quest for enlightenment.

The Jewish vision of spirituality in action is based on the performance of mitzvahs. The biblical Hebrew word *mitzvah* means to be commanded. In contemporary usage, doing a mitzvah has come to mean a good deed,

FIGURE 2.3. Rabbi Zalman Schachter-Shalomi relaxing in his backyard in Boulder, Colorado. Reb Zalman has pioneered new approaches to Jewish spirituality. Photo Rabbi Ayla Grafstein. *Courtesy of Rabbi Ayla Grafstein*

as in "help that poor little old lady across the street. It's a mitzvah." But that is not the original meaning of the word, and that is not the understanding of the concept in the classical rabbinic tradition. For those who still believe in a commanding God, the obligatory nature of the divine commandments comes from God's revelation to the Jewish people at Mount Sinai. When the people engaged in an act that God had commanded them to do, it built a bridge between them and God. But the observance of ritual was only efficacious if it was done correctly, and halacha had a vast literature describing how the 613 mitzvahs should be performed. To take the example of prayer, certain prayers must be recited in a certain order during a certain time frame. While there was room for inserting one's own personal prayer, this could not be done instead of the established text of the prayer service. The sages thus created a space for private personal prayer, but it was within the context of a highly formalized structure. But many, if not most, contemporary Jews outside the Orthodox community no longer hold this belief. As Schachter-

Shalomi puts it, "Today, any sense of commandment must come from within, from inside us."[20]

Prayer is the vehicle for the sanctification of mundane activities. Throughout history, prayer has helped Jews express their joys and sorrows, for themselves and their families, and for the Jewish people as a collectivity. It provided an emotional outlet as well as a communal framework. Prayer was obligatory only for men, since it was a positive time-bound commandment. This meant that it was a commandment that required action (rather than refraining from an action) and had to be performed during a certain time period. Nevertheless, women were allowed to and encouraged to pray if and when they could. Prayer was directed at God and included not only praise but also requests for assistance. Abraham, the patriarch, set the example for this by begging God to spare the wicked city of Sodom, since if God destroyed the entire city he would be killing the righteous as well as the evildoers (Genesis 18:23–33). Traditionally, Jews prayed three times a day because it was part of their halachic obligation. While this is still true for the Orthodox, non-Orthodox American Jews have to have a personal reason to want to pray. Now it is true that many will come to synagogue for services even without feeling that they have a compelling reason to pray, but their prayer will be more intense if they feel something inside. This could be connected to something that is happening in their lives at that time or to something that they went through in the past. Schachter-Shalomi explains that "tying a prayer to our own lived experience makes it so much more powerful."[21]

Those seeking to revitalize Jewish spiritual life emphasized that prayer needed to become more personalized—more emotional and less intellectual. Schachter-Shalomi explained that "the prayers in our siddur were collected over centuries, but the siddur is not a museum vault of liturgical music and information. It is a living document. Like a coloring book, though, the siddur gives us only the outlines. Coloring those outlines with life, context, feeling, is up to us." One way to do that is to provide more opportunities for people to pray in their own words. "We're not trying to lay the same old praises at the feet of some old man in the sky; we're trying to connect with a being, a will, a love radiating out from the center of the universe . . . that can nourish something deep in our souls, something that has gotten very hungry among us."[22]

Once the belief in a commanding God was lost and the commitment to a consistent halachic observance was abandoned, Jews had no reason to observe much of the ritual. Writing a generation ago, Marshall Sklare explained

FIGURE 2.4. Yochanan Kalisher drumming in Ruach Hamidbar–Spirit of the Desert High Holy Day services in Arizona. American Jews have become more open to new types of religious music. Photo Barry Bisman. *Courtesy of Rabbi Ayla Grafstein*

that Jewish rituals were more likely to be observed if they met certain criteria and would likely be ignored if they fell in other categories (as discussed in chapter 1). What worked were ceremonial occasions that focused on family and that occurred infrequently, usually on a festive holiday. What did not work were rituals that demanded a great deal of expertise or discipline and were weekly or even daily requirements.

People could now choose what they wanted to observe and how often they wanted to observe it. Once Jews began looking at practices as folkways rather than divine commandments, it became possible to "pick and choose" or "mix and match." They even had a name for it: "salad bar religion." Rabbi Jack Steinhorn (Elihu J. Shalem), an American-born Orthodox rabbi who led the largest Orthodox synagogue in South Africa for twenty-seven years and now lives in the Old City of Jerusalem, argues that the "New Supermarket Judaism" that has emerged from American-style merchandising "has been all-pervasive throughout the world."[23] The plethora of choice is intoxicating, but ultimately unsatisfying. Approaching religion as one would a salad bar is unlikely to provide the person with the personal discipline necessary to experience religiosity as it was intended to be experienced. There is an intense spiritual satisfaction that is the result of self-sacrifice, and the perpetual "religious tourist" is unlikely to feel that sense of satisfaction since they have never made a commitment to sacrifice. Rather, they are constantly looking and evaluating and making temporary choices, only to reverse themselves and consider yet other options.

I have visited the homes of quite a few people who could be classified as long-term religious seekers. Usually raised with a number of different religious influences in their childhood household, they dabble in one religion after another or sometimes several spiritual paths simultaneously. Their shelves are often filled with all types of self-help books, but they are perpetually hungry for something that none of their books seem to satisfy. So they keep looking. Alan Wolfe interviewed a man named Tom Rivers who "has changed his faith as many times as he has changed jobs." Rivers refers to himself as a "spiritual junkie" who is, in his own words, "all over the place."[24] Some congregations try to cater to religious switchers. One minister referred to his congregation as a "Heinz 57 church," while another compared his to Baskin-Robbins's thirty-one flavors of ice cream. Their hope is that by offering a huge variety of religious approaches and activities, they can meet the emotional needs of these searchers and keep them affiliated with their congregation. To keep these seekers interested, religious leaders need to constantly offer something new and exciting.

While new and exciting activities can be fun, what keeps the seekers connected is the sanctification of daily life. This sanctification is concretized through the performance of religious ceremonies, particularly those ceremonies that relate to important life cycle events. The traditional Jewish life cycle included rituals that were to be performed after birth, at puberty, at the time of marriage, and at death. Many of these life cycle rituals had been transformed into public occasions for the celebration of the socioeconomic status of the family, losing much of their original religious meaning. Just watch the movie *Keeping Up with the Steins* to see an example of this. Now there was an increasing desire to prepare for these religious events in a spiritual manner that would help to deepen the individual's relationship with God and bring a divine connection to the family's celebration.

Some also felt that there was the need to reintroduce ceremonies or traditional observances that had been jettisoned in earlier generations, particularly by the classical reformers. For example, the Reform movement had eliminated the need for a get, a Jewish religious divorce. The Reform rabbinate declared that a civil divorce was sufficient and that no religious document or ceremony was necessary. But this did not address the spiritual aspect of the separation from one's spouse. Divorce generates all sorts of emotions, most of which are negative and potentially destructive. One of the roles of religion would seem to be helping people cope emotionally with the vicissitudes of life. While the point that a get would no longer be required in a nonhalachic context remained valid, there were psychospiritual reasons to reintroduce, if not an actual get, then some sort of religious document that could mark the end of the couple's marriage.

The non-Orthodox have reintroduced or created from scratch ceremonies that are designed to appeal to different people at different stages of life. Some of them are brand new ceremonies that have never been done before. For example, feminist liturgists came up with a ceremony that can be performed in the aftermath of a rape to help a person deal with the emotional impact of the trauma in a Jewish spiritual manner. Likewise, new ceremonies have been developed for everything from first menstruation to the beginning of menopause. The men's movement has likewise considered whether there might be specific stages of life or physical changes that might warrant the creation of ceremonies specifically for men, but this has not been institutionalized, at least not yet. This gender imbalance may reflect the increasing feminization of American religion, a process in which women are growing increasingly enthusiastic while men are distancing themselves from what they regard as a feminized spirituality. Perhaps this is the reason that so many of the new ceremonies focus on women's issues. Others disagree with this analysis, arguing that "masculinized" Judaism is now moving toward a better balance.

It is not only ceremonies that are being rediscovered and recreated. Other types of observances are likewise being looked at in new ways. Perhaps the most interesting of these new approaches to traditional observances is eco-kashrut. Kashrut, the kosher laws, is a very complex system that governed all aspects of how to prepare and consume food. Jews were prohibited from eating certain types of food, which were regarded as nonkosher, and they were restricted from mixing other types of food together or eating certain foods following a specific amount of time after other food items. The consequence of following the kosher laws strictly was that it was impossible to eat out in any nonkosher restaurant or even at another family's house, unless they were committed to the same standard of kashrut. For most non-Orthodox Jews, however, the laws of kashrut had little meaning and were almost completely ignored. Creative thinkers considered how the concept of kashrut could be reapplied in a more meaningful manner. For example, some felt that what was important was to abstain from eating the meat of animals that had been raised under inhumane conditions, such as veal. Others argued that Jewish tradition should call for avoiding meat entirely. As Richard H. Schwartz put it, "while rarely discussed in the Jewish community, a widely accepted aspect of modern life—the mass production and widespread consumption of meat—contradicts many fundamental Jewish teachings and badly harms people, communities, and the planet."[25]

Schachter-Shalomi developed a broader approach that reinterpreted the traditional concept of kashrut. By the late 1970s, he was using the term *eco-kosher* to describe a humane approach to food and eating that was environmentally sensitive. Eco-kosher would take the ecology of the earth into consideration when deciding what to eat or not to eat. "On the one hand we have the threat of Earth's destruction, whether cataclysmic or gradual; on the other, we have the halting emergence of planetary cooperation, countries putting their heads together to control crime and disease, mediate conflict, and protect the environment. Strengthening this whole-Earth cooperation is to me the most urgent and important way we have of serving God, the holiest and most pressing invitation of our time."[26]

Rabbi Arthur Waskow argues that Jews need to consider new types of questions to ask when making decisions about not only what to eat, but what to consume in a broader sense. He believes that Jews should ask questions like "is it eco-kosher to eat vegetables and fruit that have been grown by drenching the soil with insecticides?"[27] The Eco-Kosher Project was started by Waskow in 1990 when he sent out a letter to rabbis and Jewish teachers calling for them to reevaluate the observance of the kosher laws. A group formed, and they decided to focus on four categories of individual and institutional purchase and investment. This would include evaluating how fresh and processed fruits and vegetables were grown, packaged, and marketed; the environmental impact of household consumables and in particular paper and cleaning products; how individual financial decisions affect the environment; and how the conservation and recycling of materials and energy could be achieved. "Always before, the choices seemed to be between preserving our own uniqueness, and abandoning our Jewishness to fight the universal struggles. What the Eco-Kosher Project implies is that we can strengthen our Jewish distinctiveness and serve the needs of the earth as well; that we can strive to heal ourselves by helping to heal the earth, and help to heal the earth by healing ourselves."[28] Waskow argued that if keep-

about making distinctions, then eco-kosher was consistent with the traditional concept. Of course, the distinctions would be made in a new way, but that way would be far more relevant to the new generation.

Others are embracing aspects of Jewish ceremonial practice, but combining them with elements that were previously seen as nonhalachic or even antihalachic. This was the case with the cremation service done for Louise Taub. When she died of breast cancer in December 2002, her Northern California friends conducted a taharah ceremony over her body, carefully washing and then wrapping her in a shroud. Renewal rabbi David Cooper of the Kehilla Synagogue in Oakland conducted a memorial service to mark the end of the earthly phase of her spiritual journey, reciting many of the traditional funeral prayers in Hebrew and English. Then she was cremated and her ashes were divided into eight urns. Each urn was given to a family member or close friend who scattered her ashes in places she would have been happiest—at the beach, in a forest, in the Cape Cod waters where she swam with her sister as a child, and in the San Francisco Bay.[29]

Despite the family's obvious affinity for Jewish tradition, they were violating one of the basic prohibitions of Jewish law concerning death and mourning. Traditional Judaism prohibits cremation. The book of Genesis states that human beings are created "in the image of God," and Jewish legal writings explained that this meant that honoring the dead was an important mitzvah that took precedence over many other commandments. God tells Adam, "Thou shalt return to the ground; for out of it wast thou taken: for dust thou art, and to dust shalt thou return." (Genesis 3:19). The sages interpreted this verse as requiring Jews to bury their dead. Even though the idea is not widely known today, the resurrection of the dead was one of the central beliefs of Talmudic Judaism. No one owns his own body and therefore it has to be returned to God in its natural state. At the end of days, the dead will rise up and live again.

It should therefore be no surprise that traditional Jews were horrified that Jewish cremation services were being done. Rabbi Avi Shafran, the director of Public Affairs for Agudath Israel of America, explained that "burning . . . is a declaration of utter abandon and nullification." Some halachic authorities believe that cremated bodies may not be resurrected, particularly if they chose cremation. Not referring specifically to the Taub case, Shafran said that "actually choosing to have one's body incinerated is an act that, intended or not, expresses denial of the fact that the body is still valuable, that it retains worth, indeed potential life."[30] Others believe that it is inappropriate in the aftermath of the Holocaust, where the Nazis burned Jewish bodies in crematoria. Neil Gillman of the Jewish Theological Seminary in New York—a Conservative Jew—has stated that any Jew who has their body cremated after Auschwitz is committing a terrible obscenity against the Jewish people.[31]

Despite the fact that it is prohibited by halacha and discouraged by Jewish custom, increasing numbers of American Jews—between 10 and 20 percent—are choosing cremation. Overall, 26 percent of Americans who died in the year 2000 and 32 percent of those who died in 2005 were cremated. Some believe that as many as 50 percent may choose cremation by the year 2025. One of the main reasons is financial. A cremation service can cost as little as $800, while a funeral costs $8,000 and up. Some find cremation to be more in keeping with their concept of life and nature and prefer it to burial in what they see as a sterile cemetery landscape. Others are claustrophobic, and fear being placed in a closed box. Some feel that the cemetery is a place filled with death, and that they want their final remains to be placed in a natural setting teeming with life, such as a garden or a rainforest. Others interpret the "from dust to dust" idea literally and want their remains to be immediately returned to dust. Some have fond memories of specific places, and they find comfort in the idea that their remains could be scattered in the beautiful settings they know will bring a smile to the faces of their loved ones.

Some of those who have asked for their ashes to be placed in a natural setting are environmentalists. They like the idea of being scattered in the woods or the ocean, somewhere natural and beautiful. The green crowd now requests burial in "woodland cemeteries," sometimes in eco-friendly coffins made entirely of wood fiber, 90 percent of which is derived from recycled materials held together by natural glue. In Sweden, those who desire a "freeze-dried funeral" can request that their body be dipped in liquid nitrogen, which causes it to become brittle and then turn to dust. The remains are placed in a shallow grave where they nourish the earth faster than they would with other burials. For those preferring cremation, LifeGem Company will capture the carbon from ashes and create a synthetic diamond, thus recycling the ashes in a form that will be highly sought after. Others prefer to be buried at sea. Eternal Reefs will put human remains in a module that mimics a coral reef. The "reef ball," which is guaranteed to last for at least five hundred years, is to be dropped in the ocean to help create new marine habitats.[32]

Shafran points out that there is an "ecological" aspect to traditional Jewish burial. "[It] requires that the body be 'accessible' to the elements, which is why only a simple wooden coffin is used and is traditionally, when permitted by [civil] law, broken or opened somewhat, to expose the body to natural forces of decay." Thus, traditional Judaism also encourages the "recycling" of biological material.[33] Despite Shafran's argument, many non-Orthodox Jews see cremation as a more holistic way to be put to rest. David Hershcopf of Oakland, California helped to arrange for the cremations of his close friend Louise as well as his mother and aunt and plans to be cremated himself. "I think the reason why my mother and (my aunt) Jenny and Louise all wanted cremation is they felt there was something unnatural about being in a plot next to all the other bodies. They wanted to be part of the earth, and they wanted to be scattered in different places."[34] The Taub family found solace in the idea that Louise's remains might be contributing to the ecology of a forest or other natural setting. Her elderly mother Berte explained that "watching a tree grow with my daughter's ashes, that's very meaningful."

Not everyone shared that feeling. When a reporter from *J.*, the local Northern California Jewish newspaper, told Rabbi Shlomo Zarchi of Congregation Chevra Thilim in San Francisco about the cremation, he said that cremation is "a rejection of everything that's Jewish. It's like a last slap in the face of Judaism on the way out the door."[35] Rabbi Zarchi would be correct if he was talking about a population that had been raised in traditional Jewish homes and accepted halachic norms. But the American Jews who are embracing new practices that in many cases run contrary to Jewish tradition are generally not doing these things to rebel. They are not deliberately rejecting Judaism. In fact, the Taub family wanted Louise's body to undergo taharah, and they wanted a rabbi to help them recite many of the traditional funeral prayers. But they had a different aesthetic and, in fact, a different set of core beliefs.

There are numerous other examples of this reengagement with Jewish ceremony in ways that would shock and disappoint those who believe in traditional Judaism and its system of positive and negative commandments. Like the reclaiming of formerly derogatory words such *queer, nigger* (which is now permutated as *nigga*), and *bitch*, it is seen as a positive twist on the original formulation. These acts have little or nothing to do with rebellion, although it certainly feels that way to those who have been formed and informed in a different milieu. Take the case of Hebrew tattooing. There are thousands of young Jewish people getting tattoos of Hebrew letters or Jewish themes as an expression of their Jewish identity. This is an abrupt departure from Jewish norms, because there was an explicit commandment in the

Torah prohibiting the practice. In Leviticus 19:28, it is written, "you shall not make gashes in your flesh for the dead, or incise any marks on yourselves; I am the Lord." This statement in the Torah has been interpreted as prohibiting Jews from voluntarily tattooing themselves. Yet many want to get a tattoo of Hebrew characters, a Star of David, a menorah, or any of hundreds of other identifiably Jewish symbols. Some may connect their tattoo to mystical cncepts, while others may relate their "ink" to various personal events such as the birth of a child.

There are other ceremonies that do not violate halachic prohibitions, but nevertheless would have no justification in the halachic system. The Torah passing ceremony done at most bar and bat mitzvahs is a prime example. In a traditional synagogue, the Torah was taken out of the ark in order to be read. The halacha required that the Torah reader recite a blessing before and after the reading. Since even many traditional men were not capable of reading the Torah (particularly without preparing in advance), the custom began of allowing a person to recite the blessings, but then have a professional Torah reader do the actual reading. There were honors given for removing the Torah from the ark and carrying the Torah around the congregation, but these evolved only in order to read the Torah. In recent decades, non-Orthodox congregations have begun to perform what is being called a Torah passing ceremony. The Torah is taken from the ark and is given to the grandparents, who then pass it to the parents, who then hand it to the child. The symbolism is clear to the family, their friends, and the entire congregation—the Jewish tradition is being passed from generation to generation. There is no need to read from the Torah, and so the Torah could be taken out and returned to the ark without being opened. A new ceremony has been created, one that may not violate the halacha but exemplifies the religious meaning that a new generation assigns to an ancient symbol.

Social Justice Activism as an Expression of Spirituality

Social justice has been an important priority for the American Jewish community since the nineteenth century. The Reform movement in particular pushed the idea that Jewish ethics were at the core of the Jewish religion and that putting those ethical teachings into practice was the most important religious obligation. The concept of social justice has changed over the past 150 years from primarily a support for organizing labor to a diverse agenda ranging from antipoverty to environmentalism. But whereas many in the earlier generation saw liberalism as a political agenda that would help them to ensure their place in American society, the younger generations have less need to have such a utilitarian agenda. Rather, they want to help others in order to feel that they are making a difference in the world. They want to help others because they want to believe that they are doing something productive. Having grown up with plenty of material possessions, they want to work towards a spirituality based on the performance of good works.

Traditional Judaism focused on the observance of the *mitzvot* (plural of the commandments). These commandments included not only ritual obligations, but also social justice imperatives. In the Torah, the Israelites are told "you shall do what is right and good" (Deuteronomy 6:12). Every person is created in the image of God, and this means that Jews are commanded to be concerned with the welfare of each and every soul. The Torah commands the Israelites to "pursue justice, only justice" (Deuteronomy 16:20). As a consequence of this moral mandate, all Jews are obligated to help make the world a better place. Rabbi Terry Bookman explains that "every action we take to repair the brokenness of our world, to make it a better place in which to live, frees another spark or lights it within another human being. Every time we volunteer at the soup kitchen, or work for justice legislation, or demonstrate on behalf of a righteous cause, or help make peace between individuals or nations, we are participating in the act of tikkun olam."[36]

Tikkun olam literally means "the repair of the world" and probably originated in some of the earliest rabbinic documents. The term *mipnei tikkun ha-olam*, on account of the need to repair the world, is used in the mishnah, the basic summary of the oral law that was codified by Rabbi Judah the Prince around 200 CE. The phrase was used to ensure that extra protection was offered to those people who were potentially at an economic or political disadvantage, for example, women who needed to receive a divorce document or a slave who had earned the right to be set free. Later, in kabbalistic thought, it was used to refer to the process of regathering the light that had been spread throughout the universe. The new understanding of tikkun olam traces its origins to the 1960s. Political activism became one of the most important mitzvot.

This use of the term tikkun olam has been picked up by American Jews, even those who are not necessarily involved in religious practice. New York City Mayor Michael Bloomberg cited his commitment to tikkun olam as one of the reasons for his plan to reduce air pollution in Manhattan by charging special fees for vehicles entering congested parts of the borough. "In my faith, the Jewish faith, there is a religious obligation called tikkun olam, or to make the world whole, or to correct error and end injustice. And that responsibility is found among people of good will in every faith." Some Orthodox thinkers objected to this use of the term. Rabbi Yitzchok Adlerstein wrote on the blog Cross-Currents that while Bloomberg was using the term in the customary manner of the day, "his understanding is the polar opposite of what the phrase [had] always meant."[37]

While the concept of social justice as a Jewish value was not new, the association of it with the phrase tikkun olam was a relatively recent one. It was the Reform movement that pioneered the concept of social justice as a Jewish religious imperative. The classical Reform rabbis of the late nineteenth century spoke incessantly of the mission of Israel and the need to bring the teachings of ethical monotheism to all humanity. This was a radically new approach. Orthodox Jews valued the mitzvah of *tzedakah*, which was usually translated as the giving of charity, but they were not known for their social activism and generally shied away from political causes. Neither group spoke specifically about tikkun olam, except perhaps in a narrow theological sense, but over the past twenty or thirty years the concept of tikkun olam has become synonymous with Jewish social justice activism and has even been spoken of approvingly by various non-Jewish politicians. Each of the American Jewish religious denominations eventually opened a political lobbying center in Washington, D.C. The liberal denominations consistently articulated their belief in tikkun olam as the justification for their involvement in political affairs. The model for this was the Religious Action Center of Reform Judaism (RAC), which was founded by Rabbi David Saperstein in 1961 at the peak of the civil rights movement. The RAC works closely with the Commission on Social Action of Reform Judaism (CSA, a committee of the Union for Reform Judaism, URJ). Known for its ability to organize groups with widely divergent ideologies around issues of importance to politically liberal Reform Jews, the RAC has lobbied for measures designed to make the United States a more equitable society, such as the Civil Rights Act of 1964 and the Voting Rights Act of 1965. Benjamin Hooks of the NAACP described the RAC as "the nerve center for the struggle for social justice in America today."[38] The RAC also supports human rights around the world. It supported measures designed to bring apartheid to an end in South Africa, and to ensure a stable transition to democracy in Eastern Europe after the fall of the Soviet Union. Reform Judaism in particular became so closely as-

sociated with social justice causes that Judaism and social action became synonymous. Such congregations neglected not only the traditional ritual that
classical Reform had rejected decades earlier but even the abbreviated and
truncated ceremony that had been adopted in its stead. While some felt that
the religious agenda had become too narrow, others were motivated to help
make a difference in American society. There seemed to be a terrible injustice
that was being continually perpetuated on the Negro population, particularly in the South. They responded enthusiastically to the rousing sermons
delivered by rabbis oriented toward social justice who called on them to put
the ethical teachings of Judaism into practice. It was an exciting time. Then
the interest in social justice began to wane. As the long-time secretary at
Congregation Emanu-El B'ne Jeshurun in Milwaukee, Wisconsin told me in
the late 1990s, "This temple used to be hopping with all sorts of social action
programs. We had a regular exchange with a neighboring black church, we
housed Central American refugees right here in this building, we organized
civil rights marches." The congregation was "constantly involved in several
causes simultaneously. But about fifteen years ago the stream of activities
started slowing up considerably and then ground almost to a halt."[39]

Various explanations were offered. Liberal Jewish social commentator
Leonard Fein wrote that "for some time now, the conventional wisdom has
held that Jews have been moving away from their traditional commitment to
social justice. We've become not merely too rich, but also too comfortable."
Part of the reason was that the increasing affluence allowed many to move to
the suburbs, far from the poverty of the inner city "where American injustice
is most manifest."[40] Others felt that the increasing obsession with personal
fulfillment shifted the emphasis from doing good for others to doing good
for oneself. People began to look through the warehouse of stored Jewish
ceremonies in search of activities that could make them feel good, giving
them a spiritual boost. According to this way of thinking, the renewed interest in Jewish ceremonial behavior was a negative consequence of the increasingly therapeutic culture.

Despite the increasing obsession with materialism, there were a number
of initiatives in the 1980s to express Jewish ethics in concrete ways. MAZON
has been one of the most successful social justice funds. Founded in 1985, MA-
ZON: A Jewish Response to Hunger is a nonprofit agency that allocates donations from the Jewish community to nonsectarian antipoverty organizations.
MAZON (the word means "food" in Hebrew) sees its purpose as providing

for those who are hungry today as well as addressing the systemic causes of poverty in the United States and around the world. MAZON founder Leonard Fein conceived of the idea for creating such an organization during the Ethiopian famine of 1985. He remembered that community rabbis historically did not allow celebrations to begin until the local poor were seated and fed. Fein felt that this custom could be built on by offering American Jews a symbolic way to observe this tradition by donating 3 percent of the cost of their life cycle celebrations to help feed those who were less fortunate.

MAZON is particularly determined to alleviate hunger on a long-term basis through legislative advocacy. Jeremy Deutchman of MAZON explained that "one of MAZON's great achievements has been encouraging front-line anti-hunger agencies (food pantries, soup kitchens, food banks, etc.) to dedicate resources to promoting sound public policies (for instance, strengthening the Food Stamp Program) that will have a lasting impact on the people utilizing their services."[41] Many believed that the organization did important work and passionately urged anyone having a celebration to put aside a percentage of their total cost for MAZON. Others were skeptical, forming the impression that many rabbis pushed MAZON primarily as a way of assuaging their own guilt for not doing more themselves. They organized large-scale mitzvah days in which their congregations did multiple social justice programs simultaneously or over the course of a single day. Unfortunately, most congregations held a mitzvah day once a year, and planned only irregular social justice activities. Aside from these isolated efforts, the Jewish community was, in the words of a report from the Jewish Fund for Justice, "not assertively pursuing . . . [the] mandate to pursue social justice."[42]

There are signs that this move away from a focus on social justice action has been reversing itself. Recently, there has been a dramatic increase in volunteers for organizations dedicated to tikkun olam. American Jewish leaders believe that the desire to do good for others can help young American Jews make a difference in the world and reinforce their Jewish identity at the same time. The key is in understanding the motivations of young people, particularly those young people who have an idealistic streak. Gary Rosenblatt, editor and publisher of the *Jewish Week*, pointed out that "young Jews see participation in Jewish life differently than their elders. They are not so much interested in attending services as they are in doing service." They want to take the idea of being participatory further, not just participating in a synagogue fund-raising campaign or even planning how funds might be used,

FIGURE 2.5. Young Reform Jews demonstrate against the slaughter of innocent civilians in Darfur. The Reform movement has long been known for its emphasis on social justice. *Courtesy of the Union for Reform Judaism*

but actually going to that underprivileged community and working directly with those in need of assistance.

Some are specifically interested in volunteering abroad, in a type of Jewish Peace Corps program. The American Jewish World Service (AJWS), for example, has been successful at sending young people to help in developing countries. This is not possible in all cases. A number of specific social justice causes around the world have attracted a great deal of interest because of the large number of innocent people killed or the terrible ravages caused by plague or pestilence. Thus the need is great, but the safety of the potential volunteers cannot be guaranteed. The genocide in Darfur in particular has stirred up the passions of young Jewish people who see it as a recent example of world apathy in the face of terrible yet avoidable human suffering. Despite the empathy generated for this cause, it is simply not safe to volunteer in Sudan. Many Jewish leaders see these young people as lacking loyalty and commitment to Judaism, and, based on traditional criteria, that would seem

FIGURE 2.6. Elderly Israelis waiting in line for food at a MAZON grantee in Jerusalem in November 2006. Synagogues throughout the United States raise money for MAZON: A Jewish Response to Hunger as part of their efforts to bring tikkun olam, the repairing of the world. Photo Joel Jacob. *Courtesy of MAZON*

to be a fair criticism. However, Rosenblatt suggests that "rather than berate young Jews about their obligation to join synagogues and communal organizations, we need to understand and appreciate their concerns, help them find meaningful ways of Jewish connection and embrace their efforts in hands-on commitment to social service and justice that follow in the path of the prophets."[43]

There are a number of personalities who have tried to publicize the need for social justice, both in the United States and around the world. Rabbi Michael Lerner has become the most prominent advocate of tikkun olam as a Jewish obligation. Lauded by some as a bold, brave voice for progressive Judaism and mocked by others as a self-serving egomaniac (one internet blogger rather uncharitably called him Rabbi Moonbeams), Lerner attracted a great deal of attention from the general as well as the Jewish media.[44] In his 1994 book, *Jewish Renewal*, Lerner writes that "Judaism presents the world with a challenge: that the world can and should be fundamentally changed; that the central task facing the human race is tikkun olam, the healing and

FIGURE 2.7. Rabbi Michael Lerner, editor of *Tikkun* magazine. Lerner has advocated a "politics of meaning" as part of his efforts to infuse public discourse with spiritual values. Photo Pat Allen. *Courtesy of* Tikkun *magazine*

transformation of the world. And Judaism has deep insight into how that can be accomplished." Lerner explains that despite this beautiful religious teaching, Judaism's potential spiritual impact has not been realized. "In every generation, this insight has been muted, avoided, abandoned, or outright denied by many, including those who claim to be the official priests, spokespeople, leaders, rabbis, teachers, or orthodox embodiments of Judaism."[45]

Lerner has skillfully promoted himself as a public intellectual, while avoiding some of the political pitfalls that might have discredited him. He was an obscure academic when he and his then wife Nan Fink, heiress to a drugstore chain fortune, founded *Tikkun: A Bimonthly Jewish Critique of Politics, Culture, and Society*. Lerner was frustrated because most of the people on the left that he knew were completely secular and totally failed to understand the centrality of religion in American society and the importance of spirituality in the lives of people throughout the world. *Tikkun* was intended to provide an intellectual forum to explore these ideas as well as develop the implications of applying religious concepts to liberal social values. The magazine was seen as a needed balance to *Commentary*, which was a neoconservative magazine published by the American Jewish Committee.

With *Tikkun* associate editor Peter Gabel, Lerner started speaking about a "politics of meaning," which could help raise political discourse above the level of self-interest and make it truly a tool for improving society. His work was brought to the attention of the Clintons and Hillary Clinton mentioned the expression *politics of meaning* in one of her speeches. Lerner was a controversial character, and when Clinton became aware of this, she dropped all connection to him. Despite this temporary setback, Lerner persevered. While *Tikkun* magazine could never build their subscription levels much above ten thousand, it was incredibly influential: its articles were written by some of the best-known left-wing intellectuals in the country and it had a perspective that was of great interest to a diverse readership.

Lerner traces his commitment to tikkun olam to his adolescent preoccupation with the ideas of Abraham Joshua Heschel. Lerner saw Heschel as his inspiration for Jewish Renewal, which he defined as "the process, repeated throughout Jewish history, in which Judaism is 'changed' back to its origins as the practice of healing, repair, and transformation."[46] Lerner explained that Heschel was the one who popularized the notion that as soon as God had Moses lead the children of Israel out of Egypt He revealed to the freed slaves that their religious obligation would be to perform tikkun olam.[47] Lerner thus named his magazine *Tikkun* to emphasize what he sees as the central obligation of the Torah—to transform the world into a more just and equitable place through the power of love.

In recent years, Lerner's commitment to social justice has put him in an uncomfortable situation in terms of his desire to be part of the left-wing community. He sees himself as a loyal Jew—he was ordained as a Jewish Renewal rabbi by Rabbi Zalman Schachter-Shalomi in 1995—and he believes that any criticisms of Israel that he or any of his writers make are done with the intention of helping the Jewish state become a more ethical political force.

Many Jewish leaders feel that his constant attacks on Israeli policies are terribly harmful to Israel, while left-wing activists see him as a supporter of Zionism and therefore lacking sincerity and legitimacy. The conflict between Lerner and some of his fellow left-wingers came to a head when he was forced to withdraw as a speaker at a rally because he was a "Zionist." This obviously deeply hurt him. Perhaps partially as a consequence, he began to see the truth of the old adage "you can't dance at two weddings at the same time." Lerner has announced plans to refocus *Tikkun* magazine on his original concerns of social justice and spirituality and move away from many of the politically oriented articles, particularly on Middle Eastern issues that had become an increasing presence in his magazine.

Lerner's approach to tikkun olam has evolved over the years, moving gradually from a hardcore intellectual political philosophy to a softer, more New Age–influenced Jewish Renewal religious community. He founded the Beyt Tikkun synagogue in Berkeley where he now spends a great deal of his time putting his ideas about spirituality into practice in a communal setting. "We intend to foster as many spontaneous acts of love and caring as possible and do what we can to embody our highest ideals."[48]

Finding Judaism Through Buddhist Meditation

When Americans first became fascinated with Tibetan Buddhism, Hinduism, and other Eastern philosophies, most Jews felt that they had to choose between their interest in Eastern spirituality and their involvement in the Jewish community. Many of the early American leaders of Eastern philosophical movements such as Richard Alpert, Jack Kornfield, Sharon Salzberg, and Norman Fischer regarded themselves as Jewish by birth and perhaps by ethnicity, but nothing more. Yet, they knew they had to trace their spiritual legacy back to their childhood and their families, and this prevented them from severing all ties with their people and heritage.

Meditation and Judaism were never seen as being religiously incompatible in the way that, say, Christianity and Judaism were, but it was still expected that a person would be in one camp or the other. Nan Fink Gefen, the dean of faculty of Chochmat HaLev, a Jewish meditation center in Berkeley, California, explained: "It used to be that meditation was seen as inappropriate in Jewish settings, but that has mostly changed. The American Jewish community increasingly recognizes that people have spiritual needs, and that one way of meeting them is through meditation." Gefen believes that "the transition from meditation being on the margins to being in the mainstream is happening very fast. People are hungry for connecting to find spiritual meaning within Judaism. And Judaism is enough settled in this country that it can take the risk of opening itself to this."

Classes about meditation are frequently offered at Jewish Community Centers, Hillels, Jewish summer camps, and synagogues. Gefen told me that "meditation is finding its way into Reconstructionist, Reform, and Conservative venues very rapidly. Some synagogues include it in services—for example, taking a few minutes of quiet before The Sh'ma."[49] Sylvia Boorstein, a popular meditation teacher, told the *Jewish Week* in 2001 that "ten years ago there was more of an alarm that 'it's not Jewish and will take people away from Judaism.' Now people are seeing that it can help bring people closer to Judaism."[50]

Buddhist wisdom suggests that true spirituality does not require a fixed identity. The deeper that a person becomes involved on her spiritual path, the more divergent the path becomes. Ideologies become crutches and religious traditions become part of the material world that no longer seems truly important. Buddhist spiritual practice tries to orient the person in such a way that he lets go of his preconceived notions and particularistic identities. As the novice gets more in touch with who she truly is, it becomes easier to let her subjective concepts of culture fall away. The Buddha, who is regarded as a spiritual teacher rather than a deity, said that "when I obtained Absolute Perfect Enlightenment, I attained absolutely nothing."[51] Once a person realizes that nothing truly matters, then it's possible to appreciate that everything that's happened to us in life actually does matter. That is why so many Jewish Buddhists reengage with their Judaism, even if they grew up with little Jewish tradition.

Buddhism and other similar types of Eastern disciplines are attractive to a small but intense percentage of Americans, including many Jews. One story has it that Charles Strauss, an American Jew, was the first American to embrace Buddhism in the United States after he heard a lecture at the 1893 World's Parliament of Religions in Chicago.[52] In the years following World War II, many American Jews who followed the Beat generation looked into Buddhism. Poet Allen Ginsberg generated a lot of publicity for this approach, with his high-profile involvement in Buddhism as well as episodic interest in aspects of Jewish culture. In the early 1970s, four Americans—perhaps not coincidentally all Jewish—founded the Insight Meditation Society, which began organizing meditation retreats "for the cultivation of awareness and understanding," and the Barre Center for Buddhist Studies, which focused on the "integration of scholarly understanding and meditative insight."[53]

In recent years, American Jews interested in Buddhism have been called Jubus, or sometimes Bu-Jews.[54] Likewise, a Hindu Jew is called a Hinjew, a Sufi Jew is called a Jufi, and so forth. A Jubu is usually meant to refer to a person who practices forms of Buddhist meditation and spirituality while continuing to identify as a Jew, at least in an ethnic sense and quite possibly in a religious sense as well. The term became popularly known after the publication of Rodger Kamenetz's description of a Jewish-Buddhist encounter in *The Jew in the Lotus*. Kamenetz credits Marc Lieberman, a San Francisco ophthalmologist, with being "the first person to ever describe himself to me as a Jubu."[55] Kamenetz wrote about the October 1990 meeting between a group of Jewish delegates and the Fourteenth Dalai Lama of Tibet, held in Dharamsala, a remote hill town in northern India. Despite their wildly divergent backgrounds, both the Jews and the Buddhists came away from the exchange with a new outlook on the meaning of spirituality and the role that it could play in national as well as personal identity and destiny.

The *Los Angeles Times* later interviewed Lieberman, the Sabbath-observing Jewish Buddhist who was the key organizer of the 1990 meeting of the Jewish delegation with the Dalai Lama. "I'm a healthy mosaic of Judaism and Buddhism." Being a Jubu was an example of "good old American innovation." The reporter asked him whether it was fair to either religion to try to blend Judaism and Buddhism together. "Fair schmair! It's what I am. My Jewish side is a tribal sensibility; a reflexive identity with the pain and agony of my people, and the pride and glories of their traditions. But my Buddhist side asks, 'Does that exclude others in the world?'"[56] Lieberman explained: "The contemporary Jewish world has ignored spiritual life and chosen material life. I refuse to cede the ground to the fundamentalists that the only way to be Jewish is their way. We're all pointing toward transcendent reality in our own ways."

"My personal experience is that the Buddhist expression of that reality is relatively clean and uncluttered. Once you've reclaimed that reality, returning to your own roots is the next step."[57] For many Jubus, the two identities are intermeshed. Whereas virtually every mainstream Jew accepts that it is impossible to believe in or practice Christianity and remain a loyal Jew, most believe that you can do that with Buddhism. Alan Senauke, a Jewish boy from New York who is now a Buddhist priest, explained his feelings this way: "My Judaism and Buddhism are like vines so entangled they are not separate. Because of my Jewishness, I'm faulty as a Buddhist, and because of my Buddhism, I can never really be a practicing Jew."[58]

For those worried about the potential for idolatry, there may be the need to avoid specific Buddhist practices. David Grotell, for example, is concerned that his meditative practice could lead him to violate the prohibition against idol worship that is one of the Ten Commandments. "Although I have a meditation spot in my home, as a Jew, I just can't allow myself to put a statue of Buddha there."[59] Others argue that the Buddha statue is not intended to be an idol and that the Buddha never considered himself a god—therefore the prohibition would not apply. Orthodox Rabbi Akiva Tatz disagrees: "The heart of the difference [between Judaism and idolatry] is this: true service understands that God is everything, I am only to serve; idolatry understands that I am everything, and my gods are to serve me." Tatz notes that many of the images in idolatrous worship are human in form. "Idolatry is really worship of the self, and the graven images are projections of that self."[60] It is difficult to see how Tatz's criticism of self-obsessed materialism would apply to Buddhism, which seems so self-abrogating, but his refusal to countenance any hint of religious syncretism is common among Jewish ultra-traditionalists.

Rabbi Emanuel Feldman, then the editor of *Tradition*, published by the Rabbinical Council of America, stated that, according to many halachic authorities, Buddhism is classified as avodah zarah (idolatry). "Within American Jewry there is virtually no agreement on what Jews should minimally practice or believe. Anything goes. Native American rites, Eastern religions, actual idolatry—all can fall under the rubric of America's loosely identified Judaism. The only thing all Jews agree on is what they do not accept: they do not accept Jesus as the Messiah." Feldman expresses puzzlement: "not a few Jews have been known to experiment with Buddhism (which, according to many halachic authorities, is out and out Avodah Zarah), but in the eyes of the masses of wavering American Jews, Buddha somehow seems not as bad as Jesus."[61]

Jubus obviously are not troubled by this type of criticism. They find tremendous joy in following Buddhist spiritual practice and believe that they can reconcile their Jewish and Buddhist selves. Sylvia Boorstein, one of the founders of the Spirit Rock Meditation Center in Woodacre, California, was introduced to Buddhism "at a time in my life when I was frightened by my sense that life was too hard, too fragile, to accept without despair. I doubted it could be otherwise." In 1977 she attended her first Vipassana retreat, which focused on what the Buddhist masters call mindfulness. "I think what most excited me. . . about Buddhism was that it offers a succinct explanation for suffering." While pain is a given in life, people can learn to end suffering through their own spiritual practice. There were no beliefs that had to be accepted, but rather there was a spiritual practice that needed to be taken on and tested out. Boorstein discovered that the first of the Four Noble Truths was that life is fundamentally unsatisfying because of its fragility. Since life is temporal, by definition nothing lasts. Boorstein was greatly relieved to hear this idea was one of the central teachings of the Buddha. She had spent the previous several years preoccupied with the idea that life was tragically flawed and had not found a way to relieve her obsession with this negative thought. "It was such a relief! My reading of how life is was not a personal melancholy misperception. My *response* to it was melancholy, but here were teachers who said that it was possible to cultivate wiser responses."[62]

In the mid-1980s, Boorstein was a Buddhist delegate at an international interfaith women's conference in Toronto. There was also a Jewish delegation as well as women representing many other religious traditions. On the first day of the conference, all the sixty or so delegates sat around a large rectangular table and identified themselves by name and religious affiliation. When her turn came, she stood up and said, "My name is Sylvia Boorstein. I grew up as a Jew, and I teach Buddhist meditation." Although both statements were true, she felt that neither of them told the whole story. "I felt awkward about what I said, but it was the best I could do at the time. One evening, the delegates took a field trip to visit a mosque, a Buddhist temple, and a synagogue. After the final stop of the evening, the group was hosted in the social hall of the synagogue. The president of the temple sisterhood came over and asked Boorstein, "And which group are you with?" Boorstein answered, "I teach Buddhist meditation." Boorstein noted the response. "Startled eyebrow reaction and sincerely surprised exclamation: 'That's funny, you don't *look* Buddhist!'"[63]

She wrote a book about her experiences, in part to "replace emphasis on religious *identity* with the idea of the importance of religious *aspiration*." She hoped that by telling her story and the stories of some of her friends, she could change the questions she asked herself from "Am I compromising myself as a Jew?" to "How am I progressing toward my goal of becoming a fully loving and compassionate person?"[64] She hoped that "I was no longer limited by attachment to parochial viewpoints. I discovered I was wrong." Because of her familial background, she needed to figure out a way to be both a "faithful Jew" as well as a "passionate Buddhist." "I have Jewish lineage. It began with my birth in a Jewish household that nourished it with stories and song and prayer and tradition that seem to have written themselves into my neuronal fibers. They are the language of my heart. I am thrilled to be able to tell my grandchildren stories I heard as a child. And I expect they will pass on to *their* grandchildren the stories I tell them about my grandparents."[65]

FIGURE 2.8. Sylvia Boorstein (*right foreground*) at the Spirit Rock Meditation Center. Boorstein, the author of *That's Funny, You Don't Look Buddhist: On Being a Faithful Jew and a Passionate Buddhist*, teaches both vipassana and metta meditation. *Courtesy of Karen Gutowski of the Spirit Rock Meditation Center*

The teachings of Buddha require all spiritual searchers to confront their personal histories. That is one of the main reasons so many American Jews who became involved in Buddhism have later begun to embrace at least parts of their Jewish heritage. Buddhism subscribes to the law of karma, and the karmic reality is that someone born and raised as a Jew went through those experiences for a reason, and they need to understand what that reason or reasons might be. Ram Dass, the famous spiritual master who was born Richard Alpert, has also searched through Judaism as part of his quest. From this point of view, being a Jubu is not only compatible but is spiritually complimentary. Buddhism can help fill a spiritual void left by a superficial suburban Jewish upbringing, yet Buddhism can encourage the Jew to later look for the tremendous wisdom Jewish tradition contains.

There are those who oppose the integration of Buddhist meditation into Judaism. Gefen opposes the teaching of Vipassana as a way of enriching Judaism. "People don't understand and appreciate our own tradition. They think it's only Eastern traditions; when they learn Vipassana in their synagogue, they don't learn the richness of Jewish meditation." Steven Bayme, the national director of Contemporary Jewish Life for the American Jewish Committee (AJC), goes much further: "The incorporation of Buddhist practices into Judaism is religious syncretism. We would consider chanting over some sort of statue syncretism if not outright paganism."[66]

The idea that meditation could enrich Jewish religious life was embraced by the Nathan Cummings Foundation, which began funding programs to teach Vipassana to leaders of the Jewish community. Rabbi Rachel Cowan explained that "mindfulness creates the awareness and quieting of the mind out of which the liturgy is renewed. Judaism has always borrowed from other traditions and made them Jewish, and that's what is happening with Buddhism." While some might object to integrating meditation based on alien religious sources, they might be more open to meditation that had Judaic roots.

A New Openness to Meditation Based on Jewish Sources

Traditional synagogues had allowed substantial amounts of time for worshipers to read many paragraphs of Hebrew prayers silently, and this practice was abbreviated in the non-Orthodox prayer service. Worshipers were no longer rushing to actually read through several pages of Hebrew text, and the silent time was transformed into an opportunity for the congregation to reflect silently or offer a private prayer, or just take a short break from the service. The moment of silence was usually at the end of the Amidah, the standing prayer that formed one of the central rubrics of the synagogue service.

Because most people's attention spans were so short, the amount of time devoted to the silent prayer became shorter, until it was reduced, in many congregations, to just a few seconds. With the emergence of the trend toward spirituality, synagogues have reversed direction, expanding the moment of silence and offering different types of silent prayer in various formats. Additional moments of silence were added to pray for those in need of healing or as part of a guided or unguided meditation. Different types of meditation have been used to create contemplative services or to form special segments within more general Friday night or Saturday morning services.

One indication that meditation has become more mainstream is that it has been introduced in many non-Orthodox or community Jewish day schools. The Abraham Heschel Middle School in Manhattan, for example, has an alternative morning service called the Minyan Ruach Chadasha (new spirit service), which integrates meditation into more traditional forms of prayer. That is not to say there is no concern on the part of some. When the New Jewish High School in Waltham, Massachussets announced that it would begin offering Tibetan Buddhist meditation as a prayer option, Headmaster Rabbi Daniel Lehmann said that "a couple of parents went bananas, thinking we were going to try and create Jew-Bus."[67]

The reduced focus on silent prayer was unfortunate, because the synagogue had been in possession of one of the most powerful spiritual tools without taking advantage of it. Mindy Ribner, a disciple of Rabbi Aryeh Kaplan and the author of *New Age Judaism: Ancient Wisdom for the Modern World*, explained that "the traditional way of meditating Jewishly has been the prayer book." Meditation can help people to "access the prayer book so that prayer becomes a devotional, alive and powerful way of connecting to God, which is what it was intended to be."[68] For those raised in suburban synagogues where the prayers were chanted or performed by a cantor or choir and the congregation generally ignored the services and chatted amongst themselves, this concept was truly revolutionary.

Ribner reminds her readers that the Jewish prayer book itself states that "even if our mouths were filled with song as the sea is filled with water, our tongue with melody as the roar of the waves, and our lips with praise as the break of the firmament, and our eyes were radiant as the sun and the moon" people would not have adequate words to praise God. At a certain point during prayer, "we realize that words only block the experience of intimacy with the Creator, which cannot be conceptualized in words." Meditation is the way that people can experience a personal encounter with God that cannot be articulated. "At the deepest level of truth, there are no words to talk about God for He is beyond words, no thoughts to think for He is beyond thought."[69]

Traditional Judaism and particularly Orthodoxy was not seen as open to any type of meditation until Rabbi Aryeh Kaplan—a genius who was far ahead of his time—published a series of books on the subject. A devoutly Orthodox Jew, he was able to write works that appealed and continue to appeal to a wide variety of Americans, Orthodox and non-Orthodox, Jews and non-Jews. Kaplan had been influenced by Rabbi Zvi Aryeh Rosenfeld, who encouraged Brooklyn yeshiva students to become involved in Hasidic spirituality, particularly the study of Breslov Hasidic thought. He worked together with Rosenfeld to translate *Tikkun Ha-klali*, which had been written by Rav Nachman, the founder of the Bratslav Hasidic sect. Kaplan then wrote several pamphlets on different aspects of Judaism for the National Council of Synagogue Youth (NCSY), which became popular and helped him to become known as an original Orthodox Jewish thinker. He is regarded as one of the intellectual founders of what became known as the baal teshuva movement (described in chapter 6).

Despite his premature death at the age of forty-eight, Kaplan published prolifically in a number of different fields. Many of his books were originally developed out of classes he gave in his living room to spiritual seekers who came to study with him. These talks became the basis for many of his posthumous writings. His best-known work is probably *The Living Torah*, a user-friendly translation of the Five Books of Moses into English. He wrote on numerous other subjects ranging from Maimonides to how to respond to Christian missionaries, but his most enduring original scholarly contribution was in the field of Jewish meditation. Kaplan demonstrated how many advanced meditative techniques were used by the ancient Jewish mystics and the medieval kabbalists. While a number of authors had already been exploring the theoretical Kabbalah, Kaplan was virtually the first to publish about the actual meditative techniques that were used. Kaplan attributed the lack of attention to actual meditation to the fact that the Zohar, the masterpiece of Jewish mysticism, barely discussed the subject. "Since the Zohar has little to say about meditative methods, many important Kabbalists began to ignore the subject completely. They were too involved in trying to unravel the mysteries of this ancient book that had been concealed for many centuries."[70]

In the introduction to his book *Jewish Meditation*, which was published posthumously in 1985, he wrote that "people are often surprised to hear the term 'Jewish meditation.' Otherwise knowledgeable Jews, including many rabbis and scholars, are not aware that such a thing exists. When shown texts that describe Jewish meditation, they respond that it belongs to esoteric or occult corners of Judaism and has little to do with mainstream Judaism."[71] Kaplan said that, as a result, most general books on meditation almost completely ignored Judaism. Rather, they emphasized Eastern practices and sometimes wrote about Christian meditation, but any discussion of Judaism was extremely limited and almost always restricted to the Kabbalah and Hasidism. Kaplan argued that this was a serious oversight. Not only had Judaism produced one of the most important meditation systems, but since Judaism was an Eastern religion that had migrated to the West, its exclusion meant that "an important link between East and West is lost." He added that there was considerable evidence Jewish mystics were in dialogue with the Sufi masters and the meditative schools in India.

But if the ignorance of Jewish meditation was a loss for the general religious seeker, it was an even greater loss for the Jewish community. Kaplan felt that "Jews are by nature a spiritual people, and many Jews actively seek spiritual meaning in life, often on a mystical level." Because they see Eastern religions as being mystical, many are attracted to non-Jewish forms of spirituality: "When I speak to these Jews and ask them why they are exploring other religions instead of their own, they answer that they know of nothing deep or spiritually satisfying in Judaism." When he tells them "that there is a strong tradition of meditation and mysticism not only in Judaism, but in mainstream Judaism, they look at me askance. Until Jews become aware of the spiritual richness of their own tradition, it is understandable that they will search in other pastures."[72]

Kaplan's first book on the subject, *Meditation and the Bible*, was published in 1978, and in the following years he published numerous volumes of primary sources on meditation and Kabbalah, many of which he found and/or translated himself. Most of the texts that he presented had previously been published only in Hebrew, and even material that had been published in English was usually inaccessible to all but the most determined meditation student. Rabbi Alan Brill teaches Jewish meditation, but only forms that can be traced directly back to medieval Judaic sources. In the introduction to a collection of kabbalistic visionary prayer he is preparing, Brill writes that Kaplan "did a wonderful job of waking people up to the variety of texts, including the neglected medieval traditions. . . . Yet he mixed in Luria, Bratzlav, Chabad, and biblical exegesis into his presentation of the medieval material, and he himself, did not seem [to] fully appreciate the medieval light meditations."[73]

Brill founded the Kavvanah Center for Jewish Thought and Spirituality in 2002 to "help people use the rich Jewish spiritual tradition to add meaning to their everyday lives and ritual practices." He argues that "the sages of yesteryear developed concrete spiritual practices that animated their prayers, meditations, mitzvah observances, as well as all of the 'real life' in between."[74] His goal is to reclaim the devotional aspect of the Jewish tradition through the study of the kabbalistic and Hasidic masters. He hopes that, over the course of time, the center will serve as a community resource bank for curricula, study guides, and other program materials designed to facilitate spirituality and meditation. Other traditional Jews are doing similar things throughout the United States.

The Love of Nature as an Expression of Jewish Spirituality

Despite the fact that the Torah describes a spirituality that developed almost entirely in the outdoors, institutional Judaism conducted almost all of its rituals within synagogue buildings. Ellen Bernstein, the founder of Shomrei Adamah (which the group translates as Guardians of the Earth), describes how she had to "back into" Judaism because "no one taught me that the wilderness experience was so fundamental to my tradition." Bernstein had enjoyed adventuring in the great outdoors since she was a child. "Growing up, I paddled, biked, skied, and meandered through the New England countryside. This penchant for the outdoors and the need to journey determined many of the choices I would make throughout my life." As she grew older, she began to recognize that her adventuring resembled a religious quest. "It was my chance to encounter life's mystery. It would usually take several days on the trail to leave behind the weight of my ego, my self-consciousness and all that is familiar and routine, and free my mind. In these moments, the world opened up to me."

Yet, for the longest time, Bernstein did not recognize the connection between her newly identified spirituality and her family's religion. "As a youth, I had rebelled against what seemed to be a hypocritical, archaic, and dead tradition, and I gravitated toward the universal spirituality of my New England forebears, the Transcendentalists." Given her negative Jewish experiences, "the last place I expected to find models for the spiritual journey was in Judaism. Yet, once I was able to drop my intolerance toward my heritage and yield to it, I recognized that my tradition embodied the most profound teachings about wandering. For, if anything, being a Jew is being a wanderer. Somehow what appears so obvious now took years for me to notice."

The patriarchs Abraham, Isaac, and Jacob, the matriarchs Sarah, Rebecca, Rachel, and Leah, as well as Moses and many other ancient Jewish spiritual models were all called to forsake their homes and their communities to wander in the desert where they hoped to encounter God and discover their sense of purpose in life. Bernstein realized that it was not just biblical heroes, but the entire congregation of Israel that was called to embark on a spiritual journey through the Sinai desert. As is well known, the Children of Israel would spend forty years wandering around in that wilderness. Bernstein explains that she views the biblical wilderness experience "as a metaphor for the journey we must all take to confront the unknown side of our soul and gain self-knowledge."[75]

There are a number of pioneering Jewish spiritual guides who have taken the wilderness metaphor seriously and tried to build spirituality programs based on an encounter with nature. Because this approach is intrinsically anti-institutional, they have not had an easy time. Nevertheless, the work that they do is critical for understanding the new approach to spirituality and its role in contemporary Judaism. The wilderness experience makes nature the classroom for teaching about what Judaism can demonstrate about living a full life. There has to be an outdoor activity to do in the wilderness so that the group is not just going there to walk around and say how beautiful everything looks. Ideally, the activity should require group cooperation and coordination. This is why sports like kayaking and rock climbing are usually the activities of choice, rather than, say, hang gliding. In the words of Rabbi Niles Goldstein, "it is a physical challenge designed for a *meta*physical purpose."[76]

Rabbi Jamie S. Korngold established Adventure Rabbi, which specializes in "experiential teaching of Jewish ritual, practice and theology," focusing on Jewish spiritual experiences in natural settings. Korngold takes her "congregation" on mountain minyan hikes, backpacking treks through the desert, and Rosh Hashanah retreats to a ranch in the Rocky Mountains. "There are a lot of rabbis who are good at congregational work. But few are good at using the environment as a tool, at connecting with the kind of population that isn't interested in congregations. I happen to be one of them."[77] She was taken with the idea expressed by Rabbi Abraham Joshua Heschel that "awe rather than faith is the cardinal attitude of the religious Jew." Korngold had long been involved in nature activities and worked as an Outward Bound guide. She tried a traditional congregational career path, but found that it was too constricting and thought she could create a "synagogue with-out walls" that might appeal to alienated Jews by combining the outdoors with Jewish practice. She was asked by a couple to officiate at the conversion and naming of their adopted baby, which they wanted to hold in a beautiful natural setting. Korngold had a sudden revelation that this could be some-thing far more than an occasional freelance ritual assignment and founded Adventure Rabbi in November of 2001.

She remembers visiting with an old friend who "somewhere along the line, had discarded her Judaism like a sweater she once loved but that no lon-ger fit." The friend told her that "I loved being Jewish when I was a kid, but when I grew up it didn't match what I knew intellectually and it didn't speak a language I could relate to." Shortly thereafter, she went backpacking with a group of Jewish students from Williams College, who told her that they had more interest in Buddhism than Judaism. Then she spoke to a friend of her father's who told her "I used to go to shul every week. But I could never pray like everyone around me. I couldn't talk to God. So I stopped going."

Korngold related that she heard American Jews talking like this frequently. "My heart aches when I hear words like these. And I hear them often. There are too many Jews who have inherited a Judaism that is void of meaning or relevance. There are too many Jews who don't know of a Judaism that is fulfilling, interesting, and joyful. There are too many Jews with no idea that our own religion is rich with opportunities to deepen our relationships with ourselves, with our community, and with our Creator." She defines her goal as a rabbi as working with those who understand what this type of Judaism can mean and to reach out to those who do not.[78]

Korngold and other rabbis like her want to offer American Jews, espe-cially those who are alienated from Judaism, a spiritual experience that is inspiring and dynamic rather than repackaging the formal and ossified sub-urban religion of their parents' generation. The theory behind that is that so many American Jews look for enlightenment elsewhere because they are sim-ply unaware that they could find something just as deep and meaningful in their own tradition. The question is how to inspire them, how to help them to break free from the negative experiences and prejudices they have devel-oped and to find an affirming Judaism in the context of an authentic spiritual community. "There are so many people whose religion is the outdoors, who really experience their spirituality outside of the synagogue. So what I do is say, 'You're going to be outdoors, you say it's a spiritual experience. Let me show you how it's Jewish.'"[79]

One way of doing that is to put people through an intense physical experience. Rabbi Niles Goldstein is an enthusiastic fan of "extreme religion," a phrase that he has taken from extreme sports, but which he carefully differentiates from extrem*ist* religion. Working with a Fairbanks, Alaska travel company called Arctic Wild, Goldstein put together a Jewish Outward Bound adventure that combined sea kayaking, backcountry hiking, and camping that interspersed textual study of excerpts from the Bible, the Talmud, and Jewish mysticism. They practiced "religion in the raw" in the bitter cold by observing a Sabbath on the North Slope of the Arctic National Wildlife Refuge. With the subzero winds of the Beaufort Sea blowing into their faces, they set up camp. "The winds weren't gale force, but they were strong enough to make striking my matches nearly impossible. And with the midnight sun hanging like a dim bulb directly in front of us, it was hard to determine what exactly constituted a genuine sunset." What they knew was that it was late on a Friday, and "even though we were standing on Icy Reef, a band of small islands that forms a fragile barrier between the Alaskan mainland and the Arctic Ocean, I was trying to help our group usher in a midsummer Shabbat with a pair of candles."

Goldstein stressed that, while an extremist approach to religion closes off a person's mind, an extreme approach to religion "is about keeping one's mind *open*, about experimenting with bold and unconventional techniques for transmitting spiritual knowledge and for reshaping souls."[80] "Extreme religion is lean and mean. It offers challenge rather than comfort, risk rather than conservatism. It is about pushing boundaries, not constructing them." Goldstein believes that extreme religion can lead to self empowerment and can be a powerful tool for building community in a context that can turn disaffection from Judaism into intense spiritual involvement. "But extreme religion scares the crap out of normative religion. Why? Because it calls into question, by its sheer existence, the supposed value of the comfort and security that is offered by a more conventional, bourgeois approach to religious life."

Some American Jews have tried to adapt Native American practices as part of an attempt to create a nature-based approach to American Judaism. A retired marine named Michael Murray has been attending my classes on Judaism in South Georgia and he invited me to a Lakota Sioux sweat lodge that was being held nearby. Stones were heated in a fire outside of a domed sweat lodge in the woods and the fire keeper passed them to the leader of the ceremony, who placed them in a pit in the middle of the sweat lodge. When some of my congregants heard that I had participated in such a ceremony, they wanted to know if it would be possible to create a Jewish version, which we are now working on. Goldstein, however, warns that "we need to be wary. I know firsthand the power of sweat lodges and vision quests. But it is one thing to be a respectful observer of other traditions, and another to be an active participant in them. C'mon, Jews are no more Sioux than Muslims are Mohican, and any forced, false attempt to meld our different and frequently divergent sacred systems of belief and behavior erodes the integrity of each of them."[81]

Others disagree. Jewish Renewal Rabbi Gershon Winkler and his wife Lakme Batya Elior established the Walking Stick Foundation, an educational organization dedicated to the restoration and preservation of aboriginal Jewish spirituality. Winkler has recently made a number of decisions that have alienated some supporters, but we will focus here on Winkler and Elior's approach to integrating Native American spirituality with Judaism. They share events with teachers indigenous to Native American and other earth-honoring traditions and integrate those teachings with chants, storytelling, and meditations in a wilderness setting. Their spiritual workshops are held at the Walking Stick Retreat Center on 83 remote, scenic wilderness acres in rural New Mexico surrounded by the nations of Walatowa, Zia, Jicarilla Apache, and the Dineh. "Walking Stick's programs are particularly important in our current trying times because times like these can easily disempower us, cause us to feel impotent and helpless. Vulnerability is a wholesome thing when it leads to intimacy with others and honesty with ourselves, but it is a treacherous thing when it leads to fear and hopelessness." They focus on Jewish shamanism, which they define as "ancient Jewish mystery wisdom that draws from rich, lesser-promulgated traditions of the Kabbalah that are more concerned with the teachings of birds and trees than with codes and creeds." Even though this wisdom was an essential part of ancient Judaism, it had "to go underground for many centuries due to oppressive attitudes by dominant host cultures towards earthiness and sensuality, and anything smacking of paganism and pantheism."[82]

Winkler and Elior stress that while some may find their approach to Judaism extreme, change has always been an essential element in religion. "As living beings, we are creatures of change, and as living Torah, Judaism is ever changing. Many of us are comfortable with the way it's been and the way it is, and many of us are not. But all of us need to remember that even the way it once was represented is a change from the way it was before then." It is written in the Babylonian Talmud that what "was practiced by the ancestors was not practiced by the descendants and what is practiced by the descendants was not practiced by the ancestors." They then cited specific cases: "Abraham and Sarah ate dairy and meat together, a no-no in later Judaic practice; Moses didn't wear a yarmulke, was married to a woman who wasn't Jewish, and had no problem accepting the advice of his non-Jewish father-in-law about how to lead the Jewish people." King David "played his harp on the Sabbath and Jeremiah never heard of Hanukkah and probably ate pasta on Rosh Hashanah instead of chicken and potato kugel."[83]

According to Winkler and Elior, they have to put a tremendous amount of energy into overcoming the antagonism many Jews feel toward Judaism before they could teach them about the beauty of the Jewish spiritual tradition: "We realized that we had spent most of that time dealing with the way many Jews have become alienated by it. To some, Judaism constituted a scrolling preprinted list of what God required of them, all spelled out and nonnegotiable." For others, "Judaism was filling out a synagogue membership application, raising money for Israel, and the puzzling memory of being sacrificed in their youth upon the bar or bat mitzvah altar following a year of excruciating lessons in a language totally alien to them so that they might be initiated into a way of life with which even their parents were fundamentally unfamiliar."[84] Judaism should be about a holy type of relationship that encourages "the fullest sense of Aliveness in each partner."[85] Each person should be encouraged to develop a relationship with the Creator that "is personal and not mediated through any 'authority.' A religious authority might teach us the 'correct way' to pray, for example, but God might prefer the haphazard, homebrewed gut way to pray we were accustomed to before we were taught the 'religiously correct' way."[86] This earthy Judaism is "fluid, living, breathing, ever-unfolding."[87]

Many Paths to the Rediscovery of a Vibrant Judaism

American Judaism is undergoing a remarkable revitalization. This is surprising, given the many problems that the American Jewish community has faced over the past two or three decades. The rising intermarriage rate in particular made many question whether Judaism had any future at all in the United States and, indeed, anywhere in the Western world. This pessimistic evaluation may yet turn out to be correct, but Judaism is showing a remarkable short-term resilience due in large part to the emergence of a number of new spiritual approaches to "doing Jewish."

Many of the innovative approaches to Judaism are seen by most in the Jewish community as legitimate expressions of the Jewish religion. There are, however, certain syncretistic approaches that have been condemned and shunned by virtually all affiliated Jews. The most controversial of these groups has been Jews for Jesus, which is part of a broader circle of religious organizations and groups that attempt to meld Jewish ethnic particularism with Christian doctrine and belief. These messianic Jewish groups, as they are collectively called, became popular in the 1970s, as many young Jewish college students looked for something meaningful, a spiritual wisdom and discipline they had not been taught by their parents and had not found in their family congregations.

In response to the popularity of Jews for Jesus and other messianic groups, a number of Orthodox Jewish educators created Jews for Judaism, deliberately playing on their adversary's name. Jews for Judaism sees their primary mission as responding to aggressive missionary groups and "cults" that specifically target vulnerable Jews. They provide free crisis counseling to young Jews influenced by what Jews for Judaism believe are deceptive missionary techniques and conduct seminars designed to train Jews to respond to the missionary threat. In order to do that most effectively, they encourage those with whom they come in contact to study and consider committing themselves to Orthodox Judaism. They argue that Orthodoxy is the antidote to the rampant assimilation they believe has made so many young American Jews susceptible to foreign religious ideologies. They are thus a variant of the baal teshuva organization, which will be described in chapter 6.[88]

The most successful approaches to Jewish religious revitalization all stress the spiritual wisdom that has lain hidden in Judaism, inaccessible to the emotionally semi-involved participant who was sent to Hebrew school and pushed through a "bar mitzvah factory" as part of childhood rites of initiation. A relatively small group of spiritually hungry seekers began a process that helped many American Jews rediscover the deep spiritual wisdom of the Jewish tradition. They are—or at least, they were, until recently—mostly on the edges of the Jewish community, struggling for acceptability or in some cases reveling in their reputation as rabble-rousers and trouble makers. Many of the most creative ideas for revitalizing Judaism have come from small groups of young people looking for personal ways of connecting to God. The massive Jewish organizations headquartered in fancy office buildings in

New York were unable or unwilling to provide much leadership, and it is primarily those on the periphery who provided the new models of spirituality.

Spiritual practice would be inconceivable without a vibrant sense of the sacred. This is probably, more than anything else, the reason the suburban synagogue failed to connect with so many American Jews on an emotional level. Worshipers needed to feel a sense of immediacy that they were somehow in contact with God, however they might conceive of the divine presence. In a postmodern world, it became less important that a certain theology be justified and crucial that the spiritual experience be spiritually transformative.

More American Jews are recognizing that they want to be part of congregations and Jewish communities yet their spirituality cannot be completely dependent upon the synagogue. There are still many who view the congregation as a "service station," a place where kids can be dropped off at religious school on Sunday mornings on the way to the golf course and that will provide ceremonies at the appropriate stages of life. However, increasing numbers are coming to understand and appreciate that Jewish practice requires individuals to take responsibility for their own spiritual development.

One reason for the resurgence of Jewish spirituality may be a direct response to the "crisis of Jewish identity" that erupted in the aftermath of the 1990 National Jewish Population Survey that found a 52 percent intermarriage rate. It seems logical that ethnic groups of all types would become more aware of their own distinctive identities when they feel that their communal cohesion is splintering as a result of assimilation into the host society. Many members of the ethnic group have already lost interest at that point, but others go into crisis mode and try to rally the troops. The sense of decline they began to feel so intensely helped to strengthen their interest in preserving their culture, which in the American context was primarily possible in religious terms.

There has been a growing awareness of the importance of bringing the sacred into the family, particularly into the lives of children. Jewish tradition required a great deal of time and effort to be expended in household preparations. The entire day on Friday was needed to cook and clean and prepare the home for the Sabbath. Cleaning the house for Passover took at least a week, which included taking everything out of the cabinets and searching for chametz (types of food prohibited on Passover). The sheer energy exerted in these efforts were an effective instrument of religious training because they included grandparents, parents, and children, aunts and uncles, neighbors and friends. The children saw how the entire community worked together to prepare for the holiday and they understood how important that must make it. Those days are long gone, and those parents that want their children to feel some of that spiritual energy need to consciously make plans to create it themselves.

Having a residual loyalty to Jewish ethnicity is clearly no longer enough to compel people to make the effort to preserve Judaism as a living religion for themselves and their families. They need to feel that Judaism can open up new sources of enlightenment to the complex questions they face along with their families. These are not generally metaphysical questions about how to understand the universe but rather practical issues about how to live their lives in a complex society.

Deciding to be Jewish in the full sense is not a rational choice that is derived from an objective analysis of the pluses and minuses of doing that versus doing something else. Rather, it is an emotional decision that is the result of a complex set of variables that include the relationships one formed in childhood and the experiences that one has undergone in camp, school, and synagogue. Many Americans now have multiple identities, and the American Jewish community is in the process of adapting to that fact. The stronger the pull of a Jewish spirituality, the more competitive Judaism can be in the "religious marketplace." This is crucial in a time of nonjudgmentalism, which has been one of the factors leading to widespread intermarriage (see chapter 4), and the acceptance of different types of alternative lifestyles (see chapter 5). Before turning to these dramatic changes, let us first take a step back and look at the American Jewish denominational structure that was so dominant throughout the twentieth century.

3 The Rise and Fall of American Jewish Denominationalism

Those who grew up in the fifties, sixties, or seventies saw American Judaism as divided into three major denominations. Whether they were aware of it or not, the tripartite division of American Judaism was typical of American religious organizations. Religious denominations served to reinforce the ideal of religious pluralism that was so important in the construction of American society. The very fact that there were so many different religious denominational groups seemed to be proof that there was no established church in the United States that could enforce its doctrine and practice on others. The denominations provided an institutional structure for those who sought out religious affiliation, thus providing American society with valuable civic organizations that could help perform good works in which the government could not or would not involve itself. In the two or three decades immediately following World War II, they were so central that Father Andrew M. Greeley described the United States as "the denominational society."[1] Beginning in the 1960s, the nature of American society began changing very rapidly; the divisions that had formerly seemed so rigid began dissolving. Robert Wuthnow has argued that the religious environment shifted dramatically and "denominational barriers have ceased to function as hermetic categories of religious identification."[2] While this opened up new spiritual opportunities for millions of individuals, it threatened the institutional viability of organizations built on the basis of denominational division. A number of Protestant denominations began showing the early signs of civil war, with biblical literalists pitted against social liberals on a range of issues from women's rights to homosexual marriage. While denominational leaders escalated their war of words, increasing numbers of lay people lost interest in denominational identification. Despite the storm clouds that were gathering, the denominational structure of American Judaism seemed solid. Reform temples, Conservative synagogues, and Orthodox shuls all appeared to have long and venerable histories (Reconstructionism was much newer), even though denominationalism was a relatively recent development in the history of Judaism. There was no reason for a moment to think anything would change. That is why Rabbi Paul J. Menitoff drew so much attention when, at a West Coast gathering of Reform and Conservative rabbis, he predicted the imminent death of Conservative Judaism.

In January 2004, Rabbi Denise Eger witnessed Menitoff's controversial speech. She was at a joint conference of the Pacific Association of Reform Rabbis and West Coast Conservative Rabbis where she heard a panel discussion on the future of denominational Judaism. It was a star-studded panel with many of the biggest names in the Reform and Conservative world, including Rabbi Bradley Artson, dean of the Ziegler Rabbinic School of the University of Judaism (UJ), Rabbi David Ellenson, president of the Hebrew Union College–Jewish Institute of Religion (HUC-JIR), Rabbi Arthur Green, dean of the Hebrew College Rabbinical Seminary, Rabbi Elliot Schoenberg, placement director of the Rabbinical Assembly (RA), and Rabbi Paul Menitoff, executive vice president of the Central Conference of American Rabbis (CCAR).

Eger described what happened: "The panel's bombshell moment came when Rabbi Paul Menitoff, head of the Reform rabbis, predicted the death of Conservative Judaism. You could hear the gasps in the room and the bristling all around. How can a Reform rabbinical leader sound the death toll for another denomination?" Flat out, he said that, within a few decades, "you'll basically have Orthodox and Reform." Eger later wrote in her synagogue newsletter that, "as you can imagine, his words were difficult to hear for many of us, and especially so for the members of the Conservative movement, the Conservative rabbis present in the room."[3]

Menitoff asked "Are Jews entering a postdenominational era?" He answered that, in his view, the denominations were slowly becoming obsolete and "it is probable that within the next decade or two, we will be living in an era of dual denominationalism: Orthodox and Reform." In his monthly column in the February 2004 CCAR Newsletter, Menitoff wrote that although the Conservative movement might continue to attract those for whom Orthodoxy remained "too restrictive" and the Reform movement "too acculturated," the most likely outcome will be "the demise of the Conservative movement." He predicted that both the United Synagogue of Conservative Judaism (USCJ) and the Jewish Reconstructionist Federation (JRF) will either merge with the Union for Reform Judaism (URJ) or disappear.

Menitoff listed several areas where Reform and Conservative Judaism had "core differences," but explained that "if the Conservative movement capitulates regarding these core differences between Reform and Conservative Judaism, it will be essentially obliterating the need for its existence." On the other hand, if the Conservative movement remains committed to a more traditional approach and "stands firm," then, Menitoff predicted, "its congregants will vote with their feet." Menitoff argued that young non-Orthodox Jews are mostly liberal Democrats and "will not remain in a movement that defines Jewish identity by gender, rejects homosexuals and is not open to people who fall in love with non-Jews."[4] What was so shocking about the comments that he made was not only what he said, but the fact that he said it at all.

While one could nitpick about his use of the terms *demise* and *disappear*, it seems clear that Conservative Judaism was and is in a state of rapid decline. The Conservative movement is facing tremendous pressure to move to the left, essentially adopting the set of policies that the Reform movement had embraced over the course of the previous twenty or twenty-five years. But the idea that American Judaism consisted of three strong movements, one to the left, one in the center, and one on the right, was so entrenched in people's minds that the fact that a major Jewish religious leader could publicly predict that this might not remain true in the not too distant future was incomprehensible.

Leaders of the Conservative movement immediately rejected Menitoff's prediction. "The future will make it clear that he's off base," said Rabbi Jerome Epstein, executive vice president of the United Synagogue of Conservative

FIGURE 3.1. Rabbi Paul J. Menitoff, then executive vice president of the CCAR, outside the organization's offices in New York in June 2001. The CCAR is the rabbinical organization of the approximately eighteen hundred Reform rabbis in the United States and throughout the world. Photo Dana Evan Kaplan. *Courtesy of the author*

Judaism. "His description of the future is rather silly," said Rabbi Joel Meyers, executive vice president of the Rabbinical Assembly.[5] "At the beginning of the twentieth century, all the Jewish pundits predicted the demise of Orthodoxy, and they all proved dead wrong. So Rabbi Menitoff has good company in bad predictions," said Rabbi Ismar Schorsch, then chancellor of the Jewish Theological Seminary. "The weaknesses of Reform are glaring. But I'll leave predictions for the future of Reform to the pundits," Schorsch quipped.[6]

Menitoff's comments shocked many of those who had simply assumed that American Judaism would always be denominationally based. There were, of course, many secular organizations of various types (such as B'nai Brith, the American Jewish Congress, the American Jewish Committee, and many others) as well as groups of American Jews who dissented from the communal consensus. But, for most, to be a Jew meant to belong to a synagogue and belonging to a synagogue meant defining oneself denominationally. American Jews felt they had to choose between one of the three major denominations that composed the tripartite denominational structure of American Judaism, and they would then become members of a synagogue reflecting their denominational choice. Of course, many made this important decision on factors other than religion. How close the synagogue was to their house, whether they liked the rabbi, and, probably most important, what the congregation offered for their children. But, once they were members, they identified themselves and were identified by others as "hyphenated Jews."

Each of the three denominations had originally seen itself as representing the entire or at least the vast majority of the American Jewish community. The first of the denominational organizations to be created was the Union of American Hebrew Congregations (UAHC), which was established in 1873. Under the influence of Rabbi Isaac Mayer Wise, layman Moritz Loth issued a call to congregations to come together, primarily for the purpose of funding an American rabbinical college. As indicated by the title of the organization, the UAHC was intended to be a union of American synagogues. The word *Reform* was not mentioned because the organization originally expected to appeal to a broad spectrum of congregations with various ideologies and ritual practices. Similarly, the Hebrew Union College (established 1875), the Central Conference of American Rabbis (established 1889), and the Jewish Institute of Religion (established 1922) all carried nondenominational names befitting their intended broad communal purpose.

The United Synagogue of America (USA, established in 1913, later renamed the United Synagogue of Conservative Judaism) was organized by

Solomon Schechter to encompass most of the non-Reform synagogues in the United States. Schechter modeled the new organization on the United Synagogue of Great Britain, which was officially Orthodox but, like the organization that Schechter was creating, served a broad constituency. The expectation was that the Jewish Theological Seminary would produce rabbis for those synagogues not wishing to affiliate with the UAHC.

The Orthodox were the only ones who gave their institutions and organizations distinctively denominational names. The Union of Orthodox Jewish Congregations of America (OU) was founded in 1898 to protect "Orthodox Judaism whenever occasions arise in civic and social matters." Its founders wrote that they created the organization "to protest against declarations of Reform rabbis not in accord with the teachings of our Torah." But most Orthodox leaders saw their denominational identity as temporary, believing that other American Jews would eventually join them or soon assimilate out of existence.

At the end of the nineteenth century, few of the leaders of these various religious groups expected that American Jewish denominationalism would continue to characterize American Judaism into the twenty-first century. Yet the reality was clear to those who chose to look. Even in colonial times, the tiny Jewish community varied enormously. Despite the appearance of conformity and uniformity, there was a great deal of dissent, as can be seen in their congregational minutes. They came from many different countries and expressed divergent viewpoints on virtually every social and political issue of importance. Their ritual observance varied just as much, and it was inevitable that they would break into divergent religious groups as soon as the community sufficiently grew and matured.

By the 1830s, large numbers of "German Jews" started arriving in the United States. Although most had been raised in traditional homes in Central Europe, they found out that ritual compromises and ceremonial adjustments made it easier to meet all their competing obligations. By the 1840s, there was a substantial momentum building for ritual reform and the beginnings of American Jewish denominationalism were well underway. The individualistic and pluralistic nature of American society made this inevitable. Eventually, a tripartite division developed, with most affiliated American Jews choosing one of the "big three": Reform, Conservative, or Orthodox. These three denominations (also referred to as movements, streams, etc.) dominated American Judaism for most of the twentieth century.

These denominations were present in virtually every Jewish community, including the community that I grew up in, Waterbury, Connecticut. Nevertheless, there were tremendous regional differences. Certain cities have long been bastions of certain types of communities. Philadelphia, for example, has for many years been home to a large and committed group of traditional Conservative Jews. Baltimore, Boston, and Cleveland have developed into Jewish communities with vibrant yeshivas. New York is too big to characterize in this manner, but different boroughs or neighborhoods have differing religious characteristics. Washington Heights had a great number of German Jews, who were either connected to Frankfurt neo-Orthodoxy or the German Reform movement. Queens has more recently absorbed many Jewish immigrants from the former Soviet Muslim republics, including Azerbaijan and Bukaria, who established ethnic Orthodox congregations. The percentage of Jews who regarded themselves as Reform, Conservative, Orthodox, or Reconstructionist (which eventually became the fourth major denomination) could vary substantially from city to city. In recent decades, the importance of the various denominations has begun to decline. As we will discuss in chapters 6 and 7, there are a number of new groups that have demonstrated that exciting new forms of Judaism can be developed and successfully marketed to both Jews and non-Jews. At the same time, increasing denominational choices exist—far more variation than fifty or even twenty years ago. For example, Shulshopper.com lists the following synagogue "flavors": Adot HaMizrach/Sephardi, Conservative/Masorti, Conservadox, Hasidic, Liberal, Liberal Orthodox, Litvisch, Modern Orthodox, Neo Hasidic/Carlebach, Neolog, Non-Denominational, Orthodox, Postdenominational, Progressive Orthodox, Reconstructionist, Reform, Renewal, Secular Humanist, Ultra-Orthodox (Haredi), Traditional Egalitarian, Yekke, and Yeshivish. Many of the most dynamic congregations are independent or only loosely affiliated with one of the denominations.

The future may be dominated by increasing cross-denominational cooperation rather than the dominance of the Reform movement or any single stream. In May 2007, the Charles and Lynn Schusterman Family Foundation quietly launched the Hevruta Fellowship, an interdenominational program for students from the Hebrew Union College–Jewish Institute of Religion and the Jewish Theological Seminary of America. While the stated goal of the Hevruta Fellowship was to provide the opportunity for eight students a year to work, study, and lead programs together, it was one of the first times that students from the two seminaries were involved in a sustained collaborative educational effort. Insiders pointed out that this type of joint effort could expand and might eventually create a de facto merger between the two movements.

Reform Judaism Capitalizes on Its Flexible Nature

In recent years, the Reform movement has been simultaneously moving in two different directions: temples are using more Hebrew and reintroducing traditional rituals, but simultaneously accepting new definitions of Jewish identity and religious fidelity. The Reform movement developed in the period of emancipation, a political process that gave the Jews of Europe varying degrees of civil rights. The first Reformers—usually identified as German Jews, but in fact coming from many Central European regions—were seeking a middle course between halachic Judaism, which they wanted to break away from, and conversion to Christianity, which they wanted to avoid. Looking for a way to remain Jewish while adapting to prevailing social customs, they hoped that by introducing modern aesthetics and strict decorum they could make Jewish worship services more attractive. Therefore, most of the early reforms focused on minor cosmetic changes. They abbreviated the liturgy and added a sermon in the vernacular, a mixed choir accompanied by an organ, and German as well as Hebrew prayers.

Late nineteenth- and early twentieth-century reformers stressed the importance of ethical monotheism. They believed that the unique ethical and moral message of Judaism derived directly from one all-good God who was responsible for creating everything in the world. Reform Jews prided themselves on their commitment to rational thought and therefore concluded that science explained how the universe was born. Nevertheless, most Reform Jews believed that God created the world in some way and continued to be involved in an ongoing process of creation. The acceptance of scientific theory and religious cosmology was not seen as conflicting, since the laws of science carried out God's will. The biblical account of creation was not a scientific theory of the world's origins, but rather a religious myth of great spiritual value. The Torah was a holy text because it reflected the religious perceptions of the ancient Israelites. Much, but not all, of what the ancient Israelites thought and wrote continued to be relevant and significant.

According to most Reform Jewish thinkers, God revealed the Torah to Israel in some form, but they would differ on what form such revelation may have taken. Most would agree that God revealed the divine presence to Israel not just in a one-time event at Mount Sinai but in stages over a long period of time. Such progressive revelation meant that all people had the potential to understand God's will. Rabbi Maurice Eisendrath, president of the UAHC during the Vietnam War era, explained that "God is a living God—not a God who revealed Himself and His word once and for all time at Sinai and speaks no more."[7] Every time a person studied Torah, they were continuing the process of bringing God's revelation to humankind. The study of God's ways helped Reform Jews understand the ethical monotheism at the core of Judaic theology.

The first attempt at reform in the United States occurred in Charleston, South Carolina in 1824, when forty-seven members of Congregation Beth Elohim signed a petition requesting that their leadership institute certain reforms, including the introduction of prayers in English. When their request was turned down, a small group of intellectuals decided to break away, forming the Reformed Society of Israelites. They published the first American Reform prayer book and held services for a few years, but disbanded in 1833. Shortly thereafter, the main congregation began moving toward Reform under the leadership of its hazan, Gustavus Poznanski.

Rabbi Isaac Mayer Wise arrived from Bohemia in 1846 and began leading a congregation in Albany, New York. Wise became the driving force behind the establishment of the main institutions of what became the Reform movement. In 1854, he accepted a lifetime contract to become the rabbi of Congregation B'ne Jeshurun in Cincinnati, Ohio, where he established a newspaper, the *Israelite* (later the *American Israelite*), and edited a prayer book, *Minhag Amerika*. He was the main influence behind the establishment of the UAHC, and he founded HUC and the CCAR. Wise was regarded as the leader of the moderate wing of the Reform movement, which battled with the radical Reformers, most of whom lived along the East Coast. Led by Rabbi David Einhorn, the radical Reformers eventually succeeded in creating a deritualized form of liberal Judaism, which became known as classical Reform. Classical Reform was defined by the 1885 Declaration of Principles, which became known as the Pittsburgh Platform: it minimized Judaic ritual and emphasized ethics in a universalistic context.

By the 1930s, the Reform movement was moving toward the reembracing of Jewish peoplehood and at least some traditional ritual. The CCAR

FIGURE 3.2. Congregation B'nai Yeshurun, known as the Plum Street Temple, in Cincinnati, Ohio, built in 1866. Architect James Keyes Wilson designed the building to blend neo-Byzantine and Moorish Revival styles copied from the the Leopoldstädter Tempel, built in Vienna, Austria in 1858. *Courtesy of the Jacob Rader Marcus Center of the American Jewish Archives*

adopted the Guiding Principles of Reform Judaism, better known as the Columbus Platform, in 1937, which supported the idea of Jewish peoplehood and hinted at support for political Zionism. The culmination of a revolutionary shift in the historic ideology of the American Reform movement, the Columbus Platform encouraged a greater diversity of religious opinion and a multiplicity of ritual approaches. By 1945, the Reform movement was well on its way to accepting Zionism and the soon-to-be-created State of Israel. Reform rabbis such as Stephen S. Wise (no relation to Isaac Mayer Wise) and Abba Hillel Silver were strong supporters of Zionism and worked tirelessly to build up the American Zionist movement. When World War II ended, the Reform movement was in an excellent position to draw in new groups of Jewish people who had recently moved to the suburbs or were in the process of doing so. While the Conservative movement grew the fastest, the Reform movement also grew dramatically, a fact that is frequently overlooked.

Much of the credit for the successful adaptation of Reform Judaism to the suburban environment goes to Eisendrath, who became executive director of the UAHC (later renamed the URJ) in 1943 and president in 1946. Einsendrath increased the profile of the movement significantly by moving the national headquarters from Cincinnati to New York in 1948. The House of Living Judaism was built on Fifth Avenue and 65th Street in Manhattan, right next to Temple Emanu-El. The Reform movement grew dramatically in the years after 1945. Between 1943 and 1964, the number of congregations affiliated with the UAHC increased from 300 to 656 and the number of family memberships went from 60,000 to approximately 200,000.[8] Many of the new Reform congregations were slightly more traditional than the classical Reform temples in the cities because they were founded by people coming from much more diverse backgrounds. Substantial numbers had been raised in traditional Eastern European homes, and while they cherished the flexibility Reform Judaism offered, they also wanted to feel a little bit of the Yiddishkeit (Eastern European Jewish atmosphere) of their youth.

One of the central issues facing the Reform movement was how to provide guidance on ceremonial observance without creating new halacha, a binding legal system. Any obligatory system of religious laws would have been anathema to most Reform Jews. Nevertheless, there were intellectuals in the movement who felt that it was essential to define the nature of the relationship between God and the Jewish people, not only in broad religious terms but also in specific ritual obligations. Covenant theologians in the movement dedicated their energies to restoring the centrality of the *brit*, the religious contract agreed to by God and the children of Israel. They contrasted the idea of covenant with *matan Torah*, the giving of the written and oral Torah by God to Moses on Mount Sinai. They explained that a covenant was a mutual agreement based on an organic, historical relationship; it was reciprocal and could be extended from generation to generation. What was important to the Reform covenant theologians was that a covenant could develop over the course of time. It was sacred but not etched in stone. Heavily influenced by Franz Rosenzweig, they wanted the Reform movement to explain exactly what God hoped people would do in both the ceremonial and humanitarian realms.

The idea of creating a Reform code of practice went back as far as the origins of the movement at the beginning of the nineteenth century. The earliest German rabbis to favor Reform wrote responsa (halachic answers)

FIGURE 3.3. Interior of Congregation Emanu-El of the City of New York, one of the earliest Reform congregations in the country, founded in 1845. Its landmark Romanesque Revival building on Fifth Avenue includes a magnificent sanctuary that seats twenty-five hundred people, more than St. Patrick's Cathedral. Architect Robert D. Kohn designed the 1929 building with load-bearing masonry walls that support the steel beams carrying its roof. Photo Samuel Morgan. *Courtesy of Samuel Morgan Studios*

explaining why certain practices were permitted according to the halacha. It was only later that the German Reform movement rejected the very concept of halacha, arguing that Judaism could be a religion separate from the framework of Jewish law. Nevertheless, individual Reform rabbis as well as various committees of the CCAR continued to debate halachic issues and write halachic decisions. This could border on the absurd, since they were writing learned legal arguments based on a system they rejected. Nevertheless, many rabbis felt that the lack of any framework for observance made Reform Judaism too vague. As early as 1938, the UAHC Committee on Synagogue and Community recommended adopting a "Code of Reform Jewish Ceremonial Observance." No such code was ever accepted, for obvious reasons: Reform Jews valued their autonomy too much. Individual Reform rabbis began writing their own guides in the mid-1950s, but they were careful to speak in the language of choice rather than obligation. Nevertheless, they stressed that Judaism had a series of observances that should be taken seriously.[9]

One of the most important developments in the post–World War II period was the establishment of a camping system. Reform children were exposed to an informal approach to Jewish living that they had never seen before. The classical Reform temple had been a rather austere place where children were "seen but not heard." This began to change, even before World War II, and congregations began to feel the need for increasing numbers of informal activities that could excite and motivate young people. The movement already had the National Federation of Temple Youth (NFTY), but it was felt that something more intense would be helpful. A Jewish summer camp could immerse Reform children in a total Jewish environment where they could learn the rituals in a fun way surrounded by friends. The first UAHC camp in North America emerged out of a series of weekend retreats held for Chicago-area children at a Wisconsin camp site. Two hundred acres were purchased in Oconomowoc and 39 campers signed up for what was then called the Union Institute Camp in the summer of 1951. Later renamed the Olin-Sang-Ruby Union Institute (OSRUI), they hired Debbie Friedman as a song leader in 1970, helping to produce a new type of Jewish religious sing-a-long music that soon became a staple in the neo-Reform service.

Like other religious movements, the UAHC expanded throughout the 1950s and early 1960s. But the momentum slowed and then stopped. In his history of the Reform movement, *Response to Modernity*, Michael A. Meyer wrote that "in the late 1960s, severe self-doubt and anxiety about the future displaced the ebullience that had characterized American Reform Judaism since the war. Divided and uncertain of its course, it long remained in a state of crisis."[10] Meyer suggested one of the reasons the Reform movement had trouble sustaining their momentum was that Jews felt less of a need to mask their Jewish ethnicity by identifying with a religious organization. Many American Jews were now expressing their Jewishness through their local Jewish federation, JCC, Zionist organization, or Jewish cultural group. This new openness to ethnicity remained a hallmark of the American Jewish community from around 1970 onward, but the Reform movement found ways to show its relevance. They expanded their activities, opening preprimary nursery schools, political action centers, and engaging in all sorts of programming that went far beyond religious services on Friday night.

By the mid 1970s, the Reform movement was growing again. HUC-JIR began ordaining women in 1972, and they brought an energy with them that helped make Reform temples more vibrant. There was, however, a general feeling that Reform Jews needed to update the content of Reform Judaism. The *Union Prayer Book* was a ubiquitous presence in the pews since the closing years of the previous century, and many younger people found its heavy, ponderous language to be excessively formal and its theological conceptions out of date. There was, however, no consensus on what a new prayer book might look like. The CCAR Liturgy Committee decided to allow the different theological schools to each include their own service. When the *Gates of Prayer: The New Union Prayer Book* (GOP) was published in 1975, it included no fewer than ten different Sabbath evening and six Sabbath morning services. Each congregation could choose one service to use every week or could rotate through several. The services all followed a similar prayer structure, but they differed in their wording and theological focus. Service 1, for example, emphasized the belief in an omnipotent God who created the world and continues to perform miracles, while service 2 presented the concept of God as the still, small voice of conscience and inspiration within each person. A gender-sensitive version of the GOP was published in 1994, and an entirely new prayerbook, *Mishkan T'filah*, in 2007.

Also in the mid 1970s, the CCAR decided to produce a new statement of principles, but there was so much disagreement that in the end they decided not to call it a platform but rather simply a perspective. Eugene B. Borowitz, the primary author of the *Reform Judaism—A Centenary Perspective*, explained that "as Reform Judaism entered the 1970s there was a general feeling that the movement needed to rethink its directions. The tremendous enthusiasm generated by the rapid expansion of the number of Reform congregations in the 1950s and '60s had passed." American Jewry was largely integrated into American "but the style of synagogue life that resulted, which seemed so fresh a few years previous, in the '70s, seemed somewhat stale and in need of invigoration."[11] Yet it was hard to formulate a clear religious vision in the aftermath of the 1960s, and therefore the perspective had to be deliberately vague about the nature of God. "In our struggle through the centuries to preserve our faith, we have experienced and conceived God in many ways." The historical events of recent decades as well as the challenges of contemporary society and culture had made it difficult for many to believe in a traditional conception of God. The perspective tried to spin this in the most positive way possible by explaining that "we ground our lives, personally and communally, on God's reality and remain open to new experiences and conceptions of the Divine."[12]

The Reform movement slowly became the dominant force in American Judaism, surpassing the Conservative movement numerically sometime during the 1980s or 1990s. The 1990 NJPS found that a plurality of American Jews identified with Reform Judaism, although more Jews still claimed to actually be members of Conservative synagogues than Reform temples. The 2000–2001 NJPS showed that the trend was continuing, and by that point there were more Jews claiming to belong to Reform temples than to Conservative synagogues. The Reform movement also became known for being the cutting-edge innovator. While the Reconstructionist movement had frequently adopted the same innovations with less fanfare years earlier, it was the Reform movement that garnered most of the publicity. The Reconstructionist movement was just so small that the press did not pay attention, but when the much larger Reform movement took similar stances journalists reported on the debates and decisions in great detail. For example, the Reform movement took the initiative in establishing outreach to the unaffiliated and particularly the intermarried. Rabbi Alexander M. Schindler, president of the UAHC, gave a dramatic speech in December 1978 calling on the UAHC to respond proactively to the demographic challenges facing the American Jewish community. Also, the Hebrew Union College accepted gay and lesbian rabbinical students beginning in September 1990, and the CCAR passed a resolution approving rabbinic participation in same-sex commitment ceremonies in 2000. In all these cases, it was the Reform movement that earned most of the attention for breaking down barriers, even though they were not necessarily the first group to pioneer a given innovation.

The CCAR approved a new set of principles in 1999 at their annual conference in Pittsburgh, the same place where an earlier generation of Reform rabbis had passed the original 1885 Pittsburgh Platform, which had formulated the basic beliefs and principles of classical Reform Judaism. Rabbi Richard N. Levy, then president of the CCAR, wrote a number of drafts for a new platform, the third of which was published in *Reform Judaism* magazine. This third draft encouraged Reform Jews to consider taking upon themselves new ceremonial obligations and the reconsideration of old ones, including keeping kosher and even laying tefillin. It also suggested that they consider learning at least some basic Hebrew, both in order to understand the prayers better and also to be able to relate to Israel and Israelis more intimately. I had originally written here that the final draft urged Reform Jews to do various things, but Levy wrote me that "I don't know whether 'urged' is the right word—you can judge that for yourself; it used language like 'Reform Jews who want to . . . may consider.'"[13] Whatever the intention, the general impression created was that the draft was pushing traditional practices.

Many neotraditionalists loved it, but some classical Reformers reacted with tremendous fury. Levy then recommended that the committee responsible for the platform throw out the original wording and begin from scratch. They then went through three additional drafts. The final platform, which was accepted by the CCAR membership voting in Pittsburgh, did not change direction, but was much more general than the original draft proposal. Many felt that it had been so severely "watered down" that it had lost its original focus. The final draft may have been philosophically simplistic and even logically inconsistent, but it did generate a great deal of controversy, an absolute necessity for attracting media attention. When the rabbis met in Pittsburgh to debate the proposed platform and vote on it, the *New York Times* featured the story in a front-page article, one of dozens written about the conference. Despite the bitterness generated, the final result was relatively innocuous. The platform did make it clear that Reform Jews could choose what they personally found spiritually meaningful out of the entire pool of traditional religious practices. Whereas in earlier decades certain religious acts (such as the laying of tefillin) would have been seen as inappropriate in a Reform temple, the new Pittsburgh platform indicated that the Reform movement was opened to broader spiritual possibilities.

The Rapid Growth of the Conservative Movement and the Origins of Its Decline

Conservative Judaism was "dedicated to the conservation and development of traditional Judaism in the modern spirit."[14] Conservative intellectual leaders differed from their Reform counterparts in that they held that halacha remained the most important form of Jewish religious expression. Following the halacha, they believed, was the most important part of being a religious Jew. Reform had rejected halacha in its entirety, and this dispute led to the creation of the Conservative movement at the end of the nineteenth century. Even the name of the movement derived directly from this conflict. Ideological leaders of the movement developed theories to explain how halacha could remain obligatory and yet be adapted to meet the changing needs of contemporary life. Yet what was important to most Conservative Jews was a respect for tradition rather than a commitment to follow the halacha in its entirety. Most members of Conservative synagogues were relatively liberal in political, social, and even religious terms, and so the name of the movement became a misnomer. Some Conservative leaders quietly suggested that the movement should be renamed, but that would have created considerable confusion, and so the original name remained.

Solomon Schechter, the president of the reconstituted Jewish Theological Seminary in the early part of the twentieth century, argued that the community becomes the religious authority for determining change. Judaism needed to be studied using modern methodologies so that Conservative scholars could better understand how postbiblical Judaism developed over the course of centuries. The Torah had been interpreted and reinterpreted by Jews throughout the ages, and how the Torah was understood was the determining factor in setting communal religious standards. "Catholic Israel" developed certain patterns of belief and behavior based on their instinctive response to both Jewish tradition and the external social environment. The Conservative movement ought to make changes based upon how Klal Israel developed their understanding and practice of traditional Judaism.

Conservative Judaism traces its origins to the Frankfurt Rabbinical Conference of 1845. Rabbi Zachariah Frankel walked out after the group of Reform-leaning rabbis voted that there was no objective legal necessity for retaining Hebrew in the service, even though it was subjectively necessary. There was then a second vote on the issue of whether it was objectively necessary for reasons other than legal ones. Fifteen of the rabbis voted that it was not; thirteen voted that it was. Despite the fact that most of the rabbis on both sides of this question wanted both Hebrew and German languages to be used together in the Reform prayer services, Frankel chose to interpret his defeat on this vote as indicating there was a fundamental philosophical difference between himself and the majority.[15] Frankel was appointed director of the newly created Jewish Theological Seminary of Breslau in 1854 and began to teach "positive-historical Judaism." They were positive in that they wanted to preserve the core revelation from God, and they were historical because they wanted to understand Judaism in a historic context. They accepted the idea of change, but only if that change could be justified halachically and seemed to fit in with the historical development of Judaism.

It is not easy to determine exactly when the Conservative movement began in the United States. In the mid-nineteenth century, there were a number of rabbinic leaders who were neither strictly Orthodox nor obviously Reform. These included some leaders who were outwardly completely traditional, such as the Reverend Isaac Leeser, who served as minister of the Mikveh Israel Synagogue in Philadelphia. There were also leaders of Reform congregations, such as Rabbi Benjamin Szold of Baltimore and Rabbi Marcus Jastrow of Philadelphia, who seemed to be significantly more traditional than even the moderate Reformers. Some Conservative scholars have claimed that these men were the forerunners of the Conservative movement, but this requires one to stretch the definition of Conservative Judaism quite a bit. It was only toward the end of the 19th century that leaders who were indisputably committed to Conservative Judaism emerged.

There were a number of key events that some have pointed to as the decisive moment in the founding of the Conservative movement. One of the obvious points would be the establishment of the Jewish Theological Seminary or, alternatively, the date on which it was reorganized. Some point to the date when Professor Schechter arrived in the United States to lead the reorganized seminary. Others believe that the seminal moment occurred a bit earlier at the "trefa banquet," the graduation of the first four rabbis ordained from HUC in 1883. The Jewish caterer hired by Rabbi Isaac Mayer Wise prepared a feast after the ordination service consisting of virtually every type of forbidden food except pork. The traditionalists later wrote that they walked out in disgust, and, shortly thereafter, plans were made to start a traditionalist rabbinical school. Michael A. Meyer wrote me that "I don't think the trefa banquet was historically significant. Far more important was the 1885 platform."[16] While Meyer is certainly correct, the story of how all these dignitaries were served course after course of nonkosher delicacies remains one of the most entertaining episodes in American Jewish history, and serves as a colorful episode to mark the beginning of a new epoch.

Rabbi Sabato Morais of Mikveh Israel in Philadelphia gathered a group of supporters together at Shearith Israel in New York to plan for the new seminary. Some wanted to call it the Orthodox Seminary, but the majority decided on the Jewish Theological Seminary of America, taking the name from the Breslau school. The Jewish Theological Seminary opened in 1887 and ordained its first rabbi in 1893, but, when Morais died in 1897, the school floundered. By 1901, it seemed certain that JTS would close, but a group of Reform philanthropists came to believe that the seminary was essential for the training of American Jewish religious leaders who would be suitable for the masses of Eastern European Jews then arriving on the shores of the United States. They recruited Schechter in 1902 to become president of the reorganized school. Schechter is credited with developing a vision for what became the Conservative movement, speaking eloquently about the need to balance tradition with change: "Unless we succeed in effecting an organization which, while loyal to the Torah, to the teachings of our sages, to the traditions of our fathers, to the usages and customs of Israel," must at the same time "introduce the English sermon, and adopt scientific methods in our seminaries, in our training of rabbis and schoolmasters, for our synagogues and Talmud Torahs, and bring order and decorum in our synagogues . . . traditional Judaism will not survive another generation in this country."[17]

As early as 1901, a rabbinical organization was founded to support the Conservative movement, but it was only in 1919 that it took the name Rabbinical Assembly of America, later dropping "of America." The United Synagogue of America was established in 1913, with twenty-two founding congregations. These congregations were traditional in their practices but did not necessarily have a clear theological understanding of what made them different from Orthodox congregations in terms of religious belief. They did understand that congregational members of the United Synagogue rejected radical reform, and therefore congregations that worshipped without head coverings on the men or used the *Union Prayer Book* or instituted other radical deviations from traditional practices were banned from membership. It was easier for the Conservative movement to define itself in terms of what it rejected rather than what it believed.

The movement was ideologically vague, which in part was a deliberate institutional strategy. This compromising approach proved successful at attracting individuals as well as congregations who were seeking a middle path. Yet there were serious internal contradictions within the Conservative movement. JTS professor Neil Gillman admitted this, stating that the writings of the founders were "riddled with inner tensions: Torah is the eternally binding word of God, but it is also responsive to changing times; the people decide what to change, but the scholars have to inspire the people so that they may know what to change and what to retain." If any change "can be validated only by its ultimate effects years later, how do we know at the outset what to change and what to preserve?"[18] Almost immediately, it became apparent that the vast majority of those joining Conservative synagogues in the post–World War II period were neither believers in nor practitioners of Conservative Judaism as understood by the movement's theoreticians. As Rabbi Morris Adler told a United Synagogue convention in 1948, "Multitudes of our people are untouched, uninformed, uncovenanted. They have not enough Judaism to live it, nor enough interest to reject it. They go on in routine indifference."[19] While many synagogues were very active, there was a gulf between the expressed religious goals of the Conservative synagogue and the congregational reality.

Rabbinical students graduating from the Jewish Theological Seminary took Conservative pulpits only to find that few congregants made any attempt to observe Jewish law. Even so, the atmosphere in these congregations was more traditional than the typical Reform temple. Hebrew was used much more, and religious ritual items were displayed more prominently. But, if Conservative Judaism was dependent upon the acceptance of halacha as a binding system of law, then the movement was clearly a failure. Conservative rabbis tried to cajole their congregants into observing more of Jewish tradition. They used various strategies to educate their congregants and increase the level of ritual observance in their congregations. Most were not successful. The result was a vague sense of disquietude. When Conservative Rabbi Abraham J. Karp wrote an article about the history of the Conservative rabbinate, he entitled it "The Conservative Rabbi—'Dissatisfied But Not Unhappy.'"[20]

Whereas the Reform movement was controlled primarily by its congregational organization, the Conservative movement was dominated by its rabbinical school. The United Synagogue of America took its cues from the rabbinic scholars at JTS rather than from their own lay leaders. The Committee on Jewish Law and Standards (CJLS) became the center of decision making for the movement. Its members were appointed by each of the three major wings of the Conservative movement: JTS, the RA, and the United Syna-gogue. Voting members were expected to be scholars of Talmudic literature capable of studying the primary sources and formulating practical halachic guidelines for the Conservative movement. That is not to say that they had to all have the same perspective. It was expected that members of the com-mittee would represent the various factions within Conservative Judaism. In fact, the committee could accept more than one opinion as legitimate, thus allowing for "halachic pluralism."

The appeal of the Conservative synagogue was in large part based on an affinity for tradition, and this would be undermined if the congregations made radical changes. Therefore, most Conservative synagogues wanted their services to look and sound reasonably traditional. They were looking for a prayer book that could be used in such a service, but would also look appropriately up–to-date and easy to use. In 1946, Rabbi Morris Silverman edited the *Sabbath and Festival Prayer Book*, which contained most of the tra-ditional liturgy with an English translation on the facing page. At around the same time, Rabbi Mordecai M. Kaplan published his *Reconstructionist Prayer Book*, which radically reinterpreted Jewish theology. While Kaplan faced the theological questions of the day directly, Silverman tried to sidestep contro-versial religious issues in an effort to preserve the Conservative movement's theological "middle ground." For example, the blessing praising God for res-urrecting the dead had been taken out of the Reform prayer book and was likely rejected by many Conservative Jews as well. Silverman wanted to avoid printing anything that would create controversy so he simply printed the traditional Hebrew but translated it as "who calleth the dead to life everlast-ing." Kaplan, on the other hand, edited this prayer to reflect what he actu-ally believed, deleting the reference to resurrection completely. Conservative synagogues overwhelmingly adopted Silverman's prayer book because it was endorsed by the movement even though many Conservative Jews probably sympathized more with Kaplan's approach that Judaism was a civilization that encompassed a great deal more than religion.

Despite the tendency among some Conservative intellectuals toward theological radicalism, most Conservative congregations closely resembled their Orthodox counterparts for much of the immediate post-World War II era. While many had trouble explaining the theological differences between Conservative Judaism and Orthodoxy, the most obvious distinguishing fea-ture was that the Conservative synagogue allowed for mixed seating. Soci-ologist Marshall Sklare wrote that by 1955 mixed seating of men and women

was "the most commonly accepted yard stick for differentiating Conservatism from Orthodoxy."[21] Leaders of the Conservative movement were not
necessarily enthusiastic about this innovation, but they had no choice but to
go along. Louis Ginzberg, chairman of the Rabbinical Assembly's Committee on the Interpretation of Jewish Law, told a congregation in Baltimore in
1947 that if "continued separation of family units during services presents a
great danger to its spiritual welfare, the minority ought to yield to the spiritual need of the majority." A few decades earlier, Ginzberg had written that
"the separation of the sexes [during services] is a Jewish custom well established for about 2000 years, and must not be taken lightly." But by the 1940s,
he said privately that "when you live long enough in America, you realize
that the status of womanhood has changed so much that separating women
from men has become obsolete."[22]

A second distinction was that Orthodox Jews refused to drive on the Sabbath. Traditional Jews brought in the Sabbath at dusk on Friday eve by lighting the Sabbath candles, and from that point on until nightfall on Saturday
night they followed an extensive system of religious rituals and observances.
They were prohibited from doing any of thirty-nine forbidden categories of
melacha, which was a halachic term that was usually translated as "work," but
actually referred to specific types of activities that were not necessarily intense or strenuous. These thirty-nine categories included not only weaving,
sewing, and kneading but also igniting. Orthodox halachic authorities had
ruled that it was forbidden to drive a car on the Sabbath, since that would
have meant that the spark plugs would ignite an air/fuel mixture.

Conservative rabbis faced a Hobbesian choice: allow their congregants to
come by car or condemn driving and watch them go to the shopping center
instead. In 1950, the CJLS passed a takanah (a rabbinic enactment) stating
that "where a family resides beyond reasonable walking distance from the
synagogue, the use of a motor vehicle for the purpose of synagogue attendance shall in no way be construed as a violation of the Sabbath but, on
the contrary, such attendance will be deemed as an expression of loyalty to
our faith."[23] They did not dwell on the obvious: the family would not have
moved so far away from the nearest synagogue if they were committed to
Sabbath observance, at least as understood in the traditional sense. They did
admit that those Conservative Jews who observed the Sabbath strictly "constitute but a tiny minority and a dwindling minority at that."

The CJLS wrote that "the program that we propose is not to be regarded
as the full and complete regimen of Sabbath observance, valid for all Jews,

for all time and for all places." On the contrary, "it is aimed to meet the particular situation that confronts us" in which many people live in widely scattered suburbs and simply cannot walk to synagogue. Many leaders of the Conservative movement later argued that this permission to drive was misunderstood. Conservative rabbis at the time only wanted to let people know that it was worse to give up going to synagogue entirely rather than to drive there. They never envisioned, so the later justification went, that people would think that it was permitted to drive anywhere and everywhere. But that, of course, is what happened. In 2003, JTS chancellor Ismar Schorsch bluntly criticized the decision, arguing that "the more you drive, the less chance [there is] of creating a Shabbat community. That's what we failed to see."[24]

While most members of Conservative congregations joined out of convenience, there was a small core of extremely dedicated Conservative Jews. Many developed their commitment through Camp Ramah, a group of Conservative movement-affiliated summer camps. Rabbi Moshe Davis and Sylvia Ettenberg encouraged a group of Conservative movement leaders in Chicago to create a Hebrew-speaking camp in Wisconsin in 1947. A second Camp Ramah was started in the Poconos by a group from Philadelphia. Eventually, JTS took over the Camp Ramah system and began working to promote its development. Because the campers lived and slept on the grounds, Camp Ramah had the potential to help show what Conservative Judaism could be like at its fullest. Daniel J. Elazar and Rela Mintz Geffen argued that Camp Ramah "is the most genuinely Conservative institution in the entire Movement, the only living whole community where an authentically Conservative way of Jewish religious life has been developed, one that lives up to Conservative halakhic canons."[25] Unfortunately, many of the most devoted Ramah campers found that the realities of the typical Conservative synagogue did not match the expectations that they had after spending several summers at Ramah. Indeed, many of those who became most active in postdenominational Jewish religious activities were nurtured and educated by the Conservative movement. This was simultaneously a success and a failure. The movement can take pride in the fact that so many of their "products" have grown up to make major contributions to American Jewish religious life. On the other hand, their departure from the movement seems to indicate weakness. When I spoke with Rabbi Joel Meyers, the executive vice president of the RA, he told me that I had missed the main point: "While some of those who are working in the Jewish community outside of the Conservative movement may have left because they were unhappy with Conservative Judaism, the real story is that they were inspired to serve the Jewish community as a whole and not just a portion because their Conservative Jewish education preached the importance of klal yisrael." In one sense, "it is painful that they are not active in the Conservative movement, but in another sense, it is proof that we have done our job too well.[26]

By the early 1970s, the Conservative movement was already showing signs of decline. While the early leaders of Conservative Judaism had hoped to find common cause with Orthodoxy, it had become clear that the hope that a broad inclusive traditionalist coalition could develop was not realistic. Many of the early Conservative leaders had underestimated the antipathy that Orthodox Jews felt for Conservative Judaism. Indeed, many Orthodox leaders despised the Conservative movement and missed no opportunity to attack its leaders. The main reason for this was that, unlike the Reform movement, Conservative Judaism claimed to be loyal to halacha, and the Orthodox felt this was deceptive. While many Jews from Orthodox backgrounds had affiliated with Conservative synagogues in the first few decades after WWII, there were now far fewer joining. At the same time, increasing numbers of those raised in Conservative congregations were finding Reform temples more inviting, especially those temples that had embraced more tradition. When Marshall Sklare published his second edition of *Conservative Judaism: An American Religious Movement* in 1972, he added a concluding chapter in which he wrote that "the morale of the Conservative movement is on the decline" and that, if the goal of the movement was promoting religious growth, "Conservatism has been an abysmal failure."[27]

That same year, Gerson D. Cohen replaced Louis Finkelstein as chancellor of JTS and became known for his advocacy of the ordination of women. He was originally against the idea, speaking out against it in a talk as late as 1977 to the Women's League for Conservative Judaism. He reversed his position, however, and became a strong supporter. The debate over this issue went on for many years and became extremely bitter. In May 1977, Cohen and RA executive vice president Rabbi Wolfe Kelman called for the formation of an interdisciplinary commission to study the potential role of women as spiritual leaders. The commission made a report recommending the ordination of women two years later, and the RA voted 156 to 115 in support of women's ordination in 1980.

That is not to say that there were not setbacks. In May 1983, the RA voted at its Dallas convention not to admit Rabbi Beverly Magidson into the organization. Magidson had been ordained at HUC in 1979, but wanted very much to be a Conservative rabbi. Even though she fell two votes short on the initial count, the vote indicated clearly that almost 75 percent of the rabbis of the RA favored the ordination of women. At this point Cohen announced that the JTS faculty would be asked to vote on the issue at a meeting to be held on October 24, 1983. The vote was positive, and JTS announced that women would become eligible for ordination in the 1984–1985 academic year. Amy Eilberg became the first woman to receive JTS ordination, graduating in 1985 (see chapter 5). The ordination of women was a dramatic move, one that had been opposed by most of the Talmud faculty.

The decision to ordain women deeply upset a small number of Conservative rabbis who felt that the movement was abandoning their commitment to halacha. Under the leadership of David Weiss-Halivni, they formed a lobbying group which they named the Union for Traditional Conservative Judaism. As it became clear that JTS and the Conservative movement were intent on going through with the ordination of women, the group began to refocus and developed plans to build their own movement, based on what they believed to have been the original Conservative theology and ideology. Shortly thereafter, they renamed their organization the Union for Traditional Judaism (UTJ), dropping the word *Conservative* in order to reposition themselves on the American Jewish religious spectrum. They began reaching out to representatives of the Modern Orthodox, whom they hoped would amalgamate with them.

Despite their best efforts, they were repeatedly turned down. Of course, the more fervently Orthodox would have nothing to do with the UTJ because of their involvement with academic biblical scholarship. But the Modern Orthodox were, if anything, even more hostile. Many Modern Orthodox Jews saw the UTJ as having been inconsistent or even hypocritical. Rabbi Bob Carroll, a Modern Orthodox rabbi and the former program director of Edah, who had been raised in the Conservative movement, told me that "when I look at the UTJ leadership, I see people who were always able to rationalize staying within the Conservative movement when it 'only' allowed driving on Shabbat (an indisputable and inviolable d'orayta [from the Torah itself] prohibition), Cohanim marrying divorcees, etc." but who "suddenly couldn't remain when the decision was made to ordain women (which is if anything, difficult to prove forbidden even on a d'rabbanan [from the Talmud or other rabbinic writings, but not directly from the Torah] level). To me, this is glaringly inconsistent with any kind of Halachic integrity."[28]

Ironically, many UTJ members were far stricter halachically than some of Modern Orthodox. But the Modern Orthodox wanted to maintain their designation as Orthodox Jews while simultaneously being able to experiment with various liberalizations with, in particular, feminist issues. Some felt that the UTJ was trying to demonstrate how traditional they could be in the hope of attracting Orthodox Jews to their ranks. After Edah, the Modern Orthodox flagship, think tank, and project organization, closed down in mid-2006, the UTJ tried to present itself as the logical heir, but, to no one's surprise, Modern Orthodox Jews were not interested. Carroll probably summarized the feelings of many Orthodox Jews when he told me that "I think that the UTJ people are psychologically reactionary."[29]

The decision to ordain women marked the culmination of a long process of gradual inclusion. Women had long been allowed to sit with men in virtually all Conservative synagogues. By the mid-1950s, most congregations were allowing girls to study for bat mitzvah. The CJLS issued rulings allowing women to have an aliyah in 1955, to be counted in the minyan and to vote and hold office on synagogue boards in 1973, to serve as a witness in a halachic procedure such as the signing of a ketubah, and to serve as a rabbi or a cantor in 1974. These decisions were more indicative of the direction of the movement than they were prescriptive from a legal point of view, but by the 1970s it was apparent that women were going to become Conservative rabbis eventually.

Since the landmark 1985 JTS decision to ordain women rabbis, the Conservative movement has moved—slowly but clearly—to resolve a number of other controversies that had been festering for many years, the most recent being the question whether to ordain lesbians and gay men and allow rabbis to officiate at same-sex commitment ceremonies. The new JTS chancellor, Arnold Eisen (who is not an ordained rabbi), acknowledged the terrible problems the movement was facing in a speech to the RA in April 2007. According to a *Jewish Telegraphic Agency* article sent out by JTS to their e-mail list, reporter Ben Harris understood Eisen as saying that the movement has "largely dropped the ball" by allowing halachic pluralism to become its core message. "Let's be mature about this," Eisen was reported as having said. "Agreeing to disagree is not enough to keep a movement going." The Conservative movement must find a way to build the same sort of intense communities that has made Orthodox life so attractive. "If we can't win on that count, we can't win."[30]

An Indigenous American Jewish Denomination

Reconstructionist Judaism is the only one of the four major denominations that was developed entirely in the United States. The Reform movement was founded in Germany at the beginning of the nineteenth century, the Conservative movement traces its roots to the historical school, which broke away from Reform in the 1840s, and Orthodoxy coalesced as a distinct movement in response to the perceived threat of religious reform. All these movements were the product of Jews working together over the course of many generations. In contrast, Reconstructionism was inspired by a single person: Rabbi Mordecai M. Kaplan, and developed into a movement through the efforts of a small group of his disciples. Kaplan espoused a rationalistic approach to Judaism that encompassed all aspects of Jewish civilization rather than a narrow definition of Judaism as just a religion.

The actual movement that emerged was very different from the Reconstructionism that Kaplan was teaching in the 1930s and 1940s. Many of the early Reconstructionist Rabbinical College (RRC) students who enrolled after its establishment in 1968 found the Reconstructionist option attractive because it was the most liberal theologically and hence tended to take the most tolerant positions on a broad array of social and religious issues. In 1984, they became the first movement to ordain gay and lesbian rabbis, followed by the Reform movement in 1990. More recently, they became the first movement to appoint a lesbian as head of a major rabbinical association, electing Rabbi Toba Spitzer of West Newton, Massachusetts in 2007. It also turned increasingly toward mystical spirituality, a trend that their founder would have disapproved of.

In 1909, Kaplan became a professor of homiletics and principal of the Teachers' Institute at the Jewish Theological Seminary. He also led the Jewish Center, an Orthodox congregation on West 86th Street in Manhattan. While he had grown up in a strictly Orthodox home, he found that his religious beliefs were at conflict with the Orthodoxy he was expected to preach. In January 1922, as his religious views became known, he felt it necessary to leave the Jewish Center. Kaplan moved a block up 86th Street and founded the Society for the Advancement of Judaism, later to be recognized as the first Reconstructionist congregation in the country. That same year, he conducted the first bat mitzvah ceremony, which was held for his daughter, Judith.

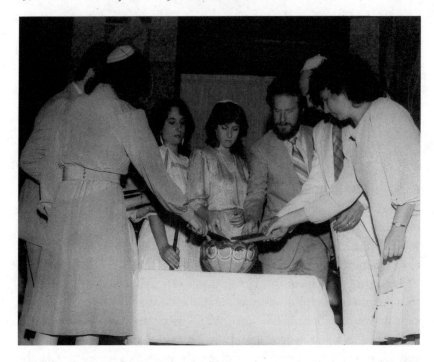

FIGURE 3.4. Reconstructionist rabbis light candles as part of their ordination ceremony at the Reconstructionist Rabbinical College in 1985. Based on the ideas of Rabbi Mordecai M. Kaplan, Reconstructionist Judaism views Judaism as a progressively evolving civilization rather than solely a narrowly defined religion. *Courtesy of the Ira and Judith Kaplan Eisenstein Reconstructionist Archives, Reconstructionist Rabbinical College*

While at first he was excited to be teaching at JTS, he quickly became frustrated by the failure of most of the faculty to apply the insights of Wissenschaft, the academic study of Judaism, to actual strategies for modernizing American Jewish life. In 1920, he published "a program for the Reconstruction of Judaism" in the *Menorah Journal* in which he wrote that a modern Judaism should dispense with supernatural ideas about God and instead emphasize the moral genius of the Jewish people. The criteria for how to reconstruct Judaism should be based on what would work—the practical needs of the times. Religious ideas and practices would need to prove their effectiveness in terms of binding the Jewish people together and keeping them interested and involved.

In 1929, Sears Roebuck chairman Julius Rosenwald offered a $10,000 prize to the person who could best answer the question: "How can Judaism best adjust itself to and influence modern life?" Sixty-two contestants submitted essays over a two-year period. Kaplan submitted what was to become his masterpiece, "Judaism as a Civilization" and won. In May 1934, Kaplan published the work, and it has remained in print ever since. Shortly thereafter, he founded the *Reconstructionist*, a biweekly magazine. In 1940, Kaplan started the Jewish Reconstructionist Foundation, a society to help promote Reconstructionism within all the existing organizations and denominations. Influenced by the educational philosopher John Dewey as well as the liberal Protestant theologians Henry Nelson Wieman and Harry Emerson Fosdick, Kaplan looked at religion through a naturalistic, empirical lens. He taught that Judaism was an evolving religious civilization rather than just a faith, as most Americans understood that term. He urged American Jews to face the reality of their existence and to bring their stated beliefs into sync with what they actually felt deep down. Kaplan personally rejected most of what he termed "supernaturalism." He particularly objected to the doctrine of the chosen people because he believed it was exclusionary, but he also rejected the doctrine of a personal messiah and traditional eschatology in general.

Kaplan did not intend to found a new denomination, but rather to influence the many Jewish Theological Seminary rabbinical students that he taught and also to spread his ideas throughout the entire Jewish community. This puzzled many of his followers, and frustrated others, because they believed that the logic of his own arguments made it clear that Reconstructionism should become a full denomination. Some believe that his movement would have been much more successful if it had been institutionalized as a full denomination in the 1930s or 1940s rather than the 1960s. A number of scholars concluded that "it appears that Kaplan was radical in thought but cautious in deed."[31] Perhaps part of the explanation was that Kaplan was deeply committed to Klal Yisrael, the ideal of Jewish unity, and he did not want to introduce further divisiveness into an already fragmented American Jewish community. He originally had hoped that Reconstructionism could "provide a rationale and a program for that conception of Jewish unity which might enable Jews to transcend the differences that divide them, assuming, of course, that they are aware of having at least one thing in common, the desire to remain Jews."[32] Rabbi Ira Eisenstein, Kaplan's son-in-law, finally created the Reconstructionist movement as a formal denomination when he founded theRRC in 1968. The pressure on Kaplan to allow his followers to create a new denomination had been building for many years, but Kaplan worried that focusing too much energy on individual congregations could dissipate much of the enthusiasm necessary for revitalizing national Jewish cultural life. By 1963, Kaplan retired from JTS, making it easier for him to go along with plans that were being formed to make Reconstructionism a separate denomination. At a meeting in Buffalo, New York that same year, a group of Reconstructionist activists persuaded Kaplan, then age eighty-three, to agree to the creation of a Reconstructionist rabbinical school. The creation of a full-fledged denomination required a shift in organizational strategy. The Reconstructionist Federation of Congregations had, ever since its creation in 1955, required that affiliated congregations be members of one of the major American Jewish religious denominations because Reconstructionism was seen as a supplementary philosophy. This requirement was now done away with. The organization was renamed the Federation of Reconstructionist Congregations, and it became a denominational organization in its own right.

The RRC set up a joint program with the Department of Religion at Temple University in Philadelphia. Originally, rabbinical students were required to enroll as doctoral students and study for both degrees simultaneously, but this requirement was modified and then later dropped. The college's curriculum was influenced by Kaplan's idea of Judaism as an evolving religious civilization. Students focused on a different period of Jewish history and culture each year: biblical, rabbinic, medieval, modern, contemporary. Many of the early graduates took pulpits in Conservative congregations, while others took positions with Jewish organizations or educational institutions. There were few Reconstructionist synagogues that could afford to hire full-time rabbis. This has changed as the Reconstructionist movement has grown. Already in 1968, the Reconstructionist movement accepted patrilineal descent. The annual convention of the Federation of Reconstructionist Congregations and Havurot (FRCH, now the JRF) that year adopted a resolution that read: "The parents of such children" born of a Jewish father and a non-Jewish mother "should be informed that in many parts of the Jewish world, their children would not be recognized as Jews without undergoing the traditional forms of conversion." The resolution recommended that "we should further inform the parents that the Reconstructionist Movement and its affiliated institutions will consider these children Jews if the parents have committed themselves to rear their children as Jews by providing circumcision for boys, Jewish education for boys and girls, and if the children fulfill the requirements of bar and bat mitzvah or confirmation."[33] This was a revolutionary policy change. According to Jewish law, a person is Jewish if he or she inherits his or her Jewish identity from their mother or converts to Judaism.

The Reconstructionist movement changed this definition to allow for a person to inherit his or her Jewish identity from either their mother or their father. This fit better into their egalitarian ethos and also seemed to be more logical, since what was important to them was how the child was raised rather than which parent had been born Jewish. The Reform movement voted to publicly accept patrilineal descent in 1983—about fifteen years later. It is true that the Reform movement maintained a long-standing practice, dating back to at least 1947, of accepting the child of a Jewish father and a non-Jewish mother as Jewish without formal conversion if the child attended a Jewish religious school and studied toward confirmation, but the Reconstructionist movement was the first to pass an official public declaration accepting patrilineal descent.[34] The issue became a full-blown controversy when the Reform rabbinate voted to accept patrilineal descent, because the Reform movement was much larger and therefore their decision affected far more people.

In recent years, the Reconstructionist movement has experienced a spurt in growth. The denomination is still small—the percentage of American Jews who identify as Reconstructionist has doubled over the course of a couple of decades, but that means that it has gone from 1 percent to 2 percent. That is still impressive and Reconstructionist Federation representatives say that the number of households affiliated with their movement is growing by between 6 and 10 percent a year. The largest Reconstructionist synagogue in the country is Congregation Kehillat Israel, in Pacific Palisades, California, with more than one thousand member households.

There are just over a hundred congregations now affiliated with the Reconstructionist federation. Many are going through a major transition in terms of their structure and function. Most started out as highly participatory groups of intellectuals and communal nonconformists. They met for prayers and studied in living rooms or basements and liked it that way. More than anything else, they wanted to avoid the "edifice complex" that they believed afflicted the other Jewish denominations. Even today, many Reconstructionist Jews still feel that building campaigns generate negative energy and should be avoided. David Zinner, a member of the Columbia Jewish Congregation in Columbia, Maryland, said that his friends in their congregation prefer meeting in an interfaith center rather than going through the difficult process of fund-raising. "A lot of synagogues see it as a major triumph when they get their own building. For us it might be a failure."[35]

As Reconstructionist congregations grew and as their members aged, they began to feel the need for many of the same services and programs that the Reform and Conservative congregations near them were offering. To do all those things, they needed a synagogue building and a full-time rabbi. This required extensive fund-raising and all sorts of decision making. Many were deeply traumatized by the apparent betrayal of counterculture values, and some of the more avant-garde members left for Jewish Renewal groups or other types of spiritual experimentation. Their numbers were more than made up for by typical suburbanites who were just as happy to join a Reconstructionist synagogue as a Reform or Conservative one. The important factors for them were the same: a quality preschool, a caring rabbi, and a short commute.

Carl Sheingold, the executive vice president of the Jewish Reconstructionist Federation, said that the movement understands the importance of growing larger but that they were being careful not to grow at the expense of what he called a "critical feature" of their movement—the willingness to experiment. Rabbi Mordechai Liebling, who had preceded Sheingold in the same position, agreed, emphasizing that "voluntaristic Judaism works." Liebling explains that "we encourage an adult, thinking Judaism and exposing people to a rich meaningful Jewish life and allowing them to bring their full cognitive facilities to bear leads them to choose to be more observant and want to learn more."[36] Sheingold saw the maturation of the Reconstructionist movement as providing a balance missing in the early years. "The origins of the movement had a lot to do with a desire for a form of religious life in Judaism that was compatible with rationality, with scientific progress." But over the past 10 to 15 years, "there have emerged approaches within Reconstructionism that are more tuned in to what has been called the spiritual aspect of life. You really become mature when you can find ways to reconcile those things and you're not debating whether it's about the mind and the heart, but you're finding ways for it to be both."[37]

The movement has published new prayer books in recent years, including a 1,275-page machzor with gender-neutral English translation prepared by poet Joel Rosenberg. The editors have tried to balance the desire for greater spirituality with the need to remain as faithful as possible to Kaplan's original religious vision. This has not been easy because many of Kaplan's religious beliefs have been reinterpreted or simply abandoned in recent years. For example, Kaplan rejected the belief in a "supernatural" God, but many of the current generation of Reconstructionist leaders are attracted to approaches that emphasize mystical emotionalism rather than philosophical rationalism. The movement prides itself on being on the "cutting edge" of Jewish life, and its membership therefore expects to have a certain degree of inconsistency, as new ideas germinate and make their way from conception to implementation.

The Surprising Survival and Revival of Orthodox Judaism

Orthodoxy is not a unified movement in the sense that the other Jewish religious denominations are. There are numerous diverse groups that share many common beliefs, including the idea that the halacha is binding in its entirety. Orthodox Judaism teaches that both the written and oral law were given from God to Moses at Mount Sinai. God made an exclusive covenant with the children of Israel, and that covenant was detailed in the laws of Moses. Orthodox Jews believe that there was an oral law given to Moses along with the written law, in which God explained verbally those laws that needed elucidation. These laws were discussed and debated by the sages and were eventually written down in the form of the Talmud. The laws of the Talmud were later codified, and the legal codes became the authoritative listings of what Jews needed to observe.

Synagogue Judaism in the American colonies and the early national republic was all traditional. While the early American Jews differed in religious background and level of ritual observance, all those who attended synagogue participated in traditional prayer. The early German and Eastern European Jewish immigrants likewise either joined an existing traditional Sephardic synagogue or, after 1820, founded their own. While the majority of these congregations slowly gravitated toward Reform Judaism, some held onto their traditionalist principles. Isaac Leeser began using the term *Orthodox* and *Orthodoxy* in his monthly journal the *Occident* in the 1840s to refer to those who opposed the incipient Reform movement, which was then beginning to grow and develop throughout the United States.[38]

The traditional element was greatly strengthened after Eastern European immigration began in 1881. There were, however, many pressures on the immigrants to abandon the strict observance of halacha and the vast majority

FIGURE 3.5. Two Orthodox men reading Torah. The mechitza, a curtain separating the women's section, is visible in the background. The presence or absence of a mechitza became one of the major distinctions between Conservative and Orthodox synagogues in the post-WWII period. *Courtesy of the Orthodox Union*

succumbed. When they were given the choice between working on Saturdays or facing severe economic deprivation, most quickly began to violate the Sabbath. There was, however, a minority who were absolutely committed to strict halachic observance, regardless of the economic or social costs. Orthodoxy was a small group that seemed to be losing support throughout the first half of the twentieth century.

Scholars of the postwar era were almost uniformly negative about Orthodoxy's future. Many Orthodox Jews likewise had grave doubts about the future of their own movement. In an often quoted comment, Marshall Sklare wrote in 1955 that the history of American Orthodoxy was "a case study of institutional decay."[39] Sociologists subscribed to the theory that conservative forms of any religious group corresponded with low social and economic standing. Therefore, Orthodoxy was incompatible with the middle-class aspirations of most American Jews and was destined to decline as they became more affluent. But those who expected Orthodoxy to disappear were to be disappointed. Most of the non-observant Orthodox faded away, but there remained substantial numbers of committed Orthodox Jews of various theological convictions. To the astonishment of those who had predicted their demise, the Orthodox began to rebuild. In an article published in 1998, Rabbi Jacob J. Schacter wrote, "With its increasing confidence, institutional strength, and extraordinary unself-consciousness, Orthodoxy has achieved a presence and a prominence in America simply and literally unimaginable even a mere four decades ago."[40]

The Orthodox, and particularly the haredim, were resolutely committed to perpetuating their traditional values without compromising with American social trends. American cultural pluralism has made it more acceptable to look and act differently. Dressing in an Orthodox style might have made one feel shame and embarrassment in the years immediately following World War II. Today, such garb would not stand out as much in what has become a highly multicultural environment. In addition, the intellectual climate in the United States has become much more conducive to Orthodox theology. While Protestant fundamentalism was still a minority view, its moral critique of American social values was taken very seriously.

The current American propensity to reshape sacred doctrines and practices to satisfy personal needs struck traditionalists as sacrilegious. Religion is not a consumer good like the latest style of polo shirts at the Gap. Tradition is immutable, and the person committed to that religion has an obligation to practice that religion exactly as it was practiced by the ancestors. Until the coming of the messiah, it will be practiced the same way in the future as well. The divine revelation that God gave to the Children of Israel is eternal and not subject to whim or fancy. Those committed to such a vision can indeed make a credible effort to live a traditional life in a nontraditional society. Much of the Orthodox community has closed themselves off from large parts of secular society, filtering what they want to allow in and censoring out everything else. Outsiders are frequently amazed that people would want to live so isolated from contemporary trends, but they are much more integrated into modern society than one might think. As politically conservative Orthodox Rabbi Aryeh Spero puts it, "haredim are not Amish. They are up to date in technology and medicine, and they are politically aware."[41]

The Orthodox community is hardly monolithic. Modern Orthodoxy was an attempt to blend Orthodoxy and modernity together in a single philosophy and way of life. The Modern Orthodox tried to show that they could observe halacha while living a modern life just like any other American Jew. In contrast, the sectarian Orthodox rejected modernity and tried to restrict its influence, if not eliminate it entirely. The modernists could be called Modern Orthodox, although some have tended to prefer the term *centrist* Orthodox, and the followers of Rabbi Avi Weiss use the term *open* Orthodox. The fervently Orthodox haredim have been called ultra-Orthodox, right-wing Orthodox, and fundamentalist Orthodox, labels that they would certainly find objectionable. Within the haredim, there are Hasidim and yeshiva non-Hasidim. There is tremendous diversity within these groups. Each Hasidic sect, for example, has its own rebbe, distinctive history, and unique customs. Most arrived in the United States after World War II or in the period leading up to the war.

Already by the 1930s, the American Orthodox community was being strengthened by the arrival of thousands of Orthodox Jews fleeing the Nazis. Legal immigration permits had been reduced drastically in 1924, and it was extremely difficult to obtain a visa of any type to the United States. Nevertheless, a few lucky or well-connected Orthodox Jews were able somehow to make it to this country, escaping the catastrophe looming over the Jews of Europe. Many were Lithuanian yeshiva students (also called Litvisch or Litvak in slang diminutive), devoted to the study of Talmud and codes. Sometimes called "black hat" Orthodox Jews because of the type of formal hat the men frequently wore, they quickly formed yeshivas modeled on the Eastern European Talmud academies they had been forced to abandon. Some of the most important black hat yeshivas were Ner Israel Yeshiva in Baltimore, founded by Rabbi Jacob Ruderman in 1933, the Rabbi Chaim Berlin Yeshiva in Brooklyn, which was expanded by Rabbi Isaac Hutner in 1939, and the Telz Yeshiva, which was transplanted from Lithuania to Cleveland in 1941, after many of the students were able to escape through the Far East. That same year, Rabbi Aharon Kotler came to the United States and in 1943 established the Beth Medrash Govoha in Lakewood, New Jersey, which was to become the largest and most prestigious center for advanced Talmudic studies in the United States.

The Litvisch yeshiva Orthodox traced their philosophy to the Vilna Gaon, the great Talmudic sage who had battled with the Hasidim. Hasidism was a pietistic and charismatic movement that began in Podolia and Volhynia and spread throughout Eastern Europe. It emphasized that true piety was not attained solely by intellectual learning, but by the outpouring of the soul in prayer and the love of God. Those against the Hasidim became known as Mitnagdim, "those who oppose," referring to those who were against the Hasidim. But over the next two hundred years, the differences between the two groups narrowed. The Hasidim began to study Talmud much more seriously, and the Mitnagdim began to appreciate the alternative approaches to religiosity taught by Hasidic rebbes.

Most immigrants did not have the background, training, interest, or time to study the Talmud intensely, but some did. As early as 1918, a group of Orthodox Jews from Poland established the Torah Vodaath Yeshiva in Williamsburg, Brooklyn. It began as a Modern Orthodox Zionist school, but in the following decade evolved into a "black hat Yeshiva."[42] Torah Vodaath was the exception; most of the major American yeshivas were established by refugees fleeing from the Nazis. There were also a number of important Hasidic leaders who arrived in these years, including the Lubavitcher rebbe, Rabbi Joseph I. Schneersohn, who came to New York in 1940. His son-in-law and future successor, Rabbi Menachem Mendel Schneerson, arrived a year later. The Satmar rebbe, Rabbi Joel Teitelbaum, came in 1946. Schneerson moved to Crown Heights, while Teitelbaum settled in Williamsburg, both in Brooklyn, New York. There were more than a dozen other Hasidic sects who were able to reorganize in the United States, mostly in Brooklyn. The surviving Hasidim flocked around their rebbes or, if their rebbe had been murdered, found a new spiritual leader.

In the years following World War II, the mainstream American Jewish community paid little attention to these Orthodox refugees. Most segregated themselves in strictly Orthodox subcommunities in Brooklyn or simi-

FIGURE 3.6. Yeshiva University students celebrating Israeli Independence Day. Many Orthodox university students spend a year or more studying in Israel, frequently returning with a deepened devotion to punctilious observance and a desire to settle permanently in Israel. *Courtesy of Yeshiva University Archives*

lar places. They participated little, if at all, in broader Jewish communal organizations or community efforts of any type. Over the next fifty years, they would come to assume a much greater importance, as the haredim began to pressure the more accommodationist Modern Orthodox leaders to withdraw from multidenominational pluralistic organizations such as the Synagogue Council of America (SCA) and the New York Board of Rabbis. Many of the sectarian Orthodox groups began to build new institutions to accommodate their growing communities. They began to publish an extensive literature, which was read eagerly by those connected to their communities as well as scholars interested in understanding their unique subcultures.

Unlike the Conservative, Reform, or Reconstructionist denominations, Orthodoxy was always diverse and never had one set of denominational institutions. The centrist Orthodox come the closest to replicating the model of having one central organization or institution to represent the union of congregations, the association of rabbis, and the rabbinical training program. The Union of Orthodox Jewish Congregations of America, also known as the Orthodox Union (OU), the National Council of Young Israel, and the Rabbinical Council of America (RCA) represent the modern or moderate congregations within Orthodoxy. The RCA represents the bulk of the more modernist Orthodox rabbis. Yeshiva University's Rabbi Isaac Elchanan Theological Seminary (RIETS) and, more recently, Yeshivat Chovevei Torah (YCT), provide professional training to future rabbis.

The various fervently Orthodox groups have numerous formal and informal hierarchies and organizational structures. The Union of Orthodox Rabbis of the United States and Canada (Agudas HaRabbonim) is a relatively small haredi rabbinical organization founded in 1902 that was once influential but has become known primarily for its periodic issuing of polemical attacks against the non-Orthodox. The main umbrella group for the haredim is Agudath Israel of America. Agudath Israel was founded in 1912 in Kattowitz, which was then in Germany and is now part of Poland, and the American branch was established in 1939. Agudath Israel is primarily an advocacy organization. Its representatives testify at government hearings and before government bodies, seeking to explain the Orthodox position on various issues to politicians, legislators, judges, and the like. It also has numerous departments that provide educational, legal, or religious programs to its members and other interested parties.

The divisions within Orthodoxy deepened in the decades following the end of World War II. The fervently Orthodox grew in numbers and influence and eventually challenged what had been called Modern Orthodoxy for primacy. The Modern Orthodox experienced a brief period of growth but then seemed to flounder, with two scholars referring to it as "a movement under siege."[43] The haredim conveyed a sense of religious confidence that appeared to intimidate the Modern Orthodox. Despite many social problems—which were described openly in their newspapers and magazines—the haredim appeared to be successfully bucking the assimilatory pressures confounding the other Jewish denominational groups.

The centrist Orthodox put much of their energies into building Yeshiva University (YU), the first and largest American university under Orthodox Jewish auspices, which proudly declared its motto to be "Torah U'Madda," the study of both traditional Jewish texts and higher secular studies. The institution traces its origins to Yeshivat Etz Chaim, a Jewish elementary school founded in the Lower East Side in 1886. Etz Chaim attracted a particularly devout clientele and was dedicated to teaching Judaic studies more intensely than the cheders that were the usual type of afternoon Jewish religious school of the time. Graduates who wanted to continue their Talmudic educations studied with Rabbi Moses Matlin in his apartment on an informal basis. In 1896, the school expanded to include a yeshiva, the Rabbi Isaac Elchanan Theological Seminary, whose first group of three rabbinical graduates were ordained in 1903. Etz Chaim and RIETS were chartered as separate educational institutions, but merged in 1915 under the name the Rabbinical College of America. There were many Jewish elementary schools opening in the 1920s and Etz Chaim was eventually eliminated so that the school could focus on the more advanced levels. In 1928, President Bernard Revel established Yeshiva College, a bachelor's degree program that included both a yeshiva education as well as a full liberal arts college curriculum. In 1949, YU launched a $150 million fund-raising campaign for a medical school that became the Albert Einstein School of Medicine. They also established numerous graduate schools as well the Cardozo School of Law.

Rabbi Norman Lamm became president in 1976, at a time when YU was experiencing serious financial problems. Lamm was an enthusiastic proponent of the Torah U'Madda philosophy, deeply believing that the primary goal of Yeshiva University should be to propound the synthesis of Torah learning and secular knowledge. Despite his enthusiasm, Lamm had to be very cautious in promoting Modern Orthodox ideas in order to avoid alienating the haredim, and particularly a number of influential right-leaning Talmudists in the rabbinical school. The Talmud faculty as a whole did not reject the concept of Torah U'Madda in principle, but they interpreted it in a conservative manner. "I went as far as I could without precipitating an ugly clash. My whole incumbency as the president of Yeshiva University was geared toward warding off civil war." Lamm contended with the ideological maneuvering during a period when the university was in dire financial condition. "My major goal was self-preservation. I did not want Yeshiva to fall apart. If I had pushed any harder against many of the determined right-wingers, it would have led to a split in the school itself which it would not have been able to recover from. I did not want that to be my contribution to Jewish history."

Many centrist Orthodox Jews felt that their movement was in crisis and that YU needed to play a stronger role in trying to revitalize it. Despite Lamm's best efforts, the more progressive centrist Orthodox, as well as many of those on the right, felt increasingly disenfranchised at YU. Finally in 1997, Rabbi Saul Berman, a professor at Yeshiva University's Stern College for Women, founded Edah. Edah was a specifically Modern Orthodox movement that was designed to help promote a more liberal—although they carefully avoided using that word—form of Orthodoxy. Edah's first conference in New York the following year attracted more than fifteen hundred delegates. The *Jewish Week*, and other Jewish newspapers as well as the *New York Times*, gave the new organization generous coverage, and the broader Jewish community formed the impression that the Modern Orthodox were on the rebound. It seemed that Edah had quickly become a dynamic and essential organization that would revitalize the Modern Orthodox community.

Despite this successful opening, Berman had a great deal of trouble administering and fund-raising for the organization. Increasingly frustrated, he attacked the "failure of will" on the part of many Modern Orthodox Jews. Some felt that he was disparaging their commitment, suggesting that the Modern Orthodox lacked the religious passion of the haredim. They had the impression that Berman was upset by the fact that when challenged by right-wing Orthodox ideologues, most of the Modern Orthodox tended to back down, refusing to engage in a sustained religious debate over the merits of the Modern Orthodox philosophy. In their personal lives, Berman felt that too many of the Modern Orthodox failed to study Torah on a regular basis or, if they did, they studied briefly and superficially. Even their observance—the hallmark of any Orthodox Jew—was shallow and lazy.[44]

But many Modern Orthodox young adults were deeply committed and wanted to devote themselves to community service. Up until this point, they had been forced to study at either RIETS or at one of several programs in Israel. There was clearly a need for an alternative American Modern Orthodox rabbinical program. In 1999, Rabbi Avi Weiss of the Hebrew Institute of Riverdale founded YCT, a new rabbinical school in Manhattan. Lamm told me that "it was a terrible thing that Yeshivat Chovevei Torah did, because they weakened—or I suspected it would weaken—the more liberal parts of Yeshiva University, but it didn't." He changed his words literally in the middle of his sentence. Rather than condemning them for weakening the more progressive elements at YU, he transitioned into the thought that they could have caused damage, but did not. "They are a very small group and they have not shown that they are a real force—despite all of their newspaper ads." The extreme right broke off as well, gravitating toward Touro College. Talmudists Yehuda Parnes and Abba Bronspiegel resigned from RIETS to take positions with Touro's Lander College. Despite these defections (or perhaps because of them), the level of conflict between the right and the left at YU declined. "The center, thank God, is holding. In fact, the center is improving."

Weiss wanted to create a training program for rabbis who would be Orthodox but at the same time tolerant. He coined the phrase "open Orthodoxy" to refer to his philosophy of an "intellectually rich, questioning, spiritual and inclusive" approach to religion. Weiss explained that "I don't like the term 'modern,' because everyone thinks they're modern. And I don't like the term 'centrist,' because when you say you are in the center, it means you are allowing yourself to be defined by the flanks."

Weiss stated that "openness for me is expressive of who we are—open to respectful and honest dialogue on a whole variety of issues. There is nothing that is off the table." This includes discussion on issues that have become controversial within Orthodoxy, including the role of feminism. The graduates accepted the principle of religious pluralism, or at the very least that of religious tolerance, and therefore cooperated with non-Orthodox colleagues. "I believe that we have the potential to transform the Orthodox community—[but] not only the Orthodox community, because our Orthodoxy is so open, ultimately it could transform the larger Jewish community. This is not an Orthodoxy which is insular. It is an Orthodoxy which is unapologetically inclusive."[45] Although some found the fact that they offered full-tuition scholarships to all their students as indicating a certain weakness, if not desperation, YCT seemed to thrive.

Edah, however, did not succeed, and Berman announced in June 2006 that it was closing down. "When we founded Edah in late 1997, we saw it as a project with a ten year mission—to reverse the separatist trend within Modern Orthodoxy which was isolating the Modern Orthodox community from the rest of the Jewish people."[46] What apparently happened was that Berman and the other Edah professionals—some of whom were his family members—had trouble raising sufficient amounts of funds to keep the organization going. There was the sense that many of the Edah supporters were "lecture junkies" who loved coming to every possible event but were reluctant to support the organization financially. Many believe that it was not so much that the conference participants were unwilling to support the organization but rather that they were not actively solicited. What funds there were may have been used inefficiently, and, since programming was increasing significantly, cost overruns mounted. Eventually, the leaders decided that the major programs with which Edah was doing well could be transferred over to YCT. This turned out to be an elegant way of closing them down, since virtually none of the educational programs, interdenominational learning projects, or conferences were continued. All that remained of Edah was the journal, which was renamed, and the Web site, which was no longer updated.

Expert opinion on what Edah's closing meant was divided. Jonathan D. Sarna felt that the demise of Edah was not a sign that Modern Orthodoxy—which he calls "Americanized Orthodoxy" in his book *American Judaism: A History*—was defeated: "If it is dead, it's because it has won rather than lost. There is a women's tefila network and some of the women's conferences have all really demonstrated the strength of Modern Orthodoxy. It is alive and well at YCT and YU, and therefore Edah doesn't really serve the purpose it did when people were afraid that YU was abandoning its Modern Orthodox moorings."[47] Samuel Heilman disagreed, arguing that its demise supports the thesis of his recent book *Sliding to the Right*, in which he argues that Orthodoxy has been co-opted by "contra-acculturative" haredim. Heilman argued that "even though Modern Orthodox [people] still constitute the majority" of the Orthodox community, "the pendulum of leadership and a sense of empowerment has swung to haredi elements. They in many ways control the rabbinate and, increasingly, the nature of how to define Jewish education" and they "seek to define what is genuinely Orthodox. What Edah was trying to do was offer a broader spectrum of definitions of what constitutes Orthodoxy. Their passing from the scene means one less voice."[48]

Lamm agreed that Orthodoxy had become more conservative with a small *c*, but he predicted that this would only be a short-term trend. "Everyone talks about the 'swing to the right,' as if we are a bunch of apes, hanging from the trees swinging right, swinging left. I don't swing; I am not a swinger, nor do I approve of swingers." He argued, however, that this trend was not limited to Orthodox Judaism. "There is a more right-wing tendency in all groups." Lamm predicted that there will be a gradual amalgamation in the future: "From what I can see in the Haredi community, in 50 or 60 years they will be us. They will have to open up to the world and they are starting to already. They are already studying in university. Right now it is only for business and computers, but eventually it will be for liberal arts as well, and they will be us." Lamm believes that the Orthodox Judaism of the future will be open to secular education and "will not be standoffish toward the rest of the community as the haredim are now. I think that in the future, the Orthodox community will be a combination of what we are now [the more modern] and the haredim and the sharp edge of each will be blunted."[49]

More than any other American Jewish denomination, American Orthodoxy is influenced by Israeli religious trends. Indeed, some believe Modern Orthodoxy has failed to build an enduring movement in the United States because so many of its leaders have moved to Israel. It would be rather ironic if "the battle for the soul of Orthodoxy" was won or lost not on the merits of arguments, or even the relative numbers in the different ideological camps, but rather on who was less likely to make aliyah (move to Israel). As Lawrence Grossman stated, "If, as seems clear, Orthodoxy will have an ever-increasing impress of the future of American Judaism, which 'face' American Orthodoxy will assume, modern or haredi, may determine the fate of the entire community."[50]

The Deteriorating Relationship Between the Orthodox and Non-Orthodox

The Orthodox and the non-Orthodox had such different conceptions of what was important in life that it was inevitable that the gulf between them would grow. Non-Orthodox Jews were determined to acculturate into American society, and that acculturation process inevitably meant that they would develop common interests with non-Jewish friends and neighbors. This would lead to higher rates of intermarriage, and many of these intermarriages would not lead to the conversion of the non-Jewish spouse. Since Jewish law recognizes as Jewish only those children that are born to a Jewish mother or who were converted to Judaism according to halacha, it was inevitable that substantial and growing numbers of American Jews would not be Jewish by Orthodox criteria.

The Orthodox have long ago recognized that this would happen, and began pulling back from the angry disputes that characterized much of the 1970s and 1980s. I have even seen a few references to "non-Jewish Jewish leaders," a reference that certain leaders of the Reform and Reconstructionist movements had non-Jewish mothers or had not converted according to halacha. The Orthodox had understood there to be an unwritten agreement with the non-Orthodox—the non-Orthodox might deviate from traditional Jewish belief and practice, but they would not change the very definition of who was a Jew. This was the bedrock upon which Jewish unity was based, because it was the determination of who was a member of the Tribe. Like any family, the Jewish people might disagree about all sorts of things, but they were still family.

But in 1983, the Reform movement officially accepted patrilineal descent as a basis for claiming Jewish identity. At their annual conference, the CCAR voted to accept the report of the Committee on Patrilineal Descent. "The purpose of this document is to establish the Jewish status of the children of mixed marriages in the Reform Jewish community of North America." The rabbis went on to say that the issue of mixed marriage was one of the most "pressing human issues" for the Jewish community. "We face today an unprecedented situation due to the changed conditions in which decisions concerning the status of the child of a mixed marriage are to be made." While the patrilineal descent resolution is regarded as the breaking point in the Orthodox/non-Orthodox relationship, it really was precipitated by the drastically increasing intermarriage rate.

The patrilineal descent resolution was worded in an awkward manner, but the purpose was clear—to allow either a Jewish father or a Jewish mother to raise Jewish children with a non-Jewish spouse who did not convert. The condition placed on the rabbinic acceptance of the children as Jewish was that the parents had to raise the children as Jewish, including having them undergo significant public acts or declarations. If the mother was the Jewish partner, the Orthodox would be willing to recognize the Jewish identity of the children, even in extreme cases where the Reform would not. But if the father was the Jewish partner, then the Orthodox would regard the children as non-Jewish. As thousands of children were being raised in Reform and Reconstructionist congregations as Jewish, even though they had non-Jewish mothers, the distance between the Orthodox and the non-Orthodox grew. Unlike an ideological issue or theological question, such a chasm concerning Jewish status could not be overcome through discussion or negotiation.

The patrilineal descent resolution and the Orthodox reiteration that halacha could never accommodate such a policy led to fears that there would be two types of Jews and two separate Jewish communities. The one hope was that a joint beit din could be established that could convert non-Jews to Judaism for all the American Jewish denominations. This would have required the rabbis of the Orthodox and non-Orthodox movements to cooperate in the creation and implementation of a unified religious court that would be formulated on the basis of Judaic principles. Since each of the movements had different and, indeed, contradictory religious principles, such an institution would have required great concessions on the part of all parties.

Efforts to build a common approach to personal status go back to the interwar period. At that time, there was relatively little concern about the intermarriage issue. What worried rabbinical authorities was the differing approaches toward *gittin*, bills of divorce. The Reform movement had done away with the need for a religious divorce entirely. This meant that if a Jewish couple were married by a Reform rabbi and later divorced, they would probably not bother to go through the Jewish divorce procedure, since their Reform rabbi would tell them that a civil divorce was sufficient. This was not acceptable to traditionalists, who followed the halacha specifying that a woman was regarded as married until she received a get (a ritual divorce). Should she have children with any other man—even though she regarded herself as divorced—she would be regarded as committing adultery, and her children could be classified as *mamzerim* (the closest English word would be *bastards*). Jewish law allows mamzers to marry only other mamzers and stigmatizes them in a number of other ways.

This concern was partially alleviated when Orthodox authorities ruled that Reform marriages were not halachically valid and therefore couples married by Reform rabbis did not absolutely need a get. In what became one of his most important halachic rulings, Rabbi Moshe Feinstein wrote a teshuva that two Jews who had been married in a Reform wedding ceremony did not require a get when they got divorced because Feinstein did not regard the ceremony as being legitimate. As a consequence of this seemingly rejectionist decision, women who had remarried without getting a get would not have mamzer children as long as their first marriage had been officiated at by a Reform (and possibly Conservative and Reconstructionist) rabbi. Therefore, Feinstein's decision served to avoid the designation of thousands or even tens of thousands of offspring as mamzers. This decision became quite important after the baal teshuva movement, in which non-Orthodox youth embraced Orthodoxy, gained momentum in the 1970s. Some of the baalei teshuva might have been regarded as mamzers if Feinstein had ruled that non-Orthodox wedding ceremonies were halachically valid Jewish rituals.

Yet there were often cases where the husband would not or could not give his wife a get. In 1935, Rabbi Louis M. Epstein recommended adding an amendment to the ketubah in which the wife would be entitled to receive a get without her husband's signature if he disappeared or refused to cooperate. Epstein, who was a scholar in the Conservative movement, hoped that

FIGURE 3.7. Rabbi Joseph B. Soloveitchik teaching Talmud students at Yeshiva University in the early 1950s. Soloveitchik, affectionately called the Rav by his many followers, advocated a synthesis of Torah study and secular scholarship. *Courtesy of Yeshiva University Archives*

his halachic argumentation would persuade Orthodox rabbinic authorities to go along with this legal innovation, but, of course, they would not. In 1953, JTS professor Saul Lieberman floated a new halachic solution to what was called the problem of the *agunah*, the abandoned wife who could not remarry because she had no get. Lieberman found new halachic justifications that he hoped would sway the Orthodox sages, and he met secretly with Rabbi Joseph B. Soloveitchik in an effort to create a joint Orthodox-Conservative beit din (see chapter 4). Soloveitchik respected Lieberman's Talmudic acumen, and he did his best to encourage moderate elements within Orthodoxy to cooperate, but this too did not lead anywhere.

Soloveitchik urged Orthodox Jews, and particularly Orthodox rabbis, to continue meeting with Reform and Conservative leaders since the non-Orthodox represented the majority of the American Jewish community and it was only possible to address communal problems through dialogue. He did, however, stress that this cooperation should only be for the purpose of meeting Jewish communal needs, rejecting any "religious" interaction. The two major motivations for such interdenominational cooperation were the search for philanthropic support and the need to combat antisemitism. Rabbis or lay leaders representing the Orthodox did sit together with non-Orthodox representatives in meetings held under the auspices of the United Jewish Appeal (since renamed the United Jewish Communities), the Conference of Presidents of Major American Jewish Organizations, the World Zionist Organization, the Jewish Agency and other Zionist groups, the Anti-Defamation League, and the Simon Wiesenthal Center. The Council of Torah Sages of Agudath Israel rejected Soloveitchik's argument for cooperation with the various denominations on communal issues, stating that organizational cooperation with the non-Orthodox was de facto recognition and endorsement and therefore prohibited. In 1956, eleven rosh yeshivas under the aegis of the Union of Orthodox Rabbis (Agudath ha-Rabbanim) signed a statement prohibiting Orthodox rabbis who accepted their authority from interacting with Conservative or Reform clergy in any joint organization or for any common religious purpose. "It is forbidden by the law of our sacred Torah to participate with them [the non-Orthodox denominational movements] either as an individual or as an organized communal body." The eleven rosh yeshivas included rabbis Aharon Kotler, Moshe Feinstein, and Yaakov Ruderman. Rabbi Eliezer Silver, a long-time leader of the haredim from Cincinnati and the president of Agudas HaRabbanim at the time, did not sign the statement. While he probably agreed with it in principle, Silver was apparently not prepared to openly support such a divisive policy.

The ban on cooperation with the non-Orthodox included the SCA, which had been established in 1926 and had members representing the full spectrum of religious life. Those who see Soloveitchik as a relative liberal believe that he refused to sign the petition, responding that there were many topics that required the cooperation of all the American Jewish denominations. Those who see Soloveitchik as more conservative believe that he was never given a chance to sign the petition. Whatever the truth may have been, both the RCA and the OU used Soloveitchik's supposed stand to justify remaining as members of the SCA.

While Soloveitchik had apparently approved Orthodox participation in the Synagogue Council of America, those more to the right continually worked to undermine that decision. After the Reform movement ordained

Rabbi Sally Priesand in 1972, some lobbied for Orthodox withdrawal from the New York Board of Rabbis. The more moderate Orthodox were able to ward off the challenge to the status quo at that time, although they felt a tremendous amount of pressure. Fears grew that the Orthodox and the non-Orthodox would split into two separate groups, two separate peoples. One Orthodox rabbi warned of "the coming cataclysm."[51] The United Jewish Appeal stopped using their slogan "We Are One" because it no longer represented reality.

After many years of criticism, the moderate Orthodox who sustained pluralistic Jewish dialogue finally buckled under to haredi pressure. They withdrew from the SCA, which then disbanded in 1994. The push to end interdenominational religious cooperation eventually caused virtually all of the multidenominational organizations and programs to stop functioning or to become de facto associations of non-Orthodox rabbis. Since then, there has been far less interdenominational dialogue. While some observers, such as Jack Wertheimer, have been surprised that the level of conflict appears to have lowered, this seems to me to be more an indication that there is nothing left to say.[52]

The Emergence of Postdenominationalism

The non-Orthodox religious movements—Reform, Reconstructionist, and the woefully misnamed Conservative movement—are, in my view, becoming increasingly similar. Their leadership maintains that they have significant theological and ritual differences, but these subtle nuances are basically invisible to the average lay person. While they each have their own reasons for maintaining their institutional independence, their synagogues are likely to resemble each other in more and more ways in the coming years. While American Jews are becoming more attuned to their spiritual needs, they are less interested in affiliating with a particular denomination.

The development of postdenominationalism was predicted by the writers of *The Jewish Catalog* as early as 1973. Of course, there had already been a number of organizations already working on a postdenominational basis. Hillel, the Jewish student organization, was perhaps the best-known example. But the passions of the 1960s promoted a new sense of spiritual energy that seemed incompatible with the existing denominational framework and to require a new type of religious structure. Proponents of a Jewish counterculture revival, the catalog editors spoke dismissively about the trivial differences between the various denominations, which spent too much energy marking their turf and not enough fostering spirituality. What the catalog came to do, they wrote, was to help interested Jews discover their religious heritage and take personal control over their ritual lives. American Jews should invest their energy in Jewish spirituality rather than defining and perpetuating useless and counterproductive denominational boundaries. At the time, many readers believed their rhetoric and felt that the religious movements were vestiges of a bygone era. While their prediction was certainly premature, their vision of a postdenominational American Jewish religious landscape may yet be in the early stages of formation.

Although this chapter has focused on a description of the four major Jewish denominations, the differences represented by these movements—the Orthodox excluded—are fading in importance. As Americans focus more of their energies on finding spiritually meaningful experiences, they are less likely to mold themselves into a denominational structure. As a result of the changing American societal environment, there is a strong desire to move beyond denominational labels and find spiritual meaning rather than promote what are perceived to be artificial boundaries and irrelevant distinctions. The astonishing growth of nondenominational churches around the country is one obvious indication that Americans are looking for content rather than a brand name.

This has encouraged many spiritual seekers, who correctly believe there to be a tremendous opportunity to take advantage of this new interest in transdenominational Jewish spirituality. To cite just a few examples: former Colorado and New Mexico circuit-riding Rabbi Gershon Winkler writes lovingly of "flexidoxy," Reform Rabbi Niles Goldstein pushes "Gonzo Judaism," and Rabbi Arthur Waskow advocates his "Down-to-Earth Judaism." What these and similar efforts share in common is a desire to transcend denominational boundaries. American Jews, so they believe, are bored with the mainstream religious menus that have been offered to them for the past several decades. They want something new, something exciting, something that redefines Jewish spirituality without building new walls.

The major denominations—which now include the Reconstructionist movement and perhaps even Jewish Renewal and Chabad as well—are still significant, but larger percentages refuse to identify themselves with any of these groups. Various terms are used: *nondenominational, postdenominational, transdenominational, cross-denominational,* and even *antidenominational.* These terms are not necessarily interchangeable, and so it is important to define what is meant. The following are my personal definitions and are not intended to be authoritative. Nondenominational Jews are those who identify themselves in telephone surveys as "just Jewish." While it's hard to know exactly what they mean by this, they clearly do not identify with any of the denominational choices offered them by the telephone interviewer. They are not Reform, Conservative, Orthodox, or Reconstructionist. In practice, this usually means that they are not terribly interested in Judaism but have a Jewish ethnic background and are willing to acknowledge that fact.

Postdenominationalism is something different entirely, referring to those individuals or congregations that do not affiliate with any of the national synagogue movements. There are at least a couple hundred congregations that are not members of any of the established denominations. Some see this as an ideological movement, while others believe that the trend is more a practical response to the high cost of such affiliation. Some postdenominational Jews believe that their approach allows them the best of both worlds; they can remain independent while drawing on the best features of each of the religious streams. Some of the most creative initiatives in American Jewish religious activities in recent decades have been postdenominational, although, as time goes on, these postdenominational Jews may evolve into a denomination in their own right.

Related to postdenominationalism, antidenominationalism is the active opposition to the concept of denominations. Antidenominationlists deliberately avoid denominational involvement, believing that the focus on denominational Judaism has tended to stifle, rather than stimulate, spirituality. They see the synagogue movements as the creation of rich, arrogant East and West Coast elite machers (self-important experts) who have manufactured phony distinctions in order to justify their honorary positions in redundant denominational organizations. They blame the movements for perpetuating the stereotype of Judaism as dull and boring. Indeed, they believe that without the constricting labels of Reform, Conservative, or Orthodox, American Judaism would have thrived.

Orthodox outreach organizations have been quick to pick up on the antidenominationalism so prevalent among younger American Jews. Beautiful full-color magazine inserts were put into the various local Jewish newspapers describing the "Ashkefardi-Ultrarefconservadox Generation" and how Judaism had a great deal of spiritual meaning that could be found if one was able to get past all these divisive labels. Those who responded to the ad were sent on to Orthodox outreach organizations, which could legitimately claim that they indeed rejected the denominational divisions; they believed that there was only one true Judaism. If others chose to refer to them as Orthodox, then so be it. They were following Judaism the way it was supposed to be followed. All the others were simply misguided.

Transdenominational refers to an approach that brings Jews of different religious outlooks together. As an example, when Arthur Waskow was preparing to be ordained as a rabbi, the Jewish Renewal movement put together a transdenominational beit din to supervise his advanced studies and then ordain him. This beit din included the leading sage of the Jewish Renewal movement, but also a Reform rabbi, a Conservative rabbi, and a feminist theologian (see chapter 6). Many if not most of the recent communal initiatives share a transdenominational goal. Also referred to as cross-denominational, this orientation stresses what American Jews have in common or what they can learn from each other. Much of the transdenominational bridge building began after the 1990 National Jewish Population Study found that there had been a significant erosion in Jewish communal cohesion. Many believe that transdenominational programs have been quite successful at helping Jews see what they actually have in common, rather than what they thought they had in common. For example, the Florence Melton Adult Mini-School and the Hebrew College Meah Program have both been successfully implemented in numerous Jewish communities, encouraging serious adult learners to take a progressive series of courses on complementary Judaic studies subjects.

In response to the changing environment, the denominations are seeking to sharpen their distinctive identities. Several of the major denominational institutions were burdened with vague, innocuous names that did not convey the actual ideology and mission of that particular group. Both the Reform and the Conservative movements took new names to emphasize who they actually were and what they actually stood for. The United Synagogue of America became the United Synagogue of Conservative Judaism and the Union of American Hebrew Congregations became the Union for Reform Judaism. Both organizations had once hoped to represent most or all of American Judaism, but they now had to face the reality that American Jewish life was becoming more diverse and that their organizations were becoming less influential. The new organizational names reflected their more modest but also more realistic self-definitions. But while the leadership of each of the movements attempts to communicate in a clear manner why their movement is distinctive, momentum is running in the opposite direction.

Many of the West Coast Jewish institutions have been far more transdenominationally focused than their East Coast or Midwestern affiliates. Thus, HUC-JIR in Los Angeles was seen by some as being more open to different types of non-Orthodox religious approaches than is HUC-JIR campus in Cincinnati. Their Skirball Cultural Center broke its ties with HUC-JIR and the Reform movement, becoming completely independent. Likewise, the American Jewish University (AJU, formerly the University of Judaism and the Brandeis-Bardin Institute), also in Los Angeles, is more pluralistic than the Jewish Theological Seminary in New York. The UJ was founded both by JTS and by the Board of Jewish Education, so it was both denominational and nondenominational from the start. When Robert Wexler replaced David Lieber as president in 1992, the UJ—including the Lee Program in Jewish and Western Civilizations of AJU—became officially nondenominational. The Ziegler School of Rabbinic Studies, the Miller Introduction to Judaism program, and Camp Ramah in Ojai, however, remained affiliated with the Conservative movement.[53]

Even in the realm of rabbinic education—formerly regarded as the most highly partisan denominational turf in existence—there have been a number of new rabbinic programs created that are completely nondenominational. The Academy for Jewish Religion (AJR) has pioneered this independent approach to rabbinic education. In its first statement of purpose it declared: "The Academy seeks to be inclusive with respect to varying viewpoints in Jewish belief and practice. It wishes to serve Klal Yisrael, the entire household of Israel, and students may choose their particular field of service in Jewish religious life. It is a house of learning where men preparing for the rabbinate may study together though espousing different points of view, and thereby bring enrichment to Jewish life."[54] It is a striking example of the change in the contemporary scene. Ignored or even opposed because it did not fit into the established denominational structure, the academy remained a tiny school for years. But in the last decade or so it has experienced dramatic growth, opening a cantorial school and ordaining more graduates than in its previous forty years combined. In 1999, it supported the founding of another transdenominational seminary on the West Coast.[55]

More recently, the Hebrew College in Boston has opened a transdenominational rabbinic program led by Arthur Green, thus fulfilling his vision for a new type of seminary, which dates back at least to the founding of Havurat Shalom Community Seminary in Somerville, Massachusetts in 1967. The mission statement of the new rabbinical program speaks of Ahavat Torah, the love of wisdom and the pursuit of Jewish learning, and the growth and development of the spiritual life. "Each rabbi needs to find his or her own way to an inner life of prayer, to communion with God, to hewing out a deep inner well of empathy and caring, on which he or she will draw daily throughout a rabbinic career."[56]

Some argue that denominational religiosity is a spent force. As philanthropist Michael H. Steinhardt puts it: "Somewhere along the way, things changed. Whether it was due to the liturgy, the practices, the synagogues, the communities, or the allures of the secular world, denominations ceased to resonate." Many of those who had grown up in the movements are now adrift. "We should be clear that the denominations were once wellsprings of creative spiritual innovation." But like many other movements of all types, the American Jewish religious denominations "have come to be more concerned with institutional survival than with innovation. The period when Reform, Conservative and Reconstructionist Judaism were vibrant, growing, intellectually exciting movements has all but ended."[57] Steinhardt is a partisan crusader against denominationalism, and he may be exaggerating for dramatic effect. Nevertheless, there is a kernel of truth in his words. The decline of the denominations has many causes, but one of the most important is the dramatically increasing numbers of interfaith families. The impact of intermarriage on American Judaism has been enormous and so we now turn our attention to that subject in chapter 4.

4 Facing the Collapse of the Intermarriage Stigma

"I created the greatest super holiday known to mankind, drawing on the best that Judaism and Christianity have to offer," explained Seth Cohen, one of the four main characters on Fox network's *The O.C.* (Orange County).[1] Cohen, the son of a Jewish father and a Protestant mother, came up with a portmanteau for his new holiday—*Chrismukkah*—as a way of helping interfaith children like himself deal with the "December dilemma." Chrismukkah joined a growing list of alternate or conglomerated holidays, many of which were first discussed on the Internet and then publicized through a television show. *Seinfeld*, for example, had Festivus, the December 23 holiday for the "rest of us." *O.C.* creator Josh Schwartz told reporters that the script tried to convey the feelings that many of his contemporaries felt. "What Jewish boy or girl doesn't feel a little jealous? They get all the good songs, the tree, Frosty and Rudolph. We get dreidels. It's not the same."[2]

In an episode in the following season, the interpersonal dramas between *The O.C.* characters all blow up on Chrismukkah. They eventually manage to reconcile and celebrate the holiday with lights, trees, eggnog, and potato latkes. The following year, they have a Chrismukkah Bar Mitz-vahkkah for Seth's non-Jewish friend Ryan where the Torah is read and everyone sways to Dionne Warwick music. The group of friends persuades the real Jew on the show, Sandy, into going along with it, and he gives Ryan an inspirational speech to encourage him to go through with the faux Jewish ceremony. Everyone has a great time, with Kirsten and Sandy proclaiming it to be the "best Chrismukkah ever."

George Washington University freshman Beth Furtwangler said that "I found out about Chrismukkah from *The O.C.*, I didn't realize that it [existed] before." But Chrismukkah is not just a mythical holiday made up for TV. It has become a real holiday or, rather, a real commercial opportunity. An entire industry is devoted to Chrismukkah. Greeting card companies sell holiday cards synthesizing religious symbols from the two religions. Some of the cards are definitely amusing, unless you find the idea of mixing the two religions together to be offensive-a decidedly minority view. Some are cutesy, such as a picture of a reindeer with a yarmulke or with antlers shaped like menorahs. One shows Rudolph the red-nosed reindeer standing in front of a menorah and another shows a driedel with a Christmas tree and a snowman on two of its sides. They also have more generic cards such as one that shows a steaming hot bowl of matzah ball soup with not only matzah balls but also a snowman floating in it.

Chrismukkah recipe books such as Ron Gompertz's *The Merry Mish Mash Holiday Cookbook* stress "the oy of cooking" for dual holiday celebrations. Other books take a slightly more serious approach, encouraging families to find personal as well as religious meaning in both of the holidays. Gompertz wrote a follow-up to his cookbook titled *Chrismukkah—Everything You Need to Know to Celebrate the Hybrid Holiday*, and Gersh Kuntzman came out with *Chrismukkah: The Official Guide to the World's Best-Loved Holiday*. O.C. producer Warner Brothers is selling the Yarmuclaus, a fuzzy red mix of a Santa Claus hat with a yarmulke. Web sites sell aprons with the greeting Merry Mazeltov, which the interfaith couple can presumably wear as they prepare recipes such as Kris Kringle Kugel and Gefilte Goose. There is a Chrismukkah holiday mug, showing a menorah with candy canes instead of candles, and there are "menorahments" such as a Christmas ball bearing the Star of David, perfectly suited for a Chrismukkah bush.

Companies are even fighting over the use of the term. Warner Brothers was litigating against Gompertz, the founder of www.chrismukkah.com, claiming that they invented the name and held the rights to it. Gompertz recalls that when he and his wife "came up with this idea to put out the line of cards it was sort of whimsical, [we] didn't intend to start a business. . . . It was going to be a fun thing for people like us in interfaith marriages." According to Gompertz, the controversy over who had created the term *Chrismukkah* first arose when *O.C.* creator Josh Schwartz began claiming that the show's writers coined it and Gompertz copied them. Gompertz argued that Michael Nathanson, a schoolteacher from New Haven, Connecticut, had been credited as the inventor of the term five years earlier on the NPR radio program *Car Talk* as well as on the Internet. Gompertz felt Chrismukkah, in addition to its connection to the Jewish experience in America, was part of his family history. "When I was a kid, we called our holiday 'Hanumas.'"[3] He has traced the Chrismukkah concept back to German Jews at the beginning of the twentieth century, who used the word *Weinukkah* as an ironic term to describe the way assimilated Jews celebrated Hanukkah with Christmas-like trees and decor.

Gompertz, the founder and president of Eco Auto, explained that "when I first registered the Internet domain name 'Chrismukkah.com' in January 2004, it was largely to stake a claim on something I saw as my personal history, saving it from the silly pop culture Fox/Warner Brothers interpretation of Chrismukkah." He considered trademarking the word, but decided that the Web site domain name was enough and that Chrismukkah's prior usage in the public domain precluded him—or anyone else, for that matter—from trying to own it via a trademark filing. In addition to the legal issues, "it just seemed like the wrong thing to do. One can't trademark a holiday. That would be so 'Grinchlike.' We were happy to share Chrismukkah with all."[4]

In October 2004 Warner Brothers filed a "global" trademark application on the word *Chrismukkah*. Gompertz had to hire a trademark attorney to protest their claim of ownership over the word. He feared that if they were successful they could restrict the usage and drive him out of business. His attorney first tried to get them to withdraw the filing, but they refused to do that. "My attorney then filed a 'counter trademark' as a legal strategy, and after two very expensive years of legal shenanigans, Warner Brothers finally backed down and cancelled their global trademark filing. So I won in a way. But it cost big bucks to defend the honor of Chrismukkah. Now with the *OC* show cancelled, I don't think Warner or Fox give a hoot about Chrismukkah."

Gompertz has had trouble with a number of Christian (as well as Jewish) organizations that have strongly protested what they see as his advocacy of

FIGURE 4.1. A Chrismukkah card from Chrismukkah.com showing a gingerbread house made of matzah. The image deliberately merges holiday practices from Judaism and Christianity in order to convey the idea that families can observe rituals and ceremonies from both religions. Photo Larry Stanley. *Courtesy of Ron Gompertz of Chrismukkah.com*

syncretism, the mixing of different religions together. He believes that some of these groups have organized spamming campaigns to try to overwhelm his Web site with e-mail denouncing Chrismukkah. "I never thought we'd get into the theological debate we have!" Gompertz notes that he deliberately removed the letter T from the word Chrismukkah in order to make it clearer that his intent is a secular rather than a religious one. Despite the problems, Gompertz continues to use the Web address to sell roughly 75,000 Chrismukkah cards each year. Gompertz says "Chrismukkah is a state of mind; a season. . . . It's about tolerance."[5]

Competitors do even better. Elise Okrend, the founder of MixedBlessing interfaith and multicultural cards, sells more than 350,000 cards each year. "I started my card line as a creative solution to 'what kind of a card do you send to a couple who celebrates both Christmas and Hanukkah?' I have both friends and family in this situation." Okrend recalls that "my first design was of a half of a Christmas tree melding half a Star of David," she said. "Everyone I showed the card to thought it was great and encouraged me to do more." Her goal is to "represent both Christmas and Hanukkah in a respective [respectful] way—one that shows symbols of the holidays side by side and celebrates our diversity."[6] Her husband Philip says that they do not use the word *Chrismukkah* in their interfaith cards. "We're not trying to create a new holiday. We're trying to portray the holidays side by side."[7] Historically, interfaith couples would try to observe both holidays, but some have found that the Chrismukkah concept allows them to celebrate the holiday season without creating unnecessary divisions. Rod Shapiro of Long Beach, California celebrates Chrismukkah with his Christian wife, Pat Wong. "Personally, I think that more and more people should embrace their similarities and tolerate their differences, and Chrismukkah is a holiday that allows couples to do that."[8]

Obviously, the mainstream religious organizations are not pleased. In the fall of 2004, the Catholic League and the New York Board of Rabbis issued a joint statement condemning Chrismukkah as "shameless plagiarism." They stated that trying to take a holiday holy to Christians and a completely separate holiday holy to Jews and combine them was wholly inappropriate. Rabbi Joseph Potasnik, executive vice president of the New York Board of Rabbis, said, "I just feel it's inappropriate to take two very distinct holidays that belong to two different faith groups and to synthesize them into one. It doesn't respect the integrity of either one." While the joint statement was directed against Chrismukkah generally, Ron Gompertz was personally attacked on a number of radio talk shows. Both Jewish and Christian radio talk show hosts criticized him for blurring, if not destroying, the distinctive elements of two separate religious traditions. A number of Jewish speakers attacked him for betraying his religion, which particularly upset him. "I'm a Jew, and I'm a good Jew," Gompertz declared. Even though he and his wife celebrate Chrismukkah, he explained, they are raising their daughter as a Jew in Bozeman, Montana.

Demographic Studies Fuel Fears of Precipitous Population Decline

The American Jewish community has crossed over a threshold, and behaviors that were once considered transgressive—such as intermarriage—are now seen as acceptable and even normative. Using the language of a recent nonfiction best seller, Sylvia Barack Fishman argues that the American Jewish community has gone over a "tipping point." In the decades following World War II, most American Jews did not see intermarriage as an acceptable option. Parents constantly told their children that they needed to marry someone Jewish, and they assumed that their kids would listen to them. Over the course of the 1970s and 1980s, that expectation began to look out of touch, and increasing numbers of young American Jews intermarried, regardless of how their parents felt. Many American Jewish leaders were caught by surprise at the rapid pace of changing social norms. Even professional sociologists did not seem to realize how quickly American society would change and how those changes would undermine what had once been ironclad communal norms.

There was always a small number of Jews who did intermarry, but they were so few as to make it easy to dismiss the phenomena as a statistical quirk. As late as the early 1960s, the intermarriage rate was still in the single digits. The person intermarrying was considered a traitor to the community and as a result was frequently rejected by family and friends. There was an assumption that he was actively turning his back on Judaism and demonstrating his determination to sever ties with the Jewish community, an assumption that would be questioned decades later. But, at the time, most parents could not see their child's choice of marriage partners as a strictly personal decision. Distressed Jewish parents screamed: "Why are you doing this to me? Are you trying to finish up what Hitler started?" The tension produced by intermarriage frequently caused permanent rifts in families. My father told me that a relative from his father's generation in the Bronx had fallen in love with his non-Jewish secretary. In order to marry her, he abandoned his business, took her to California, and cut off all contact with his family. Despite the angst created by individual cases, intermarriage was considered a marginal issue for the community.

Over the course of the 1960s, American Jewish leaders slowly began to grow concerned. In 1964, Marshall Sklare wrote an essay titled "Intermarriage and the Jewish Future" in *Commentary* arguing that intermarriage was going to become a critical problem. But the article that really shook people up came in 1977, when Harvard demographer Elihu Bergman published "The American Jewish Population Erosion" in *Midstream*. "When the United States celebrates its Tricentennial in 2076, the American Jewish community is likely to number no more than 944,000 persons, and, conceivably as few as 10,420."[9] This was shocking news, but questions were soon raised. The sociologists on whose studies Bergman had relied came forward to criticize his methodology and refute his conclusions.[10]

Much later, Bergman admitted to fellow sociologist Steven Cohen that the criticism was valid. "He said that getting the facts straight wasn't all that important. What was important was provoking Jews to sit up and take notice."[11] Despite his exaggerations and poor methodology, his general thesis seemed logical: Jews were intermarrying at much higher rates than before, and this was likely to endanger the future of the American Jewish community. This "population erosion" would threaten established Jewish institutions, which relied upon a certain number of Jews to support them by both donating money and participating in their activities. Institutional Judaism, which was based on the existence of institutions, would crumble and collapse.

There was worse news yet to come. The release of the National Jewish Population Survey in November 1990 generated unprecedented hysteria. The survey, sponsored by the Council of Jewish Federations and Welfare Funds (CJF), found that 52 percent of those who had married between 1985 and 1990 had chosen a non-Jewish spouse. Almost everyone who cared about "Jewish survival" was terribly upset about the NJPS's finding of a 52 percent intermarriage rate. Most had been aware that there was more intermarriage than before, but few had any idea that more than half of Jews marrying were tying the knot with non-Jews. Later, other sociologists not directly connected with the NJPS argued that they had miscalculated, but even the critics put the intermarriage rate at at least 40 percent.

Some argued that the 52 percent finding proved that near universal rates of intermarriage were inevitable in an open society and that the only reasonable

Jewish communal response was outreach to intermarried couples. Others felt that the lesson to be drawn from the finding was the opposite—that intermarriage needed to be discouraged more vigorously and that the intermarried needed to be excluded from communal life so as not to negatively influence those still within the community. Orthodox leaders implicitly blamed the "continuity crisis" on the American Jewish community's lack of halachic observance. They argued that, rather than redefining the nature of Jewish identity to include the children of Jewish fathers and non-Jewish mothers, every Jew needed to commit themselves to Torah and mitzvot. Rabbi Avi Shafran, the director of public affairs of Agudath Israel of America, argued that "the Jewish future lies not in redefining the word 'Jew' but in recognizing that we Jews are all joined at the soul through our Torah." He said that the "Jewish patient" needs "a megadose of Torah study and observance" rather than any arbitrary "redefinition" of Jewishness.[12] Rabbi Pinchas Stolper, then executive vice president of the Orthodox Union, predicted that "the intermarriage process will take everything Jewish with it in its wake. It will grow and grow until it engulfs the entire community. It's another Holocaust."[13]While Stolper felt that any solution other than embracing Orthodoxy would be futile, Jewish communal professionals began experimenting with strategies for coping with the new social reality.

Jewish federations as well as private foundations made plans to earmark tens of millions of dollars to what became known as the fight for "Jewish continuity." The CJF sponsored a North American Commission on Jewish Continuity to bring together the funders and administrators of the major Jewish philanthropies, the heads of the Jewish religious denominations, and other Jewish leaders and educators. Most agreed to participate, with the exception of the fervently Orthodox. Rabbi Moshe Sherer, the president of Agudath Israel of America, was one of the Orthodox leaders who declined, saying that including the Reform movement in an effort to reverse the ravages of assimilation was "like inviting the arsonist to help put out the fire."[14] Sherer later initiated a two-million-dollar campaign called Am Echad, One People, to declare that there can be no "multiple Judaisms," that only Orthodoxy was Jewishly authentic.[15]

Intermarriage rates were connected not only to how traditional a person was and how much Jewish education he had, but also to his mobility. The more mobile a person was, the more likely she was to intermarry. This is logical, because the easier it is to move away from family and friends, the easier it's likely to be to break other communal ties. Many moved from the East and the Midwest to the South and the West. The western part of the United States has the highest percentage of unaffiliated Jews in the country and in general has the most "unchurched" Americans. Jews show a particularly high rate of mobility. One group of researchers put together an entire book on Jewish internal migration, which they called *Jews on the Move*.[16] A few years later, two of the scholars edited another work, *Still Moving,* which reported that Jews from the Northeast and Midwest were doing exactly that.[17] This mobility has led to tremendous population growth in cities that have had Jewish populations for a long time, such as Denver, as well as practically creating new Jewish communities in cities such as Phoenix and Las Vegas.

As intermarriage increased, resistance to it weakened. The basic reason for this is simple—the children are going to do what they want; if the parents refuse to accept their choices, it will damage and perhaps even destroy the parent-child relationship. This was a sea change in the course of just one generation. In the immediate postwar period, relatively few Americans married outside their ethnic groups. Those who did understood that they were violating a social taboo. They expected to face parental opposition, even communal ostracization . Most were prepared for this and made plans accordingly. They might move west, possibly even breaking all ties with their family and starting over. Or they might prepare for a long period of difficult family relations, hoping to eventually rebuild love and trust.

In the Jewish community, there were stories of parents "sitting shiva" for their intermarried children. These parents would react to the news that their child was marrying a non-Jew in the same way that they would respond to the news of a child's death. Many would declare that their child was dead as far as they were concerned. Some even went so far as to actually go through the rites of mourning, including sitting on low stools and covering mirrors. The majority would do neither, but might refer repeatedly to what others did. In any case, the point was clear—marrying outside the religion was an act of betrayal that brought grief and suffering to the hearts of their loved ones.

The vast majority of American Jews wanted to perpetuate their Jewish identity, but few were willing to consider becoming Orthodox as a way of preventing intermarriage. Some suggested that encouraging the non-Jewish spouse to convert could provide a workable solution. Gary Tobin, a social scientist working out of San Francisco, wrote a book, *Opening the Gates: How Proactive Conversion Can Revitalize the Jewish Community,* in which he argued that the Jews of America were ready to engage in an organized proselytizing campaign that could bring in millions of new Jews. Most of these "Jews by choice" would be converted by Reform, Conservative, and Reconstruction-ist rabbis, or even by secular humanist spiritual leaders, and, because of this, would not be accepted by the Orthodox as legitimate converts. Tobin was not overly concerned by this, nor was he worried that intermarriage would lead to the end of the Jewish people. Rather, he suggested that increasing assimilation was a natural sociological process and actually provided an opportunity to draw large numbers of non-Jews into Judaism.

Most non-Orthodox American Jews felt that they had to make their peace with the inevitable. They understood that their children were going to make personal lifestyle choices that they might not have wanted them to make, and they felt that encouraging conversion was the optimal course of action under the circumstances. But there were those who took a more belligerent position. Rabbi Ephraim Buchwald of the National Jewish Outreach Program wrote to *Moment* magazine that "those of us out in the field know that the 'Silent Holocaust' has already most likely claimed close to two-thirds of America's six million Jews—lost to Jewish life, perhaps irretrievably."[18] Buchwald felt that most American Jewish leaders did not see the assimilatory process as sufficiently catastrophic. "There are no barking dogs, no Zyklon-B gas . . . but make no mistake: This is a spiritual Holocaust."

After Gary Tobin quoted him on the very first page of *Opening the Gates*, writing that Buchwald was comparing the Holocaust to intermarriage, Buchwald responded by correcting him. "First of all, for the record, that statement was said about general assimilation, not intermarriage." Buchwald denied that he was "hysterical," but pointed out that if a zoo keeper had been losing 40 percent of his sea lions, he would probably be pretty upset. He wrote that he was "agitated" because he had not been able to successfully mobilize or even sensitize the American Jewish leadership to do what he felt needed to be done in order to nurture the next generation of American Jews. He admitted that he was troubled that the community was spending billions of dollars on Holocaust memorials rather than investing that money in "joyous, Jewish outreach for our young people." Buchwald wrote that he was "worked up because there are millions of American Jews who desperately want to be a part of the Jewish community and they have nowhere to turn. We have failed them."[19]

Having tried to partially deny his earlier inflammatory comment, Buchwald could not resist drawing a new analogy that was almost as extreme: "Ladies and gentlemen, this is the reality: Our children are drowning. If I may continue the metaphor, while our children are drowning, the nonchurched gentiles of America are floating on an air mattress in the water. It's true, they're not swimming with God. But they're not drowning. Gary Tobin suggests that we throw the life preserver to the gentiles. Have we lost our minds?!!"

The Inreach-Outreach Debate

Rabbi Buchwald's use of Holocaust imagery in reference to assimilation if not intermarriage is extreme, but the emotions behind his inappropriate imagery are heartfelt. Buchwald believes that it is crucial to focus on "inreach," reinforcing the Jewish education and experiences of those who were already involved in Jewish life. Advocates of inreach include Steven M. Cohen of the Hebrew Union College–Jewish Institute of Religion, Sylvia Barack Fishman of Brandeis University, Jack Wertheimer of the Jewish Theological Seminary, and Steven Bayme of the American Jewish Committee. All publish extensively to defend their belief that the Jewish community should focus resources on programs designed to reinforce Judaic commitment among those already at least somewhat involved in Jewish life. The Jewish community can help the most by encouraging enrollment in day schools, Jewish summer camp, and trips to Israel.

On the other side of the debate, there are the advocates of "outreach," who include Rabbi Kerry Olitzky of the Jewish Outreach Institute (JOI) and Edmund Case of InterfaithFamily.com. Outreach supporters argue that, while all of the educational programs geared toward the moderately and heavily affiliated are important, it is crucial to reach out to the hundreds of thousands of Jews who are currently not involved in Jewish life—or only marginally so. Most are intermarried and relatively few belong to synagogues, but the advocates of outreach believe that there is hope for engaging them. The key is finding something that interests them and helping them to stimulate that interest. As Barry Shrage, the president of the Combined Jewish Philanthropies of Boston, puts it, the Jewish community needs to make Jewish life so vibrant, so magnetic, so attractive that people will want to get involved.

Those who argue for inreach believe that the future of the American Jewish community depends on the moderately and heavily affiliated rather than the unaffiliated. Those who are intermarried are unlikely to raise their children with an exclusively Jewish identity, and few of their grandchildren will identify as Jewish. The advocates of inreach believe that, by watering down standards, the outreach groups have simply made it easier for American Jews to assimilate. They point particularly to the Reform movement's 1983 patrilineal descent resolution as an example of what they see as a misguided policy that has caused more harm than good. The advocates of outreach respond by arguing that the Jewish community can welcome intermarried couples and that a warm, friendly reception encourages families that would otherwise be lost into the Jewish community. The sociological debate is fueled by a constant stream of new studies that are interpreted by the proponents of the different schools according to their already formed philosophical positions. Much of the public debate is designed to make the case for inreach or outreach to policymakers and funders, whether at the major Jewish communal organizations or private family foundations.[20]

Outreach is not necessarily targeted exclusively at intermarried couples, but rather at the broader category of the unaffiliated: people from whatever background who are not members of any synagogue and not involved in Jewish communal life in a meaningful way. They may have been members of a synagogue when their children were preparing for their bar or bat mitzvahs, but they let their membership lapse because they did not see what value they were getting from their dues. Or they may have never belonged to a synagogue, perhaps because they were not the type of people who were drawn to group activities.

Synagogues of all types have sharpened their strategies for drawing in visitors, who are seen as potential members. Congregations have found that programs for children are particularly effective for drawing in entire families. Rabbi Emeritus Alvin Sugarman of the Temple in Atlanta explained that "we are hoping the nursery school will be the entry point. We're saying to the unaffiliated that there is something very important about bringing their children up Jewish and giving them a solid Jewish education." Like other rabbis concerned about temple membership levels, Sugarman was looking for people who might eventually become members. "The unaffiliated community is a tremendous untapped market. Maybe I'm a cockeyed optimist, but if we develop meaningful relationships, I genuinely believe they will connect."[21]

Even though outreach targets all unaffiliated Jews, the focus is clearly on the intermarried. Paul Golin of the JOI writes that, while few Jewish leaders have been willing to admit that "the battle against Jewish intermarriage is over and we should instead focus solely on outreach," that is indeed the fact. "But the battle is over, and has been for a generation. What's more, Jewish outreach works, and it works best when not hampered by mixed messages that tell intermarried families we want them, but they're still second-class citizens."[22] While he does not say so explicitly, he is probably referring to rabbis who refused to officiate at interfaith weddings but then claim that they want those same couples to join their congregations. What has to be taken into consideration is that sanctifying a marriage is much more than a mechanism for bringing new couples into the synagogue. Likewise, outreach is a response to a particular theological perspective rather than just a sociological strategy. Rabbi Eric H. Yoffie, the president for the Union for Reform Judaism, argues that outreach is a theological principle central to the Jewish mission. The starting point must be the same as for all Jewish religious thought: "our unique destiny as a religious people, tied to God in a covenant that we trace back to Abraham and Sarah." Jews have the obligation to follow through on this covenant, which guides the Jewish people in a world that is redeemable but not yet redeemed. There is a biological aspect to Judaism, but it is only one dimension out of many. "Judaism speaks the language of fate, but it speaks as well the language of choice."

Yoffie emphasized that Jews who are most successful at the work of outreach are those who are familiar with the power and beauty of their heritage and can model proud and assertive religious behavior. Outreach thus begins with an act of self-definition rather than an act of inclusion, because Reform Jews must begin by affirming their particularistic identity and only then reach out to others. "The first step of outreach—and the single most important step—is to have a clear sense of who we are and of the boundary that exists between us as Reform Jews and the society around us." Reflecting on two decades of outreach, he said, "if we have learned anything at all after twenty years, it is this: you do not draw people in by erasing boundaries and eliminating distinctions. If there are no clearly defined distinctions between our Jewish values and the values of the world around us, then what reason would serious people—Jews or non-Jews—have to cast their fate with ours?"[23]

Conversion to Judaism as the Optimal Paradigm

While the Jewish tradition is profoundly ambivalent about converts and conversion, there are many biblical and Talmudic texts that speak of the convert in extremely positive terms. Many scholars believe that Judaism began as a missionary faith, but had to stop after Christianity became the official religion of the Holy Roman Empire in 315 CE. Laws were passed prohibiting

Jews from proselytizing, upon pain of death. Even before this, the Talmudic sages felt that it was only fair to warn a potential convert that he was joining a persecuted people and his action might result in persecution or even death.

In modern times, all of the Jewish religious denominations accepted converts, but the criteria used for acceptance or rejection differed dramatically. Usually the interested candidate will approach a rabbi and begin a course of study. After a six- to twelve-month period of participation the candidate is brought before a *beit din* (rabbinical court) that will ask both personal questions to ascertain the convert's motivation and religious questions to determine the convert's level of knowledge. A male convert will usually be required to undergo circumcision, although the Reform movement eliminated this requirement in the 1890s. Most rabbis will ask an already circumcised male to undergo *hatafat dam brit*, the drawing of a drop of blood from the glans of the penis to symbolically indicate that the circumcision was being done in order to bring the man into the covenant of Abraham. Both male and female converts will then undergo immersion in a mikveh, a pool of running water, and be given a Hebrew name. Once someone converts to Judaism, they are to be regarded as a Jew like any other Jew.

There are different types of converts who convert to Judaism for different reasons. The largest number were what some rabbis call "accommodationist converts" or "accommodating converts." These are almost entirely romantic partners of Jewish people who are asked to convert as part of plans to marry. The accommodationist convert agrees, but is not self-motivated. If the Jewish-born spouse is or becomes involved in Jewish religious life, they may follow, but they almost never initiate such activity. Idealistic converts, also sometimes called activist converts, are those who convert as a result of their own personal spiritual journey. Many are not married or are married to a non-Jew, but others may have a Jewish spouse. If so, they may have chosen a specifically Jewish spouse because of their interest in Judaism. One woman from a non-Jewish background now active in Temple Shalom in Brisbane, Australia, where I served as a student rabbi, told me that she had always wanted to become Jewish: that was the reason that she searched for a Jewish husband Down Under, where Jewish men are pretty rare.

Ideological converts seek out Jewish spouses as a consequence of their deep interest in Judaism, whereas accommodationist converts become involved in Judaism as a consequence of their Jewish spouse. There are ambivalent converts, who are careful not to become too involved, perhaps because of residual loyalty to the religion that they were raised with. There are also religious-switching spouses who may alternatively become enthusiastic about Judaism, then Christianity, and then Judaism once more. I have congregants in my current congregation who converted to Judaism only to return to their original faith several years later, when the children were growing up, and then reverted to Judaism after the children left home. They were torn by conflicting loyalties—to their spouses, to their parents, to their children.

When the Jewish community discusses conversion as a solution to the intermarriage problem, they are aluding to the accommodationist converts, those who could be convinced to convert for the sake of their spouse and family. Most Jewish leaders would have preferred it if those non-Jews marrying Jews would have converted to Judaism before marriage, regardless of the degree of their commitment. The problem was that, as the intermarriage rate increased, the percentage of those converting either before or after marriage declined. Thus the number of intermarried families skyrocketed. There were rabbis who were reluctant to convert people whose primary motivation was marriage to a Jew, but most would have been happy to help create Jewish families and Jewish homes. Intermarried couples, on the other hand, created a much more ambiguous situation, the consequences of which are still being debated.

While most rabbis prefer to meet face to face with candidates for conversion, there are online possibilities as well. Rabbi Celso Cukierkorn of Miami, Florida runs a Web site, convertingtojudaism.com, which includes everything that a person would need to study for conversion to Judaism. The Web site contains an online curriculum divided into eight units, each of which focuses on a different aspect of Jewish faith and practice. Cukierkorn told the *New York Times* that modern technology provides him with "a wonderful way to help people who cannot find a rabbi to convert them or who lives [*sic*] in places where they don't have a rabbi or their schedule will not allow them to convert." While he estimates the online curriculum requires between 80 and 120 hours of study, the rabbi looks to see "how they feel and what's inside them" rather than how much they know.[24] Cukierkorn told me that there is a dire necessity for Web sites such as his because "all of the doors are open for Jews to leave Judaism, but few doors are open for people to enter."[25]

In an increasingly pluralistic society, there are people coming to Judaism from an astonishing variety of backgrounds. Some convert to Judaism after a long spiritual search. They may have experimented with a number of different religions before they discover Judaism. Many had put a great deal of spiritual energy into their religious lives, and they bring that energy with

FIGURE 4.2. Adult bat mitzvah ceremony held at Temple B'nai Israel in Albany, Georgia with Florence Prisant (holding the Torah), Peggy Posnick, Gail Greenfield, Rachelle Bitterman, and Karen Stiller, May 31, 2008. Posnick (*fourth from right*) has demonstrated tremendous dedication to her adopted faith over many decades. Photo Dana Evan Kaplan. *Courtesy of the author*

them after their conversion. Others are converting because they have married a Jewish spouse. Despite the fact that there is less pressure on them today to convert, they still feel that it is important that everyone in the family has the same religion. Others are married to a Jew for years and sometimes decades and eventually decide on their own to formalize the religious commitment they've experienced over time.

While the numbers of people converting to Judaism are relatively small compared to the numbers of those intermarrying, the dedication that some converts bring to Jewish life has had a dramatic impact on many synagogues. Peggy Posnick is one longtime convert to Judaism who has made a tremendous contribution to her congregation. For the past ten years, she has played a central role in Temple B'nai Israel, the synagogue in Albany, Georgia where I have served since 2001. Posnick told me that she knew from a young age that she did not want to be in an intermarriage. "When I was growing up in the small town of Doerun, Georgia, it was Baptist and Methodist, and they were always fighting with each other. Local people thought that a mixed marriage was a Methodist and a Baptist and that that was a terrible thing." Later, when she was studying at Grady Memorial Hospital School of Nursing in Atlanta, she met her husband, Donald, who was then a medical student at Emory. He was Jewish. She resolved to convert to Judaism so that there would not be two religions in the home. "I thought back to all the families who were fighting in my hometown where I was brought up, and I thought, "Well, I'm not having that in my family."[26] Donald and Peggy married in 1949, and Peggy converted to Judaism with Rabbi Joseph Narot at Temple Israel in Miami in 1953. "We had already decided to start a family and I didn't want my children to be brought up without a Jewish mother." Posnick thought that her decision was logical and was surprised when her friends tried to discourage her. "When I was contemplating marrying Donald, the girls all got together and said that I shouldn't do it; he's Jewish and I don't know what I'm doing." She had never even met a Jewish person before Donald, and she was rather shocked by the attitude of her girlfriends. "I didn't think that they [Jewish people] were different and, when they told me that I shouldn't marry a Jewish guy, I didn't know what they were talking about. I just knew that I loved him."

Donald never pressured her to convert. Rather, it was Peggy who decided that she wanted to embrace Judaism. At that time, Temple Israel was classical Reform, and Rabbi Narot required very little in the way of preparation for conversion. He must have immediately seen her enthusiasm, and, after a brief introduction to Reform Judaism, he readily agreed to officiate at her conversion ceremony. Even without much formal indoctrination, Posnick learned a great deal from her mother-in-law, the women in the sisterhood as well as through her own explorations. She built up a deep commitment to Judaism that has lasted for more than fifty years. "I have a strong belief in God. Judaism means everything to me. . . . I really don't know how to put it into words." When I pressed her for additional details, she wrote me that "Judaism was so much a part of me I could not think of living any other life. It has given me peace and happiness and, above all, a love of my God."[27]

Whereas Posnick had no Jewish family background, many of those approaching rabbis with requests to convert have Jewish fathers. They may have even been raised as Jews, only to find out that their Jewish status was not accepted by the more traditional elements of the community. Sarah Zarrow was sent to Hebrew School and became a bat mitzvah, but was not hala-chically Jewish because her mother had never converted. Later, as an adult, she began to study for conversion with Rabbi Jeremy Kalmanofsky of Con-gregation Ansche Chesed on the Upper West Side of Manhattan. "I thought the day would come, I'd dunk, and I wouldn't feel anything. But I also knew somewhere that it wasn't like an exam, that it was more of a beginning than an ending. But the mikveh was really cool. I was terrified that I'd do some-thing wrong and that I'd nullify things. . . . It felt really good and when I came out and said the Shema, I started to cry."[28]

There are many inspirational stories of Jews who have chosen to convert and have made a significant contribution to their congregations and Ameri-can Judaism as a whole. However, the majority of non-Jews marrying Jews did not convert to Judaism either before or after marriage and the Jewish community has had to develop strategies to respond to the impending de-mographic crisis.

The Origins of Reform Outreach

The 1977 Bergman essay generated a great deal of concern for the future of the Jewish community in the United States. Most rabbis and Jewish commu-nal leaders condemned those who intermarried. They lacked commitment to the community, those leaders said, and they were apathetic toward their Judaism. Some rabbis even devoted High Holy Day sermons to attacks on those who intermarried, the majority of whom were men in their twenties and thirties.

It was the Reform movement that pioneered a new approach to the prob-lem of rising intermarriage rates. In December 1978, Rabbi Alexander M. Schindler called for a sustained effort to reach out to the unaffiliated, par-ticularly the intermarried. Schindler, president of the UAHC (since renamed the Union for Reform Judaism, URJ), spoke passionately about the crisis developing. "I begin with the recognition of a reality: the tide of intermar-riage is running against us. The statistics on the subject confirm what our own experience teaches us: intermarriage is on the rise. . . . We may deplore it, we may lament it, we may struggle against it, but these are the facts."[29]

Schindler urged the UAHC Board of Trustees to work with him to for-mulate an effective counterstrategy. "We must deal with this threatening re-ality. Dealing with it does not, however, mean that we must learn to accept it. It does not mean that we should prepare to sit shivah for the American Jewish community. On the contrary, facing and dealing with reality means confronting it, coming to grips with it, and determining to reshape it." Schindler recommended a three-pronged strategy. If possible, congregations should encourage the non-Jewish spouse in an interfaith marriage to convert to Judaism. The majority of the non-Jewish spouses were women. In 1978, according to Schindler, two-thirds of Jewish-Gentile intermarriages consisted of a Jewish man and a non-Jewish woman. About one-quarter of those women converted to Judaism either before or during their marriage. However, among the third of intermarriages that involved a Jewish woman and a non-Jewish man, only a tiny percentage of the men converted.

Schindler believed that it was possible to encourage larger numbers of both men and women to convert to Judaism. Such converts should be called Jews by choice, rather than converts, since the latter term was perceived to carry negative connotations; the term *Jew by choice*, on the other hand, was positive and affirming. Unfortunately, in my view, the new term had more problems than the original. It does not reflect the basic fact that the person is changing religions and thus appeared to be a deliberate euphemism. This emphasized rather than eliminated the supposedly negative implications of the original term. Also, all American Jews are Jews by choice since in contemporary society it is a simple matter to drop all Jewish affiliations. Because of these problems, the term *Jew by choice* has partially fallen out of favor and many have returned to the original terms *convert* and *conversion*.

Nevertheless, Schindler had a point—many Jews swallowed hard when they said the word *convert*. He bluntly revealed the well-known social reality: converts were greeted coldly; others were forced to listen to angry or intolerant remarks. The Jewish community needed to become more sensitive to Jews by choice and potential Jews by choice. "We often alienate them. We question their motivations (since only a mad man would choose to be a Jew, the convert is either neurotic or hypocritical). We think them less Jewish (ignoring that they often know more about Judaism than born Jews). Unto the end of their days, we refer to them as converts."

Schindler argued that it would not be enough to just focus on trying to increase the numbers of converts to Judaism. Rather, there had to be a concerted effort to make intermarried couples feel welcome in the synagogue, even if the non-Jewish partner did not convert. This was a revolutionary change, because up to that point marrying a non-Jew was considered a violation of communal norms and bringing a non-Jewish spouse to the synagogue was like rubbing salt in the wounds of the Jewish community. In fact, there were rabbis who cited the story from the book of Numbers about how Phinehas dealt with an Israelite who brought his paramour directly to Moses and the elders at the entrance of the Tent of Assembly, thereby sinning in public:

> Behold! A man of the Children of Israel came and brought a Midianite woman near to his brothers in the sight of Moses and in the sight of the entire assembly of the Children of Israel; and they were weeping at the entrance of the Tent of Meeting. Phinehas son of Elazar son of Aaron the Kohen saw, and he stood up from amid the assembly and took a spear in his hand. He followed the Israelite man into the tent and pierced them both, the Israelite man and the woman into her stomach — and the plague was halted from upon the Children of Israel.[30]

This was a horrible image, and even many who opposed intermarriage assiduously avoided referring to it. There were other negative images that came to mind in regard to intermarriage, and Schindler understood that this made it harder to attract intermarried couples.

Schindler hoped to encourage "Jewish drift"—where mixed-marriage couples would gravitate toward the Jewish community and the Jewish religion. One study found that almost half the non-Jewish husbands of Jewish women described themselves as Jews, despite not having formally converted to Judaism. Schindler hoped to encourage this trend, not only by welcoming intermarried Jews and their marriage partners into the Jewish community but also by inviting them to actively participate in religious activities in the synagogue. He warned that it would not be easy to bring in many of these Jews married to non-Jews. "They may feel guilty, they may feel resentful, they are almost sure to feel some confusion and ambivalence toward active involvement in the community. They may feel inhibited out of a sense of regard for their partner's sensibilities or out of embarrassment in the face of a community they think will be hostile to their partners."

The most controversial aspect of Schindler's proposal was that outreach should include unchurched gentiles, people who may have been raised as Christians or in another religion but had become alienated from it. His concept of outreach would also include people who had been raised without any formal ties to a religious community. "I believe that the time has come for the Reform movement—and others, if they are so disposed—to launch a carefully conceived outreach program aimed at all Americans who are un-churched and who are seeking religious meaning." Schindler's position re-versed two thousand years of Jewish nonproselytization policy. Because it was so revolutionary, the press focused their attention on Schindler's advo-cacy of active proselytization of non-Jews and paid relatively little attention to his overall call for outreach.

Traditionalists howled, complaining that Schindler was single-handedly repudiating the collective wisdom of the sages. Schindler defended his pro-posal, pointing out that American society had changed and that people in the late 1970s had much more of a personal choice in religious matters than did their parents. Despite all the recriminations, very little came of Schindler's idea to proselytize unchurched gentiles. Those American Jews who remained interested in Judaism were happy to share their religious customs with any-one who came to them, but they were uncomfortable about the idea of preaching to complete strangers who had not shown any interest in convert-ing. With very few exceptions, American Jews lacked the sense of religious mission necessary to galvanize such a campaign.

On the very last two pages of *The Sacred Canopy*, religious studies theorist Peter L. Berger cites Schindler's speech as a clear indication that "even in a tradition as foreign to the spirit of pluralism as the Jewish one, the logic of the market imposes itself at the point where the 'social engineering' of subcultural defensiveness becomes too difficult." Berger explains that "the fundamental option between resistance and accommodation must be faced by Judaism, particularly in America, in terms that are not too drastically different from those in which it is faced by the Christian churches." Berger says that the option is "between defensively maintaining a Jewish subculture (which may be defined in primarily religious or primarily national terms) and playing the pluralistic game along with everyone else."[31] As intermar-riage rates went up, Schindler decided that the Reform movement needed to do the latter.

The Patrilineal Descent Resolution

While the Reconstructionist movement long favored liberalizing the defini-tion of who was a Jew, the more traditional movements remained committed to the halachic standard. Although the Hebrew Bible defines Jewish identity in patrilineal terms, the Mishnah states that the offspring of a Jewish mother and a non-Jewish father is recognized as a Jew, while the offspring of a non-Jewish mother and a Jewish father is considered a non-Jew. While historians have attempted to explain why the sages reversed what appears to have been a long-standing precedent, the fact remains that the Talmudic position became normative in the halacha. Orthodox groups in particular were insistent that no change could be made. Redefining who was a Jew, they argued, would split the Jewish people into two groups that could no longer marry each other. Their vociferous objection to the patrilineal descent resolution was hyperbole to some degree, because the Orthodox did not accept Reform or Reconstructionist conversion either—even if these liberal movements had insisted on full conversion, it really would not have made any difference.

The more liberal American movements had always tried to be flexible. The Reform movement had long accepted the children of Jewish fathers and non-Jewish mothers into religious school. The child would be confirmed with the rest of their class, and this was regarded as in lieu of conversion.[32] But the numbers involved were relatively small, and there didn't seem to be any need to formalize a policy regarding the children of Jewish fathers and gentile mothers. But, by the early 1980s, the numbers involved had increased many times over, and the Reform movement felt that a more explicit policy would be helpful.

Schindler decided that the Reform movement needed to act, and he urged his fellow rabbis to pass a resolution accepting patrilineal children as Jewish. On March 15, 1983, the CCAR passed a resolution accepting patrilineal descent. "The Status of Children of Mixed Marriages" stated that its purpose was "to establish the Jewish status of the children of mixed marriages in the Reform Jewish community of North America." The rabbis wrote that "we face, today, an unprecedented situation due to the changed conditions in which decisions concerning the status of the child of a mixed marriage are to be made."[33]

They argued that it could no longer be assumed that the child of a Jewish mother will be Jewish or that the child of a non-Jewish mother will not be. Therefore, it seemed logical to them to declare that the same requirements should be applied to establish the status of a child of a mixed marriage, whether the mother or the father was the Jewish partner. They declared that "the child of one Jewish parent is under the presumption of Jewish descent. This presumption of the Jewish status of the offspring of any mixed marriage is to be established through appropriate and timely public and formal acts of identification with the Jewish faith and people."

What this meant was that, if a child was born of either a Jewish father or a Jewish mother, and raised Jewish, that child would be regarded by the Reform movement as Jewish. Children were, however, expected to participate in the various Jewish life cycle ceremonies that usually mark the stages of Jewish persons. Someone who had a Jewish parent (even a Jewish mother), but had not been raised as Jewish and had not had any public religious acts of identification such as a Jewish baby-naming ceremony, a bat or bar mitzvah, or a Jewish confirmation service could theoretically be regarded as a non-Jew despite matrilineal descent. Under such circumstances, the Reform movement would be defining Jewish identity more strictly than even the Orthodox.

The CCAR resolution on patrilineal descent did even more than Schindler's call for outreach in redefining Jewish identity. Parents of different religions could now raise their children as Jewish, even if the mother was not Jewish and did not want to convert. This allowed the Reform movement to regard the many children of Jewish fathers and non-Jewish mothers as Jewish, something that would not have been possible under the old definitions. Jewish identity was now something one chose rather than something that simply was. Children with one Jewish parent were choosing to identify themselves as Jewish. They were being asked to voluntarily undergo significant religious acts of identification as a way of showing their commitment to Judaism and to the Jewish people. While Jewish children had always been asked to prepare for their bat and bar mitzvahs, their Jewishness was never contingent upon successful completion of that ceremony or any other. The emphasis had now shifted from birth to conscious choice.

Not surprisingly, conversion rates began to fall. Some non-Jewish mothers had converted out of sincere belief, but many others had become Jewish in order to please their spouse or the spouse's parents. This type of "Jew by choice" no longer had to convert in order for her children to be raised Jewish. Nevertheless, it would be erroneous to attribute the entire decline in conversion rates solely to the patrilineal descent resolution. There was a significant shift in attitudes during the 1970s and into the 1980s, which had a tremendous impact on the rates of conversion. American society began to emphasize that each person could and should choose the spiritual path she found most meaningful and comfortable.

Converting to any religion should only be done if that was what the person really wanted to do. Otherwise, converting would be insincere and negate one's own spiritual identity. Pursuing individual religious interests became much more popular for each spouse, rather than conforming to a single model for the entire family. If one spouse felt strongly about religion, the other might accommodate by allowing the children to be raised in that faith. The other would nevertheless be more likely to remain connected to the faith of their birth or the religion they had chosen, rather than simply following husband or wife. Thus the patrilineal descent resolution probably came along at the right time.

There was a small number of Reform rabbis who opposed the patrilineal descent resolution, many of whom were socially and religiously more conservative than the movement as a whole. They were accorded a respectful hearing during various deliberations at the CCAR conferences when the subject was discussed, but the issue affected too many people for their arguments to be accepted as policy, even if some others may have agreed with them in theory. If the Orthodox rabbinate had agreed to accept the validity of Reform conversions, then perhaps a case could have been made that the patrilineal descent resolution was unnecessarily harming the relationship with the Orthodox and undermining mutual recognition of each other's conversions. Since the Orthodox rejected the validity of Reform conversion, the vast majority of the Reform movement felt they had no choice but to implement a daring but necessary innovation.

The patrilineal descent resolution was passed and became the official policy for the entire Reform movement in the United States. Progressive, Liberal, or Reform movements in other parts of the world were free to make their own religious policies, and most chose to stick with the traditional definition of Jewish identity. In the United States, the patrilineal descent resolution reaffirmed the Jewish identity of thousands or possibly tens of thousands of children in mixed-marriage families and was widely seen as a tremendous success.

In 1996, the CCAR created an eleven-member task force to interpret and develop guidelines for the successful implementation of the patrilineal descent policy. The task force recommended that the resolution be referred to as "equilineal descent" or simply "Jewish descent" rather than patrilineal descent, since the resolution accepted descent from either the mother or the father. But, aside from complaints about the name of the resolution and its convoluted wording, there was widespread acceptance of the policy itself. As Dru Greenwood, then director of outreach for the UAHC put it, patrilineal descent is "totally accepted" by most Reform congregants.[34]

While the Conservative movement has not officially accepted patrilineal descent, many (including myself) believe that their doing so is inevitable. Conservative congregations face the same social pressures that Reform and Reconstructionist synagogues do. As intermarriage grows increasingly socially acceptable, even traditionally minded Jews will intermarry. Many of their children will not be halachically Jewish if the mother is not Jewish. If the Conservative movement refuses to accept their children as Jewish, then they will very likely join a Reform or Reconstructionist congregation. The Conservative movement is acutely aware of the competitive forces they face. For this reason, the movement is moving as quickly as possible to respond within its parameters.

In December 2005, Rabbi Jerome Epstein, executive vice president of the United Synagogue, announced a *kiruv* (ingathering) initiative at the Boston biennial to make intermarried families feel welcome in Conservative synagogues, schools, and other institutions. Nevertheless, Epstein emphasized that the Conservative movement felt that outreach to intermarried families was only "a vital first step." The ultimate goal must be to inspire the intermarried non-Jew "to choose Judaism out of conviction that Jewish living will enrich their lives."[35] In an op-ed in the *Forward*, Reform Rabbis David Ellenson and Kerry Olitzky disagreed. They argued that it was important to distinguish between outreach and efforts to convert. "To focus on conversion alone as a panacea to the challenge of interfaith marriage and Jewish continuity is mistaken. Our real task is to create a community of meaning worth joining. No amount of pressure or manipulation can force this process along." Ellenson and Olitzky pointed out that leaders and organizations had "become so focused on whether or not the community should open its doors to those who have intermarried that we have forgotten that people make decisions based on what they deem best for themselves and their families, rather than on what they regard as best for a community." For these individuals , "appeals to continuity and survival will not provide decisive grounds for joining the Jewish community."[36] Rather, they argued, synagogues had to demonstrate how living a Jewish life could add meaning to people's lives and the lives of their children. And then, if they were successfully brought into the community, "we had better make sure that our institutions provide meaningful and enjoyable experiences for them."[37]

One of the more successful institutions the Conservative movement has built is the Solomon Schechter Day School system. Many intermarried couples who did not necessarily plan on being involved in Judaism found that their local Schechter would make an ideal school for their child or children. They therefore now had a concrete reason for wanting to be a part of the Jewish people. Much of this has to do with the perception that urban public schools are not suitable for middle-class white children and the parents therefore are looking for a private school alternative. It is only then that they begin to consider a Jewish day school. The problem is that since the Conservative movement does not accept patrilineal descent, such children are admitted "provisionally," on the condition that they convert before their thirteenth birthday.

Some parents are told that their children would be admitted as long as they kept the child's patrilineal status quiet. A number of critics called this policy hypocritical, and one Jewish educator who refused to be identified said the current policy promoted a "culture of dishonesty" that made patrilineal children (my term) "into closeted Jews." The Schechter system is working on changing their bylaws to admit children of non-Jewish mothers. This is already done by most of the seventy-six Schechter schools around the United States and Canada. They do so quietly in order to avoid appearing to repudiate the Conservative movement's position that only matrilineal descent or conversion makes one a Jew. Elaine Cohen, United Synagogue's consultant to the Schechter schools, said that the new bylaw proposal would be "reframing current policy in more inclusive language."[38] Now that the Conservative movement has made substantive moves toward changing their policies toward gays and lesbians, there is every reason to believe that they will soon reform their position on patrilineal descent. Most of those in the Conservative movement that I have spoken with disagree with me.

In recent years, many "half-Jewish" individuals have begun to talk of their experiences growing up, frequently caught between their Jewish and Christian families and identities. The patrilineal descent resolution provided a viable solution for some couples who felt comfortable with their personal religious differences but wanted to raise their children with a singular religious faith. It also proved a godsend for Jews with strong ethnic identities who felt attracted to and wanted to marry gentile partners.

Nevertheless the pluralistic nature of American society has increased acceptance of interfaith marriage. In such households, it becomes increasingly likely that children will develop multiple identities rather than committing to a single religious or ethnic self-definition. The patrilineal descent resolution would have little meaning for many such families and would not be helpful in defining the children as Jewish in such cases.

Will There Be Two Separate Jewish Peoples?

Pessimists warned that there were now two definitions of who was a Jew. As a consequence, there would soon be two groups of Jews who would not be able to marry one another and would basically constitute two separate Jewish peoples. In 1985, Modern Orthodox rabbi Irving (Yitz) Greenberg wrote an influential essay for CLAL: The National Jewish Center for Learning and Leadership titled "Will There Be One Jewish People By The Year 2000?"[39] Greenberg was not the first to point out that the American Jewish community was rapidly heading toward a schism, but his warning was the best publicized and probably carried the most weight.[40]

The United Jewish Appeal had long run advertisements with the slogan "We Are One." Over the course of many hundreds of years, the Jews were one people who had to face many severe challenges together. Despite obvious differences between the different factions in recent times, virtually everyone in the American Jewish community felt that this slogan expressed how they felt. Greenberg pointed out that over the previous twenty years there had been a decisive challenge to this truth. "The pattern of current demographic change and negative social interaction is leading to grim consequences." Greenberg warned that if sociological forces were left unchecked, "the Jewish people will split apart into two, mutually divided, hostile groups who are unable or unwilling to marry each other."

Greenberg predicted that "by the turn of the century, there will be between three-quarters of a million and a million people whose Jewishness is contested or whose marriageability is denied by a large group of other Jews." He complained that "at this moment, there is no brainstorming, let alone serious dialogue, between the movements to deal with the problem." He recommended that the American Jewish community establish a systematic religious dialogue among the Jewish religious denominations that could discuss the crisis facing the Jewish community and work toward solutions. Greenberg felt that too many Jews on both sides were not upset with the increasing polarization because they were convinced that their group would thrive and the other side would disappear, but, he warned, "We need each other." Even if it turned out that the extreme Reform or the extreme Orthodox managed to survive at the expense of the other side, the Jewish people as a whole would be weakened tremendously.

Greenberg warned that if each of the movements continued to go its own way, disaster would result. Yet a feeling of fear of moderation pervaded each of the denominations. While each movement had much to learn from the other movements, moderates within each camp respectively were afraid to take policy stands supporting Jewish unity, if taking such positions would require some sacrifice on the part of their own denomination. For example, Reform rabbis suffer a professional penalty for opposing intermarriage (i.e., many Reform rabbis report having trouble finding desirable employment if they refuse to officiate at intermarriages), as would Orthodox rabbis who might favor the inclusion of liberal rabbis in joint conversion courts.

Greenberg again warned that "unless all Jews stand up for unity, we may be heading for a fundamental schism. Only spotlighting the forces of divisiveness, generating strong internal pressures within each movement to take other groups into account and increased support for active dialogue and joint activity can arrest this slide toward alienation and separation."[41] He sponsored a symposium the following year, 1986, dealing with the question "Will There Be One Jewish People by the Year 2000?" Even before the conference started, there were signs that the answer to the question was clear. As a condition for attending, the Orthodox insisted that speakers not stand on the platform at the same time because they did not want to appear to give legitimacy to the non-Orthodox leaders.

More recently, Greenberg repeated his warning that religious disagreements should not be allowed to lead to a permanent split within the Jewish people. Lag B'Omer, best known as a "warm, fuzzy semiholiday with a nature-loving theme," was in the Talmud actually "a devastating reminder of a catastrophe caused by Jews' divisiveness." Over a short period of time, the Talmud recalls, tens of thousands of Rabbi Akiva's students died because "they did not treat each other with respect." The Jews rebelled against Rome but spent as much time fighting each other as they did the Romans. Three separate revolts were all crushed, and, as a direct result, the Jews spent more than eighteen hundred years in exile. "Today, Jewry seems headed for a repeat of the disaster." Greenberg argued that there was a fundamental lack of respect and a complete unwillingness to work together interdenominationally, even for the purpose of preserving Jewish unity.

Rabbi Norman Lamm, the then president and current chancellor of Yeshiva University, sounded a hopeful note when he publicly advocated the creation of a kind of joint beit din to handle issues of personal identity. Much later, he told me, "If a major, major, major part of the Jewish community slips into assimilation and disappears, it would be an incredible tragedy." Lamm wanted to do everything that he could to help, "which is why I was one of the Orthodox rabbis who was open to working with non-Orthodox groups without threatening any of our own integrity. I could not see ourselves turning our backs on the rest of the community. I think we owe it to klal Israel to try to keep everyone in the fold."[42] Lamm recalled that the Israeli government was grappling with how to handle the fact that the Israeli chief rabbinate was not accepting Reform converts who had converted in America. "Israeli Prime Minister Yitzchak Shamir called me about this and said 'what can you do for us?' I said I'll try. The truth is that the whole problem was more political than real, because there were not that many Reform converts who wanted to go on aliyah. So it affected a small handful of people, but there were principles involved."[43]

Lamm obviously had to tread delicately. "I could not make an actual halachic beit din with non-Orthodox rabbis. First of all, it would not sell, and second, it wouldn't even make sense. How can you be a judge when you don't accept the law?" Instead, he decided to recommend a bicameral arrangement in which a "mixed commission" of Orthodox and non-Orthodox rabbis would interview candidates for conversion and decide whether he had integrity and really wanted to be a Jew. If they decided that the candidate had integrity , then she "would appear before an Orthodox beit din—mostly a Modern Orthodox beit din—with the understanding that they would decide according to the Shulchan Aruch, which would not go to extremes or be exclusionary."[44] Rabbi Joseph Glaser, the executive vice president of the CCAR, accepted the proposal. Lamm told me that he got the impression that the Reform movement was split over his proposal, but that Glaser's support helped to ensure their cooperation.

"This was all done quietly, but of course it got out after a while," Lamm explained. Rabbi Ismar Schorsch, the chancellor of the Jewish Theological Seminary, heard about the negotiations and decided that he wanted to be involved as well. "So we seemed to have it all tied up nicely and it would have worked out, but a two-pronged attack was aimed at the program, one by the right and one by the left." Eventually Lamm had to abandon the plan. "I still think it was a good idea if I had support, at least from those on the left who are closer to us in our desire to solve the problem, and those on the right who were closer to us in abiding by the halacha, we could have managed it.

But you have very powerful groups that are opposed to it both on the right and the left, which is the ultimate destiny of those in the middle."

Despite his tireless work to find middle ground, Lamm worried that the unilateral steps being taken by the Reform movement were creating hundreds of thousands of people who regarded themselves as Jewish but were not according to the standards of halacha. Because of this, he felt that the patrilineal descent resolution was "the single most irresponsible act in contemporary Jewish history."[45] His views on a joint beit din were equally unlikely to please the left. He suggested that Reform and Reconstructionist rabbis could tell couples that the marriage ceremonies that they performed were not according to the time-honored traditions of Moses and the people of Israel. This would have constituted a declaration that these liberal Jewish marriages were nonhalachic. Therefore, if the marriage ended in divorce, it would be clear that no get would be required, which might have prevented the problem of thousands of the children of subsequent marriages being declared mamzerim. This might have solved a halachic problem but, in the eyes of the liberals, it would have delegitimized the non-Orthodox religious movements.

Despite his vehement opposition to patrilineal descent, he wanted to avoid any formal response that would officially make all those outside Orthodox circles *sofek mamzerim*: "Agudas ha-Rabbanim wanted to show how upset it was with the secular and Reform groups so they wanted to have a commission to establish the *yichus* [ancestry] for every Jew who wanted to marry according to Orthodox law." Lamm was horrified. "I quickly called up the chairman at the time and I said absolutely not. You may not do this, you must not do this, because I would rather have people slip through the cracks who are mamzerim than to have a whole part of the community that would be off bounds." That would have formalized the split, and he did not want that to happen. "We don't have the moral right to accelerate the deep, deep divisions that exist."[46]

There was also a possibility that the State of Israel might amend the Law of Return, the Israeli law passed by the Knesset in 1950 that guaranteed automatic Israeli citizenship to any Jew or anyone with Jewish ancestry who wanted to immigrate. The law said that anyone who had a Jewish mother or had converted to Judaism was regarded as a Jew. Orthodox and particularly haredi political parties in Israel made a number of unsuccessful attempts to amend the Law of Return to add that the conversion must be done "according to halacha." To this day, the Israeli chief rabbinate continues to lobby for such a change and has not shown any interest in compromise. Rabbi Shlomo Amar, Israeli Sephardic chief rabbi, recently told Reshet Bet Radio in Israel that "a conversion is explicitly and clearly a halachic act—not a political or a social one. Conversion is halachic. And when it is not halachic, it's not a conversion."[47]

Adding the words "according to halacha" would have allowed them to exclude all non-Orthodox conversions and therefore constituted a threat to the legitimacy of the Reform and Conservative movements in America and throughout the world. If Israel refused to accept those converted by Reform and Conservative rabbis, then the Israeli government was effectively denying the legitimacy of the Judaism of millions of American Jews. The increasing amount of intermarriage has made the potential for damage much greater. When the first of these attempts to change the Law of Return was made decades ago, virtually all American Jews were still halachically Jewish. By the early years of the twenty-first century, a substantial and growing percentage are not. The threat that the Law of Return might be amended started out primarily as a symbolic threat, but has now become a practical concern of the utmost importance. Years earlier, Greenberg had predicted that there would be two separate Jewish peoples by the year 2000. Did he feel that his prediction had come true? "Yes and no. It depends on what you want to emphasize. A lot of damage has been done and a lot of ties have been cut." Whereas a generation ago, most Reform Jews had Orthodox relatives and most Orthodox Jews had Reform relatives, now "there are four degrees of separation between most of the people on the two sides." The Orthodox and the non-Orthodox live in virtually separate religious worlds. As a consequence, there is "a tremendous psychological barrier that has been built." On the other hand, "there has not been a formal break, no formal declaration that the two groups are completely separate peoples. They have not taken the final step, which is where they would literally treat you like a foreign person." Greenberg tries to end on an optimistic note. "In the ancient kingdom of Israel and kingdom of Judah, they fought wars against each other. We obviously haven't gotten that far yet."[48]

Attempting to Develop a Unified Conversion Program

As the differences between the Orthodox and the non-Orthodox widened in the 1970s, the fear grew that there would be two types of converts and that non-Orthodox converts would not be recognized as Jews by the Orthodox. Numerous rabbis from both camps tried to devise various plans to avoid this situation, since there was still hope that the entire Jewish community could remain united, at least on the basic question of who is a Jew. This turned out to be an overly optimistic expectation.

The most sophisticated and long-lasting attempt to create a communal conversion program that would be acceptable to all was in Denver, Colorado. This was not a surprising location for such a daring effort. Denver had one of the highest intermarriage rates in the country, according to some estimates exceeding 70 percent at a time that the more conservative East Coast cities had rates of around 30 percent. There was a significant Orthodox presence in Denver, but much of it was relatively liberal. In fact, the largest Orthodox synagogue in the city preferred to call itself "traditional." They hired Orthodox rabbis and had men and women sitting separately, but they had no mechitza, the physical barrier between the men's section and the women's section that is required in a strictly Orthodox worship service.

For these and other reasons, Denver became the site of the most extensive experiment in interdenominational cooperation. In 1978, a number of Denver-area rabbis decided to form a joint board to supervise the conversion process. This board organized a study program in which everyone participated, but then delegated authority to an Orthodox beit din, three Orthodox rabbis who performed the actual conversion rites. The goal was to create a system that could convert individuals in a way that would make them and their children "kosher" in the eyes of almost all Jewish religious authorities. The difficulties of creating such a program were immense. Orthodox Judaism requires a convert to accept *kabbalat mitvzot*, the yoke of the commandments. While this is not defined in the Talmudic literature, most Orthodox rabbis interpreted this as meaning that the convert must believe in Orthodox Judaism and commit themselves, at least in principle, to observing all the commandments. Because of this problem, none of the haredi rabbis in Denver would participate, but three rabbis with Orthodox ordination—Daniel Goldberger, Jerome Lipsitz, and Stanley Wagner—agreed to participate in the joint conversion program. Each rabbi could send his conversion candidates to the joint conversion program. If he preferred, or if the candidate requested it, each rabbi could still do his own conversions independently.

Generally, a perspective convert would approach a rabbi of a specific synagogue. In most cases, such individuals would gravitate to a rabbi they liked or the synagogue with the warmest services or the institution where their partner's family belonged. Denominational ideology usually played only a small role in such decisions. The emphasis was on integrating new Jews into the Jewish community. As Rabbi Stanley Wagner told me, "the point was that there were no Reform, Conservative or Orthodox candidates." Perspective converts had to agree to join a synagogue, but they would do so after the conversion. There was no specification as to which type of synagogue to join.

Each perspective convert would study in a twenty-week basic Judaism course that was sponsored by the Denver Jewish community. Rabbis and other lecturers from different perspectives would teach during the course of the program. There would be educational and social programming as well, and the sponsoring rabbi would continue to meet with the candidate on a regular basis. A panel of Reform, Conservative, and Orthodox rabbis would convene with the candidate at the end of the program to evaluate his suitability for conversion to Judaism. If the panel approved the candidate, he would then appear before a beit din consisting of three Orthodox rabbis. All male converts were to be circumcised and, if they were already circumcised, they would undergo a hatafat dam brit. All converts would then go to the mikveh for a ritual immersion. The Orthodox rabbis would then sign a conversion certificate, which they hoped would be recognized by Orthodox as well as non-Orthodox authorities.

The biggest concession that the non-Orthodox rabbis agreed to was that they would not actually be qualified to serve on the beit din certifying the conversion itself. The beit din present at the actual conversion ceremony would consist of three Orthodox rabbis. This was necessary because virtually every Orthodox rabbi in the country would only accept a convert if the conversion certificate indicated that only Orthodox rabbis had supervised the conversion. The Orthodox rabbis accepted extensive Reform and Conservative participation in the program, and the non-Orthodox rabbis agreed to let the Orthodox handle the actual conversion ceremony. The Orthodox rabbis participating in the joint conversion program were concerned about how the Orthodox colleagues elsewhere might react. As a result, they decided to avoid publicizing their involvement. This created, as Goldberger put it, a great deal of "guilt, guilt, guilt." He expressed "guilt about acting apart from the [Orthodox] movement" and "doing something that wouldn't be approved of" by the Orthodox rabbinic establishment. Wagner added, "I felt like a person walking the middle line of the highway. You could get hit by a car going in either direction."[49]

The continuation of the joint conversion program was dependent upon a delicate balance. Each of the rabbis had to meet their colleagues' minimal requirements without compromising their own beliefs and values. They also wanted to avoid anything that would jeopardize their standing in their own denominational hierarchy. When the CCAR adopted the patrilineal descent resolution on March 15, 1983, tthe Orthodox rabbis in Denver then came under tremendous pressure to end their association with their Reform colleagues in their joint endeavor. To make matters worse, Denver was chosen by the UAHC as a pilot community for their new outreach program. On June 17, 1983, Goldberger announced to the Denver Rabbinical Council that the Orthodox rabbis were withdrawing from the joint conversion program. They had conducted between 175 and 200 conversions over the course of six years.

Denver's joint conversion program had been kept quiet to prevent outsiders from criticizing and pressuring. Most rabbis and Jewish professionals only became aware that there was such a community conversion effort when it was announced that the program was being stopped. Predictably, haredi leaders were outraged that Orthodox rabbis had been willing to participate in the joint beit din. The *Jewish Observer* wrote that "it is time that all Orthodox rabbis recognize that Reform and Conservative are far, far removed from Torah, and that Klal Yisroel is betrayed—not served—when Orthodoxy enters in religious association with them." The haredi publication argued that the Denver Orthodox rabbis "have been party to an outrageous fraud." Wagner, the Orthodox rabbi most closely associated with the Denver joint conversion program, wrote me that "almost anywhere I go, in 'informed' Jewish circles, my name immediately is associated with the plan. So, I am a 'marked man' as a result of it. But, frankly, I wear the banner proudly. My commitment to it has not waned in the twenty years since [the program was stopped]. Indeed, now residing in Israel as I do, I am more convinced than ever of its validity and desirability."[50]

In the aftermath of the breakup of the joint conversion program, any rabbi in Denver who wanted to be regarded as Orthodox had to be cautious in terms of officiating at future conversions. When an Orthodox group built a new mikveh in East Denver, they instituted a no-conversion policy, no matter who the sponsoring rabbi might be. Rabbi Hillel Goldberg explained that "it was felt strongly that Denver needed a tikkun (healing) and that therefore the new mikveh in East Denver should allow no conversions whatsoever. This would ensure that no non-halachic conversion was performed in the mikveh—and that many new people would come to use the mikveh who might have been frightened away by the stigma of possible ritual misuse." Another reason the Orthodox rabbinic authorities decided not to allow any conversions at all was that they wanted a beis din kovu'a vechoshuv [a permanent rabbinic court with extremely learned judges], something that was not practical for a moderately sized Orthodox community such as the one in Denver.[51]

Multidenominational conversion program ideas would be revived over and over because it seemed to be the only possible solution to, as one moderate Orthodox rabbi put it, "the coming cataclysm."[52] Substantial numbers of influential rabbis within the Rabbinical Council of America (RCA) tried to lobby for support for such a plan. But the more "right-wing" rabbis strenuously opposed any such efforts. In November 1990, eleven Roshei Yeshiva at RIETS, YU's rabbinical school, wrote an open letter opposing a joint beit din. Any rabbinical court "which includes even one member who is not an Orthodox Jew . . . is without halakhic authority."[53] Rabbi Aaron Soloveitchik, the brother of the revered Rabbi Joseph B. Soloveitchik, compared the idea of Orthodox cooperation with non-Orthodox religious movements to the sin of the golden calf because it would "mislead ignorant Jewish masses to worship the idol of Reform and Reconstructionist Judaism."[54]

Eventually, the non-Orthodox movements gave up hoping that the Orthodox would reconsider and work together with them. Instead, they have launched a number of joint conversion programs for the Reform, Reconstructionist, and Conservative movements. In Los Angeles, for example, the Sandra Caplan Community Beit Din was established to officiate at conversions accepted by these three non-Orthodox movements. But since the Orthodox were not participating, the main purpose of such a program was undermined. Unlike the Denver joint conversion program, the Southern Californian effort would not produce conversions with any chance of being accepted by the chief rabbinate of the State of Israel, which only recognizes Orthodox conversions. Neither will their conversions be accepted by most Orthodox rabbis in the United States or by most Orthodox synagogues elsewhere in the world. Rabbi Meyer May, president of the Orthodox Rabbinical Council of California, explained that "the basic issue is that a potential convert must accept the mitzvot and Torah as being divine and must accept the written and oral law as the absolute truth." Since non-Orthodox converts do not accept these beliefs, "we would not accept [such] a conversion as valid."[55] The Caplan Community Beit Din has not been successful and plans are underway to reorganize it, but few hold out much hope.

Rabbinic Officiation at Mixed-Marriage Ceremonies

In the days when the community stigmatized those who intermarried, the rabbi played an important role in reinforcing community pressure. He (the rabbi in those days was always a man) would tell the couple what the Jewish community felt—that they were betraying the covenant of Abraham and breaking their parents' hearts. He would scold them for making a rash and immature decision that would certainly bring nothing but sorrow to their families and categorically refuse to play any role in the wedding ceremony itself. There were a small number of Reform rabbis who had been officiating at intermarriage ceremonies for decades, but they catered to a German Jewish elite that had little contact with the Jewish masses. For most American Jews considering intermarrying, there was no one to whom they could turn.

Even as late as the 1960s and early 1970s, there was a consensus that intermarriage was damaging to the Jewish people and therefore could not be condoned. Rabbis who tried to buck this trend were regarded as mavericks and radicals. They might find congregations that would tolerate their "deviant" policies, but they were kept out of mainstream Jewish organizations. For example, when Rabbi Mayer Selekman came in 1971 to Temple Sholom of Broomall, a suburb of Philadelphia, he was not admitted as a member of the Philadelphia Board of Rabbis because he officiated at interfaith weddings.[56] Throughout the 1970s, Rabbi Albert Axelrad, the Hillel rabbi at Brandeis University, was repeatedly attacked because of his willingness to officiate at certain interfaith ceremonies. The critics were not mollified by the fact that Axelrad set stringent conditions that had to be met before he would agree to officiate. Critics of intermarriage felt that the individual rabbi's officiation policy should conform to communal standards.

But, over the next two decades, attitudes toward intermarriage steadily shifted. As attitudes began to change, intermarriage rates began to escalate. In the years following the 1983 patrilineal descent resolution, communal resistance all but crumbled. Most Americans no longer felt that they owed their community blind loyalty. They felt they had the right to seek out happiness wherever they could find it. The Jewish community had no right to demand that they marry a certain person of a certain background just because it might meet communal needs. Rather, what was important were the individual's desires. The non-Jewish spouse was now less likely to convert before marriage. Previously, Jewish people who cared about Jewish survival and continuity would usually ask their beloved to consider converting. This

FIGURE 4.3. Jewish Interfaith Wedding Network officiant Rabbi Gershon Steinberg-Caudill and Father Gerald Caprio performing a Jewish-Catholic ceremony in Los Gatos, California. Such dual officiations, once regarded as scandalous, have now become relatively commonplace. Photo Yehudit Steinberg-Caudill. *Courtesy of Yehudit Steinberg-Caudill, Jewish Interfaith Wedding Network, and David Senk*

was, in many cases, an awkward demand because what was important to many of these Jewish spouses was their ethnic identity. Yet the only way they could perpetuate that ethnic identity was by asking their future spouse to convert to Judaism, a religion most knew little about and practiced only sporadically. Despite this inherent hypocrisy, that was the way things were done. But, by the 1980s, each marriage partner was expected to accept the other as they were. It became far less acceptable to ask one's spouse to convert to his or her religion. Some of the couples agreed to support each other in practicing their respective religions, but many put aside any religious training they had received growing up and made a new beginning together without any religion. As Rabbi Harold Schulweis put it, many of these "interfaith" marriages were really "interfaithless." This made it easier for rabbis to officiate at such wedding ceremonies.

Most of the rabbis who officiated were either Reform or Reconstructionist. These were the most liberal streams, and most rabbis with liberal views were affiliated with these two denominations. This continues to be the case. Also, these were the movements that allowed rabbis to make their own decisions. Conservative rabbis were prohibited from officiating at interfaith weddings. If they did so, they could be expelled from the RA. Obviously, Orthodox rabbis would be violating the halacha if they officiated, and could also face sanctions from the RCA or other Orthodox rabbinical groups. As intermarriage rates increased, rabbis came under greater pressure to officiate at intermarriage ceremonies. "It is becoming more and more uncomfortable to be a Reform rabbi who does not officiate at intermarriages," said Rabbi Howard Jaffe of Temple Isaiah in Lexington, Massachusetts. Jaffe still refuses to officiate at interfaith weddings, but many others have shifted their positions. Rabbi Judy Shanks of Temple Isaiah in Lafayette, California began officiating in 2003. She told the Jewish Telegraphic Agency that "if these people are making themselves part of us, then I want to be there for them at every important life-cycle event."[57]

Among Reform and Reconstructionist rabbis, there are still substantial numbers who refuse to officiate. Yet, they face a difficult situation. Many congregations would not hire a rabbi who refused to officiate at intermarriage ceremonies, because they felt that that would be one of the most important functions of their congregational leader. Many of the families in their temples had children who were intermarrying, and it was important to them that they have a rabbi who could represent them at the wedding ceremony. Rabbi Deborah Bravo, formerly of Temple B'nai Jeshurun in Short Hills, New Jersey and now of Temple Emanu-El of Edison, New Jersey, said that when she was going through placement in 1998, every congregation asked her whether she would officiate at an intermarriage. "It has become the litmus test for placement."[58]

Some rabbis who had previously refused to officiate at intermarriages tried to meet the new expectations by blessing the couple at the beginning of the wedding ceremony, but having a judge or justice of the peace actually officiate at the legal part of the service. This may have satisfied some of the older members of their congregations for a short while, but it soon became apparent that these rabbis were trying to pretend that they were not doing something they were actually doing or, even worse, that they were pretending to be doing something they actually were not. Either way, it was felt that they were not meeting the couple's need for validation and approval. The question for many rabbis today is no longer whether they will officiate, but whether they can set any sort of preconditions. Rabbi Irwin Fishbein, the

FIGURE 4.4. "The Interfaith Wedding Rabbi," David Gruber, ordained Orthodox but now a secular humanist, officiates at interfaith weddings without preconditions. Most interfaith couples request certain Jewish wedding practices, especially the breaking of the glass, which the groom in the photo is preparing to do. Photo Jennifer Yarbro. *Courtesy of Jennifer Yarbro Photography*

director of the Rabbinic Center for Research and Counseling in Westfield, New Jersey, maintains a comprehensive list of rabbis who will officiate under different sets of circumstances. A couple planning to get married can access the list via the center's Web site and can search for a rabbi in their area who will officiate under conditions that they might find acceptable.[59] For example, if they want the rabbi to co-officiate with a Christian minister, they can search the list for those rabbis who have checked off that possibility.

Requiring preconditions became more and more difficult. Increasing numbers of couples felt that they were doing nothing wrong, and they were quick to resent any implication that they needed remedial education or behavioral modification. They felt they had a right to make whatever personal decisions they wanted, and they expected the clergy to validate their choices without hesitation. Any attempt to set conditions might be viewed as critical and judgmental. In 1990, almost two-thirds of Reform rabbis who officiated at interfaith marriages required that the interfaith couple make a commitment to having a Jewish home and raising Jewish children. Only five years later, that percentage dropped to significantly less than half. Fishbein explained that this was due to the fact that more rabbis recognized that the commitment to making a Jewish home was "not something that rabbis can really require. You are dealing with the future. Very often the couple themselves do not know what they are planning to do."[60]

Many of the rabbis who did officiate felt that they were helping the couple and that this might improve the odds that they would want to affiliate with the Jewish community. Rabbi Jacques Cukierkorn from Kansas City told me: "In my eight years as a Rabbi, I have yet to have a couple come to ask for my permission to get married. They all come to ask for my help. I have to decide if I want to help them or not, if I want to bring Judaism to this very important event in their lives [even if one of them is not Jewish]." By doing their wedding, "I believe I am enhancing the probability of them raising Jewish kids. If I turn them down, then some minister will happily welcome them and probably their children as well."[61]

The Possibility of Creeping Syncretism

Jews have been marrying non-Jews in large numbers for more than forty years. Many of the non-Jewish spouses do not practice any religion, and they may agree to raise their children as Jews. Some even embrace Judaism, either formally converting or simply adopting Judaism as their exclusive religious practice without any formal ceremony. But substantial numbers do practice another religion, in most cases Christianity. As the boundary between Judaism and the general society around it continues to blur, it is possible that Christian theological and/or ritual elements may be absorbed into the synagogue. The advocates of outreach argue that it is possible to influence intermarried couples to make it more likely that they will raise their children as Jewish without any other supplementary religious identity.

Bruce Phillips of the Hebrew Union College–Jewish Institute of Religion found that there were several "key predictors" that determined which children would be raised as Jewish in intermarriages: the Jewish parent was responsible for the child's religious upbringing, the intermarried couple had a substantial network of Jewish friends and found that to be a positive thing, the Jewish parent had siblings who were in-married, and the couple had relatively little contact with the non-Jewish side of the family. Some of these factors are causes, and others are effects. For example, is the intermarried couple influenced by their Jewish friends to raise their children as Jews, or do they seek out Jewish friends because they have already decided to raise their children as Jewish and they want support for that decision? Are the children raised Jewish because the Jewish parent was given responsibility for their religious upbringing, or was the Jewish parent given responsibility for the religious upbringing because the couple decided to raise them as Jewish?

The most startling finding that Phillips reported was that there is a rapidly declining number of Jews who report that their religion is Judaism. "Largely as a result of intermarriage, the once seamless overlap between Jewish ethnicity and Judaism has begun to unravel."[62] American Jews had been an "ethnic church" in which the ethnic group all professed the same religion and all members of the religion had the same ethnic background.[63] This is no longer the case. Only 62 percent of Jews who were born Jewish identify Judaism as their religion. Many of those who were raised in intermarried households, even those who were supposedly raised only as Jewish, do not see Judaism as their religion. Increasing numbers see themselves as Jewish by ethnicity, but as Christian by belief. To what degree these "Jewish Christians" will influence American Judaism in the future is an unknown. Up to this point, they are regarded as complete outsiders, but this could potentially change in the coming years.

Parents who themselves were raised with the idea of multiculturalism find it logical to teach their children about both religions. There are a handful of interfaith schools in certain cities that function much like a Jewish or Christian religious school except they teach both religions simultaneously. The Bay Area Interfaith Sunday School is one. Lessons open with the Sh'ma, followed by the Lord's Prayer, emphasizing the dual religious curriculum. Most of the classes are taught by two parents, one Christian and one Jewish. But, unlike most of the other interfaith schools where parents teach their own religion, the Bay Area parents all try to teach both religions.

The parents understand that most of the Jewish community (and the Christian establishment as well) opposes raising children in two religions, but they feel that that is the best way that they, as interfaith parents, can respond to their own interfaith relationships. The children feel warm and secure in a small, tightly knit community of interfaith families where it seems safe to discuss their attachments to both parents' religions. The families have a number of different ways of dealing with their personal religious identities. Some of the children have been confirmed in the Catholic Church, and others go to synagogue on the High Holy Days. Many integrate significant aspects of both Judaism and Christianity into their belief systems. What seems natural to them would be astounding to many outsiders. To take just a single example, one little boy said that he sees Jesus as his savior but also feels Jewish.[64]

Those who see syncretism as a mortal threat to Judaism frequently point to the Dovetail Institute for Interfaith Family Resources as a prime malevolent influence. Dovetail is seen as promoting the two-faith option, even though its founder and longtime leader, Joan Hawxhurst—a Methodist—is raising her children as Jews with Jewish husband Steve Bertman. "I was completely horrified by what I heard at this conference, which attempts to set decades of outreach efforts by the Jewish community into complete reverse." This was the initial reaction of Anna Rachael Marx, a recent college graduate who was asked to speak at a Dovetail conference "Rejoice in Your Choice: Finding Common Ground in Interfaith Families" as the program associate of Project Welcome, the Reform movement's Bay Area outreach effort. Dovetail asked her to describe the opportunities offered for involvement in the local Jewish community. Marx agreed to speak, but, after attending the two-day conference, "I learned that Dovetail does not promote nonjudgmental education, but instead presents arguments meant to convince families to practice two faiths concurrently." They do this, according to Marx, "by openly discussing the downfalls of single-faith homes."[65]

The leaders of the Dovetail Institute certainly do not see themselves in this light. They explain that their organization is devoted to helping Jewish-

Christian couples make decisions about how to raise their children. What makes them controversial in the Jewish community is that they support parents who want to raise their children in both Judaism and Christianity. Dovetail does not officially advocate this approach, but they do encourage those who are so inclined to pursue that option. Mary Rosenbaum, Dovetail's executive director, estimates that about half the families that are active members are raising their children in two faiths. Most of the other half are raising their children as Jewish. A small number choose a more neutral path such as Unitarianism, ethical humanism, or Unity.

Rosenbaum says that "raising children in both faiths only works if both partners are actively involved in their own religion. To do it successfully you have to be really interested in religion and willing to spend a lot of time and energy. It's not just Christmas and Chanukah." Mary and her husband Ned have done just that. Ned remembers that when they got married in 1963, they told the Catholic priest who officiated that they planned to raise their children in both the Catholic and Jewish religions. "He said that was perfectly awful." This is certainly the view of most Jewish leaders as well. Edmund Case, the president and publisher of InterfaithFamily.com, also opposes raising children in two religions. "First, I don't think it's possible to be both Jewish and Christian. There is a theological inconsistency. Second, we hear from children that it's confusing. They feel torn between two religious communities, and are not really part of either. If their parents say they can choose one religion when they are older, they feel torn between their parents or grandparents."[66]

Dru Greenwood, the former director of outreach for the URJ, said that the goal of Reform outreach is to encourage the couple to choose Judaism for the family. If that is not possible, the Reform movement urges the couple to choose one religious identity for their children. "There are good ways to honor and respect the cultural heritage of both parents in an interfaith home. Raising children to be both Jewish and Christian is not one of them." Ned Rosenbaum actually agrees with Greenwood, with a subtle distinction. "We raised our kids *with* both religions, not *in* them." Mary Rosenbaum disagreed with my characterization of this as a "subtle" distinction. "In our view, raising children with an education in both faiths is not the same thing as encouraging them to think that they belong to both. [This is] a core difference that our children, for instance, never had any trouble grasping."[67]

The Rosenbaums hoped that when their children grew up, they would choose one religion. Their daughter, Sarah, has done so, formally converting to Judaism. But their other children are still conflicted. Ephraim, one of their two sons, considers himself "half-Jewish." He explains that "I don't think I seriously contemplated being one or the other. That's one of the disadvantages of being raised interfaith—it has kind of a paralyzing effect."[68] He added that there are benefits: "One tremendous advantage (and burden) in having parents of different faiths is that it has compelled me actively to search out a system of belief that I could feel comfortable with."[69] None of their children have tried to incorporate Christian elements into Judaism, but one can see how some people raised with two religions might want to do so.

Even if some Jews or non-Jews active in the synagogue try to bring in certain Christian beliefs or rituals, it is extremely unlikely that the non-Orthodox American Jewish denominations are going to become forms of so-called messianic Judaism. Many Americans (hopefully most) are aware of the basic differences between Judaism and Christianity (although probably not the more obscure theological distinctions), and those involved in synagogue life are going to want to preserve a distinctive Jewish approach to religion. A Judaic approach can mean a lot of different things, but, as everyone knows, what it cannot include is a belief in Jesus. Rather, any syncretism that might occur will—at least at first—involve small details that do not obviously cross the line into another religion. It is not likely that anyone is going to put up a giant crucifix in a synagogue sanctuary.

The so-called messianic Jewish movements claim that they are fulfilling the words of the prophets by embracing Jesus and the belief that Jesus was, is, and will be the messiah. Every mainstream Jewish group rejects that argument and regards any type of "messianic Jew"—no matter how much Jewish ritual they practice—as beyond the pale. On this point, virtually all rabbis—Reform, Conservative, Orthodox, and Reconstructionist—agree. As Rabbi Eric H. Yoffie, the president of the URJ, put it: "There's no such thing as a 'messianic Jew.' The whole notion is a fraud." Rabbi Yoffie's position is consistent with the historic Jewish view on the limits of religious pluralism. But, as other limits are tested and broken, why should this one taboo remain? A number of Jewish writers have asked that exact question.

Dan Cohn-Sherbok and Carol Harris-Shapiro—the former a Reform rabbi and the latter a Reconstructionist rabbi—have described the position that messianic Judaism is no more a deviation from traditional Judaism than any of the non-Orthodox movements.[70] Harris-Shapiro argued "that other movements could [also] be seen as deviant from different traditional Jewish perspectives throughout history." She explained that, "theologically and halachically, one could argue (and I do) that the kinds of Judaism that are practiced by secular humanistic Judaism, Jubus, and even Reform Judaism are problematic" and are seen as "deviant either by specific contemporary groups within Orthodoxy or in light of premodern Jewish standards enshrined in significant texts." Her ultimate argument is "that given the disparate centers of power and authority to determine who is a Jew and who is a good Jew, that drawing some kind of consistent 'he's in and he's out' position becomes impossible. As I say in the book, 'We are all, from a Jewish perspective somewhere, heretics.'"[71] Needless to say, this is not the establishment position. Yoffie speaks for most American Jews, arguing that "the overwhelming majority of Jewish leadership in all of the religious movements sees messianic Jews as outside the pale and indeed not Jews at all. Those who suggest otherwise speak for a tiny fraction of the Jewish community."[72]

Maintaining boundries between Judaism and Christianity is necessary, but cannot be the central component of Jewish religious identity. Michael Medved, the Orthodox film critic and conservative political activist who has worked closely with evangelical Christians, believes that the so-called messianic Jewish groups are singled out for disapprobation because "the chief distinguishing characteristic of most American Jews is not what they do believe but what they do not believe. They do not believe in Jesus as the Messiah."[73] If American Judaism is to thrive, American Jews are going to have to develop a serious, positive theological structure and not simply rely on a reaffirmation of what they do not believe. Alan Laufer, former president of Little Neck Jewish Center, put the choice starkly. "Will we see to it that Hanukah, and all of our holidays, are celebrated in a manner that dignifies and glorifies the four-thousand-year-old tradition that has been passed down to us? Will we pass this tradition down to our children and grandchildren? Or, will Hanukah and indeed all our Jewish holidays deteriorate into just another Festivus?"[74]

5 Inclusivity as a Social Value

In the winter of 1979, the Jewish Women's Group at the University of California at Berkeley invited Rebbetzin Hinda Langer from the local Chabad House to speak on women and halacha. In the course of the discussion, the listeners heard Langer mentioning that she thought that while lesbianism was prohibited according to Jewish law, it was a relatively minor transgression, much less serious than eating bread during Passover. The statement—which Langer denies making—was just a side comment and nobody paid too much attention to that particular point at the time. "I only found out that I was being written about after my children Googled my name. I'm a little bit in shock."[1] She seemed to regret having become the inspiration for a lesbian Jewish practice. But that is exactly what happened. When the group was planning their Passover seder a few months later, they began talking about Langer's comment and how they felt that lesbianism was much more "transgressive" than Langer understood. The end result was the creation of a new symbol—the orange on the seder plate. The history and meaning of this symbol was and remains contested.

FIGURE 5.1. The traditional Seder plate with the addition of an orange. The orange symbolizes the contemporary desire to be inclusive. Photo Ann Silver. *Courtesy of Ann Silver*

In the traditional Passover ritual, there are a number of ceremonial foods placed on the seder plate. In a spirit of rebellion, they decided to place a crust of bread on their seder plate that year as a symbol of the difficulty that Jewish lesbians experienced being accepted in the Jewish community.[2] By adding a piece of bread—which would stick out as something completely foreign to the traditional ritual—Jews could acknowledge that gay and lesbian Jews had been excluded from Jewish religious life. By incorporating bread into the seder, they would be acknowledging that they likewise wanted to include those who had previously been marginalized. The marginalized groups soon included not only gays and lesbians, but also heterosexual women.

While the bread would seem incongruous and likely offensive to anyone familiar with the traditional seder, its presence was very much in keeping with the pedagogic purpose of the evening. Traditionally, children are encouraged to ask why certain things are done differently on Passover evening in contrast to the way they are done the rest of the year. Perhaps the most famous section in the entire seder is the Mah Nishtanah, which asks the question "why is this night different from all other nights?" Also called the *fier kashes* (four questions, in Yiddish), the text was originally read by the seder leader, but since the later Middle Ages has been recited by the youngest child present, who is encouraged to sing it. Each of the four questions begins by noting that on the evening of the seder there is a specific practice that is not found during the rest of the year. The presence of the bread would provide the perfect justification for asking a new question.

The story about the "crust of bread at the seder table" was retold at lesbian seders and incorporated into lesbian haggadahs written in the early 1980s. The primary source came from *A Women's Haggadah*, which had been edited by Shifrah Lillith. Lillith, a New York Jewish feminist whose original name was Susan Fielding, had read an article in a feminist newspaper in 1982 that described a woman going to a rabbi to ask him about the place of lesbians in Judaism. He told her bluntly that lesbians have as much place in Judaism as bread does on a seder plate. This story, perhaps apocryphal, became a powerful legend that generated tremendous indignation and a great determination to right a wrong and correct an injustice.

Shortly thereafter, when Lillith wrote the text for her haggadah, she asked one of the traditional questions, but added a new twist: "Why is this night different from all other nights and this Passover from all other Passovers?" The text answered that just as there was no place for *chametz* (leavened bread) on the seder plate until that year, so too there was no place for lesbians. Now there would be room for both. The lesson the haggadah teaches is that there are pharaohs in every generation who would perpetually enslave women. Women must not passively accept this treatment, but rather break free from this servitude, liberating themselves from their own personal Egyptian slavery.

Feminists throughout the country found this symbolism intriguing, but many were uncomfortable with actually putting bread on a seder plate. It was too blatant a violation of traditional Jewish norms, broke a taboo that made it uncomfortable for those who had kosher-style seders, and was impossible for those who had strictly kosher-for-Passover kitchens. That, of course, was the point—to be shocking by transgressing a sacred prohibition. Many moderates felt that this same point could be made without sticking chametz smack in the middle of the Passover home liturgy. Various groups experimented with alternative approaches. Some added Miriam's cup to supplement the traditional cup of wine reserved for the Prophet Elijah. The cup of Miriam was a wine goblet devoted to remembering the role of Moses's sister Miriam, the singer and prophet in the Passover story. A feminist seder at Oberlin College left a space on the seder plate marked with the Hebrew word *makom*, which literally means "space" in Hebrew, but also refers to God as an abstraction rather than as a masculine entity. They felt that by doing so they emphasized that, just as they were leaving a space on the seder plate for other ritual foods, so too were they leaving space at their seder table for Jewish lesbians as well as others who had felt excluded in the past.

Susannah Heschel, a professor of religion and the daughter of Abraham Joshua Heschel, is credited with first suggesting that an orange be placed on the seder plate. She later explained that the orange represented the fruitfulness of inclusivity that can result when women and other previously excluded people lead and participate in the seder. The orange represented her personal struggle for inclusivity as well. "My life was one of struggling to be part of Judaism—struggling for a Bat Mitzvah, an aliyah, the right to say kaddish, inclusion in the minyan. All the barriers that my generation of feminists was able to pull down needed public markers, and women's seders became a central occasion for celebrating these changes and honoring those who brought them about."

Heschel had grown up feeling conflicted between her father, who presided over the seder with a dozen friends and colleagues, and her mother, who was occupied in the kitchen before and during the Passover holiday. "I never quite knew where I belonged. I wanted to be with my father, listening to his explanations of the haggadah, reading the Hebrew texts, enjoying the splendor of the beautiful table. But I also wanted to stay in the kitchen, helping my mother, and urging her to sit down with the guests, to rest, and to enjoy the seder. Wherever I was, I felt guilty for abandoning the other parent."[3] She later found books on feminist theory that helped her understand the conflict she felt between the two roles she wanted to assume. Particularly helpful was Mary Daly's *Beyond God the Father*, which "rescued me from the confusion I felt over Judaism's conflicted honoring of religious study and synagogue observance and its exclusion of women." Daly had written that "if God is male, then the male is God." Heschel began to understand that "the problem was not a series of laws relegating women to second-class status, but a deeper problem of a symbol-system that placed holiness in the male domain."

In the early 1980s, the Hillel Foundation invited her to speak on a panel at Oberlin College. While on campus, she saw the feminist haggadah that had been written by a group of Oberlin students. One of the rituals that they had included was the placing of a crust of bread on the seder plate. Their hagaddah told a story about a woman rebbe at her own *tisch* (table) who is asked by one of her disciples why a crumb of chametz was included. She answered that it was because a woman had asked the local rebbe about how much room there was in Judaism for a lesbian, and the rebbe had screamed at her, "There's as much room for a lesbian in Judaism as there is for a crust of bread on the seder plate!" The idea of adding a crust of bread to the seder plate was inspiring to her, "but I couldn't follow it literally." Nevertheless, Heschel liked the idea of concretely showing the need for greater inclusivity, so "at our next Passover, I decided to place an orange (actually, I used a tangerine!) on our family's seder plate." "During the first part of the seder, I asked everyone to take a segment of the orange, making the blessing over fruit, and eat it as a gesture of solidarity with Jewish lesbians and gay men and others who are marginalized within the Jewish community."

Heschel explained that "celebrating women's inclusion in the synagogue had become, even at that time, a mainstream, conventional act, whereas gay and lesbian Jews were still behind barriers." While the feminist movement had already achieved a level of respectability in the Jewish community that made it "unacceptable to ridicule its efforts, Jewish attitudes—even in the years after the Stonewall riot (the major gay revolt against homophobia, in New York City in 1969)—remained hostile and mocking toward gay liberation." Heschel preferred an orange rather than bread not only because she did not want to break one of the central laws of Passover but also because she wanted to avoid a symbol that was entirely negative. "Bread on the Seder plate brings an end to Pesach—it renders everything chometz. And it suggests that being lesbian is being transgressive, violating Judaism." In contrast, she felt that an orange was suggestive of "the fruitfulness for all Jews when lesbians and gay men are contributing and active members of Jewish life. Since each tangerine segment has a few seeds, we had the added gesture of spitting them out at that seder, recognizing and repudiating the sin of homophobia that poisons too many Jews."

Heschel found that after she started mentioning her custom of putting an orange on her family's seder plate in her lectures, "the typical patriarchal maneuver occurred." Rather than crediting her with the idea of placing an orange on the seder plate as a way of affirming gays and lesbians, the focus of the story shifted. A man is reputed to have shouted at Heschel during a speaking tour in Florida that a woman belongs on the bimah in the same way that an orange belongs on a seder plate. Heschel found this infuriating. "A woman's words are attributed to a man, and the affirmation of lesbians

FIGURE 5.2. African American Jewish woman reading from the Torah at the biannual convention of the Jewish Reconstructionist Federation in Portland, Oregon, November 2004. Non-Orthodox women are now allowed to read from the Torah, lead services, and perform other public rituals that were formerly restricted to men. Photo Wanya F. Kruyer. *Courtesy of Wanya F. Kruyer, www.wfknl.com*

and gay men is simply erased. Isn't that precisely what happened over the centuries to women's ideas?"[4]

Popular author Anita Diamant suggests that the orange should be on the seder plate so that a child can ask, "what's that thing doing on the seder plate?" "The orange is a symbol of the struggle by Jews who used to be ignored by our tradition"—like gays and lesbians, women, Jews by choice, African American, Asian, and Latino Jews, handicapped Jews, crypto-Jews, and so forth—to become full partners in religious life. "The orange is a sign of change, too, because now all kinds of Jews are rabbis and cantors and teachers and leaders. And the orange is a mark of our confidence in the Jewish future, which means that some day maybe you too will bring something new to the seder plate."[5]

The Changing Roles of Women in Contemporary Judaism

Of all of the major social changes that have occurred over the past one hundred years in Western society, the most significant is the changing role of women. Feminism, along with the civil rights movement, emerged out of the 1960s, although both have roots that go back much further. As women began to move into positions of responsibility that had traditionally been assigned only to men, there was a great deal of conflict and dissonance. Feminist leaders tended to come from backgrounds that allowed for new ways of thinking and had a conscious awareness of the possibility that different expectations existed. Perhaps for this reason, many of the leading feminists were Jewish. Whether or not they were practicing Jews, these early feminist leaders became role models for many Jewish women who saw new possibilities open up before their eyes. Some of these Jewish women wanted to apply the principles of feminism to the Judaism that they cared so much about. This chapter will focus on the impact of feminism and gay rights on American Judaism, both because they were trendsetters and because they can serve as examples of how American Jewish religious life could become more inclusive.

In 1970, Betty Friedan (born Naomi Goldstein) organized the Women's Strike for Equality, a march down Manhattan's Fifth Avenue. Addressing a primarily Jewish crowd, she spoke of the traditional blessing recited by Jewish men every morning in which they thank God for not having been created a woman. Friedan told those assembled that she dreamed of a day when women all over the world would be able to say "I thank Thee, Lord, I *was* created a woman." Friedan was already a well-known feminist leader. In 1963, she published *The Feminine Mystique*, a highly influential book that chronicled the discontent many American women felt. They had gone to college and sometimes graduate school, but were expected to fit into a society in which they got married, raised a family, and devoted their time to PTA meetings, carpooling to little league, music lessons, and Sunday school. "We can no longer ignore that voice within women that says: 'I want something more than my husband and my children and my home.'" That same year, Congress had passed the Equal Pay Act. One year later, the 1964 Civil Rights Act included title 7, which banned discrimination in employment on the basis of sex as well as race. Women suddenly had unheard-of opportunities. In 1966, Friedan established the National Organization for Women (NOW), which became the most important feminist advocacy group in the United States.

Many of the early feminists believed that religion was a repressive influence and that women could achieve equality only by breaking the hierarchical power of traditional religious institutions. Later, some began to feel that religion and feminism could be reconciled, and a number of pioneers began to develop feminist theological approaches. Jewish feminists have struggled to develop opportunities to express their religious needs while at the same time trying to integrate themselves into the broader framework of Jewish religious life. The perception was that the organized Jewish community was less than welcoming. Rachel Adler, one of the early Jewish feminists, summarized the feelings of many women "Being a Jewish woman is very much like being Alice at the Hatter's tea party. We did not participate in making the rules, nor were we there at the beginning of the party. At best, a jumble of crockery is being shoved aside to clear a place for us. At worst, we are only tantalized with the tea and bread-and-butter, while being confused, shamed and reproached for our ignorance."[6]

Traditionally, women's religious activities were centered in the home. Women were expected to make sure that the kosher laws were observed properly in the home. They were also obligated to make sure that *taharat hamishpachah*, family purity, was observed. According to the halacha, all physical contact between a husband and his wife was forbidden from the first sign that she was beginning to menstruate until seven days after her period ended. During this time she was regarded as a niddah, ritually impure. After the niddah period ended, she was obligated to go to the mikveh and ritually immerse. Only then could she resume any physical contact with her husband, including sexual relations.

In the classical rabbinic tradition, the halacha makes a fundamental distinction between men and women. While both men and women are obligated to obey all the negative commandments such as "Thou shalt not murder," only men are required to observe positive, time-bound commandments. Those who were not obligated to observe a particular commandment could not do that commandment on behalf of others. As a consequence of this, men dominated the public sphere of Jewish religious life.

Because women were not obligated to observe positive, time-bound commandments, they could not serve as witnesses. When a couple got married, the witnesses attesting to the marriage had to be observant Jewish men over the age of thirteen. If a couple had to go through a divorce, the get would be given by the husband to the wife, who would simply accept it. If the husband refused to send a get to his wife, she became an agunah, a woman regarded as still married and therefore prohibited from having sexual relations with any other man. If the husband disappeared or refused to sign off on a get, the wife might remain permanently "chained". As Orthodox Jewish feminist Blu Greenberg put it, the agunah problem is "an outright abuse and violation of Jewish ethics." As such, 'it should have been resolved yesterday.'" She explains that "the fact that the agunah is still an unresolved issue is due, in part I believe, to the fact that Orthodox women (and men) are not demanding that halachists end such injustice through reinterpretation and repair of this law."[7]

The worshipper was presumed to be a man since public worship was an obligation only for men. The obligation to pray with a minyan in the morning, afternoon, and evening was a positive time-bound commandment. Only men were obligated to observe positive time-bound commandments because the sages presumed that many women would be busy with household duties and the children and it would therefore be impractical to obligate them to drop everything during a specified time period. According to traditional interpretations of halacha, only a person who is obligated to do a specific practice can lead others in the performance of that particular act or count as part of the minimum number necessary to do that act in a religious quorum. Since men were the only ones obligated to pray in a minyan, women could not be counted as part of the ten people necessary for group prayer.

Women were separated from the men in the synagogue. This was based in part on the precedent set in the Temple in Jerusalem, where the sexes were usually (but not always) divided. There is some debate over whether the earliest synagogues had an *Ezrat Nashim* (a women's gallery), but in any case the sages determined that women must be kept separate from men during prayer. In many communities, women simply did not attend services, but focused their ritual attention solely on the home. When they did go to a synagogue, the congregation erected a mechitza, a physical divider separating the men from the women. Various reasons were given for this practice. One thread of thought held that free mingling would lead to sexual transgression. Even being able to see women would distract the men from their prayers. The distinctive gender roles developed by the sages in the Talmudic period were maintained without revolutionary change throughout the medieval period and, to a large degree, even well past the enlightenment and emancipation.

While the role of women in Judaism did change to some degree in other parts of the world, it was in the United States that these changes were most apparent. One of the most notable ritual innovations was the introduction of the bat mitzvah. Jewish boys had traditionally been called to the Torah when they turned thirteen. They would bless and perhaps read the Torah for the first time, a ceremony marking their coming of age in the community. In traditional Jewish society, girls reached mature status at age twelve, but there was no religious ceremony in the synagogue parallel to that of the bar mitzvah for boys. That changed in 1922, when Mordecai M. Kaplan arranged for his daughter Judith to become a bat mitzvah. Even though Judith's ceremony was hastily planned and rather minimal, it became a precedent-setting event. At first, only a few families followed Kaplan's lead but by the 1950s, the bat mitzvah had become wildly popular. Like their male counterparts, young Jewish females could now bless and read from the Torah and lead worship. In so doing, they publicly affirm their commitment to Judaism as well as demonstrate their scholarly accomplishments.

Despite the growing popularity of the bat mitzvah ceremony and many other signs of greater participation for women, progress toward complete religious equality between the sexes was slow in coming. Societal attitudes remained relatively conservative until the middle to late 1960s. Even those American Jewish religious denominations that accepted the equality of women in theory found it difficult to make actual changes. For example, the Reform movement was unable to build a consensus to allow for women rabbis until the early 1970s. Many of the changes made were slow, tentative, and ambivalent. Nevertheless, the role of women in Judaism was transformed over the course of only two or three decades, a remarkable accomplishment by any standard.

As we saw in the introduction to this chapter, some of the most influential ceremonial changes were introduced by small groups of cutting-edge feminists rather than by (male) rabbis leading mainstream congregations. These small groups focused on creating meaningful liturgy for holidays that they celebrated together. Since Passover had an established tradition of reading a haggadah, many of the most interesting ideas were originally proposed as innovations to the traditional seder. Passover focused on liberation, and this theme resonated strongly with women seeking exactly that. Their mothers had busied themselves with the manifold preparations necessary for the holiday—cleaning the house thoroughly to remove all the vestiges of chametz, and cooking for the seder and for the entire Passover week. Their daughters now wanted to apply that energy in a new direction. Their goal was to look at the exodus from Egypt not only from the perspective of Moses and Aaron but also from the viewpoint of Miriam, Yochevet, Shifra and Puah, and other Israelite women involved in the exodus drama.

Letty Pogrebin hosted an influential seder in New York beginning in 1976. "Seder sisters" already had access to E. M. Broner's *The Women's Haggadah*, which had been published in *Ms.* that spring, and they brought their copies with them. Gloria Steinem, who began attending Pogrebin's seders, was impressed. "The whole idea of remaking religious ceremonies to include women I found very magnetic." Steinem had previously kept her distance from religious activities because of her impression that it reinforced the social structure that had oppressed women. "Religion in general did make me feel excluded. But it was only through the seder that I came to realize that the ceremony in and of itself was less hierarchical than Christian ceremonies; everybody read and participated. I came to appreciate the democracy of it, the cyclical nature of it, the lack of emphasis on an afterlife. The feminist seder gave me whatever Jewish education I have."[8]

Feminists were eager to stake their claim to dates and times that had special meaning for women or could be interpreted as validating the importance of women's spiritual experience. Rosh Hodesh, the celebration of the new month, became a central opportunity for women to celebrate an emergent feminist Judaism. The new month had many obvious connections with femininity and contemporary feminists could draw on ancient precedents for their innovative ideas. The Talmud spoke of the new month as a holiday that had special meaning for women and urged them to take time off from their household chores on Rosh Hodesh in order to celebrate. Feminists wanted to develop new forms of ritual to help women to formalize the sacred nature of the day and to remind them of their inherent spirituality. Rosh Hodesh groups began meeting in more progressive cities in the early 1970s, coming together for prayer on the evening of the new moon. Some of the celebrations were standard prayer services, but others were funky and artistic, ranging from readings in praise of menstruation to women's mythology-writing exercises. While many of the Rosh Hodesh groups drew from the traditional ritual, the primary focus was on the individual religious needs of the women present. As Judith Plaskow pointed out, this "structural openness" seemed to define a ritual as feminist.[9]

As women became more involved as participants and leaders in synagogue Judaism, they sought to expand the breadth of ceremonial activities in which they were engaged. An obvious area of interest was the wearing of ritual items. In a traditional synagogue, the men wore a yarmulke, a head covering, and a tallit, a prayer shawl. In most Modern Orthodox synagogues, the practice of married women covering their hair at all times in public had fallen by the wayside and was restricted to the synagogue, where married women would wear a hat. Many did not even do that, but simply picked up a small, round, white piece of cloth that they stuck on their heads with a bobby pin. The practice of wearing a head covering to show that the worshipper was respectful of God is already mentioned in the Talmud. Perhaps because men were obligated to pray three times a day, this practice was limited to males. Some women now wanted to adopt the practice, and artists began making feminine yarmulkes that would be appropriate for female heads. The tallit had been developed because the Torah requires tzitzit to be placed on all four-cornered garments. Since people did not normally wear four-cornered garments, the tallit was developed specifically to meet the Torah's requirements in order to allow men to observe this particular commandment. Since it was only required during the daytime, it was only incumbent upon men. Women now wanted to start wearing tallits as well, and soon a vast array of beautiful, multicolored tallits were being offered by various Jewish artists.

Susan Weidman Schneider, the editor of *Lilith*, a Jewish feminist magazine, remembers that a button was given out reading "it's not just tallis envy" at a Jewish feminist conference in 1974. Many of the women at that conference were already in the habit of wearing a tallit, but they were certainly pioneers. Over the following three decades, the practice became more common, spreading to different types of women in all sorts of synagogues. Nevertheless, many women felt uncomfortable usurping what they still sensed was a male prerogative. Perhaps the most masculine ritual item was tefillin, the prayer boxes containing parchment scrolls with biblical citations that are placed on the forehead and wrapped around the left arm. Tefillin were traditionally put on every weekday morning by adult Jewish men as a sign of the covenant between God and the Jewish people. Relatively few women began laying tefillin, either because they saw it as an intrinsically masculine act or because outside of Orthodox circles, very few people of either sex performed that ritual.

Women also began training to be ritual functionaries. As non-Orthodox movements began to accept women as rabbis and cantors and synagogue presidents, it became logical to consider the possibility of having women as mohels as well. Most non-Orthodox synagogues used physicians to perform the brit milah, so a woman physician would be eligible. Eventually, programs were created to train medical personnel in the ritual requirements of brit milah. Jewish doctors and nurses could enroll in a short course to learn the history and philosophy of brit milah and would be given a certificate indicating that they were now a trained Jewish ritual officiant. Halacha discouraged women from performing milah, ritual circumcision. In Yoreh De'ah 264:1 of the *Shulchan Aruch*, the sixteenth-century code of Jewish law, two opinions are brought down. One states that a ritual circumcision performed by a woman is kosher, meaning acceptable, and the other says that it is not. However, both agree that a woman should only perform a brit when a male mohel is not available. This preference has become a custom that assumed the force of law, and, as a result, women did not traditionally serve as mohels.

But even in the Orthodox world, there were circumstances in which a woman would be encouraged to circumcise a newborn Jewish male. For example, an Orthodox Jewish nurse circumcised the newborn babies of Holocaust survivors in DP camps right after World War II and an Orthodox woman physician performed numerous circumcisions when visiting Jewish communities in the Soviet Union, when communist repression of religion was still at its height. These women performed circumcisions because there was no male mohel available, but there is a biblical precedent for women. Zipporah, Mose's wife, circumcises their son. Some Orthodox commentators, concerned with the implication, write that Zipporah only began the circumcision but then had a male relative take over in the middle. But there is nothing in the text to indicate that that is what happened. Dr. Emily Blake, a female mohel from Nyack, New York, says that she is frequently asked whether it is acceptable for a woman to perform a brit. "I tell them there are just two instances in the Torah that mention [the practice], Abraham and Zipporah. So the way I look at it, 50 percent of mohelim should be women."[10]

New ceremonies were created to welcome baby girls into the covenant of Israel. Intended to match the brit milah ceremony for boys, the baby-naming ceremony can be held on the eighth day after birth. The Simchat Bat or Shalom Bat was primarily a celebration, sometimes without any formal liturgy, while the brit bat and b'ritah not only included a full baby-naming ceremony but also might include a substitute for the act of circumcision, such as washing the baby's feet in water or immersing her in a body of water.

FIGURE 5.3. Savina Teubal's Simchat Chochma ritual for those who reach senior status, conducted on November 10, 1986. New ceremonies and rituals are being created to spiritually mark milestones and events both joyous and traumatic. *Courtesy of Marcia Cohn Spiegel*

While there is no medical procedure matching the male circumcision, the baby naming is a ritual designed to bring the female child into the covenant utilizing a variety of liturgical rituals. Feminists have also created liturgy to recognize the sacred nature of a woman's biological cycle. These ceremonies are much less common, but they provide a ritual outlet for those wanting to mark such occasions as first menstruation, a miscarriage, menopause, or even recovery after a rape.

Rethinking Liberal Jewish Theology

Perhaps for the first time in all of Jewish history, women thinkers were free to contribute to Jewish thought on an equal basis. Some thinkers looked at issues of religious innovation from a feminist point of view that challenged the accepted notion that male experience could be extrapolated as universal. The more radical argued that Jewish theology was designed to reinforce male power and justify traditional gender roles. They outlined an entirely new theological approach that would consciously reject patriarchy and substitute instead a new paradigm.

Feminist theology looked beyond ritual innovation to the core beliefs that constituted the Jewish religion. Some feminist thinkers felt that Jewish theology needed to be broadened to encompass the whole of women's experience as well as continuing to include the masculine viewpoint, while others felt that basic Jewish theological concepts needed to be completely rethought since they were developed in a patriarchal mode. Feminist thinkers formulated new paradigms to explain how religion could reinterpret ancient text in a modern or postmodern world. Women theologians also proposed new models for thinking about God and describing religious experience. They saw spirituality as involving communion with God and obeying God's teachings, in particular those mitzvot that focused on morals and ethics. But other women built theological systems that focused on new understandings of halacha. Others brought substantial amounts of experience from Eastern approaches to spirituality.

One approach was to uncover aspects of traditional Jewish thought that were proto-feminist. Instead of rejecting aspects of Judaism or recreating new ones, this type of thinking tried to resurrect theological dead ends and liturgical fragments in order to emphasize the continuity between what was being done today and what had been done in the distant past. The Shechina, the mystical representation of God's immanence, became one of the central metaphors for a more female and feminist reconceptualization of God. Other feminist scholars found this insufficient. While they were happy to use whatever feminist material the classical rabbinic tradition might provide, they reserved the right to supplement it with new feminist imagery that could supplement or replace traditional masculine symbolism.

Some of the feminist theologians rejected central aspects of Jewish theology as a part of their feminist critique of Judaism. Judith Plaskow, for example, rejected the idea that God is transcendent on the grounds that this was a masculine theological construct that manifested a male hierarchial worldview. Plaskow wrote that the image of God as a transcendent being was an essentially male understanding of reality and one of the root causes of inequality in Judaism. She went far beyond simply advocating a greater role for women in Judaism, launching a theological attack on many of the basic religious concepts of traditional Judaism. Jews needed to reconfigure their religion rather than just try to patch up the current structure, which was based on hierarchical models of society and inherently unequal and unjust.

In 1986, Plaskow wrote *Standing Again at Sinai: Judaism from a Feminist Perspective*, in which she argued that the Torah had been written by men using the language of patriarchy. This religiously marginalized women and could no longer be tolerated. Modern Jewish women had to reclaim the Torah by redefining its contents. "We must render visible the presence, experience, and deeds of women erased in traditional sources. We must tell the stories of women's encounters with God and capture the texture of their religious experience." Jews must expand the notion of Torah "to encompass not just the Five Books of Moses and traditional Jewish learning, but women's words, teachings, and actions hitherto unseen. To expand Torah, we must reconstruct Jewish history to include the history of women, and in doing so alter the shape of Jewish memory."[11] Jewish religion is indeed deeply rooted in the collective memory of the Jewish people, and that memory is based on a patriarchal structure.

"The central Jewish categories of Torah, Israel and God are all constructed from male perspectives. Torah is revelation as men perceived it, the story of Israel told from their standpoint, the law unfolded according to their needs. Israel is the male collectivity, the children of Jacob who had a daughter, but whose sons became the twelve tribes."[12] Nevertheless, Plaskow was hopeful that that very memory can be used as a tool for building a new hermeneutic for understanding Judaism differently. "Both the patriarchal character of Judaism and resources for transforming the tradition are grounded in the Jewish past. Feminists cannot hope to understand women's marginalization within Judaism without understanding where we have come from."[13]

Plaskow's feminist critique of Jewish theology extended to halacha. Jewish law may have developed in response to the Jewish historical experience, but that experience was molded primarily by men in a patriarchal culture. A Jewish feminist religious perspective has to look at halacha differently. Plaskow can do that because she accepted the assumption that the halacha itself was not given directly by God to Moses at Mount Sinai, and therefore was not divine. If it was developed by men working in a male-dominated cultural environment, then contemporary Jews can reformulate the halacha based on a more egalitarian approach.[14]

While Plaskow tried to rethink the concepts of Torah, Israel, God, sexuality, and tikkun olam from a feminist perspective, Rachel Adler focused on reinterpreting traditional legal arguments. Adler argued that non-Orthodox Judaism must accept the premise that "Jews beget Judaism," meaning that the Jewish community of a given time and place reshapes the religion according to its particular needs. Since Jews living in Western countries want to integrate the Western ethical ideal that women are equal into their theory and practice, they can and should do so. Even though she is theologically less radical than Plaskow, Adler nevertheless also believed that Jewish theology needed to evolve substantially. She argues that halacha is androcentric, with the Talmudic sages placing the masculine perspective at the center of their view of the world. However, she was concerned with men as well as women and was careful not to lump all women together. She does not use the term *women's experience* but rather women's experiences, since women do not all have the same experiences.

Adler is interested in expanding boundaries rather than simply shifting the focus from men to women. "I think one of the differences between Judith Plaskow and me is that I see the creation of an egalitarian Judaism as a project which women and men have to share. *Engendering Judaism* is not addressed solely to women. It is an inclusive theology."[15] Borrowing the term *methodolatry* from Mary Daly's *Beyond God the Father*, Adler argued that Jewish law was developed by "elite men," as opposed to "non-elite men," including *amei ha-aretz* (the uneducated), male slaves, and others who were "not participants in jurisgenesis." Therefore, men as well as women can benefit from a broader conception of Judaism.[16]

Adler had embraced Orthodoxy as a young woman and studied it intensely, only to reject it and return to Reform Judaism twenty years later. Because she had studied traditional texts, Adler was able to bring an in-depth knowledge of the complexity of the halachic system to her theological writing. She critiqued the way halachic questions were asked in Talmudic discourse, arguing that they were geared to a masculine understanding of legal categories. For example, she was shocked to find that post-WWII Orthodox rabbis had seriously debated the halachic question whether a Jewish man could continue his marriage after the Nazis had raped his wife. According to the halacha, any sexual contact between a woman and a man who is not her husband might make her permanently forbidden to her husband. But there were obviously extenuating circumstances in this particular case that would seem to render any such discussion pointless. Yet these extenuating circumstances were not regarded to be a deciding factor in the *shealot u-teshuvot*, the responsa literature produced by the Orthodox rabbinate, since the legal categories focused only on the men.

She also was able to bring the emotional investment of someone who had struggled as a woman and as a feminist to find a place for herself within the traditional framework of Judaism and failed. After reading some of her work, I began to think of her as a theologian driven as much by personal passion as by theological interest. When I told her this, she dismissed my comment, noting that "postmodern scholars would say that everyone is situated in a particular context from which they view their subject, and everyone chooses subjects in which they have personal investments of some sort. I have simply been transparent about my situation and investments."[17] Adler argued that the problem of women could be used as an example of what was wrong with halacha in general.[18] "I was not only talking about laws concerning women. I was asking what a tradition is and how one joins the conversation of tradition and how one might build a halakha that is proactive rather than reactive."

Adler explained how her theology had evolved. "When I was Orthodox, I thought that God's Torah was as complete as God: inerrant, invulnerable, invariable truth. I thought that I, the erring, bleeding, mutable creature, had to bend myself to this truth." If God is perfect, then it is human beings who are not worthy. "Whatever I was or saw that did not fit had to be cut off, had to be blocked out. The eye—or the I—was alone at fault. I tried to make a theology to uphold this truth, and as hard as I tried to make it truthful, it unfolded itself to me as a theology of lies."[19] Adler saw her theological ideas as a response to her experiences and freely admitted that her temporary embrace of Orthodox Judaism had been an influential factor. "For me, trying to live with integrity is a theological process. Thus I don't believe that I 'failed' to be an Orthodox Jew. I think that I succeeded at determining when Orthodoxy was no longer a position I could maintain with integrity." What she brought away from it "was an understanding of the need for a holistic Jewish praxis, a love and reverence for classical texts, and a new respect for Reform Judaism's willingness to assume the risks of change."

When she was Orthodox, Adler wrote "Tum'ah and Taharah: Ends and Beginnings," published in the *Jewish Catalogue* and in the first Jewish feminist anthology, *The Jewish Woman*.[20] She tried to build an argument to justify the traditional laws of menstrual impurity by constructing a feminist justification for the categories of purity and impurity. The essay was especially influential among traditional women who were trying to reconcile the laws of family purity with their feminism. But, by 1993, she felt the need to repudiate what she had written. "As a feminist Reform theologian," she wrote that she could no longer "in good conscience endorse" what she had written earlier. "I have had to ask myself, what is the responsibility of a theologian when she no longer believes what she has taught to others as Torah?"[21]

She revisited the question of whether tum'ah and tahara could have meaning for a modern feminist and whether human beings would be able to actually achieve religious purification. Her conclusions shocked many of her earlier readers. She built a theological anthropology that renounced not only purity, but wholeness and perfection as well. "Human is not whole. Human is full of holes. Human bleeds. Human births its worlds in agonies of blood and bellyaches. Human owns no perfect, timeless texts because human inhabits no perfect, timeless contexts. Human knows that what it weds need not be perfect to be infinitely dear."

In 1998, she published her feminist theological classic, *Engendering Judaism*, in which she struggled to reconcile her feminist theology with her continuing interest in halacha. Adler focused on the question of how rabbinic texts that appear to denigrate women can be read by a modern feminist. How does one broaden theological conceptions to encompass the human experiences of all people? What does it mean to engender Judaism?

The Impact of Feminism on Non-Orthodox American Jewish Liturgy

Traditional liturgy imagines God as a king, warrior, judge, and father. God is referred to by the pronouns *He, Him, His*, and the like. The traditional prayer book was intended primarily to be used by men, who would come to the synagogue and pray not only for themselves but on behalf of their wives and children. As Judaism changed in response to American social developments, women became more involved in the synagogue, and they wanted a spiritual experience that was more inclusive. But change took a long time, in large part because the liturgy of the prayer book had to be rewritten.

Most American Jews could no longer read Hebrew, or, if they could read it, they could understand very little. The translation thus became much more important. Until the 1970s or even later, the translations portrayed God in entirely masculine terms. Feminists found the language of the traditional prayer book unacceptable. Both the Hebrew and English portrayed God in masculine terms, almost never referring to the Shechina, the feminine aspect of God in mystical conceptions of Judaism. The problem with masculine references to God is that the language not only reflected but also shaped the way that people understood God, religion, and the world. Feminists argued that the traditional religious language was a reflection of the patriarchal rabbinic culture. As society changes, the language used to refer to religious concepts must change as well. There were various ways that prayer book editors could change the Hebrew prayers, or at least the translations, to make the prayers less masculine centered. First, they had to overcome the residual hostility to any liturgical change. Some people had memorized the prayers in English and opposed any alteration that would break their historical connection with the liturgy as they remembered it from their childhood. Others objected to losing their cherished image of God as a kindly, elderly old man, sitting on a big throne with a crown on his head.

Once such opposition was overcome (or ignored), the editor could try any one of a number of strategies. Some wanted to replace masculine pronouns for God with gender-sensitive or gender-neutral forms for the divine name. Gender sensitive refers to language that takes into account the need to avoid representing God entirely as a male entity, but does not necessarily eliminate all gender references, while gender neutrality is, as the words imply, completely devoid of masculine or feminine references. For example, *Sovereign* or *Ruler* could replace *Lord* or *King*. These words would convey a similar theology, but in a gender-neutral phrasing. "God of our fathers" could become "God of our ancestors," achieving the same goal. Alternatively, the words could be rendered "God of our fathers and mothers," including men and women in the formulation, making it gender inclusive rather than gender neutral.

Other feminists wanted to search for divine metaphors that were more explicitly feminine. *Mekor hachayim*, for example, literally meant "the source of life," but had the symbolic implication that God was a female who gives birth to everything in the world. Others portrayed God as a goddess, a theological conception that critics felt was dangerously close to pantheism. Nevertheless, Judith Plaskow spoke positively of these metaphors. To her, they contained "a sense of fluidity, movement, and multiplicity, [a] daring inter-weaving of women's experiences with Jewish, Native American, and God-dess imagery that leaves the reader/hearer with an expanded sense of what is possible when speaking of/to God."

The prayers were designed to help worshipers draw closer to God, but imagery that conveys out-of-date and perhaps even offensive notions of fam-ily or society could stifle rather than nurture spirituality. Some religious lan-guage that might once have been comforting had become jarring. For exam-ple, the Sabbath hymn "A Woman of Valor" praises the Jewish wife for being so devoted to her family and husband. When this hymn was composed, it was intended to compliment the Jewish wife and mother for her devotion to the central institution of the Jewish family, but a modern feminist might take offense at the notion that a woman's worth is derived from her domestic chores. Many other examples could be cited about how family and commu-nity life have changed, and the symbolism inherent in certain descriptions now strike some differently than they did their ancestors.

Particularly irksome was the opening prayer of the Tefillah. Also called the Shmonah Esrei, the Eighteen Benedictions, or the Amidah, the standing prayer, the Tefillah was regarded as one of the central rubrics of every prayer service. It began with the following words: "Praised be our God, God of our Fathers, God of Abraham, God of Isaac and God of Jacob." This seemed exclusionary. Where were the matriarchs? In 1972, a Reform task force on equality argued that such exclusionary language could mislead worshippers about the true nature of both human beings and God. They recommended altering masculine references in the various prayers and substituting egalitar-ian phrases that were called "gender sensitive" or "gender neutral." Neverthe-less, it took a long time for the national movement to act on that recommen-dation. Finally, in the early 1990s, the CCAR redid their 1975 *Gates of Prayer* to offer gender sensitive translation of the Hebrew prayers. The beginning of the Amidah was altered to read "Praised be our God, the God of our Fathers and our Mothers, God of Abraham, God of Isaac and God of Jacob; God of Sarah, God of Rebekah, God of Leah, and God of Rachel."[22]

Rewording the names of God framed in the masculine form was more difficult. In English, most prayer books had referred to God as *He* and *Him* and called God *The Lord*. Most worshippers who attended synagogues where these prayers were read regularly had become accustomed to the accepted texts. Any changes, no matter how minor or how justified, were likely to upset creatures of habit. Furthermore, many congregations were unwilling or unable to replace prayer books that they had only recently purchased. One solution was to develop a list of gender-sensitive words that could be verbally substituted for masculine references to God. Thus, the word *God* might be used to replace *The Lord* every time it appeared in the prayer book. This is what was done at Temple Jacob in Hancock, Michigan, where I served as a student rabbi in the early 1990s. When the prayer book had the word *Lord*, some congregants said "God," others said "Adonai," and still others said any one of a number of other names for the divine. I found it confusing and can only imagine that many of the worshippers had an even more difficult time.

Feminists felt, for the first time in recorded history, that Jewish women had the opportunity to express their religious sentiments liturgically. Women began writing new types of prayers, including creative prayer books that reflected a distinctive female voice. In 1976, Rabbi Margaret Moers Wenig and Naomi Janowitz edited *Siddur Nashim: A Sabbath Prayer Book for Women*, perhaps the first prayer book to use feminine imagery for God. While some of their translations of prayers simply substituted female pronouns for male ones, Wenig and Janowitz did introduce metaphors that imagined God as a female entity who gave birth to the world and whose womb protects all creatures. *Siddur Nashim* was credited with popularizing female religious imagery, opening up new liturgical possibilities for women who had never seen an alternative to the traditional wordings. Nevertheless, some felt that it did not fundamentally alter the conception of God as a domineering divine being who imposes Her (instead of His) will through sheer power.

Much of the liturgy being written at this time became influential in feminist circles only, but a number of works achieved mainstream success, notably Marcia Falk's *The Book of Blessings*.[23] Falk is best known for critiquing the traditional Jewish blessing formula: *Baruch atah, adonai eloheinu, melech haolam* . . . " (Blessed are you, Lord our God, King of the universe . . .). She argued that this opening formula was sexist, hierarchical, and even possibly "idolatrous." In order to correct this, Falk looked for new metaphors that could present God as an immanent presence who contributes to the restoration of the natural order rather than reinforcing masculine dominance. Falk had been writing Jewish liturgy for many years, but she first presented her creative prayers publicly in 1983 at an educational conference held at Rutgers University and then at a Jewish women's conference in Los Angeles the following year.[24]

Falk wrote that she was gratified to see that her blessings were being adopted by communities from a wide range of theological orientations and that some were using them as models from which to create their own personal liturgies. "But the results were not quite what I had anticipated. My early blessings were, for me, starting points in the creative process; I had never intended them to be used as blue prints or formulas."[25] So she was taken aback when she heard that people were inserting the phrase *eyn ha-hayim*, the source of life, which she had been using in some of her prayers, instead of *adonay eloheynu, melekh ha'olam*, Lord our God, king of the universe.[26] Falk did see the traditional phrase *adonay eloheynu, melekh ha'olam* as an example of "dead metaphor," a "greatly overused image that no longer functions to awaken awareness of the greater whole." Furthermore, she had argued that the image of God as a king with absolute power had "reinforced forms of patriarchal power and male privilege in the world." Nevertheless, "I have never believed that the alternative to this icon is a substitute image for the divine, since any single name or image would necessarily be partial" and could potentially become the basis for a different type of theological distortion. What she wanted to do was "set in motion *a process of ongoing naming* that would point toward the diversity of our experiences and reach toward a greater inclusivity within the encompassing, monotheistic whole."[27] Falk saw her liturgical writings as "a kind of midrash" because "I crafted my theological metaphors to connect specifically to the occasions they marked" and because "my language was rooted in biblical and rabbinic sources as well as other texts from later Hebrew literature." Her earlier work was based closely on the traditional form of Hebrew blessings, but was theologically radical because of the new images for the divine presence. She was hoping to "apprehend the divine" by presenting new ways of expressing gratitude to God. The process of finding the best words to express the appropriate theological position was delicate and had to be undertaken carefully. For example, Falk had written a "Blessing Before the Meal" in which she replaced the phrase *barukh atah*, blessed are you (masc. sing.) with an active, first-person-plural gender-inclusive form, *n'vareykh*, let us bless. She then found what she felt to be a perfect metaphor from Deuteronomy 8:7: "A land of watercourses, wellsprings, and depths emerging from valleys and from hills." The Hebrew word she selected was *ayin*, wellspring or fountain, with the figurative meaning of "source." "In the springing up of the fountains, I saw an arc of motion that mirrored the description in the traditional blessing of *hamotzi*, the psalmist's image of bread drawn from the earth."[28] Falk saw her blessings as creative expressions of love for God that were meant to inspire rather than become canonized liturgy. As a poet, "I sought to create an organic whole with each new blessing." As a liturgist, "I firmly believed that no convention of prayer ought to become completely routine, lest it lose its ability to inspire authentic feeling."[29]

Ordaining Women Rabbis in the Liberal Movements

The most important leadership position in the Jewish community was that of the rabbi. The rabbi had traditionally been a judge who made decisions on questions of Jewish law, but in modern society the role had evolved to become a much broader one, encompassing everything from giving sermons to helping develop strategic visions to speaking at interfaith functions. The exclusion of women from the rabbinate was upsetting not only because of its symbolism but also because it deprived young girls of positive female role models. Having seen only men leading the congregation in prayer and numerous other roles, these young women had no model of feminine leadership that could help them form their own aspirations for leadership in the Jewish community or in other fields.

The Jewish community was not the first to ordain women. The first female Congregationalist minister, Antoinette Brown, had been ordained way back in 1853. There were other cases of women serving as ministers in the late nineteenth and early twentieth centuries, just as there were a handful of Jewish women who led congregations as quasi rabbis, such as Ray Frank and Paula Ackerman. The Presbyterian Church accepted the principle of women's ordination in 1955 and ordained their first woman minister in 1956, but the number of women ordained in the following years was small. One of the branches of the Lutheran Church granted women the right to be ordained in 1970, as did the Episcopalians in 1976.

The growing influence of feminism strengthened the argument for women's ordination. Women's primary role did not have to be that of wives and mothers. Women who felt the calling should be allowed to try to become anything they have the talents and abilities to be. The civil rights movement created an atmosphere in which it was increasingly unacceptable to be seen as discriminating. Even though religious organizations were exempt from the civil rights laws that prohibited discrimination, they were expected to behave according to the highest standards, and those standards included treating women fairly. A third reason that women became increasingly able to enter the ministry in general and the rabbinate specifically was that the massive move to suburbia created a huge number of new churches and synagogues who needed ministers and rabbis.

When Sally J. Priesand arrived at the Hebrew Union College–Jewish Institute of Religion (HUC-JIR) in Cincinnati in February 1964, "they didn't take me very seriously at first. Few people at the college paid much attention; they thought I came to marry a rabbi rather than be one."[30] Priesand was not the first woman to study at the Hebrew Union College. Founder Rabbi Isaac Mayer Wise had allowed women to enroll from its founding in 1875, but none had been ordained. A few had tried to complete the program, but had been discouraged and, in one case, rejected by the Board of Governors at the very end of the process. A few others had taken congregations without having been formally ordained. A "lady rabbi" served for a number of years on the West Coast, and the widow of a rabbi took over her late husband's congregation in the Deep South. These were exceptional situations and the women were seen as filling in on a temporary basis or serving congregations that no "real" rabbi would want. There was still no woman who had graduated from a recognized American rabbinical school and taken a mainstream congregational pulpit.

Priesand had decided in 1962, when she was sixteen years old, that she wanted to be a rabbi. The problem was that only men were eligible to be ordained as rabbis. She was not completely alone; there were a handful of other women studying in the HUC undergraduate department, as well as women from the University of Cincinnati who participated actively in HUC activities. Most were planning for careers in religious education and many were hoping to marry future rabbis. By the time she entered the rabbinical program in 1968, she was the only female studying at that academic level. In 1972, Priesand had become the first woman to be ordained as a Reform rabbi at HUC-JIR. This was a revolutionary breakthrough. Even though the Reform movement had been committed to egalitarianism from its origins in the early nineteenth century, it had never before allowed any of its rabbinical seminaries to ordain a woman. "On June 3, 1972 I was ordained rabbi by Hebrew Union College–Jewish Institute of Religion in Cincinnati, Ohio. As I sat in the historic Plum Street Temple, waiting to accept the ancient rite of s'micha [rabbinic ordination], I couldn't help but reflect on the implications of what was about to happen." She thought back on the status of Jewish women in ancient and medieval society. "For thousands of years women in Judaism had been second-class citizens. They were not permitted to own property. They could not serve as witnesses. They did not have the right to

FIGURE 5.4. Rabbi Sally Priesand being ordained by Rabbi Alfred Gottschalk at the Hebrew Union College–Jewish Institute of Religion in Cincinnati, Ohio on June 3, 1972. Priesand was the first woman to be ordained as a rabbi in the United States. *Courtesy of the Jacob Rader Marcus Center of the American Jewish Archives*

initiate divorce proceedings. They were not counted in the minyan." Even in the Reform movement, women " were not permitted to participate fully in the life of the synagogue. With my ordination all that was going to change; one more barrier was about to be broken."[31]

Although Priesand was the first woman to be ordained by a rabbinical seminary, the Reconstructionist movement had been the first to formally accept women into their rabbinic program. In 1967, when the Federation of Reconstructionist Congregations and Fellowships (renamed the Federation of Reconstructionist Congregations and Havurot in 1983) decided to raise the money necessary to open a Reconstructionist rabbinical school, it was simply assumed that applications would be accepted from both men and women. According Rabbi Ira Eisenstein, it "never occurred to us even to debate the matter" because it was the "obvious thing to do."[32]

Sandy Eisenberg (Sasso) became the first female Reconstructionist rabbi, graduating in 1974. She had been raised in Congregation Keneseth Israel in Philadelphia, a Reform temple led by Rabbi Bertram Korn. "When I decided that I would be a rabbi, I was 16 years old. It was 1963 and there were no women rabbis then. In many ways, it was a simple decision. I was in love with Judaism and wanted to teach and serve the community just as my rabbi did." But in certain other ways, it was a difficult choice. "For many years I told no one of my secret ambition except the rabbi of my congregation, who was my beloved teacher and mentor. Who knew, I told myself, maybe this too would pass. I would find another passion, another career goal. Actually, throughout college, I tried. I looked into English, to the academic study of religion. But these did not satisfy me."[33]

When Sasso was in university, Korn invited her to help lead a service. The congregants responded positively, and this helped her make the decision to go to rabbinical school. Sasso decided to go to the Reconstructionist Rabbinical College in large part because she found the religious thought of Mordecai Kaplan to be inspiring, particularly the idea that people have the responsibility to "look upon ourselves not merely as descendants but as ancestors of posterity, responsible for preserving and creating symbols and rituals for future generations."

Women, Sasso felt, were now able to do just that. Speaking at an event celebrating the thirtieth anniversary of women rabbis in Toronto in 2002, she recalled how excluded she felt as a woman. "What struck me the most was the absence of text, the lack of female voices, women's thoughts and stories. I read of men's struggles with God, but not women's. What I read either did not understand who I was as a woman or excluded me. No one was answering my questions, in fact, no one was asking them." She felt torn between feminism and Judaism, neither of which fulfilled her completely. "Just as I felt ill at ease in the emerging feminist culture that did not address my Jewish soul, I felt marginalized in the Jewish community I sought to serve because it did not embrace my woman's soul."[34]

When she married fellow rabbinic student Dennis Sasso in June 1970, Rabbi Korn said that "for the first time in the story of Judaism, two students for the rabbinate are being wed."[35] Not everyone shared Rabbi Korn's enthusiasm. Some just found it odd. "You look like a normal American girl," one person remarked. Others found her to be a novelty. One reporter focused on the "rabbi in mini-skirts." Many were upset. "What would prompt a Jewish girl to have the chutzpah" to do something so radical? Some suggested that she should set her ambitions on what they saw as the more appropriate role of teacher in her husband's religious school.[36] When Sasso was ordained in 1974, she took a job as rabbi of the Manhattan Reconstructionist Havurah. Three years later, she and her husband were elected to separate rabbinical positions at Beth El Zedeck, an Indianapolis, Indiana congregation affiliated with both the Conservative and Reconstructionist movements. They were the first husband and wife rabbis to serve the same congregation. This arrangement was quite successful, and they have been working at Beth El Zedeck for more than thirty years.

In the Reform and Reconstructionist congregations, some women rabbis found that they were greeted warmly and treated fairly. Others complained that they had to break through "stained glass ceilings." It is true that relatively few women were appointed as senior rabbis of large congregations in the years following women's ordination. In 1992, Rabbi Paula Reimers of Arizona commented sadly that "it's the same old story. Everyone is in favor of women rabbis—until it comes time to hire one. A congregation would rather take an incompetent man than a woman. Women are picked last."[37] Such complaints, frequently heard in the 1980s and early 1990s, have substantially diminished if not disappeared. Many of those who originally resisted the idea have now warmed up to women rabbis. Part of the change may be simply that they have become accustomed to the idea. They have seen women rabbis in action, and many have been impressed. There have even been women rabbis playing fictional roles on TV, and this too has made them not only more acceptable but even glamorous.

Women rabbis made a number of attempts to organize. The Reform movement's Women's Rabbinic Network (WRN) became a powerful lobbying organization within the CCAR. The WRN held their own meetings within the CCAR conferences, planned various special programs, and issued their own publications. They also raised substantial amounts of funds to promote Jewish women's studies, which included creating the Rabbi Sally J. Priesand Visiting Professorship at HUC-JIR in New York, launched in the fall of 1999. Rabbi Janet Marder became the first woman president of the CCAR in March 2003. Marder explained that women rabbis value three important characteristics: balance, intimacy, and empowerment. Women were determined to balance their career responsibilities with their familial obligations. They wanted to develop close personal relationships in the workplace rather than rely on power dynamics. As a consequence, they wanted to share responsibility rather than perpetuate the traditional hierarchy.[38]

Rabbi Laura Geller, senior rabbi at Temple Emanuel in Beverly Hills since 1994, believes that she exemplifies a feminine approach to the rabbinate. "My style is one of shared leadership—I would argue that's a feminine model of leadership. Our congregation is not a hierarchy, but a series of concentric circles. One of my very clear goals is to empower lay people to mentor young people, lead services, teach, and really take responsibility for their own Jewish life."[39] Many believe that this approach works substantially better than the older power-based model. Michael and Linda Lieberman, members of Congregation Shir Hadash in California, told me how Rabbi Melanie W. Aron had unified the Los Gatos temple: "From the time that we were founded, there was constant conflict between our [male] rabbis and various segments of the community. And then Rabbi Aron came. "She made more of an effort to work with people. Everyone liked her and the bickering just stopped."[40]

The Struggle for Egalitarianism in the Conservative Movement

While women were accepted as religious equals relatively easily in the Reform and Reconstructionist movements, the inclusion of women has been more controversial in the Conservative movement. Some changes were made rather organically without too much dissent, but others set off protracted struggles. Going back to the beginnings of the Conservative movement, deviations from traditional practice included the removal of the mechitza, the barrier that separated men from women during prayer, the adoption of the practice of mixed seating, and the establishment of mixed choirs with women as well as men. By the 1950s, most Conservative synagogues accepted these practices as normative, and did not see any inconsistency between these liberalizations and their refusal to count women in a minyan, let them lead services, be called up to the Torah for an aliyah, be ordained as rabbis, or invested as cantors.

The Conservative movement accepted the idea that halacha could evolve and put the responsibility for evaluating possible changes into the hands of the CJLS. In 1955, CJLS chairman Rabbi Aaron Blumenthal wrote a responsum permitting women to be called to the Torah. Blumenthal admitted that "there is no recorded instance of a woman called to the Torah either in the Talmud or in the Gaonic literature. However, there is a medieval decision that seems to be practical halachah." He cited a medieval responsum written by Rabbi Meir of Rothenburg where it is written that, "in a city whose men are all Kohanim and there is not one Israelite among them, it seems to me that one Kohen takes the first two aliyot and then women are to be called, for 'All may ascend.'"[41] Some traditionalists ridiculed Blumenthal's logic, arguing that Rabbi Meir of Rothenburg was only presenting a hypothetical situation that could not possibly be used to determine practical halacha. But, as Elliot Dorff has recently written, "The Conservative Movement's commitment to be honest to the historical context of Jewish law in the past and present . . . requires us . . . not to be too constrained by specific texts that limit the role of women, for they were only giving retroactive legal justification for what common practice was at the time."[42]

Most Conservative congregations accepted the idea of giving women aliyot and promptly instituted the practice. This was important in itself for women who wanted to be able to bless the Torah, and it opened the way to include a Torah reading as part of the bat mitzvah ceremony. Many Conservative synagogues began moving the bat mitzvah from Friday night to Saturday morning, where the bat mitzvah was expected to chant Torah blessings and even read from the Torah. The status quo was maintained throughout the 1950s and 1960s, but many Jewish feminists involved in the Conservative movement felt that the denomination was not sufficiently sensitive to their concerns. A small Jewish women's group named Ezrat Nashim presented a Call for Change to the RA on March 14, 1972. Ezrat Nashim, which had been founded the previous year as an outgrowth of the New York Havurah, had a name that was a double entendre. Literally, *ezrat nashim* means "help for women," but the phrase was generally used to refer to the courtyard in the Jerusalem Temple where women congregated. Later, the term was used to refer to the women's section in the synagogue, which was sometimes located in the back and other times upstairs in a balcony. The women's group adopted the name with an ironic intention. The name reflected the dual goals of the group—to provide support for women interested in becoming more involved in Jewish religious leadership and to enrich Jewish religious life itself.

The young women traveled to the Concord Hotel in Lake Kiamesha, New York, for the annual convention of the RA, but they were not put on the official program, so they organized their own meeting. This worked out nicely, because there were many women at the RA convention, mostly wives of rabbis who were traveling with their husbands but not planning to attend the official program. They were hyped up because Sally Priesand was scheduled to graduate from the rabbinic program of the Hebrew Union College just a few months later, and her ordination gave them hope that women could make inroads in the Conservative movement as well. The women insisted that the separate-but-equal concept that relegated women to the sidelines must end immediately. Jewish tradition, which had once been so far ahead of most other societies and cultures, had fallen behind, and this was disgraceful. "Life-patterns open to women, appropriate and even progressive for the rabbinic and medieval periods, are entirely unacceptable to us today."

The Call for Change argued that positions of leadership should be open to women and men on an equal basis. Ezrat Nashim also called for broadened religious participation for women, accepting the commitment to observe certain commandments as a condition for religious equality. Paula Hyman, one of the members of Ezrat Nashim, wrote that "we recognized that the subordinate status of women was linked to their exemption from positive time-bound mitzvot, and we therefore accepted increased obligation as the corollary of equality." If women were willing to accept upon themselves the obligation to observe positive time-bound commandments, then they should be able to be considered qualified for any religious role. Specifically, the Call for Change demanded that women be accepted as eidim, witnesses. This was a key stumbling block to the equality of women in Jewish law. If women could be accepted as witnesses, then they could sign ketubot, marriage documents, and gittin, bills of divorce. As long as they were not eligible to serve as eidim, men would continue to have monopolistic control over important areas of ritual that determined personal status.

While there was no dramatic breakthrough, the CJLS continued to issue responsa that broadened the scope of permissible religious activity for women. In 1973, the CJLS accepted women as eligible to be part of a minyan. The following year, they passed yet another responsum that allowing women to lead synagogue services as prayer leaders. In large measure because of these rulings, many Conservative congregations began moving to allow women to take on new ritual responsibilities. In 1972, only 7 percent of Conservative shuls allowed women to bless the Torah. By 1976—only four years later—fully 50 percent of all Conservative congregations did. The decision to count women in a minyan was made relatively easily, but the issue of ordaining women was considerably more controversial. The JTS Talmud faculty refused to give their approval, and they retained substantial religious authority in a movement that drew its legitimacy from its rabbinic scholarship. Also, most traditionalist Conservative Jews were dead set against the idea. Even though they comprised only a small percentage of the movement, right-wing Conservative Jews were the ones most likely to send their children to Solomon Schechter day schools and Ramah summer camps. They were also the most likely to observe kashrut and Shabbat and thus formed the majority of the "serious" Conservative Jews who participated weekly and even daily in religious activities. Leaders feared that a decision to ordain women would alienate this group and that they might defect to Orthodoxy or form their own movement.

In 1977, JTS chancellor Gerson Cohen appointed a Committee for the Study of the Ordination of Women as Rabbis, and in 1979 they issued their report. Eleven of the fourteen finding that there was "no direct halachic objection" to the ordination of female rabbis. Nevertheless, the vote to ordain women rabbis was put off after sixteen of the most distinguished JTS professors threatened to boycott. They argued that "Jewish law forbids the participation of women as rabbis." They objected to the whole idea of letting all faculty members vote. How could a professor of Hebrew literature, for example, vote on a halachic issue? Surely this was a question that had to be decided by the halachic experts, meaning the Talmud faculty. It was that same year—1979—that Sandy Eisenberg Sasso accepted a joint rabbinic post with her husband at Temple Beth El Zedeck, a congregation that was affiliated with the Conservative as well as the Reconstructionist movements. While the situation was rather unusual, Sasso was thereby now a rabbi leading a synagogue affiliated with the Conservative movement. Although this precedent did not seem to influence the course of the debate, it was already obvious that women were going to enter the Conservative rabbinate and become rabbis of Conservative synagogues whether JTS ordained them or not. Even so, the position of JTS had enormous symbolic importance. Pressure continued to mount. In 1980, the RA voted 156 to 115 in favor of ordaining women as rabbis. Still, the question was not decided.

Later in 1979, Rabbi Linda Joy Holtzman graduated from the Reconstructionist Rabbinical College in Philadelphia and was hired as the solo rabbi of Beth Israel congregation in Coatesville, Pennsylvania. While there were already approximately a dozen women rabbis who had been ordained by the Reconstructionist or Reform movements, they were all either assistant rabbis, Hillel directors, or hospital chaplains. When she came to New York to shop for a white robe for the upcoming High Holy Days, she told the *New York Times*, "the fact that I have an appointment in a small town and that they have entrusted me with functions they believe are important is very significant for women and for the Jewish community." The newspaper reported that Holtzman's appointment was "a marked breakthrough for the growing numbers of women who have faced obstacles in becoming a rabbi-in-charge."[43]

Rabbi Wolfe Kelman, the executive vice president of the RA, called Holtzman's appointment "an historical breakthrough and simply fantastic. The real significance is that many congregations that have been leaning toward appointing a woman, and have been reluctant to be the first, will be encouraged to do likewise." Women who had already become rabbis in other movements looked at the Holtzman precedent and hoped that they might now be acceptable to the RA. In 1983, Rabbi Beverly Weintraub Magidson became the first non-JTS female ordainee to petition the RA to be admitted to membership. Magidson had studied at HUC-JIR because JTS was not admitting women, Ordained in 1979, she was hoping the RA would now admit her as a member. Her application was rejected, falling short of the three-quarters majority necessary by only four votes. Even so, Magidson was able to find a position at a Conservative synagogue. The movement was at risk of having large numbers of women rabbis enter the Conservative rabbinate through the "back door," studying at other rabbinical seminaries and then taking positions in Conservative synagogues.

The Conservative movement hierarchy was at an impasse. There was too much respect for the Talmud professors to ignore their vociferous objections and yet there was a groundswell of support for social change that reflected contemporary American reality. This impasse was broken not by any brilliant essay or masterful organizational intervention, but rather by a death. Saul Lieberman, long considered the greatest Talmudist at JTS, and a man of immense influence, had a heart attack on a plane trip to Israel and passed away. Without Lieberman's forceful presence, the momentum toward a vote was now unstoppable. On October 24, 1983, the JTS faculty voted thirty-four to eight to admit women to its rabbinical program. In September 1984, twenty-three women entered JTS as members of the seminary's first class to include female rabbinical students. There were already several women studying at JTS, hoping that the path would be cleared for their ordination.

Amy Eilberg, the daughter of a Pennsylvania congressman, was the most advanced, and she became the first woman to be ordained by JTS in May 1985. Some of those who opposed the decision believe that Joel Roth, a professor of Talmud, consented to the ordination on the condition that Eilberg agree not to serve as a witness. Partisan sources claim that she did agree to this, but then broke the agreement as soon as she took her first pulpit, but

Eilberg brusquely denied this. "What you were told is not true. The truth is that I was asked whether I would be willing to abstain from serving as a witness, and I immediately said that I would not be willing to make such a commitment. I did not go back on this agreement, because I never agreed to it."[44] Roth refused to confirm that there had been any agreement, writing me that "while I then and now have urged women not to serve as witnesses in matters of Jewish law, I have no recollection whatsoever that her ordination, or that of anyone else, was conditional upon their agreement not to do so."[45] While most rabbis rarely served as witnesses, women rabbis were now able to assume that role when necessary. Women began entering the rabbinical school at JTS in large numbers, precipitating the departure of those who were most opposed to the ordination of women. Women graduating from JTS automatically became members of the RA. Those who had been ordained in other seminaries became eligible to apply for RA membership and most were admitted, including Beverly Magidson.[46]

The Impact of Feminism on Orthodoxy

There has always been a relatively small but determined group of Modern Orthodox women who have pushed to introduce feminist ideas into Orthodox Jewish life. They did not want to undermine traditional Jewish values, as they understood the term, but they wanted to help expand the role of women in Orthodoxy. What was important to them was that their efforts should be completely compatible with the halacha. The problem with this was that the determination of what might be compatible halachically was in the hands of mostly haredi poskim, rabbinic legal scholars with sufficient expertise to make policy decisions, almost all of whom were hostile to both their methods and goals. The poskim worried that allowing women to make any changes might lead to the destruction of the halachic system in its entirety. Orthodox Jewish feminists disagreed, arguing that Orthodoxy could be more flexible. They were determined to push as hard as they could for change, as long as that change could be justified in a halachic context.

In order to understand the struggle for a greater role for women in Orthodox Jewish ritual, we must remember that Orthodoxy is structured differently from the other denominations. As we discussed in chapter three, Orthodoxy is incredibly variegated, and no single set of organizations and institutions represent the whole. Perhaps even more importantly—in dramatic contrast with the non-Orthodox movements—American Orthodoxy was and is greatly influenced by religious trends in Israel. As a result, Orthodox Jews in the United States refer to Israeli Orthodox institutions, programs, thinkers, and decisions during the very early stages of their own deliberations on any given topic. Yet, American Orthodoxy is tremendously influenced by the American environment as well. This is certainly true for the Modern Orthodox (many of whom now prefer to be called centrist Orthodox) but it is also true for the haredim, the fervently Orthodox who try to limit their exposure to American culture. Any controversial issue, including that of allowing women to play a greater role in synagogue ritual, has to be acceptable to rabbinic leaders in Israel as well as the United States. Since the sages that dominate decision making in the various subgroups are generally extremely conservative, achieving consensus on any ritual innovation is virtually impossible.

The American Orthodox synagogue played a more important role in the American Orthodox community than the synagogue did in Israel. Whereas the American synagogue was a center of intellectual activity and social life, the Israeli synagogue was generally seen as a place to pray and not much more. Because of this, American Orthodox feminists placed their emphasis on women's prayer groups and greater inclusivity in the synagogue service, whereas Israeli Orthodox feminist-oriented women were more concerned with advanced Talmudic study. Already in the late 1960s, Rabbi Steven (later Shlomo) Riskin of the Lincoln Square Synagogue in Manhattan allowed women to celebrate Simchat Torah by dancing with the Torahs in a separate area. As long as they were not dancing in front of men, Riskin reasoned, it would be halachically permissible. He even allowed them to read from the end of one Torah and the beginning of another just as the men did. This innovation was then copied by other liberally leaning Orthodox congregations.

During the course of the next decade, Orthodox women's prayer groups were organized on the Upper West Side of Manhattan and a number of other Modern Orthodox enclaves. Some of the women involved decided to create an organization to support women's prayer groups, which they called the Women's Tefillah Network. These prayer groups became popular among women who were traditional in religious practice but feminist in ideological orientation. Most identified themselves as Orthodox, but others were not completely observant and shied away from that label. These tefillah groups provided an opportunity for Orthodox women to lead prayers, read from the Torah, and perform various other ritual acts that they would normally not be allowed to do. They were careful to restrict themselves to ritual activities that had the appropriate heter (rabbinic dispensation). For example, they were able to find a precedent allowing women to read Megillat Esther on Purim, if there were no men present, and received a heter from a sympathetic rabbi permitting them to hold their own public megillah reading.

In addition to Riskin, the women were encouraged by Rabbi Avi Weiss at the Hebrew Institute of Riverdale, Rabbi Haskel Lookstein of Congregation Kehillat Jeshurun in Manhattan, and a number of other progressive Orthodox leaders, but the vast majority—and virtually all haredi rabbis—opposed any type of women's prayer groups. Agudath ha-Rabbanim, the Union of Orthodox Rabbis of the United States and Canada, issued a strongly worded statement condemning these groups in the *Jewish Press*, an Orthodox Jewish newspaper published in Brooklyn. While Agudath ha-Rabbanim loved to dramatize their opposition to various modern innovations, the substance of their position was not that different from most other haredi groups. "God forbid this should come to pass. A daughter of Israel may not participate in such worthless ceremonies that are totally contrary to Halacha. We are shocked to hear that 'rabbis' have promoted such an undertaking which results in the desecration of God and His Torah." Because of the severity of the infraction, they issued a stern warning. "We forewarn all those who assist such "'Minyonim'" that we will take the strictest measures to prevent such 'prayers,' which are a product of pure ignorance and illiteracy. We admonish these 'Orthodox rabbis': Do not make a comedy out of Torah."[47]

The opposition to women's prayer groups and other liberalizations came not only from haredi yeshivas but even from Yeshiva University, long considered the "flagship" of American Modern Orthodoxy. In 1985, a group of five Talmudists teaching at RIETS, Yeshiva University's rabbinical school, published a responsum prohibiting any sort of organized women's prayer group. This brought a long-simmering conflict out into the public. Rabbi Avi Weiss, one of the strongest supporters of the women's prayer groups, published a response reaffirming his support for the concept. Along with Rabbi Saul Berman, Weiss apparently saw the RIETS Talmudists as obstructionists, determined to block legitimate halachic activity just because it was contrary to their social norms. The conflict was not restricted to the issue of women's ritual activity, but it was certainly the most prominent. Eventually, Weiss established a new rabbinical seminary which was dedicated to being "open" to numerous liberalizations, as long as they were halachic according to his determination.

The founding mother of Orthodox Jewish feminism is Blu Greenberg, who, in 1981, wrote an impassioned polemic entitled *On Women and Judaism* to try to convince Orthodox Jews that feminism and Judaism were compatible. "There is much that we can learn from the women's movement in terms of our own growth as Jews." On the other hand, "there is much that feminism can gain from the perspective of traditional Jewish values."[48] Greenberg tried to push the Orthodox community to find ways to allow women to participate more broadly in Judaism without violating Jewish law. She wrote that "though the truth is painful to those of us who live by Halakah, honesty bids us acknowledge that Jewish women, particularly in the more traditional community, face inequality in the synagogue and participation in prayer, in halakhic education, in the religious courts, and in areas of communal leadership."[49]

In order to begin rectifying the inequality that she saw, Greenberg founded the Jewish Orthodox Feminist Alliance (JOFA) to advocate for women's increased participation in Orthodox Jewish life. JOFA began holding biannual conferences at the Midtown Hyatt Hotel in Manhattan in 1997. The first conference attracted about two thousand people, mostly Orthodox women. Like many of the organizations created by the modern Orthodox, JOFA found it hard to turn their short-term enthusiasm into permanent institutional structures. Nevertheless, Orthodox Jewish women had made tremendous strides. Greenberg remembers that "when I was growing up in the 1940s and 1950s, even the word *bat mitzvah* was off-limits in Orthodoxy, signaling the celebrant as Reform or Conservative. Today, no self-respecting Modern Orthodox family would refrain from marking its daughter's Jewish maturity with a *bat mitzvah* celebration." While the changes in Orthodoxy may not seem as dramatic as the changes that have been made in the more liberal denominations, "they are more remarkable in some ways because they represent a greater shift from the status quo." In just one generation, "Orthodox women's roles have shifted from exclusively private to increasingly public, from the household and *mikvah* to houses of study and prayer, and religious courts of law."[50]

As Greenberg suggested, prayer could only go so far without the Talmudic learning to support halachic decisions. Orthodox women had traditionally been excluded from advanced rabbinic studies, and their education was focused primarily on the study of the Hebrew Bible. However interesting and important, the Tanach was not the primary basis for Orthodox decision making. There needed to be a school for advanced Talmudic studies that would accept women or even a program intended specifically for women. In 1979, Rabbi David Silber founded the Drisha Institute in Manhattan. Drisha's goal was to provide advanced Jewish studies to women, including Talmud. In addition to many other educational initiatives, Silber organized a three-year program leading to a certificate that gave women graduates authorization to teach Talmud at the high school level. While Drisha was careful to avoid issuing feminist manifestos, the program had opened up not only a new type of scholarship to Orthodox women but also an entirely new realm of possible leadership roles.

During the 1980s, higher Torah learning institutions for women expanded their programs. While some of these midrashot were strictly one-year programs intended for girls straight out of high school, others developed into multiyear educational programs that include *mechonim gevohim*, a female equivalent of the *kollel*, where a married male student receives a fellowship to study Talmud full-time. The midrashot managed to remain on good relations with the Israeli chief rabbinate and the national-religious Zionist Orthodox establishment because they were seen as a natural extension of the Ulpana girls' intensive high school study programs. Despite their commitment to advanced Jewish studies, it was only later that some Orthodox women began to embrace feminism in Israel. Whereas American Orthodox women first got interested in feminism and then began to work toward the development of advanced study programs, the process went in the reverse direction in Israel. Part of the reason for this was linguistic. Israeli Orthodox women obviously read Hebrew fluently and could use this knowledge to learn Aramaic and other related languages quite easily. In contrast, even a relatively well-educated Orthodox American Jewish woman would have to spend years developing the language skills necessary to master the various types of rabbinic texts.

By the early 1990s, women were being certified for the first time as *toanot*, legal advocates for women dealing with divorce cases in batei din. They also were training to become yoatzot halacha, experts in Jewish law in areas directly pertinent to women. Nishmat, the Jerusalem Center for Advanced Jewish Study for Women, established the Keren Ariel Program in September 1997 to train female halachic experts in the laws of niddah. The laws of female ritual purity were chosen as the study area because having women who were highly trained in the intricacies of the laws of taharat hamishpachah would make it possible for women to pose halachic questions directly to other women. Nishmat ran the program over the course of two years. Women studied half the week for a total of more than one thousand hours of study. It included intensive *chavruta* study as well as a daily *shiur*, and bimonthly evening lectures on issues concerning medicine and halacha. Nevertheless, they were cautious to avoid giving the impression that these women were talmudic scholars who were making original decisions. Rabbanit Chana Henkin, the founder and dean of Nishmat, explained that "the title yoatzot halacha—halachic consultants or advisers—was selected to convey that these women are not rendering original halachic rulings."[51] When they needed to convey a decision on an issue that had no precedent, they referred the issue to recognized male halachic authorities. Already in 1984, Blu Greenberg speculated that there might be Orthodox women rabbis some day. Several years later, Haviva Ner-David (originally Krasner-Davidson) tried to apply to the rabbinical program at Yeshiva University. In an article for *Moment* magazine, she claimed that she never even received an acknowledgment that her application had been received. The rabbinical school denied this, but explained that their program was limited to males only. She later studied privately for ordination in Israel with Rabbi Aryeh Strikovsky, an Orthodox rabbi who taught at Pardes, a coed yeshiva in Jerusalem. She wrote a book describing her quest called *Life on the Fringes*, a play on the fact that Orthodox men wear tzitzit, ritual fringes, and that women were traditionally exempt from this obligation.[52] Ner-David settled in Israel and therefore never assumed a public role in American Jewish religious life. This hurt her credibility, as did her husband's connection to Marc Gafni, a charismatic Jewish Renewal rabbi who was accused repeatedly of sexual improprieties. Worst of all, Strikovsky later claimed that she was "ordained" as an educator rather than as an actual rabbi.[53] Nevertheless, she has made a contribution to the progressive Orthodox circle in Jerusalem that is engaging in a creative struggle to reimagine the halacha.

Some expected Rabbi Avi Weiss to allow women to study for the rabbinate in the new rabbinical school Yeshivat Chovevei Torah that he launched in the fall of 1999. This turned out not to be the case, at least initially, but hopes were raised at the time because of his passionate support of a greater role for women in the Orthodox synagogue. The previous year, Weiss had hired Sharona Margolin Halickman to work as a "congregational intern" at his synagogue, the Hebrew Institute of Riverdale. Rabbi Adam Mintz of the Lincoln Square Synagogue in Manhattan started a similar program at the same time and appointed Julie Stern Joseph as congregational intern. Sharon Liberman Mintz explained that Modern Orthodox women saw that they could "be astrophysicists, or neurosurgeons, but in the [Orthodox] Jewish world, they did not have a prominent role in synagogue leadership." Liberman Mintz, who was involved with the process of defining the role of the congregational intern, said that "the idea of this program was to show young women that there was a possible leadership role for them in the synagogue; that women could play an active role in [Orthodox] Jewish life."[54]

All parties involved stressed that although the congregational intern idea was new, it was not an attempt to pioneer a role for women in the Orthodox rabbinate. At the time, Joseph said that "my goal is not that I want to achieve a title. I want to provide a service." She denied that there was any plan to expand the congregational intern role into a quasi-rabbinic position. "There's no thought that this role will evolve into a rabbinic position for women. If there was, then I wouldn't be involved." Weiss also denied that the congregational intern position in his congregation was intended to evolve into a rabbinic role for women. "It is a distinct role in which and through which women can make a spiritual impact. The call for women to be rabbis is unhelpful. It has halachic problems." His language could be interpreted as indicating that he was against talking about the issue, not because he was against the ordination of women, but because he worried that such talk might solidify opposition. Certainly, many of the roles assigned to the two women were tasks that were routinely done by assistant rabbis.

Weiss felt that one of the advantages of having female synagogue professional staff was that they could counsel women who felt more comfortable with a female, such as in the actual case of a twelve-year-old girl who was converting to Judaism. Halickman was able to be with her at the mikveh, something that a male rabbi could not do for obvious reasons. Halickman had studied at the Azrieli School of Education at Yeshiva University, which was a popular program for rabbinic students thinking about going into Jewish education as a career. "If I have the background of a rabbi, but don't want to be a rabbi for Orthodox reasons, I should not be shut out of opportunities."[55] While Joseph did not play any role in the main service at Lincoln Square Synagogue, Halickman delivered periodic sermons at the Hebrew Institute. As Weiss put it, "when the occasion arises, [Halickman] is welcome to teach Torah on Shabbat morning." Not only was she to be allowed to address the entire congregation, but she could do so from the pulpit, something that was highly unusual in an Orthodox context.

While Lincoln Square quickly ended the congregational intern experiment, the Hebrew Institute has continued it to this day. Halickman served part-time for a few years, then became the full-time *madricha ruchanit* (religious mentor), a completely new type of position. In addition, they continued to hire congregational interns. Sara Hurwitz was the fourth intern, beginning work in the summer of 2003. She then replaced Halickman as *madricha ruchanit* in September 2004. "There are probably five percent of the things that a rabbi does that I cannot do in my role as madricha ruchanit. Those five percent happen to be very public, meaning that I cannot lead public rituals such as davening [leading services] on Shabbat morning." What she could do was "be a presence on the women's side of the sanctuary, greeting women when they enter, helping them find a seat and a prayer book, making them feel as if they are participants in the service rather than observers." Hurwitz believes that participation is important for women in an Orthodox synagogue. "I think that the spirituality of the sanctuary increases tenfold when women feel like they have a role and, rather than just observing, they can feel part of the service. Their voices are louder, they feel more comfortable, they [feel that they are] part of what is going on."[56]

Hurwitz is currently studying under Weiss's auspices with the goal of receiving a certificate that will have "the same language as rabbis graduating from a semicha program" and will "hopefully give me a title that will indicate that I have the same job responsibilities as a rabbi." She and one other woman study the same curriculum as the YCT semicha students. They do much of it on their own, but they go twice a week to the YCT campus to study in a shiur (Talmud lecture) with Rabbi Ysoscher Katz. They are currently discussing what title they will use for the female equivalent of an Orthodox rabbi.

Some people believe that Dina Najman-Licht is already serving as the first Orthodox woman pulpit rabbi. In fall 2006, Congregation Kehilat Orach Eliezer (KOE) hired Najman-Licht as its rosh kehila (head of community).[57] Najman-Licht was a Drisha fellow, a Torat Miriam fellow, and had learned at Nishmat; indeed she had studied in virtually all of the innovative programs that had been set up to allow Orthodox women to study advanced Jewish law. A few liberal Orthodox women saw this as a tremendous step forward, but some Orthodox bloggers dismissed the appointment as being irrelevant since the congregation was not regarded as completely Orthodox. Hirhurim, one of the most widely read bloggers, wrote that "this has nothing to do with Orthodoxy." His reasoning was that since the congregation had been established by people coming out of the Conservative movement and had been led by a former JTS professor, the congregation was tainted by the impure ideology of Conservative Judaism.

KOE was founded by members of the JTS community to help Rabbi Louis (Eliezer) Finkelstein make a minyan after he became ill in 1983. Rabbi David Weiss Halivni, a Talmudic scholar who taught at the Jewish Theological Seminary before resigning in protest over the decision to ordain women, was their rabbinic adviser. KOE calls itself a "halachic community." The synagogue has a mechitza down the middle of its sanctuary, but allows the Torah to be passed through the women's section, allows women to lead the Kabbalat Shabbat service, and allows women to read from the Torah in a separate chapel. Once in a while, the congregation has even allowed for what they call "mixed kriah," which means that a woman or women would read from the Torah with men as well as women present.

Najman-Licht teaches classes, gives sermons, and answers the community's questions about Jewish law. Her job description specifically does not include any function that would require her to serve as a religious witness, such as officiating at any life cycle event. She also does not sit on any beit din. Since congregants lead services most of the time anyway, Najman-Licht will not be expected to do that either. Both the congregation and Najman-Licht assiduously avoided referring to her as a rabbi or referring to the position as a rabbinic placement, but it nevertheless could be seen as equivalent. The congregation is struggling but this may be because of its ideological position to the right of the Conservative movement and to the left of Orthodoxy rather than to anything related to the gender of their spiritual leader.

There are two levels in the debate over whether women could and should become Orthodox rabbis. There is the halachic level, in which the relevant question is "can a woman perform the various duties that a rabbi is called upon to do?" Then there is the sociological level, where the relevant question is "can and will Orthodox communities accept a woman as their spiritual leader?" The answer to the first question is that she can at least perform most rabbinic functions, including visiting the sick, counseling congregants, representing the congregation at communal events, giving advice on religious issues to the board of directors, and teaching classes on Judaism. There are certain ritual and legal roles that are controversial. But even if it is decided that women cannot perform a number of these acts, that would not disqualify her from becoming a rabbi. Male rabbis likewise cannot always perform every role that a rabbi may do, for a number of different reasons, and accommodations can be arranged. For example, a rabbi who is a kohen is prohibited from entering a cemetery unless one of his own close relatives has passed away. Therefore, rabbis who are kohanim find colleagues to perform the graveside service and find other ways to be there for the family. A woman Orthodox rabbi could and would make similar arrangements for someone else to perform those tasks that she could not.

Nevertheless, critics are not assuaged. Even if they accept that halachic accommodations can be made, they worry about the sociological implications. Rabbi J. David Bleich, a professor of Talmud at Yeshiva University, well known for his articles on arcane halachic difficulties, told the *New York Times* that "a lot of people focus on the now without being terribly concerned about the future. That's being shortsighted."[58] While he admitted that a woman might be able to play the roles that the congregation had delineated for Najman-Licht, he said that there was no formal training program that would enable a woman to achieve a high level of competency in halachic decision making. He also implied that allowing women to move into this field might cause unspecified sociological problems that could seriously damage Orthodoxy in America.

While some Modern Orthodox women have been disappointed that they have not made more progress, others think that preserving the traditional sex roles is far more advantageous than overthrowing them. They believe that traditional Judaism provides them with a special role, one that they cherish, and they have no desire to be treated as equal. Many of the women who become baalei teshuvah speak of how the female role in traditional Jewish families was one of the main attractions that drew them to become Orthodox. Perhaps battered by their experiences in the highly competitive and unforgiving contemporary American economy, they find the Orthodox emphasis on marriage and children with the goal of creating a warm and happy Jewish home to be far more enticing. Rebbetzin Tzipporah Heller, for example, writes that "modern feminism quickly atrophied into 'careerism,' which left us a society in which women's contributions are unrecognized by men and, more painfully, by women themselves."[59] Heller points out that, after three decades of feminism, many women seem more miserable than they were before they got all of their hard-earned gains. Her answer is, not surprisingly, that they should turn to Orthodoxy. Specifically, she emphasizes that Judaism believes in "wholeness," in being part of a society while remaining a unique people, in being part of a community while maintaining one's individuality, and in being a full-fledged member of society while also being a woman.

While feminism has generated a great deal of controversy and stimulated debate, it has been extremely difficult to achieve substantive goals. Over the years, Blu Greenberg seems to have begun to accept the limits of what she could accomplish. "Years ago I thought everything had to be equal; that less than equal meant sexism, discrimination, hierarchy, and disability. I now believe that distinctive roles can be compatible with equality and equal dignity, and that not everything in life has to be taken to its logical conclusion." She speculates that perhaps Orthodoxy "may turn out to be the best testing ground for a theology of distinctive-but-equal gender roles."[60] Writing in 2000, Greenberg reflected on the potential impact of Orthodox Jewish feminists on the future of Judaism. "Although ultimately we want what is best for Judaism and best for women, it may take time to discern exactly where this convergence lies. How will the changes affect relationships, the family, the ways we raise our children, the definitions of sexuality, and ultimately the Jewish future? What is the staying power of women in traditionally nurturing roles?" She admits that the early feminist thinkers may have overestimated their ability to overcome nature. "Perhaps biology counts for more than feminism has allowed, and there is a reason that society has not restructured itself to accommodate the new ideology. We are the first generation to write the book on new gender relations, and we want to write and read it at the same time."

The Sea Change in Attitudes Toward Gays and Lesbians

The eighteenth chapter of Leviticus, which condemns male homosexual acts as an "abomination," is read aloud in traditional synagogues as part of the Yom Kippur afternoon service. When Orthodox Rabbi Steven Greenberg would hear the part condemning sexual relations between men, "At first, I felt guilt and contrition. Later, I felt a deep sadness for being caught up in gay desire, and I would petition heaven for understanding. After the reading, I would sob in my corner seat of the shul, acknowledging the pain of those verses on my body and spirit." He tried to connect himself with the Jews of the past, "listening in shul to their deepest feelings of love and desire turned abhorrent, ugly, and sinful." He wanted to formulate an appropriate response to what he was hearing, but he was feeling so many different emotions that he had trouble making sense of them all.[61]

Greenberg began to stand for the reading, crying quietly. It was part submission to the Torah's condemnation and part protest against it. "Wrapped in my kittel and with my tallit over my head, I stood up for a single portion of the Torah reading and sobbed." On Yom Kippur 1996 Greenberg decided that he wanted to be called up to the Torah for the reading of the very verses that condemned him as a sinner and labeled his sexual behavior as an abomination. "I arranged with the shammes that I would have the proper aliyah, and when it was time, I went up to the bimah in the center of the shul. My heart was pounding as I climbed the steps to the table where the scroll is read." He felt "as if I were standing on top of a mountain in a thunderstorm. My head was swirling as I looked out at the congregation seated around me. The men standing on each side of me at the podium were intent on their jobs, oblivious to me. Before me was the scroll."

Greenberg felt intense emotion standing in front of an open Torah scroll. The Torah possesses the highest level of religious sanctity, and to stand before it as it is rolled open is both a great honor and a huge responsibility. "I have studied this scroll for years. On Simcha Torah I have danced with it. I kiss it weekly as it passes through the congregation on Shabbat. The plaintive and magisterial melody of the reading on Yom Kippur is both ominous and comforting. I say the blessing, the scroll is rolled opened, and I feel as if my arms too have been rolled aside and my heart is exposed." Greenberg holds onto one of the handles of the Torah scroll for balance. The chapter first lists all of the prohibitions concerning incest. And then the verse that he dreads is in front of him. "Thou shalt not lie with a male as one lies with a woman, it is an abomination."[62] Standing in front of the Torah, "I feel the eyes of many on me. I am looking not at them, but at the scroll. And for the first time that I can remember, I feel it looking back at me."[63]

Greenberg has so far been the only American Orthodox rabbi to come out as a gay person. He did his bachelor's degree and studied for his ordination at Yeshiva University and then began working at CLAL: The National Jewish Center for Learning and Leadership. Virtually no one knew that he was gay. Then in 1993, he wrote an article "Gayness and God" under the pseudonym Yaakov Levado (Jacob Alone) for *Tikkun*.[64] This article attracted a great deal of attention, and people began to speculate who he might be. Eventually, he revealed his true identity and published a book-length treatment of the subject, *Wrestling with God and Men: Homosexuality in the Jewish*

Tradition, in which he tried to reinterpret the Bible and Talmud in order to find a way to legitimize monogamous homosexual relations. Greenberg described his experiences at Yeshiva University and Yeshivat Har Etzion in Israel, both single sex educational institutions. "I was welcomed into a monastic world of sorts, where hundreds of twenty-something men studied and debated in pairs for twelve hours a day. The emotional and intellectual intensity of these young men sequestered away from women was likely fueled by a good deal of sublimated sexual energy." He remembers that "For me the male camaraderie and physical affection, the spiritual passion and intellectual head butting was for many years wonderfully nourishing. But over time, as my sexual repression wore thinner every year, male closeness itself became a strange frustration, and the consciousness of desire bubbling up from inside me became undeniable."[65]

As Greenberg became more aware of his attraction for men, he became increasingly troubled. Finally, he decided to visit Rav Yosef Shalom Eliashiv, a haredi sage who was well-known for giving people advice. Greenberg told him simply, "Master, I am attracted to both men and women. What shall I do?" The sage responded compassionately. "My dear one, my friend, you have twice the power of love. Use it carefully." Greenberg was calmed by the sage's words, at least temporarily. He still hoped that he was bisexual rather than homosexual and that his bisexuality might actually be helpful in his rabbinate. "In an amazing turnaround I began to feel that this piece of my soul might actually make me a better rabbi. As a bisexual I could have a wider and richer emotional life—and perhaps a deeper spiritual life than is common—and still marry and have a family."

After Greenberg returned to New York in 1978, he began looking for someone to marry. Half of his friends were engaged or married and he likewise wanted to settle down. Since he was becoming an Orthodox rabbi, the women that he dated were not surprised that he didn't make any sexual advances toward them. He writes that he fell in love three times, but each time began to realize that he wasn't attracted to the woman. Finally he had a disappointing episode with a woman in a romantic spot on Roosevelt Island at a lighthouse where he couldn't even get himself to kiss her. "The next week I was a wreck. The humiliating failure to feel any desire for a woman I cared so much for left me confused and deeply depressed."

Shortly thereafter, Greenberg started acknowledging his homosexuality. After having dinner with some friends in Greenwich Village, "I pulled my yarmulke off my head, bought a baseball cap to put in its place, and took my first steps toward Christopher Street." For those unfamiliar with New York, Christopher Street was where a lot of gay bars were located. While this decision to acknowledge his attraction for other men helped Greenberg resolve his sexual dilemma, it left his religious identity in limbo. "The sexual discoveries, as amazing as they were, offered no credible life trajectory." He continued to date and became seriously involved with a number of women. But each time the relationship floundered because of his fundamental lack of attraction. With his last girlfriend he decided to tell her the truth, which she seems to have dealt with fairly well. But, while his honesty helped them to become closer in one sense, it of course drove them apart in the way that counted. Even at that point, he was still struggling to come to terms with his sexuality and what his attraction to men might mean. "Only after many years of persistent denial, knocking my shins again and again into the hard truth and then coming back for more, was I able to fully acknowledge that I am gay."

Greenberg's determination to stay Orthodox despite his sexual orientation created tremendous psychological dissidence for him in part because he had so little information. There was almost nothing written about gay and lesbian Jews before the 1960s, even from a liberal perspective. Sexuality in general was not spoken about as openly as it is today. There was certainly no ongoing debate about how Judaism should approach homosexuality. Same-sex sexual relations were prohibited, and there was a tremendous stigma attached to even the faintest suggestion that someone was so inclined.

Even completely nonobservant Jews accepted the basic premise that the Torah had condemned homosexual behavior as *toevah* (an abomination). The key passage was Leviticus 18:22: "Do not lie with a man as one lies with a women: It is an abhorrence." Sifra 9:8 states that "you shall not copy the practices of the land of Egypt where you dwell, or of the land of Canaan to which I am taking you. What did they do? A man would marry a man and a woman would marry a woman." The prohibition against homosexuality was considered so clear-cut that no one even considered suggesting otherwise. The same situation was true for virtually all the Christian denominations in the United States, although, being much larger and more diverse, there was a bit of tolerance to be found at the very edges of American Christianity.

By the beginning of the twenty-first century, the LGBT (lesbian, gay, bisexual, and transgender/transsexual) movement had achieved considerable respectability, but thirty years earlier, the situation was very different. Rabbi Lionel Blue, of the Liberal movement in Great Britain, was a well respected

FIGURE 5.5. Rabbi Steve Greenberg wearing tefillin during morning prayers outdoors. Greenberg was the first and only Orthodox rabbi to come out of the closet and continue to identify as Orthodox. Photo Steven Goldstein. *Courtesy of Rabbi Steve Greenberg*

radio personality known to be gay, but there was no comparable figure in the United States until Allen B. Bennett, a Reform rabbi, came out of the closet in 1978. "My coming out was not directly connected to anything happening in the Reform movement. Rather, it was a result of the anti-homosexual teacher initiative."[66] The Briggs Initiative proposed barring gays and lesbians from working as teachers in the California public school system. People working in the campaign against the proposition knew that Bennett was gay and asked him if he would be willing to be one of a series of gay and lesbian clergy willing to declare themselves and publically oppose the initiative.

Bennett agreed, but the campaign organizers changed their mind when they found out that there was no openly gay rabbi anywhere in the United States. They felt that if Bennett were to declare himself gay, the tremendous publicity about Bennett's sexuality would overshadow their attempt to derail the proposition. Meanwhile, a local paper ran a series of stories on gay life in Northern California that featured Bennett, identified only by a pseudonym. Later, with his permission, the paper revealed Bennett's name. Other newspapers and magazines picked up the story about "the first gay rabbi." Bennett was even written up in *Time* magazine.

Shortly after he came out, Bennett met with Rabbi Alexander Schindler, the president of the UAHC. "How many gay Jews do you think there are in North America?" Schindler asked him. Bennett replied that he didn't know the exact numbers, but that most people thought that about 10 percent of the general population was gay. "So that would be about six hundred thousand gay Jews then? Now that's interesting!" Schindler explained that he was looking for groups of people who might be interested in joining Reform synagogues. He had recommended that outreach to intermarried couples be intensified and he was trying to determine whether there were other groups that could be brought into the Reform movement. "How many gay and lesbian Jews are already members of synagogues?" Schindler asked. Bennett thought that the number was small, perhaps only about two thousand. "Now that's interesting!" Schindler thundered.

Bennett also met with Rabbi Joseph Glaser, the executive vice president of the CCAR. At the time, Glaser was a well-known, outspoken opponent of gay rabbis. "I want to talk to you," he told Bennett sternly. "What you have done has caused a great deal of difficulty for the movement and will probably cause a great deal of difficulty for you as well. Why would you do something like this?" Bennett simply replied, "Because it's the truth. Why would you want me to lie as a rabbi?" Glaser's tone softened and he asked Bennett to tell him what it was like to be a gay rabbi. "I told him not only what it was like for me, but more importantly, what it was like for all those people who were still afraid to come out." Glaser slowly began to shift his position.

Bennett went to a service at the then-new Sha'ar Zahav, a gay and lesbian outreach congregation founded in San Francisco in 1977. He spoke with Bernard Pechter, one of the founders of the congregation, who asked him what he was doing. Bennett told him that he was a graduate student at the Graduate Theological Union in Berkeley, which was true, but not the whole story. "I swallowed hard and told him the truth—that I was a rabbi." Pechter hugged him. "We have been waiting for you." Bennett eventually became their first rabbi, and the congregation grew. Several other Reform rabbis followed him.

Progress was rapid. Rabbi Stacy Offner became the first lesbian rabbi to come out in a mainstream pulpit in 1987. She was Minnesota's first woman rabbi when she became the assistant rabbi at Mt. Zion Temple in St. Paul in 1984 and associate rabbi in 1987, right before she came out as a lesbian. "My 'impetus' for coming out was when I was asked directly by the Executive Committee if I were lesbian and I said yes. I had never lied about my sexuality—but in a closeted world we were partners in maintaining a secret. They didn't ask and I didn't tell."[67] Shortly after she answered their question, Offner told me that she was asked to leave her position. A group of her supporters broke away from Mt. Zion, and, in May of 1988, Offner became the rabbi of Shir Tikvah Congregation of the Twin Cities, the first mainstream congregation to knowingly and enthusiastically hire a rabbi who was a lesbian. By the early 1990s, more than fifty women rabbis identified themselves as lesbians—close to a third of the total number ordained.[68]

In 1990, the Hebrew Union College–Jewish Institute of Religion (HUC–JIR) began accepting openly gay and lesbian applicants for their rabbinic program. They thus became the second American Jewish denomination to do this, after the Reconstructionist movement in 1984. The CCAR passed a same-sex marriage officiation resolution at its annual conference in Greensboro, North Carolina, in March 2000. The Reform and Reconstructionist movements were willing to reinterpret, or even reject, biblical and rabbinic condemnations of homosexual behavior, and social prejudice against gays and lesbians was easily overcome. Rabbi Denise L. Eger believes that "by bringing women into the circles of decision making, as well as smashing our notions of God and gender, the atmosphere was ripe for other innovations as well."[69]

FIGURE 5.6. Rabbi Rita Sherwin presides over a same-sex wedding at Temple Israel, Springfield, Missouri, while the couple exchanges rings. Photo Robert E. Anderson III. *Courtesy of Robert E. Anderson III*

In December 2006, the CJLS adopted three conflicting opinions on the acceptability of homosexuality and the specific question whether gays and lesbians could become Conservative rabbis and cantors. Since one of the papers accepted allowed for the ordination of gays and lesbians and the rabbinic officiation at same-sex union ceremonies, the Conservative movement effectively reversed its long-standing ban. The University of Judaism in Los Angeles announced almost immediately that, in light of the ruling, they would begin to accept openly gay and lesbians students to their rabbinical program. The following March, the Jewish Theological Seminary in New York announced that they would likewise accept gay and lesbian students into their rabbinical and cantorial programs.

In their introduction to the book *Lesbian Rabbis: The First Generation*, Rabbis Sue Levi Elwell and Rebecca T. Alpert asked the questions "how can a lesbian speak in the name of a patriarchal tradition that silenced women? How can she represent a culture that denies her very existence? How can an individual whose choice of a life partner challenges heterosexuality stand for a tradition that celebrates traditional notions of marriage and family?" They argue that the first generation of lesbian rabbis reflect "a bold insistence on living with contradictions, and forging sometimes tenuous truces between seemingly irreconcilable principles and beliefs."[70] Over the past couple of decades, substantial progress has been made toward reconciling those contradictions. In *Standing Again at Sinai*, Judith Plaskow had cited Pirkei Avot: "It is not incumbent upon us to finish the task, but neither are we free to desist from it altogether" (2:16). She expressed the feeling that the efforts being made were leading toward a new synthesis. "As we work toward the creation of a feminist Judaism as part of a larger struggle toward a more just world, we place our small piece in a mosaic that will finally provide a new pattern—a new religious and social order."[71]

6 Radical Responses to the Suburban Experience

David Ingber spent much of his twenties practicing yoga, tai chi, shiatsu, Reiki, Alexander Technique, Feldenkrais, gyrotonics, Zen meditation, martial arts, integrative body psychotherapy, and postural integration. He was a spiritual searcher and quasi-religious switcher, a common type in his generation, as described in chapter 2. This was not the way he had been raised. His family prayed at the Great Neck Synagogue and sent Ingber to the Ramaz School, a Modern Orthodox day school on the Upper East Side of Manhattan. But, by the age of fourteen, he rejected Orthodoxy and spent most of his time bodybuilding. "I was huge. I was going to go out for Mr. Long Island." Ingber reembraced Orthodoxy in his later high school years, becoming what is called a baal teshuva, a returnee to Judaism. He spent his senior year of high school in Israel at an American yeshiva called Beit Midrash L'Torah, undergoing what young, American, Orthodox Jews studying in Israel call a "flip," becoming intensely Orthodox. "I was learning eighteen hours a day, memorizing Mishna, praying at sunrise at the [Western Wall]. I became hyper-religious."

When Ingber returned to the United States, he enrolled in the Rabbi Chaim Berlin Yeshiva in Brooklyn, where he was expected to devote himself to full time Talmudic study. But he felt himself drawn to meditate, a practice that was looked down upon in the Litvak yeshiva. He also became interested in mysticism, a topic of study that was regarded as esoteric and appropriate only for specific advanced students. It was not only the yeshiva that was making him feel restless and unsatisfied. "Unhappy sibling models and unhappy parental relationships are hardwired into the very nature of certain approaches to Judaism which leads to unhappy relationships to God and ourselves. It's a Judaism of 'never good enough-ness.'"[1] Ingber left Judaism again at the age of twenty-three and spent the next decade pursuing other spiritual quests, eventually ending up as a Pilates instructor and astrologer in Israel. After a little while, he began to feel the desire to return to Judaism and soon enrolled in Yeshiva Chovevei Torah, the open Orthodox rabbinical school on the Upper West Side. He picked an Orthodox school because, even though he had rebelled several years earlier, he still "felt that the only valid expression [of Judaism] was Orthodoxy." But after two years there, he met Reb Zalman, as Jewish Renewal founder Rabbi Zalman Schachter-Shalomi was affectionately called. "He's deeply Jewish and deeply universal. I've never met someone who loves God so much in my life." He immediately became a disciple of Reb Zalman.

Schachter-Shalomi had long understood the limitations that language imposed on humankind's ability to grasp the infinite. He believed that allowing the names of God, and the ways of speaking about God and to God, to evolve was a central necessity for making a spiritual connection. One problem was that the word *God* was a noun, as were most other appellations for the Divine Being. "I have for many years encouraged my students to think of God as a verb. Imagining God in terms of action, of process, opens up new ways of connecting to the infinite. Take the expression "infinite Being." . . . If we think of God as a process of Be-ing, of *is*-ing, of infinite existing, we open up new ways of relating." Students of Torah can begin to imagine a "godding," a process "that the universe is doing, has been doing, and will continue to do—at least on our scale of comprehension—forever." In the broadest sense, "we can say that as part of that universe we are 'godding' in everything we do. In the more limited, human sense, we could wake up in the morning and consider how we might "god" most effectively today."[2]

It was Reb Zalman who had formulated the central critique of contemporary American Jewish life: "Judaism today is ooververbalized and underexperienced." He discovered that many of the Eastern philosophies were better than the Western religions were at encouraging people to experience life and not just think about it. "It is in the nature of the situation that people will turn away from something that is not satisfying to them." Schachter-Shalomi found that this lack of spiritual satisfaction was pushing many young people away from Judaism. Yet, while they discovered Eastern meditative disciplines to be spiritually fulfilling, they felt them to be rather foreign. Repeating a Buddhist mantra over and over could come off as ridiculous. Many of them asked Reb Zalman for a Jewish mantra, something they could integrate into their meditative practices that would also make them feel they were connecting with the Jewish historical experience. Ingber was also attracted to Jewish Renewal because it drew heavily on Kabbalah, which had a lot of similarities to some of the non-Jewish spiritual disciplines he had studied earlier. Jewish Renewal seemed to bring together various social and political concerns with an intense mystical orientation that melded traditional Judaism and the counterculture together. It combined the spiritual intensity of the Hasidic movement of the 1760s with the sincere social justice agenda of the Reform movement of the 1960s. After years of searching, Ingber had finally found an approach to spirituality that fulfilled him and brought him inner peace.

After Reb Zalman ordained him, Ingber decided to establish a Renewal-style congregation on the Upper West Side. Naming it Kehilat Romemu, Ingber had high expectations-he hoped it would transform people physically, emotionally, intellectually, and spiritually. In order to have an impact on how people feel, he created a service that centered on "fully embodied, ecstatic and contemplative prayer." He explained that "one reason people don't go to shul is because it's antiquated." In order to attract young people, services have to help them answer the existential question that they are asking, "What does this all mean?" He implied that many synagogues stress intellectualism when that is not appropriate. "A service is like a restaurant. We're not trying to give people a book about eating; we're trying to give them a meal to eat. You know when you've had a great meal, and you know when you've been to a great prayer service. I want people to walk into this and feel alive."[3]

Ingber's goals were certainly ambitious. It was not going to be easy to create an environment in which jaded Upper West Siders were going to feel moved. His new service was well-attended, but received mixed reviews. An anonymous blogger named Shteeblehopper commented that, given the emphasis at Romemu's Web site on the concept of individual "freedom" and the description of "a community that expects and relies upon your active partici-

FIGURE 6.1. Caption: Rabbi David Ingber holds the Torah while marching with followers in Falls Village, Connecticut. Photo Sam Feinstein-Feit. *Courtesy of Sam Feinstein-Feit, www.eights.org*

pation," she was surprised and disappointed by how "top-down" the service was. "The vibe I picked up from Rabbi Ingber was 'I'm going to tell you and show you how to pray and how to be spiritual.'" But even such a critic could not help but be impressed by the singing, which was "high-energy and contagious." She liked the meditations and *kavanot* about the prayers that Ingber led in between the songs and could see how the vision for the congregation built on and expanded what had been done earlier in various Jewish Renewal and other progressive Jewish spiritual settings.

Ingber had spent many years searching for a path that could bring him peace and he was now at a point where he felt that he had found it. He had instinctually sensed that the Judaism he inherited was somehow stale and spiritually stagnant. For a long time, he was unsure whether he would ever find a way to express his Jewish spirituality in a meaningful manner, but he knew that he could only reengage with his ancestral religion if he could reinvent it. "I had to wait until I could teach a Judaism that was transformative and exciting and healing and courageous. A Judaism that isn't fear based. A Judaism that is unabashedly devoted to spirit."[4]

Responses to the Perceived Superficiality of Suburban Judaism

Ingber became involved at various points in his young life with both the baal teshuva and Jewish Renewal movements, two different responses to the perceived superficiality of post–World War II suburban Judaism. Both the followers of Jewish Renewal, who found their way to an alternative Jewish spirituality, as well as the baalei teshuva, who embraced Orthodoxy as adults, shared a frustration with the institutional religion in which they were brought up. To the dismay of their parents, they found the Judaism being taught in their suburban synagogues to be both sterile and vapid. Seeking something more spiritual, they looked for alternative beliefs and practices. Some found it in a havurah and later in Jewish Renewal; others found it in the baal teshuva movement; some became involved in serious adult Jewish learning; and many tried out various other paths they hoped would be intellectually authentic and emotionally satisfying. Their quests had a similar motivation, but their paths and endpoints were quite different.

Despite the fact that Jewish Renewal and the baal teshuva movement have different approaches, beliefs, and cultures, they drew from the same sources of inspiration and, at least in the early years, from much the same population pool. Many of those who became interested in an alternative Jewish spirituality were motivated by their reading of the three *Jewish Catalogues*, which were published between 1973 and 1976. They may have joined one of the early havurot and eventually moved in one direction or another. Shaul Magid wrote me that "many of these folks [who were part of the havurah movement] became baalei teshuva, while others retained allegiance to the counterculture and formed Renewal. Hence, it is hard to see these movements as utterly distinct." Magid remembers "hanging around Crown Heights and Boro Park", two predominately haredi neighborhoods in Brooklyn, "yet [I] went to see Zalman and Shlomo on their retreats in rural Pennsylvania." He thus lived in a haredi community and at the same time was going to Jewish Renewal conferences-something that would be almost inconceivable today. "It was a real mix then, before the baal teshuva movement was taken over by Aish HaTorah and Ohr Somayach." Magid supports his contention that the two movements drew in large measure from the same group of people. "The first real baal teshuva yeshiva, the Diaspora Yeshiva in Jerusalem (that began in 1968) was full of hippies and House of Love and Prayer people. There are also many refugees from that early baal teshuvah movement that ended up later in Renewal."[5]

Why were many young American Jews in the late sixties and early seventies looking for something religiously different? The problem was that the American synagogue needed to build a tight-knit religious community in order to develop a strong sense of communal spirituality. To do that, the community had to have common values and a willingness to make a long-term commitment to a full set of religious obligations. With the exception of the Orthodox and small pockets of highly committed religious seekers, this did not prove practical. As a consequence, young American Jews who grew up in the fifties, sixties, and seventies often found their parents' suburban Judaism to be spiritually vacuous. Rabbi Michael Lerner, the founder of *Tikkun* magazine, already discussed in chapter 2, wrote me that "Judaism in America failed to turn people on not because it was too different but because its values were too similar to the mainstream values of self-interest and 'looking out for number one' above all else."[6] The young adults were looking for something with meaning, a religious path they could embrace with their whole hearts. It was a deeply personal quest. Many hoped that the currents of their hearts would lead them back to their own true selves, but they could not be sure. What they knew is that they wanted to escape from the kind of religion they were exposed to as young people.

It is almost universally agreed that young American Jews found their religious education to be incredibly uninspiring. There are numerous accounts of adults who turned away from Judaism as a direct consequence of their Hebrew school experiences. Others remained committed to Judaism, but resolved to find a more effective way of communicating the joy and beauty of their religion. Lerner's entire generation was turned off by Hebrew schools that were unable to communicate a clear vision. The students reluctantly went twice a week after "regular school," as well as Saturday mornings. Most dropped out as soon as they could. There were 125 students in Lerner's bar mitzvah year, but only five continued their Jewish education all the way through Hebrew high school, graduating from the four-hour-per-week program four years later. "Most of them looked back on Hebrew school as an ordeal that they went through to please their parents, and once they were free to make choices of their own, they ran from the Jewish world as fast as they could."[7]

Writing decades later in his book *Jewish Renewal*, Lerner argued that the Jewish community had "a smug and self-satisfied message" to explain why so many young Jews abandoned their heritage. Lerner mockingly assumed their voice: "Of course these people left their Jewishness, because being a

Jew is very difficult. They live in a society that encourages people to seek their own pleasures and to take the easiest path, the path of assimilation to the mainstream values of American society." Only those who understand the importance of Judaism can withstand the pressures of assimilation. "You, who have stayed connected, are very special and different, and morally and spiritually on a higher plane than those who have left. Meanwhile, don't worry, because many of those who have gone away will come back once they see how empty that world really is."[8] Lerner believes that this argument is self-serving and fallacious.

Young people were fired up with idealism from the radical ideas that took shape in the sixties. Consequently, they were driven away by what they saw as the repellent values they encountered in their parents' suburban synagogues. Despite liberal lip service, Lerner argues, their parents were narrow-minded, sexist, and homophobic. Many of the adults in the suburbs craved crass materialism, while their children felt a terrible spiritual emptiness. Suburban Jews flaunted their exclusivity, while wallowing simultaneously in the joylessness of an unending Holocaust trauma. Lerner wrote me that "'Never Again' about the Holocaust could have meant 'let's stop the oppression of all peoples before it turns in a genocidal direction,' but instead, in the hands of American Jews, became 'never again to Us—and screw everyone else, because they didn't care about us when we were victims, so why should we care about them now?" The suburban Jewish community emphasized conformity and was intolerant of dissent, particularly about Israel and Middle Eastern politics. "Imposing an orthodoxy in regard to support for Israeli policies has had, particularly when wedded to the tactic of describing critics as 'self-hating Jews' or antisemites," an extremely negative impact on American Jewish life.[9]

By the late 1960s and early 1970s, increasing numbers of young Jews were seeking to respiritualize Judaism. Many were inspired by Rabbi Abraham Joshua Heschel, the charismatic Polish Jewish philosopher who taught at the Jewish Theological Seminary in New York. Small but influential numbers of American Jews began insisting on more emotional content in their Judaism. They wanted intimate and spiritually satisfying worship rather than the staid and hollow services that were offered at most establishment synagogues. In contrast to the shallow suburban religious practices, Jewish Renewal and other neo-Hasidic religious approaches sought out authenticity and depth of spiritual experience.

This feeling led idealistic young American Jews in a number of different directions. Many became involved in democratic, populist causes that stressed the need for equality and self-expression. Some became hippies, focusing on Eastern philosophies, including meditation. Some of those who later returned to Judaism wanted to bring the spiritual insights they had achieved with them. They gravitated toward charismatic religious leaders who could understand where they were coming from as well as bring a deep sense of Judaism to their spiritual practice. Believing that most of the great teachers of a truly spiritual Judaism had been wiped out in the Holocaust, they felt that American Jewish life preserved the external forms of Judaism, such as the synagogue, but had somehow lost (or never had) the inner spiritual message that was so essential to truly connecting with God.

They led spiritually hungry young people into a new way of approaching Judaism that became known as Jewish Renewal. As Magid explains, "Jewish Renewal is essentially an attempt to revive, recontextualize, and reform Jewish spiritualist movements that have most recently manifested in Hasidism but have roots in pre-modern Jewish pietism. It is a reformation of Jewish spiritual practice in the spirit of humanism and global consciousness."[10] Its goal was to bring a sense of vitality to a Judaism that had become overly institutionalized. Both Reb Zalman and Reb Shlomo, as Rabbi Shlomo Carlebach was known, wanted to nurture the soul of American Judaism, deepening its spiritual content while rejecting the status consciousness that had turned so many off. They wanted to open their hearts to the emotions that lay within, emphasizing music and artistic expression, rather than dry scholarship or pedantic and rote ritual observance. Jewish Renewal incorporated contemplative practices including meditation and chanting, and tried to encourage a euphoric and ecstatic atmosphere in worship. It also sought to encourage a spirit of reflection that was not ecstatic, teaching individuals how to engage in deep contemplation, inner meditation, and meaningful silence. Lerner explains that "instead of rushing through the prayers (as you'll find even in the synagogues of the ba'alei teshuva), Jewish Renewal would rather do fewer prayers but fully experience them, find ways to go into them in a deep way, stay in the consciousness state that the prayer seeks to elicit."[11]

Other young American Jews took an entirely different turn. They also felt uninspired by the synagogue experience of their youth, but they were not interested in going the hippie route. Rather, they wanted a completely traditional form of Judaism, a Judaism that actually demanded the full observance of the mitzvot, just as described in the *Shulchan Aruch* (code of Jewish law) and based on the Torah and the Talmud. They wanted to study in schools that would explain the actual beliefs of traditional Judaism, without reinterpreting everything to allow for maximum flexibility. These young people began observing more of the commandments, something that was not easy to do in the suburban environment. It was difficult to walk to synagogue because most houses were many miles away from the nearest house of worship. Few families kept kosher, and, unless they were lucky enough to live in or near an Orthodox suburb, there were not likely to be any kosher restaurants nearby. Their parents were probably well-meaning, but completely uncomprehending. Most eventually left home for what became known as baal teshuva yeshivas, religious seminaries which specialized in teaching adult beginners.

Jewish Renewal and the baal teshuva movement thus differed enormously in the type of individual who was attracted to them, as well as the beliefs and practices of those who identified with each group. What they shared in common was that both saw the suburban Judaism of their youth as superficial and lacking in spirituality. They wanted something more intense that would bring them a sense of fulfillment—that would seem more "religious." Magid was one of many young people who became involved in these movements. "In the 1970s, the answer for many disaffected Jews was Orthodoxy through the Baal Teshuva movement." Magid was among them. "The next phase was the rise of Jewish Renewal (beginning with Bnei 'Or in Philadelphia, Havurat Shalom in Somerville, Massachusetts, the Aquarian Minyan in Berkeley and the Jewish Catalogues in the 1970s) as a spiritual alternative to the existing movements that lacked creativity and courage." Magid was also among them. [12] Although both draw from the Jewish spiritual tradition, they are deeply influenced by American society. As Magid states in reference to Jewish Renewal, it "is a theology that grows as much out of late twentieth-century America as out of Judaism. It is, perhaps, the second stage of an indigenous American Judaism born in America's transition from late pluralism to multiculturalism following the Second World War." [13]

The Development of Jewish Renewal

Some describe the Jewish Renewal movement as feminist neo-Hasidism because it draws on both feminism's social and political perspectives as well as the mystical joy of the Eastern European Hasidic world. A few others dis-

FIGURE 6.2. Group blessing at Elat Chayyim Jewish Retreat Center, Accord, New York. Photo Rabbi Ayla Grafstein. *Courtesy of Rabbi Ayla Grafstein*

pute this characterization, arguing that Jewish Renewal has certain antifeminist tendencies and has moved away from its original neo-Hasidic model. All agree that it has had an influence on American Judaism vastly out of proportion to its actual numbers. The beginnings of the Jewish Renewal movement can be traced to the development of the havurah, which was named for the Jewish fellowships that Jewish pietists had organized in the early rabbinic period. The havurah was an experimental fellowship set up by young political and social activists who wanted a community in which they could engage in heartfelt prayer and study. Many of the early havurah members had seen how groups of hippies had formed communes and they wanted to create a Jewish religious alternative.

They placed the stress on kavanah, which is the intention to concentrate and really pray. A person who was able to pray with great kavanah was said to be "davening well." In addition to the regular Hebrew prayers, they sang nigunim, wordless Hasidic melodies, with great fervor. They hoped that communal prayer could bind them together, but they differed on what type of community it should be. Some had the idea of creating rural communities, others hoped to create residential urban centers, and still others were inspired by the monastic life of the ancient Dead Sea Scroll sect.

The original members spoke of their desire to engage in a deep and sincere search for the meaning of life and expressed the sentiment that the Jewish religion could provide them with a framework for this. But, in order for that to happen, they needed to reinvent Judaism as a revolutionary religious force that could work toward the liberation of the individual. Unfortunately, their previous experiences with Judaism had been in what they saw as superficial, materialistic suburban settings or through smug, self-satisfied, arrogant institutions. They wanted to create an "authentic Jewish community" that took tradition seriously but was willing to make the types of changes they thought were necessary. This included gender equality and also an array of other political and social causes important to the New Left, such as peace activism, social justice, and, for some, vegetarianism.

Havurat Shalom Community Seminary was the first such commune, established in Somerville, Massachusetts just outside Cambridge in 1967, with funding from the Danforth Foundation of St. Louis. The use of the word *Seminary* in the title may seem strange, but it may have been deliberately included in order to make the havurah members eligible for a draft exclusion. Arthur Green, a recent graduate of the rabbinical school at JTS, did envision the creation of a counterculture seminary for serious Jewish textual study that would transcend denominational divisions. He planned to include the then almost unheard of subject of mysticism as well as specific topics of contemporary importance such as the Jewish roots of pacifism and antiwar activism. This idea was never realized, and the havurah members eliminated the goal of creating a seminary from their mission statement at the end of their first year. They instead decided that their havurah would become a nonresidential religious community devoted to prayer and study. (Decades later, Green opened a nondenominational rabbinical school at the Hebrew College in Boston that fulfilled many of his earlier goals).

Other havurot were soon created in most of the other large cities. They each had their own focus, but they all shared a number of things in common. In particular, they were resolutely nondenominational. While many of their members had come from Conservative backgrounds and spent their summers at Camp Ramah, the communities were determined to create a new type of Judaism that was neither Reform, Conservative, nor Orthodox. Most of all, they wanted a Judaism that was vibrant, and they criticized the existing denominations for making synagogue members passive "consumers" of a commodity, rather than active participants who would create and build.

The havurot initially attracted little attention. But, in 1973, Michael and Sharon Strassfeld and Richard Siegel published *The Jewish Catalog*. Subtitled *A Do-It-Yourself Kit*, it was modeled on the recently published *Whole Earth Catalog*, which began publication in 1968. *The Jewish Catalog* stressed that readers could actually do Judaism rather than just watching rabbis and synagogue elders do it. It also suggested that they could incorporate Jewish ideas and rituals into their own lives, transforming both Judaism and themselves in the process.

The original havurot were led by men, but the influence of feminism soon led to a reconsideration of this policy and most became fully egalitarian. Eventually, gender egalitarianism became one of their characteristic features. The havurot gathered together for Shabbat and holiday prayer services, sharing communal meals and frequently studying together. They spent a lot of time debating how their Judaism should manifest itself, and many of these debates influenced later developments, not only in the Jewish Renewal movement but in all segments of American Jewish life. Establishment synagogues even tried to adapt the style of worship within their congregational structure. Rabbi Harold Schulweis of Encino, California pioneered the idea of building havurot within his large suburban Conservative congregation. While Schulweis reported considerable success, other congregations found that the havurah model did not translate easily to a conventional structure.

The early havurot referred to their desire for "religious renewal," and are seen as the precursors to what became known as the Jewish Renewal movement. The exact relationship between the havurah movement and Jewish Renewal is difficult to describe. Many of the same people were involved in both groups, and much of their basic thinking is complementary if not identical. The main difference was that the havurah movement focused primarily on the havurot, whereas Jewish Renewal encompassed many different aspects of alternative Judaism.

By the early 1980s, the havurah movement and Jewish Renewal were closely aligned, but then they began to diverge again. Rabbi Mitchell Chefitz, who brought the havurah spirit to a formerly classical Reform Temple Israel in Miami, explains that "Renewal and Havurah parted ways . . . around the topic of leadership. Renewal chose charismatic leadership—Zalman, Arthur Waskow, Marc Gafni—and the havurah chose to focus on the development of autonomous community."[14] There were also charismatic women leaders including Rabbis Marcia Prager, Shefa Gold, and Tirzah Firestone, all of whom studied with Reb Zalman. Gafni was a brief and marginal figure in American Jewish Renewal, although his tremendous charisma made him incredibly popular with a segment of their constituency, at least for a short while. Susan Saxe of ALEPH suggests a variation of Chefitz's distinction between the two approaches: "While Renewal does indeed embrace charisma, we are also very committed to community building. We are informed by a feminist model of communal and individual empowerment that makes it pretty hard for someone who wants to abuse his or her charisma to get very far." She is probably referring to Gafni, who was later accused of sexual improprieties. "So the difference between us and the Havurah movement is more subtle than 'we're into charisma and they're into community.' I'd put it more like this: Havurah and Renewal are both committed to community building. Havurah rejects charisma because of its shadow side, and creates structures to avoid it. Renewal accepts that charisma happens and builds structures to contain and, if you will, domesticate it."[15]

The Jewish Renewal movement began to coalesce organizationally after many of the most important figures found themselves in the Philadelphia area in the 1970s. The Reconstructionist Rabbinical College had been founded there in 1968, and many progressive-thinking young religious Jews were attracted to Philadelphia for that reason. As is true with any type of group, once you have a considerable number of highly motivated people in one place, it tends to draw others. Arthur Waskow became one of the unifying figures for what was a very disparate group of people. In 1982, the RRC invited him to Philadelphia to teach courses in practical rabbinics, then helping him to establish the Shalom Center, a study/action institute originally dedicated to the development of Jewish thought and action related to the nuclear arms race. In 1995, the Shalom Center merged with P'nai Or, the lead institution of the Jewish Renewal movement, to create ALEPH: Alliance for Jewish Renewal; in 2005, ALEPH became an independent transdenominational organization.

Waskow had been a student activist and an important leader in the counterculture. Like many young Jewish activists, he had rejected Judaism, or at least ignored it. But he had a "conversion experience" and decided to reengage with his spiritual roots. This led him on a search for a more intense relationship with God, which he described in his book *Godwrestling*. Later, in 1978, he founded *Menorah*, a magazine devoted to exploring issues relating to the renewal of Judaism. Waskow's life turned around during Passover week 1968. He had been involved in the antiwar movement and other left-wing

FIGURE 6.3. Rabbi Arthur Waskow speaks with fellow members of Clergy and Laity Concerned About Iraq after an early morning interfaith on-the-street prayer vigil in New York City on April 29, 2006. Photo Kate Anne Brennan. *Courtesy of Kate Anne Brennan*

causes, and was close with the black militant movement. The Reverend Martin Luther King Jr. had been assassinated April 4 in Memphis—just ten days earlier—and riots had erupted in black neighborhoods throughout the country. Police were called out to maintain order. In Washington, D.C., federal troops were put on the streets. Waskow had spent the day of the seder bringing relief supplies to black neighborhoods that were under curfew. "That evening, I was walking home to my family's seder, past detachments of the army patrolling the streets. My guts started saying, 'This is Pharaoh's army, and I'm going home to do my seder.' I thought of all the black spirituals about Pharaoh's army and Israel in Egypt land, and it all kind of erupted in me."[16] Reminiscing later, Waskow wrote that "when we reached the part about how each of us must look upon himself as if he himself had come out of Egypt, we stopped the seder and just talked. It was a life-turning moment for me." As a result of his experience, he decided to edit his own version of the Passover liturgy, which he called *The Freedom Seder*. The central narrative was a retelling of the Exodus story in which Moses is a labor organizer among non-union Hebrew bricklayers. Waskow included passages crying out against the inequality of American society and protesting the unjust Vietnam War.

The new haggadah was presented at a "freedom seder" held at an African American church in downtown D.C. The seder was broadcast live on a New York radio station and a video recording of the event was then shown on Canadian television. The seder generated a tremendous response from the many Jewish student radicals who felt alienated from the Jewish establishment on one hand but also were increasingly uncomfortable with the anti-Zionism and borderline antisemitism of much of the new left. Waskow's *Freedom Seder* spawned a host of imitations. "There was just an explosion of different haggadahs." Beyond the cultural contribution of the *Freedom Seder*, Waskow's words showed many student leftists that it was possible to combine Judaism with activism. Waskow was one of a whole group of students—many of them older—that Schachter-Shalomi had begun training for the rabbinate, a course of action that upset the established rabbinical schools. He studied under the supervision of a unique transdenominational committee of four: Rabbi Zalman Schachter-Shalomi, the former Hasid who had become a key teacher of Jewish Renewal; Rabbi Laura Geller, a Reform rabbi; Rabbi Max Ticktin, a Conservative rabbi; and Judith Plaskow, a feminist theologian. Waskow was ordained as a rabbi in 1995, when he was sixty-two years old.

Fortuitously, Schachter-Shalomi, usually called Reb Zalman, had moved from Winnipeg, Manitoba to Philadelphia to teach in the Department of Religion at Temple University. Schachter-Shalomi, who became recognized as the most important leader of a broad coalition of spiritual seekers who wanted to reinvigorate Judaism by incorporating mystical insights and meditative practices, argued that renewing Judaism required a "paradigm shift."[17] Schachter-Shalomi first tried to help people bring emotion into prayer, creating davenology, a system for praying that was designed to "learn how one moves on the inside, because it doesn't have external markers." Then he tried to address what he saw as Judaism's antiquated theology. Most American Jews had a "reality map," and that understanding of the world did not correspond to what they understood to be the Jewish belief system. "After Hiroshima and Nagasaki, Auschwitz, Birkenau, moonwalk, fifth-generation computer, the whole story of the universe has changed. We are not talking about fields; we are talking about string theory. We're talking about a whole other thing in quantum stuff, and that hasn't yet been incorporated in our theology. A theology that's out of date cannot get the loyalty of the people in the present."[18]

Many of those involved in Jewish Renewal admire Schachter-Shalomi in part because he was born and raised in Europe and is therefore their connection with a lost and destroyed European Jewish culture. He has managed to combine what they see as the best of Old World Judaism with the most sensitive understanding of contemporary spirituality. Schachter-Shalomi was born in Poland and raised in an Hasidic family that nevertheless had a great interest in Western culture. The family moved to Vienna, where they lived until the Nazis took over. His religious background was Orthodox, but certainly eclectic. "I went to yeshiva, and at the same time attended a leftist Zionist high school, where I learned Latin and Modern Hebrew. I danced the Horah with Marxist Zionists and also celebrated the farewell to the Sabbath with Orthodox anti-Zionists." He remembers his father urging him to go both to gymnasium, which was a secular coed high school, as well as Orthodox yeshiva. "My own life—not only my father's—was always full of contradictions."[19]

Schachter-Shalomi and his family fled to an internment camp in France in 1940, after which they were able to immigrate to the United States. He became a student at the Central Yeshiva at 770 Eastern Parkway in Brooklyn, where he was ordained in 1947. With the Rebbe's blessing, Schachter-Shalomi toured various colleges and universities with Reb Shlomo Carlebach, who later became famous because of his beautiful singing. He also dabbled in nonrabbinic work, trying his hand as a furrier and even as a kosher butcher. He was then appointed a Chabad shaliach in Massachusetts and Connecticut, one of the first to be sent out on such a mission. But, even so, he was an unconventional Chabad shaliach, stressing religious experimentation at the possible expense of Orthodox conformity. He wanted to explore the religious commonalities that Judaism had with people of other faith traditions. He was also intensely mystical and understood Jewish mystical doctrine as transcending halacha.

In 1956, he became first a Hillel director and then professor of Judaic studies at the University of Manitoba in Canada, where he remained until his move to Philadelphia. In 1969, Schachter-Shalomi went to Boston on a sabbatical at Brandeis University. Rabbi Arthur Green was in the process of establishing Havurat Shalom, and Schachter-Shalomi immediately became involved. In 1975, Schachter-Shalomi moved to Philadelphia to teach at Temple University. Schachter-Shalomi was already known for his interest in Jew-

FIGURE 6.4. Rabbi Zalman Schachter-Shalomi leading followers during prayers at Elat Chayyim, Jewish Retreat Center, Accord, New York. Photo Rabbi Ayla Grafstein. *Courtesy of Rabbi Ayla Grafstein*

ish spirituality because he had written the article in the first *Jewish Catalogue* on Jewish prayer, "The First Step". Schachter-Shalomi described how a complete beginner could delve into the holiness and intensity of Jewish prayer. Over the next several years, he emerged as the spiritual guide for a relatively small but extremely dedicated following. Despite his charisma and fervent message, he was never able to have a major influence on the broader Jewish community, at least not directly. Part of the reason may be that he uses a freely associative speaking and writing style with New Age terminology and even computer jargon that can be difficult to fully comprehend.

As his religious views became more liberal, Schachter-Shalomi gradually broke with Orthodox Judaism. In addition to various non-Orthodox approaches to Jewish thought, he has also been influenced by disparate types of New Age spirituality, such as transpersonal psychology, the literature of psychedelics, and James Lovelock's Gaia hypothesis. Even so, the influence of Chabad on his approach to Judaism is still marked. Schachter-Shalomi "graduated" Chabad in 1966, which led him to search out independent ways of practicing Judaism in America. What apparently happened was that the Lubavitch movement severed all connection with him after he wrote an article in *Commentary* praising LSD as having sacramental potential. He had hoped that the Rebbe would support his "spiritual explorations" because he believed that the drug experimentation of the 1960s was, at its roots, a search for transcendence that had precedents in kabbalistic thought. Unfortunately, the Rebbe or his advisers felt that Reb Zalman had crossed well over the line and they could no longer tolerate his countercultural speculations, particularly after they appeared in writing in such a respectable publication. His desire to explore new spiritual realms stemmed from a universalistic approach that was not compatible with Chabad or other forms of Orthodox Judaism. "I do not believe that anyone has the exclusive franchise on the truth. What we Jews have is a good approximation, for Jews, of how to get there. Ultimately, each person creates a way that fits his own situation." While there are differences between Jewish and non-Jewish approaches to mysticism in terms of specific methods, "there are no differences in the impact of the experiences themselves. When it comes to what I call the 'heart stuff,' all approaches overlap."[20]

Schachter-Shalomi founded the B'nai Or Religious Fellowship, which he envisioned as "part Qumran and part ashram". The name was taken from one of the Dead Sea Scrolls, in which the children of light battle against the children of darkness. Schachter-Shalomi was deeply touched by the story of the Essenes and inspired by the discovery of the scrolls. Early researchers were convinced that the Essenes had lived in the community of Qumran, storing their scrolls in the caves nearby, and Schachter-Shalomi used the name to convey his vision of a modern semimonastic religious commune. The group established a retreat and training center called the B'nai Or House on Emlen Street in Philadelphia, where some of the most dedicated followers lived and others came to pray and study. Yonassan Gershom, who was involved with B'nai Or in its early phase before breaking away, describes how Reb Zalman was hoping to attract Jews looking to live a contemplative religious life. The original B'nai Or fellowship was more traditional than the Jewish Renewal movement today. Gershom writes that it was quite close to what is now called traditional Judaism or Conservadox Judaism, except that it was more mystical and so might best be called neo-Hasidic. According to Gershom, Reb Zalman intended the fellowship to be "a repository of Chassidic knowledge that would preserve and renew the Jewish spirituality that was destroyed in the Holocaust—similar to the way that the Essenes retreated to the wilderness to preserve their knowledge from being lost under persecution of the Romans."

Gershom and his wife Caryl (Rachel) lived in the B'nai Or House in 1982 and 1983, and, although never an insider, he studied and traveled with Reb Zalman. "The community never really came together. . . . I think part of it was due to Reb Zalman himself. He admired the contemplative monks he met in the various ashrams of the 60's, but he himself was too restless to be a leader of that kind of community. He was always on the road, so the B'nai Or community lacked continuity on the local level. People came and went, but few stayed for the long haul."[21] Virtually all those who continue to identify themselves as Jewish Renewal believe that Gershom came away with a distaste—Arthur Waskow calls it dyspepsia—for the movement that is not reflective of what anyone else experienced.[22] Rabbi Phyllis Berman, another early follower of Reb Zalman, explained that "what Zalman has done in promoting the Va'ad (the council that determines the process for the granting of smicha [rabbinical ordination]) and the hevra [group] is not to repudiate "discipleship"; quite the contrary, it is to expand the base of discipleship, finding it among many of Reb Zalman's musmachim [rabbinic graduates who studied under him] and not just in him, now in his mid-eighties."

Perhaps Reb Zalman's greatest talent was in nurturing the potential for spiritual leadership in others. Berman recalls that "even twenty years ago, Reb Zalman would gather us in a circle, teach some Torah, and then ask everyone to move one chair to the left so that each of us would take our place in the "rebbe seat" to find within us Torah worth teaching. He has done deep teaching about the quality of listening and respect that we give to one another as the medium in which great teachers are brought into being."[23] She objects to what she sees as the implication that many of Reb Zalman's earliest followers have defected. "From my personal experience with Reb Zalman since the 1960s and seeing only a small number of the thousands of people over the years with whom he made contact, most of us who were touched by him at some point in our lives have remained connected and loyal to him to this day; he has changed the spiritual lives of countless numbers of people."[24]

Schachter-Shalomi developed an intense style of prayer service that mesmerized his devoted followers. The group would chant prayers in Hebrew or, alternatively, in English while retaining the traditional Hebrew melodies. Gershom says that "as far as I know, Reb Zalman invented the technique of chanting the English prayers with the Hebrew davening cadence. The purpose was to give non-Hebrew readers a feel for the inner dynamics of traditional davening." The service included long meditations and substantial periods of silence. They also danced and utilized other types of movement. Instead of a sermon, Schachter-Shalomi engaged worshippers in a theological dialogue. Tirzah Firestone describes how Reb Zalman turned her on to the worship experience: "Prayer became a new adventure. The prayers and their traditional order were revered in Jewish Renewal, but they were enhanced by melodies, movements, and intentions that brought out their depth and personal relevance."[25]

Many of his followers were awed by the intense devotion they were guided into while saying the Shema Yisrael, the central credo of Judaism. The Shema is a proclamation uttered by Moses to the children of Israel, urging them to remember that at the source of all creation is the one God, but, in most modern American synagogues, the prayer is passed over very quickly. Gershom remembers that, in the original B'nai Or fellowship, they said the Shema "with a full breath for each word, and our voices blending together in a crescendo which felt as if it pierced the very gates of Heaven."

Firestone describes how Reb Zalman led the prayer: he asked everyone to recite the Shema four times, each time with a specific kavanah, intention. The first time, everyone was to say it very slowly, and to feel as if they were hearing it through Moses's lips. They paused to absorb the message. They were then asked to recite the Shema, but to put their own names in the prayer instead of Israel and say it through the voice of their own highest Self. Firestone began the prayer "Hear, O Tirzah . . ." She realized that "suddenly it became a personal reminder of our inclusion in the wholeness of the higher power." The third time they recited the Shema with the name of a person with whom they had a fractured relationship in order to lay a foundation for healing and wholeness. Again they paused to feel the power of what they were doing spiritually. Finally, they were asked to recite the Shema Yisrael as if they were on their own deathbeds, preparing for their final transition into the world where all is clearly one. Firestone remembers that she "was shaken by this way of praying. It was entirely different than anything I had ever experienced in a Jewish context, and much more akin to the in-depth meditations I was used to from the world of Arica" and other similar psycho-spiritual practices. "My exposure to these liturgical innovations began a long process of releasing me from the narrow view I had previously held of Jewish traditions." During the mid-1980s, the movement underwent a major shift in orientation. At the 1985 B'nai Or Kallah, it was decided to change the name of the organization from B'nai Or, disciples of light, to P'nai Or, faces of light. The prima fascie reason was that *B'nai* meant "sons of" and this was not respectful of the women in the group. The change in name was just one indication that the movement was redefining itself ideologically and reorganizing itself administratively. What had formally been a neo-Hasidic style rebbe's court was becoming a more politically active, humanistic religious movement. Gershom was skeptical. "Some saw it as a circumcision (lopping off the B to make a P), but I wondered at the time if it was not more of a castration." Like many other movements of its kind, Jewish Renewal was maturing and defining what its core values were. To his credit, Reb Zalman was willing to be influenced as well as influence others. Reb Zalman had not intended to establish a new religious movement. Gershom recalls that "I remember hearing him say that he wanted it to be like in the days of the Maggid of Mezeritch, who trained disciples and then sent them out to found their own communities. He did not envision a new denomination or a centralized movement, but rather, a network of independent communities of many different flavors, but all grounded in observant Judaism." This vision did not materialize, at least not in the way that Gershom believed that Reb Zalman originally conceptualized it.

By 1986, B'nai Or had become P'nai Or and the concept of Jewish spiritual renewal had become the name of a nascent movement called Jewish Renewal. Gershom, who later became a Bratslaver Hasid, was horrified by the changes. "The new generation were not disciples in the old sense, and they were not Chassidim in any sense." Critics charged that the new P'nai Or seemed to draw heavily from Reconstructionism, and appeared to disavow miracles, revelation, chosenness, the afterlife, and other "superstitious" beliefs, preferring to view Judaism as a human-made folk culture. Some felt that they no longer focused as much on inner-directed contemplative mysticism, putting excessive emphasis on ecology and social justice. According to critics, the entire neo-Hasidic style was abandoned and the concept of discipleship repudiated. Reb Zalman appeared to renounce his role as rebbe and from that point on preferred to be called Zayde (Grandfather) Zalman. While a small number may have become alienated, the Jewish Renewal movement has continued to grow in both numbers and influence. Their neo-Hasidic approach has introduced ecstatic practices into Jewish prayer that were previously almost completely unknown. Reb Zalman has produced dozens of students who have gone on to make their own contributions to American Jewish spiritual-

FIGURE 6.5. Reading Torah outdoors at an ALEPH retreat. Photo Ann Silver. *Courtesy of ALEPH: Alliance for Jewish Renewal* © *2005*

ity, founding congregations, writing thoughtful books, and contributing to social movements for the betterment of the country and of humanity.

The Hippie Rabbi Who Created New Paradigms

Another charismatic personality who became associated with Jewish Renewal was Reb Shlomo Carlebach. Credited as "the father of new Jewish music," Carlebach was able to draw from the European Jewish musical tradition, but, at the same time, bring a distinctly personal touch to his songs.[26] He emphasized the need for everyone to join in the singing. "I think my voice is just good enough to inspire people to sing with me. If I would have a gevald [incredible] voice like, let's say, Moshe Koussevitzky, then nobody would want to sing with me, because then they'll think they don't want to miss my voice, but my voice is just good enough to make them sing."[27]

Like Schachter-Shalomi, Carlebach was one of the earliest Chabad shluchim, joining Lubavitch after graduating from the Beth Medrash Govoha in Lakewood, New Jersey. He began singing publicly in Greenwich Village, where he met Bob Dylan and other folk singers who later became well-known performers. He traveled to Berkeley for the 1966 folk festival and decided to stay in the San Francisco Bay area to reach out to "lost Jewish souls," many of whom were gravitating to Northern California. In 1967, Carlebach opened the House of Love and Prayer in Haight-Ashbury, an outreach effort that was criticized within the Lubavitch movement for being too tolerant toward countercultural lifestyles. Nevertheless, the House was wildly successful, drawing on the model of the commune, which was then in vogue. Carlebach disagreed with his critics, arguing that his House of Love and Prayer was an important accomplishment that was not in conflict with the values of Chabad, but many of his colleagues saw it as a break with Orthodox Judaism.

Carlebach placed his emphasis on love rather than concern with the minutiae of halachic observance. "I feel there is not enough love between people, their emphasis is not on loving. . . . You walk in Orthodox circles, who's called an Orthodox person? His wife wears a sheytl [wig] and buys glatt [the strictest] kosher meat. I never heard somebody say, "This man is really Orthodox, have you ever seen the way he talks to people, the way he talks to children?" Carlebach was careful not to negate the importance of ritual observance, but simply to emphasize the need to be loving. "We need both, God needs the whole thing."[28] Nevertheless, his approach was regarded with suspicion by some. As one journalist put it after his death, "he operated outside traditional Jewish structures in style and substance, and spoke about God and His love in a way that could make other rabbis uncomfortable."[29]

Carlebach said that he was amazed at how many young people would come to his House of Love and Prayer in San Francisco shortly after he opened it. He believed that thousands of college students were receptive to the religious message of Judaism, but that they had been turned off by what they had seen growing up. "I said to the Jewish establishment, 'We have to do teshuvah [repentance], We must have done so much wrong that these kids left us.' They are the real tzadikim [righteous ones]."

Like Reb Zalman, Reb Shlomo taught that Judaism was a spiritual path that had something profound to say to every human being. When he was asked why there was antisemitism in the world, he said that perhaps the world is angry with Jews because they have something very special to share and are yet reluctant to do so. Determined to reverse this tendency, he developed a number of effective strategies for bringing the message of Judaism to a broad audience. Carlebach loved to go to eclectic multidenominational meetings and conferences, which gave him the opportunity to teach Torah to the uninitiated. For Jews on the fringes, this was an exciting act of interfaith interaction, and they responded to Reb Shlomo's message with great enthusiasm. Numerous people spoke of how they had been involved in a cult and returned to Judaism after meeting Reb Shlomo at a spiritual gathering of one sort or another. But that was not his primary purpose—he just wanted to share his love of Judaism with people of all backgrounds.

Carlebach and his twin brother Eli Chaim became co-rabbis of Congregation Kehilath Jacob, also called the Carlebach Shul, the small synagogue on West 79th Street that his father had led. He also worshipped at the agricultural settlement that he founded in Israel, Moshav Mevo Me'or Modi'in. As a rabbinical student in Israel, I was fortunate to have taken a class in comparative religion with Professor Yaakov Ariel where we attended a Friday night service on the moshav during one of Reb Shlomo's visits. Kabbalat Shabbat was like nothing I had ever seen, with much overt emotion. We could see immediately that he was a charismatic religious figure as well as a gifted musician. His singing of Am yisrael chai (The nation of Israel lives) in front of the Soviet mission to the United Nations in the mid 1960s made that song into "a contemporary Jewish liberation anthem." He took other verses from the Torah and made them into memorable songs, especially "Pischu li" (Open for me [the gates of righteousness) and "Barchi nafshi" (May my soul bless God). He first recorded his music in 1959, something that was completely unheard of at that time. The album was a success, and he was able to record more than twenty-five albums, which included almost a thousand melodies. His success led to the creation of an entirely new genre of music—Jewish popular music composed and sung by individual American Jews that was intended to be recorded and sold. He traveled constantly and founded numerous organizations and a number of congregations that he visited from time to time. Because of his short attention span and his constant desire to try new things, he never focused on building a movement that might institutionalize his philosophy after his death. He died of a heart attack while flying to Canada at the age of sixty-nine in 1994. The story goes that he was sitting next to the Skverer Rebbe on the plane, with the two of them singing "Chasdei hashem ki lo samnu" (God's loving-kindness does not end).

After his death, many of his disciples claimed to be the heirs of his spiritual and musical legacy. They vied for legitimacy, each claiming to represent the true spirit of Shlomo. Carlebach's synagogue on the Upper West Side was appropriately called the Carlebach Minyan. There are now other synagogues that proudly publicize themselves as "a Carlebach minyan," meaning that their services are conducted with the spiritual effervescence and musical enthusiasm that characterized the services led by Carlebach himself during his lifetime. Each of the Carlebach minyans tried to build devotion and exuberance that would hopefully create a euphoric religious environment. They use many of Reb Shlomo's distinctive tunes, but supplement them with other compositions as well. There are thirteen Carlebach shabbat minyans in Jerusalem, more than fifty throughout Israel, ten in New York, nearly fifty throughout the United States, and others throughout the world.[30]

His followers were enchanted by the wordless melodies that had the emotional intensity and religious fervor of a Hasidic tisch, the third Sabbath meal where the disciples sat at their rebbe's table and sang their hearts out. Carlebach loved singing soulful, Hasidic nigunim, and he would use these nigunim as an opening to share personal stories that could bring out the insights he believed were contained in every prayer in the siddur. Carlebach took three different types of music—Hasidic, Israeli, and American—and created something that was uniquely his. His overt display of devotional ecstasy was distinctively Hasidic, but his folk music was borrowed from America and his use of the *shirah b'tzibbur*, group sing-alongs, was taken from Zionist and Israeli practices.

One of his chief ambitions in life was to avoid being judgmental. Reb Shlomo told *Tikkun* magazine about a man who came to services on Friday night at the House of Love and Prayer right after it had opened. At the end of the service, the man pulled out an instrument and started to play. "Of course, that is not what we do in an Orthodox shul on a Shabbat, but I said nothing, because he was coming on Shabbat and I was glad he was there. He did it again the next week, and the week after that, and then he came to me and said, "Thank you for not saying anything to me. I was testing your patience, and I now see that you really would accept me here." Now, he is a doctor and president of the PTA of an Orthodox yeshiva. I never, never tell people what to do."[31]

Carlebach was spontaneous, almost impetuous. One evening on Hoshanah Rabbah, he announced that there would be *hakafot* the next morning. All the Torahs would be taken out of the ark and everyone in the synagogue would dance around, celebrating the end and beginning of the Torah reading cycle. But as he concluded his announcement, he suddenly seemed inspired by a new idea. With great excitement, he announced that he believed that the Hallel had not been sung with full musical accompaniment since the destruction of the Second Temple—almost two thousand years earlier. He told everyone that the next morning would be the perfect time to do this and that they should all bring their musical instruments.

Reb Shlomo taught a Judaism that merged heart and mind. He did not, or he did not seem to, deliberately set out to pioneer a new spiritual approach to Judaism. Rather, he was just conveying his emotion: Judaism was a deeply personal spiritual path that spoke to his soul and that he wanted to share with everyone around him. He taught that every moment was a unique opportunity to connect to God and to one another. If he felt his congregation was not immersing themselves as deeply as they could, he might even stop prayers and tell everyone that the only thing that mattered was that the current Sabbath had to be the best Sabbath they had ever experienced.

For all his inspiration, Reb Shlomo left a mixed legacy. His reputation was badly marred after his death when several women accused him of inappropriately touching them. None of these allegations were made publically during his lifetime, and so Carlebach never had any opportunity to respond. His defenders cited the fact that he was a very "touchy" person, showing his emotions by constantly stroking and hugging and kissing. Many remember the incredibly charismatic guitar-strumming man who seemed to love everyone who came anywhere near him. They remember his enthralling Hasidic stories and his tight bearhugs, giving them a sense of acceptance and love. But there was concern even during his lifetime. A group of Jewish women apparently confronted Carlebach privately in Berkeley, California in the early 1980s. He initially denied everything, but then eventually admitted to a problem, saying, "Oy, this needs such a fixing."[32] Despite his apparent private admission, he never made a public statement.

The accusations first became public in a 1998 article published in *Lilith*, the Jewish feminist magazine. Several women described private meetings with Carlebach in which he allegedly inappropriately touched them. The Awareness Center, an advocacy group for Jewish victims of sexual abuse, organized a campaign to remind people of his alleged inappropriate actions when a proposal was made in 2004 to name a street in Manhattan "Rabbi Shlomo Carlebach Way." Awareness Center director Vicki Polin argued that giving him such an honor would be humiliating to his victims. "They also deserve to have a voice. It would be very difficult for them to walk down a street and see that it was named after him."

Despite this controversy, Carlebach remains a spiritual model for many American Jews inspired by Jewish Renewal. Naomi Mark, one of Carlebach's long-time students, said that he had "never wanted to be a flawless guru." What made him so special was that "he really understood our lives and the sense of alienation people sometimes feel living in the modern world, trying to juggle spirituality and Judaism in the context of the many contradictions they feel. He understood what those struggles are like and that's what made him different from other traditional rebbes."[33]

Carlebach is a fascinating figure because he was an important part of Jewish Renewal as well as a pioneer of the baal teshuva movement. As far back as the 1960s, Carlebach was inspiring hippie youth to embrace their Jewish heritage. Many of his outreach tactics were viewed as too liberal by Orthodox leaders, and Carlebach's practices were not always consistent with halachic standards. This made him suspect in Orthodox eyes, and they have generally ignored his contribution to the development of Orthodox outreach. While he is today seen as more of a Jewish Renewal figure, the reality is that he straddled both worlds.

Carlebach did not like to use the term *baal teshuva* for a person who had embraced Orthodox Judaism as an adult. "I hate the name baal teshuvah, because it implies that these young people were doing wrong and now they are repenting." Carlebach felt that the way in which they were confronted was unpleasant and untrue. "They came back to Orthodox Judaism, and the first time they were told that up until now you were a sinner. No." He also objected to the common practice of telling baalei teshuva that the other religions and philosophies they may have tried out were false. "Every religion is a flashlight. We in Judaism have a psychedelic light, but there is no need to knock any other religion, I love a girl and want to marry her, I don't have to say that every other girl is ugly."[34]

Reb Shlomo felt stymied in his efforts to bring people to Judaism by the lack of spiritually aware yeshiva programs. As Jewish religious leaders, "the most we can do is keep our hearts open, and when people come and want to learn, we can tell them where to learn, I have to tell people to go to yeshiva to learn, and unfortunately after a few weeks either they leave the yeshiva or you don't recognize them anymore because the spark is gone from their eyes and they don't care for the world anymore."[35]

The Baal Teshuva Phenomenon

The baal teshuva movement began attracting notice in the late 1960s and early 1970s when growing numbers of young Jews who had been raised in non-Orthodox homes started showing an interest in "becoming religious." Much of the enthusiasm was a result of the startling victory of the State of Israel in the Six-Day War, fought in June 1967. In the weeks leading up to the outbreak of hostilities, many assimilated American Jews who had never previously experienced a visceral connection with the Jewish state suddenly felt as if their own lives were at risk. Orthodox believers saw Israel's victory as the beginning of the messianic redemption from *galut*. They considered strict ritual observance to be one of the necessary prerequisites for the coming of the messiah and they were determined to help those nonobservant Jews who expressed an interest in learning more about traditional Judaism.

Rebellion was a central theme of those years. Many Americans were beginning to search for existential meaning as a response to the counterculture and the hippie movement. The Vietnam War was beginning to look like a quagmire from which the country would never be able to extricate itself, and people were looking for something to give their lives direction. Often, those drawn to the baal teshuva movement were trying to rebel against their parents. Perhaps surprisingly, they believed that, by becoming strictly Orthodox, they could establish independent identities and show their disapproval of their parents' materialistic suburban lifestyles. Many parents interpreted their children's decision to become Orthodox as a repudiation of everything they stood for. Rabbi Yitz Greenman of Aish HaTorah in New York explains that "a lot of parents react harshly to their children becoming observant. They see it as a slap in the face. A rejection of their values."[36]

While many counterculture types were obviously living lives very far from that of Orthodox Judaism, there was a fascination with ritual practice. Just as some found various exotic spiritual practices attractive, others felt that it was cool to observe the Sabbath and follow the other mitzvot. In an atmosphere where some were becoming Buddhists and others Hindus and many were getting involved with the various new religious movements, popularly called "cults," Orthodox Judaism was just one of many weird but fascinating spiritual journeys.

The word *baal teshuva* is a Hebrew term that means "a person who has repented." The term historically referred to a Jew who had been raised in a traditional home, but had then chosen to willingly transgress the halacha, only to later repent and return. It can also be used in a general sense to refer to anyone who has done a bad thing and then repented. From the 1970s on, the term was popularly used to refer to a non-Orthodox Jew, frequently coming from a secular background, who decided to embrace Orthodoxy. They might become Modern Orthodox or haredi: there is only one term referring to either ideological destination. Baalei teshuva saw themselves as returning to the faith of their ancestors, recreating themselves as well as reconnecting to the Judaism with which they had lost touch. The baal teshuva refashions an identity, creating a new persona as well as a new lifestyle. They may also take on the obligation of maintaining the tradition for their parents. Dina Green lights two Shabbat candles even though the Orthodox custom is for a young, unmarried woman to light only one. "My mom doesn't like candles, so I do it in her place. It's a tradition that many religious kids with secular parents take on."[37]

Herbert Danzger of the Graduate Center of the City University of New York explains that most baalei teshuva were young adults, having just graduated from high school or in the middle of studying at university. "Often, they are at a point in their lives when they are free of social ties and free of parental supervision."[38] This was true for Phillip Slepian. Slepian grew up in a congregation that had been formed through the merger of an Orthodox and a Conservative synagogue in Bridgewater, New Jersey. His family was not observant, although they kept kosher at home, initially so that his grandparents could eat in their house. His parents sent him to public school, and he, like most young American Jews in the 1970s, got whatever Jewish education he was going to get through an afternoon religious school and synagogue youth group. It was at United Synagogue Youth shabbatonim that he participated in classes taught by college students who had themselves grown up in USY, but had become baalei teshuva during high school or in the first year or two of college. Slepian was impressed with these young, idealistic counselors, who seemed to have tremendous dedication as well as a great deal of personal charisma. After the formal educational program would end, he and a few of the other more motivated participants would ask these counselors all sorts of questions. What did they believe, how did they practice, and why had they made the change?

Slepian's parents had come from a typical Eastern European Jewish Brooklyn background, but they had stressed the importance of universal culture to their children. "My parents were very big on exposing us to the secular culture. They took us to lots of Broadway shows, museums, and that sort of stuff. They were very big on exploring the world in general."[39] Perhaps as a reaction against their universalism, Slepian was looking for a deeper, more intense, particularistic Jewish identity. His interest was encouraged by the kindly Orthodox rabbi emeritus at his now Conservative synagogue in Bridgewater. "I began a process of just logically thinking things through, asking myself if I could make that leap of faith to accept that Torah, both written and oral, was issued to us by God at Mount Sinai. It took several years, but I gradually increased my observance. There was a point where faith just took over." By the time that Slepian finished high school in 1978, he was ready to make the commitment. As soon as he could, he went to study at Yeshivat Hamivtar, a baal teshuva yeshiva headed by Rabbi Chaim Brovender in Jerusalem.

Jerusalem became the center of the baal teshuva movement. In the 1970s, a young American man named Baruch Levine began recruiting young Jewish tourists who were visiting Israel. He would stand at the entrance to the Western Wall area and approach anyone who looked like a young Jewish student, asking them if they would like a tour of the Orthodox neighborhoods in and around Meah Shearim or be received at the home of an Orthodox family. Most of those he approached were happy to accept, seeing it as a chance to get an insider's view of what was going on or, at the very least, as a way to get a home-cooked meal. Later, Jeff Seidel took over from Levine and continued to expand the original concept, which became known as Jeff Seidel's Jewish Student Information Center, offering educational tours around the Old City and throughout the country. Seidel also provided a free copy of his *Jewish Traveller's Resource Guide*. This proved to be one of the most effective ways of recruiting potential baalei teshuva.

Many stories began to circulate about young American Jews from Reform or Conservative backgrounds who suddenly embraced Orthodox Judaism. *Rolling Stone* even did a feature story on Chaim Willis, an intelligent but unfocused young man who stopped in Jerusalem as part of a long trip abroad. His sister Ellen became alarmed at his sudden "conversion" and went to visit him, later writing a touching and generally positive account of what she saw at Aish HaTorah (as mentioned in chapter 1). Like Willis, many had dropped out of universities or refused to enroll in them, preferring to study full-time in Israeli yeshivas.

Virtually all baalei teshuva have detailed stories about how they "became religious." Being Orthodox, most identify Jewish religiosity solely with Orthodoxy and therefore see their lives before their transformation as having been secular. In most cases, they were not deeply involved in Reform or Conservative Judaism, but their families frequently belonged, at least nominally, to some kind of synagogue. Like those who found themselves attracted to Jewish Renewal, they found the suburban Judaism with which they were raised to be superficial and resolved to find something more intense and spiritually fulfilling.

This was the case with Jack Abramoff. His name is familiar to many readers not because of his religiosity, but rather because of the central role he played in a corruption investigation during the George W. Bush administration. He had become a successful lobbyist with close ties to many of the top Republicans. But on January 3, 2006, he pled guilty to charges of conspiracy, tax evasion, and fraud in a plea bargain with prosecutors as part of a larger corruption investigation. "I had lost a sense of proportion and judgment. God sent me 1,000 hints that He didn't want me to keep doing what I was doing. But I didn't listen, so He set off a nuclear bomb."[40] Abramoff was photographed leaving the courthouse in a black hat identical to the ones traditionally worn in the yeshiva world. Blogs speculated whether the hat was his way of trying to mobilize Orthodox support on his behalf or whether it was covering a yarmulke that he did not want to show so as not to commit hillul Hashem, disgracing Judaism publicly.[41]

Abramoff was raised in Beverly Hills, north of Santa Monica Boulevard. His parents joined Temple Emanuel, and Abramoff was sent to the religious school there. But by the time of his bar mitzvah, he was alienated from Reform Judaism. "I quickly came to the conclusion that what they were saying was gibberish." Abramoff told his father, "that's the last time I'll be involved with that sort of tradition." He felt that he wanted something more authentic, but the only thing he knew about traditional Judaism came from watching the movie *Fiddler on the Roof*. Abramoff started going to services at Sinai Temple, the large and influential Conservative congregation in Los Angeles. He began to study Judaism and was particularly influenced by Hayim Halevy Donin's best-seller *To Be a Jew*. "I read that book cover to cover several times over and decided that if I was going to be a Jew, that's the kind of Jew I was going to be."

He decided to observe the fast day of Tisha B'Av for the first time when he turned thirteen, but did not yet understand the proper way to observe such a day of mourning. Abramoff somehow thought that, rather than just leather shoes being prohibited, no footwear was allowed, and that it was a rest day, when all the restrictions of the Sabbath would apply. "So I walked to Temple Sinai, 5 miles down Wilshire Boulevard, night and day, in my socks. Somebody at the temple asked me if I wanted a ride. I thought, 'Hey, what's wrong with these guys?'"

Some baalei teshuva rejected their families and felt themselves to be—forgive the expression—"born again." They believed they had been re-created as new people and had no reason to maintain familial relationships. This was not encouraged by any of the baal teshuva organizations, although they did worry that home visits might be a bad influence on the baal teshuva. When I was in high school, I was invited to visit Mirrer Yeshiva for a week. One of the students I met was a boy just a little bit older than I named Chaim Cohen, and we became friendly. But, when I went back to visit a few months later, he was gone. I was told that he went home to Springfield, Massachusetts frequently to visit his family and they had pressured him to give up the Orthodoxy he had recently embraced. He changed his name back to Mitch, grew his hair long, and enrolled in a premed program. The baal teshuva yeshivas have to carefully balance the need to prevent what could become a potentially bad influence, from their point of view, with the human need to maintain good parent-child relations. Even with the best of intentions, some baalei teshuva cause a great deal of pain to their secular families. *Newsweek* reporter Joshua Hammer writes, in his memoir about his brother becoming a baal teshuva, "for years my brother's religious transformation filled me with a rage and embarrassment so profound that even today I struggle to understand it."[42]

While some baalei teshuva may reject their past and everything associated with that past, others are able to integrate their talents and experiences into their new lives. Matisyahu, the Hasidic reggae rapper, is a perfect example, finding that becoming a baal teshuva helped his career bloom. Matisyahu's 2005 album *Live at Stubb's* was ranked number 2 on Billboard's Reggae chart, going platinum. *Youth*, his third album, peaked at number 4, and his single "King Without a Crown" made the Top 40. In the song, he sings in a lilting pseudo-Caribbean patois: "I want Moshiach [messiah] now." In the song "Got No Water," he talks of God, using the Orthodox pietistic term *Hashem* meaning "the name." The words are as follows: "Hashem's rays fire blaze light my way light of my life / And these days well wait no longer night / reaching for my G-d like skyscrapers in the night / I said I know it's hard inside is empty *galus* (exile) cuts like a knife/ Internalize Torah vibes bound to feel alright." Perhaps his most famous line in the song "King Without a

Crown" is "Me no want no sensimilla. . . . / Torah food for my brain," a reference to his feeling that Lubavitch Hasidism gives him a greater high than marijuana ever could.

Matisyahu was born Matthew Miller and grew up in a typical non-Orthodox Jewish home in White Plains, New York. In his later teenage years, he became a dreadlocked Phish fanatic and was immersed in that type of cultural and social environment. He enrolled at the New School and one day met a young Lubavitcher in Washington Square Park. Matisyahu became an enthusiastic follower of the Rebbe, and soon moved to Crown Heights. What is telling is that, even after becoming Lubavitch, he was able to keep up with his music. Chabad did not force him to reject his previous interests and devote himself only to the study of Torah. Rather, they seem to have taught him about Judaism while letting him absorb the new ideas into his already formed personality and culture. While he has recently broken publicly from Chabad-Lubavitch, he and his family remain Hasidic Jews. "I was full on Chabad for about four years." He complained to the *Jewish Week* that many of the articles written about his break from Chabad "make it seem like I just woke up and said Chabad is not for me, but it has been a process for the last four years. Not that I want to come down on Chabad, but I started learning things in a new way." Matisyahu emphasizes that "I need to do Judaism in a way that makes me feel more alive, not less alive."[43]

Institutional Developments

Orthodox outreach became known as *kiruv*, which is the Hebrew word for bringing people closer, in this case, closer to Torah. An entire profession arose of kiruv workers, Orthodox rabbis and rebbetzins, as well as educators and social workers, who specialized in working with non-Orthodox young people. Chabad pioneered what became known as outreach, sending recently ordained young Lubavitch rabbis all over the world to interact with and influence non-Orthodox Jews. Rabbi Menachem Mendel Schneerson, the Lubavitcher Rebbe himself, began sending out a handful of shluchim already in the 1950s. We will be looking at Chabad in more detail in the next chapter. At this point, suffice it to say that they were an important part of Orthodox outreach. The NCSY, a youth group movement created by Rabbi Pinchas Stolper of the OU to reach out to non-Orthodox high school students, became quite popular in certain circles and positively influenced many students from homes where tradition was respected, but halacha was not observed.

Outreach consisted of creating informal educational programs that could touch the hearts and souls of non-Orthodox youth and then convincing them to begin living as Orthodox Jews. The success of early outreach efforts created hundreds of newly Orthodox young people who knew relatively little. No matter how effective the outreach programs were, it was not reasonable to expect them to make up for twelve years of Jewish day school and a rich Orthodox Jewish home life in just a few months of sporadic extracurricular activities. The need for intensive educational institutions that could provide beginning and intermediate-level programs for baalei teshuva, as well as some who had been raised Orthodox but needed remedial work, was pressing.

Many Orthodox educators believed that the best place for such an intensive educational institution was in Israel. Israel was an inspiring place to be, particularly in the years following the Six-Day War, and could be a positive influence on the baal teshuva in the making. The Diaspora Yeshiva, one of the first programs specifically designed for baalei teshuva, was founded on the Mount of Olives in 1967. They developed an enthusiastic following, becoming famous for their student musicians, the Diaspora Yeshiva Band. But, by the early 1970s, they lost much of their popularity to the newer baal teshuva yeshivas, Ohr Somayach and Aish HaTorah, who have remained dominant over the past four decades. All these schools were specifically focused on working with young adults who were considering becoming observant.

In its early years, outreach was focused on individual programs or schools that were loosely linked together in an informal network of referrals. Rebbetzin Esther Jungreis was the first Orthodox educator to focus on building a worldwide outreach movement, rather than just a single yeshiva, youth retreat, or home hospitality program. Beginning with a column in the *Jewish Press*, an Orthodox weekly newspaper published in Brooklyn, she started a career as a conference headliner and motivational speaker. She became famous for her parables and stories and her ability to remind diverse audiences of simple but timeless truths. Perhaps the closest thing the Orthodox community had to a televangelist, Jungreis traveled worldwide giving talks to large enthusiastic gatherings. "We just ask that Jews look within their souls and find their roots by discovering Torah."

During her public appearances, she cried out: "To be a Jew is the great[est] privilege. To be unaware of it is the greatest catastrophe—spiritual genocide."

Her choice of language is deliberate. Born in Szegad, Hungary, she survived the Bergen-Belsen concentration camp. The rebbetzin determined "to devote her life to combating the spiritual holocaust that was occurring here in the United States." Although this analogy has been made by others as well, it sounded extreme, and I expected that the rebbetzin would refrain from repeating it in conversation with me. That turned out not to be the case. She bluntly told me, over the phone, "we're in a spiritual holocaust right now."[44] She believes that the rampant assimilation occurring in the United States today is comparable in its impact to what happened in Nazi-era Europe, although she clearly understands that there are tremendous differences. "We had a generation that surpassed expectations in every field. But when it came to spirituality—we, the People of the Book—were Jewish illiterates. Something constructive had to be done."

Jungreis began her crusade after being disturbed by the tremendous amount of alienation she saw in the aftermath of the 1960s youth revolution. She believed that, without Orthodox Judaism, young Jews exposed to the corrosive influences of the counterculture were spiritually rudderless. "It is our mission to create a better world. To bring healing to the world. But if the Jew does not have the knowledge of Torah, a vacuum is left in his soul and he will gravitate to any-ism."[45] Her message was well-received by parents who had been pained by their children's rejection of Judaism, frequently in favor of some sort of Eastern philosophy. "If you study the recent history of American Jews, you see that the majority of hippies, yippies, and the left were dominated by Jews. Buddhism? A tremendous amount of Jews." Other New Age practices and various new religious movements, ditto. She resolved to "rescue" the young Jews who had fallen into the many spiritual traps just waiting for them in contemporary American society.

She established an outreach organization called Hineni, which means "here I am," to promote "spiritual outreach," issuing a call at the Young Israel Collegiate Youth Convention for a "rally for neshomas [souls]." Shlomo Carlebach just happened to be speaking at the bar mitzvah reception for her son which was held the following day, and he urged the guests to start planning what became known as the "Rock and Soul" event right away. It took a long time to implement the plan, but in November 1973 Hineni was officially born at the Felt Forum in Madison Square Garden, the very place where Billy Graham had launched his own international crusade. Displaying similarities with the Christian revival model, the Hineni event was deliberately staged at a neutral location because most of the target audience would not want to go into a synagogue or any other type of Jewish communal building.[46] Thousands of previously uninvolved Jews sang and danced to the rebbetzin's entreaties. Jungreis gave an impassioned address urging the mostly young crowd to open up the Torah and "learn who you are!" In a dramatic whisper, the rebbetzin told them, "You are a Jew. God spoke to you at Mount Sinai. Have you not forgotten? The fact that you are here—that you are searching shows that there is still some of the 'pintele yid,' some of the spark of Judaism still left in you."

Although she obviously focused on Jewish youth, the rebbetzin made an attempt to universalize her message as well. Jungreis has written four books, including the best-selling *The Committed Life: Principles for Good Living from Our Timeless Past.* The book is filled with inspirational stories about people inviting God into their lives and discovering the beauty of virtues such as forgiveness, compassion, faith, hope, and gratitude. The Hineni Web site likewise focuses on issues of universal concern. The flashing headline states that "life is a test" and informs the Web surfer that the rebbetzin has a new book explaining how to meet life's challenges successfully.[47]

A whole genre of literature was created to cater to baalei teshuva. Written in English, these books were designed to explain the beliefs and practices of Orthodox Judaism to readers who were presumed to lack even basic knowledge. Other authors wrote on a more sophisticated level, relying on the many baalei teshuva who had extensive secular educations. The works of Rabbi Aryeh Kaplan (already discussed in chapter 2) were considered particularly influential. In his short life, Kaplan wrote close to fifty books on numerous subjects, including groundbreaking works on the spiritual significance of Kabbalah. His best known book is *The Living Torah*, a translation of the Five Books of Moses into English, one of the first to be structured around the weekly Torah portions.

Kaplan's writings influenced many baalei teshuva who were interested in understanding the philosophy behind Orthodox Judaism. What is truly remarkable was that this same man was capable of writing books that became central works in the Jewish Renewal movement. While Kaplan was always strictly Orthodox, he had an openness that enabled him to teach and influence many disciples outside of Orthodoxy as well as within. Rabbi Pinchas Stolper eulogized him as a man who "saw harmony between science and Judaism, where many others saw otherwise. He put forward creative and original ideas and hypotheses, all the time anchoring them in the classical works of rabbinic literature."[48] Despite his portrayal by many today as a model of a haredi Jew, Kaplan went through a series of religious stages and apparently even served a Conservative congregation for a brief period of time. Rabbi Alan Brill, an expert on Jewish mysticism, wrote me in amazement: "Many of the baalei teshuva now pretend that Kaplan and his followers were always haredi!"[49]

Artscroll is the best known and most prolific Orthodox Jewish publisher of religious books that cater to the baal teshuva market. They have published hundreds of books, including translations and commentaries on the entire Hebrew Bible and the many folios of Talmud. *The Artscroll Siddur* has become the standard prayer book in most Orthodox synagogues, even Modern Orthodox congregations. It features a beautiful layout and detailed notes and commentary, far surpassing anything else available. They also publish *The Chumash: The Stone Edition*, a Torah translation and commentary that has become the best-selling English-Hebrew Torah translation and commentary in the United States. Even my Reform temple in Southwest Georgia uses this edition for their Torah study group on Saturday mornings.

The popularity of Artscroll alarmed many Modern Orthodox leaders not only because of its fundamentalist (using the term in a broad sense) theology and anti-academic approach but also because it seemed to be one more indication that the haredim had achieved total domination over the entire Orthodox community. Some blamed the influx of baalei teshuva for what those critics saw as a negative development. William B. Helmreich and Reuel Shinnar, for example, wrote that "the growth in the baal teshuva movement has certainly fueled the rightward shift. New to the faith, such individuals often need constant reassurance that they are genuinely doing God's will and humrahs (strictures) provide that reassurance."[50] Artscroll has certainly done a great deal to popularize a haredi world view. Their commentaries assume that the Torah was given from God to Moses and then passed on from generation to generation without any change or corruption in the text. They understand Judaism as ahistorical and ignore modern scholarship on biblical dating, textual criticism, archaeological finds, and other scientific discoveries leading to academic reinterpretations.

Once a student decided to become Orthodox, they were encouraged to go study. Special schools were established to cater to students with high levels of conceptual abilities but little if any textual background. Yeshivat Ohr Somayach was founded in 1970 by Rabbis Mendel Weinbach, Nota Schiller, and Noah Weinberg. Originally called Shema Yisrael, it focused on teaching beginners how to "learn" classical rabbinic texts. The goal was to provide students with a foundation on which they could go on to study Talmud in a regular yeshiva environment. To do that, the student needed to become familiar with a couple hundred key Aramaic words and phrases and to learn enough about the concepts of Jewish law that they could go into a *beit midrash* (study hall) with a *chavruta* (study partner) and prepare a *daf* (page) of Talmud without help. In 1979, Ohr Somayach opened a branch of their yeshiva in Monsey, New York, which enabled those who could not go to Israel for whatever reason to develop their Talmudic skills.

Rabbi Dovid Refson founded Neve Yerushalayim in 1970 as a girls' seminary for baalot teshuva (the plural of the Hebrew term for female returners to Orthodoxy), which became the unofficial sister school of Ohr Somayach. While many of the girls arriving at the school were not observant, they had to follow the rules of Orthodox Judaism while they were there. Girls attending Neve had to wear the modest dress typical of Orthodox women, including sleeves below the elbow and long skirts. They did not have to cover their hair because most of them were not married. Some of the girls looked almost comical in this garb, having been used to wearing baby tees and midriffs for their entire lives. The curriculum at Neve stressed practical halacha that an Orthodox woman would need to know. This included kashrut, taharat mishpacha, and Sabbath and holiday rules that would apply to the family and home. The girls also studied Tanach and other types of Jewish religious literature, but not Talmud. While men may have been attracted to Orthodoxy because of its theology or ritual, substantial numbers of women found the emphasis on traditional sex roles to be reassuring. Having grown up in a secular society where divorce and other types of family instability were rife, many were looking for a way to live that they hoped would guarantee them personal happiness in a warm and nurturing family environment.

In 1974, Rabbi Weinberg broke off of Ohr Somayach to establish Aish HaTorah. Aish HaTorah differed from Ohr Samayach in that it focused more on convincing young men to embrace Orthodox Judaism, rather than on preparing them to enter high-level yeshivas where they would study Talmud independently. The yeshiva developed an extensive program to teach extremely basic Orthodox Judaism—and to do so in an interesting and persuasive manner. Unlike Ohr Samayach, learning methodology was secondary. Weinberg reasoned that if he could truly convince young men to devote their lives to Orthodox Judaism, there was plenty of time for them to learn how to study Talmud, but if he overemphasized the technical aspects too soon, the young man might drift away from Judaism entirely.

Aish HaTorah stressed that embracing Orthodox Judaism was not an all-or-nothing proposition. They were concerned that many baalei teshuva accepted a tremendous burden of responsibility upon themselves too quickly and would then start to feel overwhelmed by the pressure. Weinberg wanted the students to understand that, while the goal was to become an Orthodox Jew, each person had to do this at his own pace. Since Torah was a profound philosophy that provided a great deal of practical wisdom for living a good life, if they persevered they would embrace more and more mitzvot over the course of time.

The name Aish HaTorah literally means "Fire of the Torah," and was inspired by the Talmudic story of Rabbi Akiva. Akiva was an illiterate shepherd who came across a stone that had been carved out by the constant drip of water. He was in awe of how something so soft could carve a hole in something so hard. If that was so, he reasoned, how much more could Torah, which is comparable to fire, do to his heart? Even though he was forty years old, he began studying and eventually became one of the greatest sages of his generation. Later in life, he became a supporter of the Bar Kochba revolt (132–135 CE), and was tortured to death by the Romans, becoming one of the most famous martyrs of the Jewish people.

Aish HaTorah was located in the Old City and was particularly focused on backpackers and casual tourists who would be offered a meal and then invited to stay for a longer period to study. Since Ohr Somayach did not need to be as visible, they built a "campus" in Ramat Eshkol, one of the newer Jerusalem suburbs. In cities across North America, both established centers that offered educational programs as well as services and encouraged participants to consider enrolling in a yeshiva for full-time study.

To draw interest from unaffiliated young Jews, Aish HaTorah created the Discovery Seminar, a four-hour program presenting an overview of the entire gamut of Jewish history and philosophy from an Orthodox point of view. More than one hundred thousand people worldwide have attended the seminars, including celebrities such as Kirk Douglas, Ed Asner, and Jason Alexander. The Discovery Seminar offered a fundamentalist (again used in a broad sense) view of the world. The universe was created less than six thousand years ago. God performed all of the miracles described in the Torah. They purported to use scientific methods such as the supposedly infallible Bible code to prove the authenticity of Orthodox Judaism and its direct relevance to specific events in today's world. This was designed to convince young secular Jews to embrace Orthodoxy, and it may have been effective in doing that, but it also drew the wrath of Orthodox thinkers who objected, arguing that this was a dangerous and possibly erroneous claim.

Aish HaTorah also engaged in outreach that was not directly focused on religious education. They are credited with inventing what they called SpeedDating, eight-minute round robin interview-style dates with large numbers of men and women gathering together in a trendy coffee shop for a few hours. Their success with SpeedDating indicates one of the main motivations of many individuals for becoming involved—the desire to meet an attractive Jewish mate. Like so much in the baal teshuva world, this may appear to be counterintuitive. Why would young singles willingly enter a gender-segregated society to improve their social lives? But the reality is that modern society has made it increasingly difficult to find suitable mates, and the Orthodox world is well prepared for this task and does it with remarkable efficiency.

Certain Orthodox synagogues became known as centers for both baalei teshuva and singles. Lincoln Square Synagogue on the Upper West Side of Manhattan was one of the few Modern Orthodox congregations to become heavily involved in outreach. In 1964, Rabbi Steven Riskin took over a small, struggling Conservative congregation and transformed it into a vibrant community center that drew in hundreds of what were then called yuppies (young upwardly mobile urban professionals). Most were not from Orthodox homes, but were attracted by the dynamic programming as well as the opportunity to meet members of the opposite sex. The singles aspect was important in their initial success- cynics felt that few in the congregation had a real commitment to the full observance of Jewish law. People half-jokingly referred to the "tefillin date" in which a young man would bring his phylacteries with him in anticipation of spending the night. Nevertheless, there was a great deal of (nonsexual) excitement generated. Rabbi Ephraim Buchwald became the Lincoln Square specialist in outreach, developing beginners' services and educational programs designed to introduce the uninitiated into Orthodoxy without frightening them away.

In 1987, Buchwald founded the National Jewish Outreach Program, which was designed to take the most successful programming ideas from Lincoln Square and apply them on a national basis. The NJOP differed from the baal teshuva yeshivas in that they were nondenominational and worked with all types of synagogues. The NJOP has had particular success with their crash courses in Hebrew reading, basic Judaism, and Jewish history. They have also publicized their "Turn Friday Night Into Shabbat" and "Shabbat Across

America," a yearly date on which hundreds of synagogues of all denominations throughout the United States promote Sabbath observance by offering a beginners' service and a traditional communal Shabbat meal.[51] Buchwald's goal is to reach much greater numbers than he could working out of just one synagogue. Because of the nature of the NJOP, however, many of those he reaches are not potential baalei teshuva.

Both the baal teshuva and the Renewal movements have influenced and inspired different American Jewish religious groups, many of which are far removed ideologically. There was a widespread consensus that the Jewish establishment was not innovative enough and had tried to use force when they needed to be flexible and creative. In contrast, the baal teshuva and Jewish Renewal movements had developed cutting-edge responses to the new challenges that the Jewish community faced. Mainstream synagogues are now playing catch-up, as will be discussed in chapter 8. They are finding that, while nothing comes easy, there are imaginative strategies that can capture the imagination of people who had previously shown no interest. Judaism in America faces unprecedented challenges, and the mainstream denominations and establishment institutions of the Jewish community were slow to react. The baal teshuva and Jewish Renewal movements have demonstrated that inspired leaders with substantive religious knowledge and personal charisma can successfully pioneer new approaches. Drawing on the concept of the need for innovation as a vital source for renewal, Zalman Schachter-Shalomi compares Judaism to an ancient tree. "The core of any mature tree is old wood. The old wood is crucial to maintaining the tree's structure, its ability to withstand the changing winds, but no growth is going on there. The living processes that are the *growth* of the tree, its message to the future, take place only in the tree's newest and outermost ring. We today are that outermost ring, and the growing is up to us."[52]

7 The Popularization of Jewish Mystical Outreach

Many Americans believe—correctly, to a large extent—that religion played a greater role in their grandparent's lives than it does in their own. While they do not want to return to the world of their grandparents—and have to give up all of the technological innovations and the many comforts of modern life—they sense that something important has been lost along the way. They want to affirm that life is sacred and that it should be experienced with the appropriate reverence. Yet they feel a vague disquietude with the current exclusion of the sacred from modern society. Hand in hand with the nostalgia for an idyllic world that has seemingly been lost, there has also been a growing interest in "miracle and mystery." Many people feel that the uncertainty of the times has contributed greatly to the fascination with the miraculous and mysterious. While most Americans continue to tell pollsters that they believe in God, it is not necessarily clear to them what they mean by this. They desperately yearn for a god who can protect them, but they are not sure that the traditional God of the suburban church or synagogue can do that. As a result of the increasingly unstable economy, Americans worry that they may not have the money that they need to live comfortably and take care of their families. In the aftermath of September 11, Americans are fearful of all sorts of physical threats, including the fear of being wounded or killed in a terrorist attack. Such fears may be exaggerated, but they are deep within the subconscious and not easily uprooted.[1]

Many overeducated secularists find the concept of supernaturalism ludicrous and cannot understand why anyone would possibly want to believe in that sort of thing. The reason for this attraction may actually be quite simple—many Americans are drawn to the supernatural because it makes them feel happy. While these people may have had negative experiences growing up in a mainline denomination, they have been drawn into the experiential realm of miracles and mysteries because it seems to not only explain evil but actually banish it. The comfort that many derive from the supernatural contrasts dramatically with the negative emotions frequently associated with more conventional religious beliefs. The existence of miracles reinforces the person's sense that human nature is essentially good and the forces governing the universe are primarily benign.

What constitutes miraculous and mysterious experiences covers a wide spectrum. What they all have in common is the belief that the person is able to come into direct contact with a supernatural force that cannot be rationally understood. This can be comforting for people who are living in a highly secularized, ultramodern, twenty-first century society that relies heavily on technology. Postmodern theorists explain that daily life in contemporary society is a "constructive reality," which makes sense most of the time but breaks down at certain critical points, such as when there is a natural catastrophe or a human tragedy. Some Americans need an alternative reality to make sense of these events, whether they have had to live through one or have just experienced it vicariously through the media.

Part of this need for an alternative reality manifests itself in an interest in the mysterious and the magical, including a fascination with mysticism. Mystical concepts dovetail nicely with certain aspects of popular culture, and this serves to reinforce the initial interest on the part of some and create a curiosity in the minds of others. Jewish mysticism has become one of, if not the most, prominent forms of mysticism in American popular culture. This chapter was going to focus on two organizations that teach different forms of Jewish mysticism, the Kabbalah Centre International Incorporated (KC, formerly the Kabbalah Learning Centre) and Chabad-Lubavitch. Unfortunately, due to legal considerations, this chapter will be restricted solely to a discussion of Chabad.

The interest in Jewish mysticism has been building slowly since Martin Buber's writings on Hasidism were translated and published in the United States in the 1950s. The first mainstream American Jew to publicize the importance of Jewish mysticism was Reform Rabbi Herbert Weiner, who in 1969 published a classic travelogue called *Nine and a Half Mystics: The Kabbala Today*. Weiner, who called himself a "half mystic," went to see the gamut of Jewish mystics in the United States and Israel. He met with Rabbi Menachem Mendel Schneerson, the Lubavitcher Rebbe, at a time when the Chabad leader was still meeting with interested outsiders, and he spent time with an obscure kabbalistic scholar named Setzer who wrote on mystical themes from his gritty, walk-up New York apartment. What made Weiner's book so appealing to a wide spectrum of readers was his ability to intersperse historical background and clear explanations of mystical and Hasidic beliefs with colorful descriptions of eccentric personalities.

Even though there were obviously tremendous societal changes during the 1960s, a prejudice against nonrational approaches to religion persisted. American Jewish scholars inherited the German-Jewish academic perspective called *Wissenschaft des Judentums*, which looked down upon the Jewish mystical tradition as primitive and not worthy of study. Religious leaders of the various denominations likewise saw Jewish mysticism as the scandalous underbelly of Judaism, something to be ignored or even hidden. This began to change gradually, as Americans felt freer to experiment with alternative spiritualities. Jews were particularly attracted to Eastern approaches to living, including various types of mysticism. Some eventually found their way back to Judaism, as we have seen with those who became JuBus or the members of havurot who later began developing what became known as Jewish Renewal (see chapters 2 and 6).

This interest in mysticism was generally ignored by the Jewish establishment, including the main Jewish religious denominations. Most Reform, Conservative, and Orthodox rabbis felt that these spiritual yearnings were beyond the scope of what their synagogues were intended to offer (see chapter 3). If it seemed to have a mystical basis, they were wary. But, as it became clear that a huge percentage of the younger generation was opting out of mainstream Judaism, Jewish communal leaders slowly began to recognize that what had met the needs of the older generation was no longer terribly effective (see chapter 2). If young people became involved in Jewish life, it was because they found something in Judaism compelling.

Many of these spiritual searchers came back to Judaism on individual paths and developed their own unique approaches to Jewish spirituality. Some became involved through unconventional paths; certainly most found something meaningful that they had not seen in the Judaism being presented in their suburban synagogue. Two of the most successful organizations were Chabad and the Kabbalah Centre. Writing in the *Jerusalem Post*, Jay Michaelson argued that, based on the success that these two groups have experienced over the past three decades, they could serve as models for successful outreach. What were they doing that was so attractive to the previously alienated and disaffiliated? Michaelson stressed that both focused on spirituality, rather than Jewish survival for its own sake, and this was the key to understanding why they were able to grow and thrive. "Go to a Chabad House or the Kabbalah Center [*sic*], and the message is much deeper [than simply survival]: This is about ultimate reality, about asking deep questions and searching for answers. Again, one may disagree entirely with a Chabad shaliah's view of the universe, but look into his eyes, and anyone can sense the earnestness." They have a passionate belief in God that can be felt. "Not only does the Hasid believe in God; he believes there is nothing but God: that this moment is charged, filled and energized by the Divine Presence. And that mystical belief translates into enthusiasm, open-heartedness and devotion." Similarly, "amid all the commercialism," of the Kabbalah Centre, Michaelson writes that its teachers sincerely believe that they are revealing the secrets of the world's oldest and most powerful wisdom. "The light is real and can be experienced here and now. That which we normally experience is but the surface of reality. Would you like to look deeper?"[2]

Unfortunately, the section in this chapter dealing specifically with the Kabbalah Centre International, Inc. had to be removed. Let me explain why. In the process of writing this book, I contacted the Kabbalah Centre, as I did numerous other organizations and individuals, and provided them with an early version of the relevant chapter so that they might be able to make factual corrections or suggest possible interpretive changes. I also wanted to interview at least one of the leaders of the organization personally. Rabbi Yakov Travis of the Tiferet Institute had just finished organizing a conference on contemporary Kabbalah at which Rabbi Michael Berg, one of the leaders of the Kabbalah Centre, had spoken. Rabbi Travis volunteered to contact

Rabbi Berg for me and recommended that he talk with me. After exchanging a number of e-mails with Rabbi Berg, we scheduled a telephone conversation for July 11, 2007.

I had sent the Kabbalah Centre the relevant chapter and requested they look it over and had also asked them if they had any high-resolution photos I could reprint in the book. I was hoping to discuss the contents of this chapter with Rabbi Berg, but, before we actually talked, on July 9, 2007, I received a six-page letter from Peter E. Nussbaum, an attorney at Wolff and Samson PC, Counsellors at Law, representing the Kabbalah Centre. In response, Nussbaum wrote me that they were denying my request to use their photographs and were also demanding that I not publish the part of the chapter that dealt with the Kabbalah Centre, at least not in the form that they had received. Nussbaum wrote that, in his client's view, the section was inaccurate, misleading, and damaging to the KC's reputation. He further wrote that the Kabbalah Centre fully intended to take further action if the chapter was indeed published.[3]

In response to my further inquiry via e-mail on July 16, Nussbaum explained that in the view of the KC it was unlikely that merely providing corrective language would alleviate their concerns. Nevertheless, I rewrote the chapter to try to respond to Nussbaum's points. I sent the revised chapter to Bob Stein, my intellectual rights lawyer, who recommended a number of additional changes. I then sent the chapter back to Nussbaum. This made me uncomfortable because it was asking the subject of the section to approve what I had written about them, rather than just suggest potential improvements that would be entirely at my discretion, but I had little choice if I wanted to ensure there be no legal repercussions after publication. On September 24, 2007, Nussbaum reiterated that his client remained deeply concerned that my revised chapter was still inaccurate and damaging. He wrote that they reserved the right to act on claims that they might have against me if and when the section of the chapter was published, even in its revised form.

Stein contacted Nussbaum directly, but, despite my attorney's best efforts, he was unable to receive any further specific information about the nature of the KC's ongoing concerns. This put me in a difficult situation. It was possible that the revised chapter addressed all of their objections, but I could not be sure. After numerous additional attempts at communications and various deliberations, I reluctantly decided to remove the material. The legal fees—despite a generous discounted rate—had reached a prohibitive level. I was also feeling a tremendous amount of stress and did not want the possibility of a hugely expensive lawsuit hanging over my head.

Right before the manuscript was scheduled to go to press, I sent another batch of e-mails to the various parties and, to my surprise, Rabbi Michael Berg responded. Although he wrote that he would be willing to work with me on the chapter over a two-week period, I did not hear from him again. I wrote to him and he did answer, citing his work and travel and promising to get back to me. On December 24, 2007, Nussbaum sent a follow-up letter to my lawyer, saying that the KC remained offended and believed that they were misrepresented throughout the part of the chapter in which they were treated. Nussbaum also wrote that they believed there were numerous false inferences and defamatory comments, although, in contrast to his original letter, he did not cite any specific examples. Nussbaum concluded by emphasizing that I had interwoven misleading as well as false content in the chapter and that, if I should publish it, the KC would vigorously defend its reputation by legal means.[4] While I feel that the ten thousand words I had written about the KC were accurate (as well as fascinating), I felt I had no choice but to remove them. I believe that the rest of the chapter remains coherent and that despite the omission the reader will still come away from this book with a full understanding of the most important trends in contemporary American Judaism. The rest of this chapter will therefore focus on Chabad-Lubavitch.

Chabad has emerged as a bold innovator whose followers have literally gone where no one else would go—whether it be Alaska or Nepal. There is a joke that when the first astronaut lands on Mars he will be greeted by a Chabad shaliach. Some even see Chabad as an emerging denomination within a dramatically reconfigured twenty-first century American Judaism. Whether this actually will happen is obviously unknown, but one thing is clear: they are capable of touching people's hearts. Chabad has shown a remarkable talent for reaching out to people who are alienated from regular synagogues. Many are angry with their home congregations for not being more accepting or with their childhood rabbi for showing little interest in them as adults. They may have other reasons for being upset and confused as well. Although it has been apparent for some time that many American Jews were not finding the mainstream religious offerings satisfactory, it was not at all clear that a mystical Hasidic approach to outreach would work any better. I remember seeing my first Chabad shaliach in Waterbury, Connecticut in the mid-1970s. I thought this gentleman was wasting his time, trying to peddle something so old-fashioned to people who were moving so decisively in the other direction. I turned out to be completely mistaken. In an era of contraction and consolidation, Chabad has constantly expanded, opening new branches in cities and towns across the United States.[5]

Because Chabad can draw out emotions that have long been dormant, philanthropists are willing to give large sums of money to finance their activities, even when those programs are intended for people on the other side of the globe. While a traditional-style synagogue requires families to "join," paying many hundreds or even thousands of dollars a year simply for the privilege of "membership," Chabad welcomes everyone without any obligation or commitment. While this has been one of the primary reasons that many—particularly those who have a vested interest in the traditional economic structure of Jewish religious activity—have criticized this group, it is also one of the primary reasons that it has been so successful. Even in my small town of Albany, Georgia, there are unaffiliated Jews who have an interest in Judaism but do not want to make the commitment of joining the local synagogue and being obligated to that institution forevermore. Some of these individuals would love a local Chabad House they could visit when they wanted to hear a lecture, engage in heartfelt prayer, or share a Sabbath meal.

The overabundance of enthusiasm generated by new, unconventional religious and cultural groups has frustrated some mainstream Jewish leaders, who believe that these organizations are problematic for various reasons. Nevertheless, Chabad seems able to touch souls in ways the established Jewish denominations can not. Mainstream *macher*s still find this fact unbelievable. As Michaelson puts it, the leaders of the Jewish establishment cannot believe "that these weird guys in beards are doing a better job reaching the unaffiliated than smarty Ivy grads with master's degrees in public relations." That is not to say that everyone is impressed, but even detractors and natural competitors have had to acknowledge that Chabad has been wildly successful. Rabbi Eric H. Yoffie, the president of the Union for Reform Judaism, lavishly praised Chabad (while simultaneously criticizing them for two specific policies) in a *Jerusalem Post* blog: "Chabad is one of the great wonders of the Jewish world." Perhaps thinking about how Reform rabbis are generally less than enthusiastic about taking positions in remote locations, Yoffie notes that "Chabad's monumental contribution to Jewish life has been its willingness to serve Jewish populations not served by others."[6]

Chabad-Lubavitch Draws on Mysticism and Messianism

The Chabad-Lubavitch movement is based on mystical beliefs. Chabad is also well known for messianism, both because it was a central component of their well-publicized theology, and because of the controversy surrounding the claims that the seventh Rebbe was or would become the messiah. The Lubavitch Hasidim followed seven rebbes, until the death of the seventh Rebbe, Rabbi Menachem Mendel Schneerson, in 1994. He passed away without leaving any sons who could take over the hereditary position or any daughters who could marry someone who could become the new rebbe. As a result, the Lubavitch movement has been without a spiritual leader ever since. Many Lubavitch apparently believed and believe that the Rebbe is going to return from the dead to be revealed as the messiah and they may not, therefore, feel that a new spiritual leader is needed. Despite concern that the lack of a rebbe would doom their movement, Chabad-Lubavitch has thrived.[7]

Chabad-Lubavitch traces its origins to Rabbi Israel ben Eliezer, the founder of the Hasidic movement. He emphasized pure, unadulterated joy, in addition to the study of the halacha (Jewish law). Even though it was originally seen by its opponents as a heresy that threatened traditional Judaism, Hasidism did not end up by breaking the halachic framework. Nevertheless, those devoted to Talmudic study alone vigorously opposed the Hasidim and for that reason were labeled *Mitnagdim* (those who opposed the Hasidic movement). Rabbi Israel ben Eliezer, known as the Ba'al Shem Tov (abbreviated as the Besht), the Master of the Good Name, became known as a faith healer. Following the Talmud, he taught that God wanted human beings to be joyful and that self-denial was a sin because it weakens the body, which has to be strong in order to serve God. Stories and legends were woven around the person of the Besht, who was said to have been incredibly empathetic and perhaps even a miracle worker with the power to see into the future. The Besht was able to become the founder of a new movement because Eastern European Jewish society was structured like a pyramid, with the Talmudists occupying the apex. While recent scholarship has debunked the myth that the Talmudists were uninterested in the suffering of the Jewish masses, they nevertheless constituted an ideal that the vast majority of Jewish working folk could not possibly emulate. As a consequence, the masses felt devalued because they could not achieve even 1 percent of what the Talmudists had accomplished scholastically. The Besht offered an alternative model of ideal religiosity. Contrary to the stereotype, his Judaic ideal did not de-

FIGURE 7.1. Rabbi Menachem Mendel Schneerson, the seventh Lubavitcher Rebbe. *Courtesy of Dovid Zaklikowsky of Chabad.org*

value learning, but it stressed the important religious contributions of the common man and woman. He offered an approach teaching that God rejoices when His children are joyful. To achieve that joy, the Jewish poor just had to carry out God's commandments, regardless of how much time they might have for learning.

The Hasidic movement revolved around rebbes, charismatic leaders who attracted Hasidim, followers. The rebbe was regarded as a *tzaddik*, a man whose righteousness went far beyond the goodness that could be expected of a normal mortal. The tzaddik sometimes became a miracle worker, a holy man, a mystic, a saint, or a prophetic voice. Just being in the presence of their rebbe, the tzaddik, was enough to make his Hasidim feel contented. Around 1740, the Ba'al Shem Tov set up court in Miedzyboz, a town in Podolia. Disciples flocked to his side in order to be in proximity to his aura of holiness and how to grasp the spiritual lessons that he had mastered. The Ba'al Shem Tov taught the simple folk primarily through parables. Even the simplest and most poverty-stricken Jew could take something away from these stories, while the more educated could interpret them on deeper mystical levels, influenced by Lurianic Kabbalah, that would not have made sense to the simple folk.

After the death of the Ba'al Shem Tov, Rabbi Dov Ber of Miedzyboz, also called the Magid (a preacher or storyteller), worked to solidify the Hasidic movement. When he died, his disciples became rebbes of different groups in towns and villages throughout Eastern Europe. The rebbe was the leader of his Hasidim, but he was primarily their spiritual mentor rather than their halachic authority or organizational manager. According to the Hasidim, the first and greatest rebbe was the Ba'al Shem Tov himself, but this use of the term may be anachronistic. His disciples were called magidim, preachers. Rabbi Boruch of Miedzyboz, the grandson of the Ba'al Shem Tov, was the first Hasidic leader to be called rebbe during his lifetime. Each rebbe attracted their own disciples, and each group of Hasidim developed their own style and in many cases, distinctive teachings.

Chabad originated as one of the many Hasidic courts that emerged, drawing its inspiration from traditional Jewish sources, classical mystical texts, Hasidic teachings, and its unique theological writings. The rebbe established a court, which was a spiritual center where his disciples could come to be withhim. They would eat and drink at the rebbe's *tisch* (table), spending long hours on the Sabbath singing, dancing, and sharing the rebbe's food. Each Hasidic court took the name of the town in which it was centered. Lubavitch was founded in Liadi, a small town in Belarus, then in imperial Russia, by Rabbi Shneur Zalman of Liadi in the late 1700s. His son established the movement in the town of Lubavitch, and so the movement was called Lubavitch rather than Liadi. These Lubavitchers were known as Chabad, which is a Hebrew acronym for Chochmah (wisdom), Binah (understanding), and Da'at (knowledge). Rabbi Schneur Zalman of Liadi taught that this acronym reflected the intellectual accessibility of the mystical teachings of the Kabbalah.

The central text in Lubavitch Judaism is the *Tanya*, a unique blend of Jewish psychospiritual wisdom written by Rabbi Shneur Zalman in 1797. Properly titled *Likkutei Amarim*, the *Tanya* serves the Lubavitch as a fundamental guide to avodah, the spiritual service of God. They believe it is their sacred duty to study and teach the *Tanya*, but, because of the difficulty and complexity of the content, this is not an easy task, even for a student well-versed in Aramaic and Rabbinic Hebrew. Even more problematic, the *Tanya* was seen by some to reveal mystical secrets that were not meant for the masses. The *Tanya* argues that even an average person can get in touch with the divine soul within and build a close relationship with God. Every person faces a struggle to keep their evil inclination in check and avoid negative influences that could lead to terrible deeds. The *Tanya* draws extensively from Kabbalistic thought, but introduces many religious concepts that are unique to Hasidism.

While the esoteric teachings of Chabad are obscure to most outsiders, what is well-known about contemporary Lubavitch is that they are keen exponents of outreach. The *shluchim* (religious emissaries), who can be found virtually everywhere, are friendly and nonjudgmental. This welcoming approach to their less observant brethren is a central part of their ideology. In chapter 32 of the *Tanya*, the first Rebbe, Schneur Zalman, wrote that no one is capable of seeing a soul's greatness from its exterior "garments." Lubavitch Hasidim believe that nonobservant Jews have a greatness in their souls that simply needs to be nurtured. They associate Schneur Zalman's statement that "one must attract with small cords of love" with the obligation to do outreach to nonobservant Jews.

The goal of the shluchim is to help Jews, no matter how detached or alienated from the tradition, to perform individual mitzvot and feel good about what they have done. Many people first notice Chabad when they see a *shaliach* (singular of *shluchim*) standing in the middle of a busy airport or bus station. The Chabad Hasid, usually a young man in a black hat and white shirt with tzitzis (ritual fringes) flying in the wind, will turn to them with a big smile and ask them one simple question: "Are you Jewish?" If they answer "no," then the Hasid thanks them for their time and ends the conversation, but if they say "yes," he asks the person to do a mitzvah right on the spot. During Sukkoth, the Feast of Tabernacles, in the fall, they drive a mobile sukkah around and offer people the opportunity to fulfill the mitzvah of sitting in it without having to disrupt their daily schedule. During the rest of the year, they drive a mitzvah mobile where they offer Jews the opportunity to perform various mitzvot.

Chabad has become much more mainstream than it was when the Rebbe first started sending shluchim out to various communities in the late 1950s. One reason is that the Chabad emissaries have successfully reached out to large numbers of Jews and non-Jews in virtually every community in the United States. At a time in which outreach has become one of the key elements in the Jewish community's strategy for survival, Chabad has been the pace setter. As Samuel Heilman, a sociology professor who studies Orthodox Jews, puts it, "In the market of outreach, Chabad looms large."[8] Between half and two-thirds of the Lubavitchers live in large Lubavitch communities, such as Crown Heights, Brooklyn, with the rest on *shlichut* (communal service) throughout the world. In contrast, most other Hasidic groups live almost entirely in a handful of locations.

The success of Chabad-Lubavitch has been part of a larger trend toward a revived and strengthened Orthodoxy. As I mentioned in my review of post–World War II developments in chapter 1, Orthodoxy appeared likely to diminish or even collapse. As late as the 1960s, sociologists predicted that Orthodoxy was destined to disappear within a generation. But this did not happen, and, beginning in the early 1970s, Orthodoxy began to revive. Lubavitch was well-positioned to take advantage of this trend. Rabbi David Eliezrie of Chabad in Orange County, California told me that this was not accurate. "We didn't take advantage of this trend, we caused it!"[9]

The Shluchim of Chabad

Virtually everyone—no matter what their religious views—is positively impressed with the sincerity and enthusiasm of the shluchim. They model a selfless idealism that seems almost unbelievable in today's self-centered world. Russian chief rabbi Berel Lazar explained that the shluchim are guided by the principal that "no Jew is too small, no effort too big, no result insignificant."[10] The Lubavitch believe that each individual mitzvah helps to bring the coming of the messiah that much closer. Rabbi Joseph Telushkin explains that "Chabad models more powerfully than any group I know the Talmudic teaching that 'whoever saves one life it's as if he saved an entire world.'

They really and consistently treat each individual as sacred. And they do so joyfully and uncomplainingly, and to not complain is not such a common thing in Jewish life."[11] Not everyone agrees. One New Yorker told me, "I didn't get an elevated or particularly generous sense from the recent crop of young mitzvah mobile recruits I've met here in Manhattan. . . . A lot of them seemed simply aimless and dutiful—fitting the role of bored soldiers." Furthermore, the same ideological fervor that has helped them to build a vibrant worldwide movement also spawned a theological crisis over the question of whether the rebbe was the messiah, a controversy so serious that it not only threatened to split the movement but had the potential to destroy it.

The first Chabad shluchim in the United States were dispatched by the sixth Lubavitcher Rebbe, Yosef Schneersohn, in the 1940s. He sent out only a handful of people to do a few specific tasks. One rabbi was sent to Nashville, Tennessee to take the pulpit of an Orthodox congregation, another was sent to California to become a roving emissary, and several Chabadniks were sent to open Jewish day schools. The principle of shlichut was established, but the implementation was only in the embryonic phase. The seventh Rebbe dramatically expanded the work of his father-in-law. Already in the 1950s, the Rebbe started sponsoring outreach campaigns to promote observance of specific Jewish holidays. "Mitzvah campaigns" soon followed, which focused on individuals' private Jewish observances. Schneerson chose mitzvot that were considered both centrally important and easy to perform, such as lighting Shabbat candles, putting up mezuzahs, giving charity, and other singular acts that were unlikely to intimidate those unfamiliar with the myriad laws of Orthodox Judaism. While critics argued that isolated acts had little significance, the Lubavitch reiterated that each and every mitzvah in and of itself is an act of cosmic significance. When a Jew does a single mitzvah, it lights up that person's *neshama*, a part of their soul that can then connect to part of the Godhead. Even if people then commit ten violations of Jewish law in quick succession, it does not nullify the mitzvah that they have done, nor the spiritual significance of that act.

In the early years of shluchim, Chabad sent single yeshiva students on summer outreach assignments. This did not always work out. Some of them felt a lot of pressure being in an irreligious environment for the first time. Even married couples felt that moving from a cocooned Lubavitch community in Brooklyn to a non-Orthodox environment was difficult and potentially disruptive. Adding to their concerns was the fact that two of the best known of the early shluchim broke with Lubavitch because they absorbed

FIGURE 7.2. Young Chabad volunteers help passersby put on tefillin on the streets of Manhattan. *Courtesy of Dovid Zaklikowsky of Chabad.org*

too much of the attitudes and behavior of the people they were being sent to influence. Rabbis Shlomo Carlebach and Zalman Schachter-Shalomi both went on to become well-known Jewish religious personalities, but both broke with Lubavitch in the 1960s and, especially in the case of Schachter-Shalomi, left Orthodoxy entirely.

The outreach campaign broke new ground. Schneerson placed advertisements in not only Jewish newspapers but secular ones such as the *New York Times* as well. The Lubavitch took to the streets, literally, to help spread the word of their Rebbe. Lubavitch yeshiva students would take Friday afternoons off from studying to stand on downtown street corners, trying to identify Jewish passersby and ask the men to put on tefillin (phylacteries) and the women to consider lighting Shabbat candles. This campaign traces its origin to the Six-Day War of 1967, when the Rebbe first asked Jewish men all over the world to "lay tefillin" before praying for the welfare of the State of Israel. He followed up on this special appeal with ten major mitzvah campaigns between 1967 and 1976. Tefillin can be put on in just a couple of minutes, so it is not likely to inconvenience men walking by. Yet it was sufficiently unusual that few non-Orthodox men were likely to have put them on that morning or, indeed, in the previous months or even years. Thus it had a certain exotic appeal, allowing Jewish men to experience "authentic" Jewish religiosity quickly and easily, without undue commitment.

The shluchim first studied at the Lubavitch yeshiva and, after they received their rabbinic ordination, were given a mandate from the Rebbe to go to a specific locale in order to do a certain type of outreach work. This could involve creating a Chabad community, establishing a Chabad House on a college campus, teaching in an already established Jewish school, or even social activism. Since the Rebbe's death, a small group of Chabad leaders working out of the Lubavitch headquarters at 770 Eastern Parkway in Crown Heights, Brooklyn have taken over the responsibility of directing Lubavitch yeshiva graduates and their wives to communities that can benefit from their work. These couples go to places they may never have visited before with the idea of settling permanently in their new community. They are given a small start-up fund and a modest salary for the first year. After the initial subsidy period, they are expected to become self-supporting. Some establish summer camp or nursery school programs that can provide income, while others take part- or full-time jobs working in the local Jewish community. Ideally, they will be able to make enough of a contribution to the Jewish community so that local donors feel it is worthwhile to fund their programming.

Lubavitch placed a great deal of emphasis on bringing Judaism to college students. They established Chabad Houses on college campuses throughout the country, based on a model campus outreach center established by Rabbi Boruch Shlomo Cunin at UCLA in March 1969. Some of the smaller Chabad Houses are in shluchim's homes, while larger ones are expansive Jewish student facilities, with full synagogues and programming centers. While they have become part of the Jewish landscape, Chabad initially had to overcome a great deal of opposition. Many in the Jewish community felt the Chabad Houses were directly competing with Hillel, the Jewish student organization. Chabad was able to demonstrate that they drew many students who would not go to Hillel. Other students began going to both places, adding to the quantity of Jewish programming on campus. While there was certainly a degree of competition, it did not seem to harm Hillel. In recent years, Richard Joel, then national director of Hillel and now president of Yeshiva University, engineered a reorganization of Hillel to better reach the current generation of university students. He has said that he believes that Hillel and Chabad serve different constituencies and are complementary rather than redundant.

Even if they do compete for some of the same students, many feel that a little bit of competition is good for Jewish life, particularly on campus.

Sometimes Chabad shluchim can apply for small grants from the local Jewish Federation. With enough charm and the ability to demonstrate concrete results, they can find one or more wealthy donors who can provide them with a substantial funding base. This is crucial, because Chabad's approach is to provide religious programming without charging and without coercing donations from newcomers. Many people have stories of how Chabad shluchim came to their offices with requests for tens of thousands of dollars, but these are supporters who are well familiar with the organization. They hope that eventually people will come to see the value of their activities and will begin to support them, but, in the initial phases, they tell people that they are there to teach and host without any expectation of remuneration. To do that, they need extensive funding.

Chabad has amazed the leaders of other Jewish organizations with their ability to raise huge amounts of money. According to Aryeh Rubin, the founder of the Targum Shlishi Foundation, Chabad knows how to raise money better than almost anyone else. "There is a certain amount of genius in their fund-raising. While most organizations get one swing at a donor, be it AIPAC, or Jewish National Fund, or the Jewish Theological Seminary, the donation goes to the home office. Chabad, on the other hand, relies on each local chapter and institution to do its own fund-raising." This allows them to solicit donations several times. "Many patrons give a donation to their local Chabad chapter, to the rabbi in Milan whom they met on a trip, to the day school in Nice, and to the soup kitchen in Jerusalem. And if you nibble they will keep fishing, and if you bite they will always be back." It is their passion that resonates with donors who keep filling the till. "Many consider them today's version of the tribe of Levy." Just as the Levites served in the Temple in Jerusalem on behalf of the Jewish people, so too Chabad is seen as serving the Jewish people as holy emissaries of God. "They fill a void, and the Jewish people recognize, applaud and support that effort."[12]

Many of Chabad's largest funders are from foreign countries, where they may have been raised in more traditional environments or faced greater antisemitism. Among Chabad's largest donors are Lev Leviev, a Uzbeki-Israeli diamond merchant, Rabbi Joseph Gutnik, a Melbourne, Australia mining magnate, and the Rohr family, Colombian American real estate investors. Sami Rohr has been involved with Chabad since the 1950s and with his son George has given tens of millions of dollars to build up the organization throughout the former Soviet Union. They underwrite the salaries of about five hundred shluchim and set up a foundation to help build Chabad Houses on American college campuses. But the Lubavitch is not primarily funded by foreign-born donors. There are also many American-born Jews giving huge sums of money to Chabad to help them build programs right here in the USA, including well-known names such as Ronald Lauder of Estee Lauder and Ronald Perelman of Revlon. Most of the money raised is by local shluchim.

This does not please many of the non-Orthodox religious groups. Reform leaders in particular are irritated that many of the wealthiest Reform Jews in the United States give impressive sums to Lubavitch, which has actively campaigned in Israel in favor of changing the "Who is a Jew" law. That law gives automatic Israeli citizenship to any person born of a Jewish mother or who has been converted to Judaism. At certain strategic moments over the past thirty years, the Lubavitch have pressured the Israeli government to add the words converted to Judaism "according to halacha." This would have allowed the Israeli government to discriminate against Reform and Conservative converts and thereby demonstrate the supposed illegitimacy of the heterodox religious movements. By funding Lubavitch, these Reform philanthropists are indirectly working to undermine their own religious movement.

Even many Orthodox Jews are unaware of the political lobbying undertaken by the Lubavitch. David Berger told me that "I once discussed my position on Reform conversion in a talk at an Orthodox synagogue in Great Neck. A listener informed me that I took a more stringent position than would be taken by the local Chabad shaliach." Berger had supported the change in the law and had commented that virtually every Orthodox leader would take the same position. The listener had disagreed, suggesting that Berger was far to the right of Chabad. "He refused to believe that Chabad had spearheaded the effort to exclude Reform converts from the Law of Return and invited me to speak to the inclusive, tolerant, lovely, pluralistic fellow who runs the Great Neck Chabad House."[13] Many funders are aware of this problem, but feel that Lubavitch's contribution to American Jewish life far outweighs this one problematic political position. They want to fund organizations that can show qualitative as well as quantitative results, and Lubavitch has clearly been able to deliver.

Another reason that many non-observant American Jews are willing to donate money to Chabad is that the shluchim do not pressure people to

FIGURE 7.3. Bob Dylan praying with tallit and tefillin at the Western Wall in Jerusalem. Dylan was in Israel to celebrate his son's bar mitzvah on September 20, 1983. Photo
Zavi Cohen. *Courtesy of the Associated Press*

become observant. This is one of the key factors in their success. As one
Chabadnik told me, "we're not necessarily trying to get people to become
Lubavitch. They don't have to wear clothes like we do, and they may not
want to accept upon themselves the same standards of kashrut and other
mitzvot. All we want them to do is to do one mitzvah, one mitzvah at a
time." Nonobservant donors can participate in Chabad activities without
feeling that they are being looked down upon. Chabad accepts people where
they are and helps them derive religious meaning from individual ritual acts.
This has prompted criticism from both the right and the left. More traditional Orthodox leaders feel that the Lubavitch are tolerating nonobservance,
almost becoming like a new form of Conservative Judaism, where the rabbi
was held to one standard and the congregation to a much laxer one. On the
other hand, religious liberals attack Chabad for being disingenuous. They

argue that although Chabad shluchim talk as if they are pluralistic, they really are not because they believe that all Jews should become observant and that observance must be Orthodox.

One of the most important "converts" credited to Lubavitch was Bob Dylan. Dylan is enigmatic and, like many of those attracted to Chabad, his involvement is sporadic. At times, he has appeared to embrace their approach to Judaism wholeheartedly; at other times, he has made comments that indicate that he remains "like a rolling stone." In 1997, in response to a question about a completely different subject, he told the *New York Times*, "that's just the nature of my personality. I can be jubilant one moment and pensive the next, and a cloud could go by and make that happen. I'm inconsistent, even to myself."[14] Although he clearly has a strong spiritual side, he has said that he does not find meaning in organized religion. For example, Dylan said to *Newsweek*, "Here's the thing with me and the religious thing. This is the flat-out truth: I find the religiosity and philosophy in the music. I don't find it anywhere else. Songs like 'Let Me Rest on a Peaceful Mountain' [a song by Ralph Stanley] or 'I Saw the Light' [a song by Hank Williams]—that's my religion." Dylan emphatically rejected the concept of traditional religious leadership. "I don't adhere to rabbis, preachers, evangelists, all of that. I've learned more from the songs than I've learned from any of this kind of entity. The songs are my lexicon. I believe the songs."[15]

Dylan was born with the name Robert Zimmerman in Hibbing, Minnesota, but he has cultivated an image of a rootless cosmopolitan, avoiding being labeled as a Jewish singer. Nevertheless, everyone in the Jewish community knew that he was Jewish and they were proud of him. But in the late 1970s Dylan suddenly became an evangelical Christian, a source of much tsuris (Yiddish for worry, distress, or sorrow) for many Jewish folk music fans. He released two Christian gospel albums, *Slow Train Coming* (1979) and *Saved* (1980), touring extensively in order to publicize his new faith, sometimes preaching the gospel in between songs. Many of his old fans, who had come to hear the Bob Dylan they thought they knew and loved, began to boo him. At a concert at the Orpheum Theater in Omaha, Nebraska, in January 1980, he told the audience, "there aren't gonna be any old songs tonight. So if anyone wants to leave they can leave right now! Anyone at all, please leave now because there's someone outside wants your seat." Later that evening, he expressed frustration that many of the critics and fans who had once so admired him had turned against him. "Years ago they used [to say] . . . I was a prophet. I used to say, 'No I'm not a prophet.' They said, 'yes you are, you're a prophet.' I said, 'no it's not me'. They used to say 'you sure are a prophet.' They used to convince me I was a prophet." Now, "I come out and say Jesus Christ is the answer. They say, 'Bob Dylan's no prophet.' They just can't handle it."[16]

By the end of the 1980s, the rumor started to spread that a Lubavitch rabbi from St. Paul, Minnesota had successfully brought Dylan back to Judaism. Rabbi Manis Friedman somehow convinced Dylan to renounce his Christian beliefs and start attending Jewish religious services. Friedman encouraged Dylan to put on tefillin in the morning and observe other Jewish rituals. Dylan began studying with Friedman and Rabbi Moshe Feller, another Lubavitch shaliach in Minnesota. He would attend Shabbat dinners in their homes, one year showing up unannounced at Rabbi Friedman's house on the night of the Passover seder wearing a leather jacket and motorcycle boots.[17] Almost every year, he appeared at a different Chabad High Holy Day service, one year in Toronto, one year in Woodbury, New York, another in Encino, California, and, most recently, in Atlanta, where he attended Yom Kippur services and then performed a concert with Elvis Costello and Amos Lee. The Chabad Web site reported that Dylan, who arrived with a ski cap on his head and a tallit around his shoulders, was called up to the Torah. Rabbi Yossi Lew reported that Dylan "said the blessings in Hebrew, without stumbling, like a pro."[18] One congregant wrote a blogger that "when he had his aliyah you could hear a pin drop but he muttered so softly that only the guys on the bima could hear him." When a Mi Sheberach was recited, the gabai asked him who he would like to have blessed and he gave the names of four children. When the gabai then asked him, "any other children?" He responded, "I have a lot of kids, just go ahead."[19]

On several occasions, Dylan visited the Lubavitch headquarters for Sunday dollars, when the Rebbe would give out crisp new dollar bills. From 1986 until March 1992, when he suffered a stroke at the age of eighty-nine, he would stand for seven or eight hours in an alcove outside his office in Brooklyn. Visitors would line up and approach him one by one. The Rebbe would speak with each person for a moment and would then hand over a crisp new dollar bill, which the recipient was supposed to then donate to charity, thus fulfilling the mitzvah of tzedakah (charity). The Sunday dollar program was an excellent illustration of how the Rebbe was able to relate to acculturated Americans in terms they could understand and appreciate. Rabbi Alan Brill explained that "the moment when one returned the dollar to charity was a moment of dedication and commitment, and that moment of resolution typified the essential dedication to God; an act of essence, atz-mus." The Rebbe's act of giving the dollar bills was not just a silly gimmick, but aimed to transform a mundane activity—the handing over of a small amount of money—into an exceptional moment when the person receiving the gift can feel God's presence. Brill explains that this "dovetails with many American religious trends that place an emphasis on finding God through personal resolution and the creation of peak moments—many times in public—of acceptance of God in the heart."[20]

Consistant with kabbalistic doctrine, Chabad believes that Jews have a special soul, a Jewish neshama, which has the capacity to bond with an aspect of God. Individual Jews have a special religious relationship with each other that goes back all the way to the giving of the Torah on Mount Sinai and, indeed, perhaps even further back to the creation of the world. While each Jew has an independent will, all Jews share a common fate and destiny. If the Chabadniks can convince even one Jew to commit to do even one commandment, the merit from this single act can affect the lives of other Jews and will have an impact on the fate of the Jewish people. Here too, Chabad has expertly managed to emphasize the right message with the right audience. They promote their good citizenship when talking to the broader American public, but stress the unique role of the Jewish people in history when talking with Jews looking to reconnect with their heritage.

Chabad has done a great deal to promote Judaism in the public sphere. Critics have been horrified, fearing that they have contributed to the breeching of the wall between church and state. Supporters deny this and emphasize that their activities have done a great deal to publicize Jewish observance. Rabbi Yehuda Krinsky, the long-time secretary of the Rebbe and de facto administrative leader of the Lubavitch movement since the Rebbe's death has said, "I think Hanukkah has become one of the most widely celebrated holidays by Jews in the world today—probably singularly because of the Chabad effort."[21] Most would argue that the proximity of Hanukkah to Christmas is far more important. Nevertheless, it is beyond dispute that Chabad has pioneered the public observance of Jewish holidays. Lubavitch has taken a significantly different position on issues of church and state than most of the established American Jewish community historically did. Most American Jews believed that any activity that breaches the wall between church and state, no matter how slight, would threaten the position of American Jews in a country with such an overwhelming Christian majority. Chabad has ignored this concern, eagerly building menorahs on public property as part of their overall strategy of publicizing Judaism. These activities were fought by a coalition of liberal Jewish organizations for years. Despite numerous law suits, Lubavitch has managed to prevail. Eventually, most other Jewish groups have become more accepting of this practice, even participating in some candle lighting ceremonies along with Chabad.

This increasing acceptance of Chabad menorahs on public property is indicative of a broader acceptance. Many non-Orthodox Jews participate in Chabad activities and give them large donations. They feel that Chabad has been enormously successful at reaching alienated Jews, people who would have been completely lost to the Jewish people. In addition, Chabad appeals to affiliated Jews who simply prefer a nonjudgmental attitude combined with traditional practices. Phil Kaplan of Orange County, California is one non-Orthodox Jew who likes going to Chabad services. "It seems like a lot more of the people we know are attending services with Chabad. I'm talking about mainstream people; I barely know any Orthodox people. In my opinion, it's because Chabad is very open and accessible. . . . With Chabad you can find your level and there's encouragement."[22] Jewish federations are increasingly willing to fund Chabad projects, something that they would not have considered just a few decades ago. Federations have seen the value of Chabad and have become convinced that they are not duplicating programs already in existence.[23]

The breakthrough occurred in the early 1990s. Between 1990 and 1994, Chabad put up large advertisements on billboards overlooking highways in the largest American cities, including Los Angeles, Miami, and Chicago, urging Jews to perform specific mitzvot, such as lighting Sabbath or Hanukkah candles. In New York they put up posters in the subways, since most New Yorkers did not travel by car to and from work. These posters had catchy headers such as "Don't Pass Over Passover" or "Start the Year Sweet—Celebrate the High Holidays." The billboards and posters gave the date of the holiday as well as a local phone number that people could call for a free holiday guide. Those who responded were directed to one of the Chabad centers in their area and put on a mailing list to be sent promotional material. This advertising campaign was just the right approach at just the right time. Along with their other outreach activities, the campaign helped Chabad to raise awareness of the group's existence and their potential for reversing the deleterious consequences of assimilation.

Chabad showed a flair and sophistication in the area of public relations. Of particular note, the Lubavitch pioneered Jewish propagandizing on the

Internet. Krinsky speaks proudly of their Web projects. "We're trying to create a marriage of new technology and 3000 year old ideas."[24] Unlike many of the reclusive Hasidic groups, the Lubavitch have moved proactively to build a prominent Internet presence, which includes more than seven hundred Web sites headquartered in fifty-two countries. Rabbi Zalman Shmotkin, who supervises the Chabad Internet effort, told *Wired* magazine that there is nothing intrinsically wrong religiously with using the Internet. "It's not the medium itself that is kosher or not kosher. It's how it is utilized."[25] The Internet is a terrific way for Chabad to present Judaic texts. Shimon Laber explained that "the Torah jumps around. It is the original hyperlinked text. Nothing can bring it out like the web."

There is a long history to Chabad's involvement with the Internet. Rabbi Yosef Kazen began producing Internet material as early as 1988. He distributed it on Fidonet, an online discussion network that was part of the early computer communication systems preceding the development of the World Wide Web. Kazen would distribute a regular e-newsletter to several thousand subscribers, foreshadowing the much more massive Chabad computer communications efforts in recent years. He also digitized some of the most important Chabad texts, including the *Tanya* in English translation. These texts became part of what Kazen called a Jewish Web library.[26] He included an interactive Ask the Rabbi column, which later became a popular staple of almost every Jewish Internet site, as well as Jewish sections on AOL, MSN, and so forth.

Shmotkin oversees more than a dozen editors, writers, and designers who work six days a week to create new material for the various Web portals. Once content is created by the team in Brooklyn, they upload it onto servers housed in New Jersey and e-mail a list of the updated material to Lubavitch representatives throughout the world. Each Chabad center gets their own domain name. They can use this domain to personalize their Web site, adding local content and acknowledging individual donors. Programmer Moshe Berghoff pointed out the importance of what they do in Brooklyn. "If the rabbis [out in the individual communities, far from the central headquarters] had to learn HTML, this would never happen."[27] Local Chabad representatives can decide what material is most suitable for their particular constituency, selecting particular features that they want to have automatically uploaded onto their individual Web sites. Other Jewish religious movements have likewise adopted this approach, in some cases years after Chabad. Language is, of course, a primary consideration. Lubavitch Web sites appear in numerous languages, not just the English and Hebrew that is frequently seen on other denominational Web pages. This reflects the fact that Chabad is truly a worldwide organization.

Since the Rebbe's death, there has been a massive effort to publish and popularize his thought. Rabbi Simon Jacobson is the director of the Vaad Hanochos Hatmimim, a foundation dedicated to perpetuating the Rebbe's teachings. Jacobson organized the publication *Toward a Meaningful Life: The Wisdom of the Rebbe*, which was published by the major commercial press William Morrow.[28] Publishing some of the Rebbe's more universal messages in a secular medium was one way of exposing a wider audience to Chabad thought. Devoted followers were interested in reading the Rebbe's individual speeches and letters. Assembling the Rebbe's lectures has been a difficult task. First off, he always spoke in Yiddish. Unlike previous rebbes, who wrote out their lectures, the seventh Rebbe never did. As a result, his talks had to be reconstructed and edited after the fact.

The Rebbe's talks and teaching were first translated into English in the 1950s and distributed in brochure form. In 1962, the Rebbe himself edited a Yiddish version of the first two volumes of *Likkutei Sichot*, a collection of his speeches and sermons. This was followed by additional volumes in Yiddish. In 1980, Rabbi Immanuel Schochet translated a volume of the *Likkutei Sichot* into English. The Kehot Publication Society is now trying to sift through all of the available material, determine the best and most accurate version, and publish the Rebbe's lectures in an organized and coherent way. They claim to have already distributed one hundred million volumes in twelve languages, including not only the Rebbe's lectures but also a wide variety of Lubavitch-inspired Judaica.

The Messianic Crisis

The Lubavitch movement is dominated by the personality of Rabbi Menachem Mendel Schneerson. Even though he is long gone and buried, his presence is still very much felt not only at the Lubavitch headquarters at 770 Eastern Parkway but also at every Chabad House, synagogue, or center anywhere in the world. During the later part of his life, a cult of personality developed around the Rebbe. Despite his outward modesty and workaholic habits, he became revered as a holy man and possible messianic candidate.

During his lifetime, many Chabadniks believed that the Rebbe was the messiah, and substantial numbers believe that he will return from the dead to become the messiah in the coming years. Others believe that the Rebbe never died, and some believe in his full divinity. Whether he himself believed that he was the messiah and whether he took actions that may have promoted this belief are matters of dispute. What is clear is that a vicious struggle developed after the Rebbe's death centering on the question of whether he was indeed the messiah. The controversy could have destroyed the movement he worked so hard to build, but it did not. Chabad has thrived.

Schneerson was born in 1902 in the Ukrainian town of Nikolaev. In 1927, he married Chaya Mushka Schneersohn, the daughter of the sixth Lubavitcher Rebbe, who was also a distant cousin. According to his official biography, he went to Berlin to study philosophy and mathematics at the University of Berlin and then to Paris, where he studied at the Sorbonne. In 1941, he was able to immigrate to New York, where the sixth Lubavitch Rebbe had moved the previous year. When his father-in-law died in 1950, he became the movement's leader. Schneerson was proclaimed to be the new rebbe in January 1951, and, already that year, he told a magazine that he was planning to adopt a much more assertive outreach policy. Almost immediately, he sent out his first shluchim, including a foreign emissary to Morocco. "Orthodox Jewry up to this point has concentrated upon defensive strategies. We were always worried lest we lose positions and strongholds. But we must take the initiative and wage an offensive. This, of course, takes courage, planning, vision, and the will to carry on despite the odds."[29]

By the mid-1960s, shluchim had been sent to Los Angeles, Miami, Philadelphia, and Minneapolis in the United States, as well as England, Brazil, Italy, and Israel. In 1967, the Rebbe proclaimed his first mitzvah campaign, and the pace of expansion increased rapidly. Today there are more than four thousand shluchim around the world. The Rebbe not only expanded the shluchim program, but also brought many non-Lubavitchers to Crown Heights. Both Jews and non-Jews came from all over to consult with him. American politicians arrived at 770 Eastern Parkway to pay their respects and get their picture taken with the Rebbe. He became one of the most influential religious leaders in the world, though he rarely traveled. And, while he never visited Israel, the Rebbe grew to be one of the most important people deciding Israeli coalition politics. His followers built an exact replica of the Brooklyn headquarters in Kfar Chabad, the Lubavitch agricultural settlement outside of Tel Aviv. Apparently, many of his followers expected the Rebbe—during his lifetime—to declare himself the messiah and move to the Chabad community in the land of Israel.

Much of the messianic controversy developed because the Rebbe had a series of strokes and was unable to express himself during the last two years of his life. In March 1992, Schneerson developed expressive aphasia and was unable to communicate. As a consequence, his followers were able to lead the Rebbe rather than the other way around. It is therefore unclear whether a healthy Rebbe would have emphatically put an end to the messianic speculations or whether he might have openly endorsed them. Even before his first stroke, the Rebbe appeared to graciously accept his followers' chanting that he was the messiah. On yet other occasions, the Rebbe seemed to discourage anyone who identified him as the messiah. *New York Times* reporter Ari Goldman remembers seeing Rabbis Yehuda Krinsky and Laibel Groner, another of the Rebbe's secretaries, pulling and tugging at his wheelchair while they were standing on the special balcony built for the Rebbe in the synagogue at 770 Eastern Parkway. Goldman saw their pulling of the wheelchair in different directions as symbolic of their desire to pull the Rebbe in different theological directions.

The messianic conflict deepened the following year. In February 1993, Rabbi Shmuel Butman, the director of Lubavitch Youth International, announced that the Rebbe would reveal himself as the messiah during the celebration of his forty-third year as the leader of Chabad. Butman, who had created an organization called the International Campaign to Bring Moshiach, set up a satellite feed through which he hoped to announce that the Rebbe had been crowned as the messiah. The rest of the Chabad leadership stayed away from the cameras, coming down only when the Rebbe was wheeled into the synagogue. After the celebration ended, Krinsky spoke with the many reporters who had come expecting to hear a dramatic announcement. "Tonight was like every other night. The Rebbe just wanted to be with his people."[30]

In the early months of 1994, the frail ninety-one-year-old Rebbe lay dying in Beth Israel Hospital, without any children or designated heirs. It seemed that his movement would sputter and falter without his leadership. Not having designated a successor, no one within the Lubavitch world had the authority to claim that he was the legitimate leader, and without leadership it seemed inevitable the movement would either wither or, alternatively, split into warring factions. Adding to the likelihood of catastrophe was the incipient messianism that dominated the movement. Even his death was not regarded as an insurmountable obstacle to this eschatology. Contrary to what I had always believed, there apparently are rabbinic sources that suggest that a messiah could die without having completed his mission and later return, rising from the dead to bring on the messianic era. However, David Berger explained that "even the tiny number of sources that speak, or may speak, of a messiah who could come from the dead provide no legitimation for the belief in the second coming of a figure who initiates a messianic mission and dies without bringing it to fruition." He emphasized that "no Jewish source (outside Christianity and Sabbatianism) allows for the possibility that God will send the true Messiah to affirm, as the Rebbe repeatedly did, that the redemption would come in his generation, and then die in an unredeemed world, only to complete his redemptive task after his resurrection." Berger points out that "this is precisely what Jews through the generations have seen as classic, Christian-style false messianism."[31]

Berger became the most outspoken critic of Chabad, writing a book, *The Rebbe, The Messiah, and the Scandal of Orthodox Indifference* in which he accused the non-Chabad Orthodox communities of ignoring what he felt was an unpardonable departure from classic Jewish belief.[32] According to Berger, Chabad has erased a central theological distinction between Judaism and Christianity by its belief in the second coming of the Rebbe as the messiah. Berger believes that the Lubavitch are a terrible threat to the future of Judaism because of their deviationist theology. "I consider this to be a historic catastrophe." The reason is "not that Lubavitch Hasidim believe these things, but that even those who say them publicly continue to be treated as Orthodox rabbis. That means that these beliefs are not disqualifying, i.e., they have come to constitute a legitimate option, within Orthodox Judaism." In light of this, "it is not even true that my criticism is based on my assessment that many or most Lubavitchers believe this; Orthodox legitimation of the believers is the issue. Nonetheless, the fact that a majority are indeed believers surely matters."[33]

Other scholars disagree. Rabbi Immanuel Schochet, a follower of Chabad, feels that Berger has failed to differentiate between Judaism and Christianity on two counts. "According to Christianity, the redemption started with the first coming of Jesus Christ, and therefore they changed the laws. In Judaism there is no first and second coming, but once the Messiah comes he starts and finishes his task there and then." Christianity is rejected by mainstream Jews "not because Jesus Christ died, but because he is prior disqualified from being the Messiah for not living up to the criteria of the Messianic persona."[34] Shaul Magid takes a third position, arguing that "David Berger is right that it [the idea that the Rebbe might be immortal] is not Orthodox, but he's wrong that it is not Jewish."[35]

Many Lubavitch insist the messianic fervor is being highly exaggerated. Krinsky states that, while there are Chabadniks who do believe in the resurrection of the Rebbe, the numbers are far smaller than Berger believes. Overall, the level of Chabad messianism is "very overstated." Krinsky suggested that the repetitive discussion about this issue is "just used by some people to confuse others." Krinsky obviously has a vested interest in damage control. Contrary to his claim, there are indications that the number of messianists is significant. Some Lubavitchers refer to 770 Eastern Parkway as Bes Moshiach (house of the messiah). They have a bookstore selling Schneerson's books and tapes called the International Moshiach Center. It is possible to still find signs that read, in Hebrew, "Welcome, the King Messiah." Berger is convinced that "Rabbi Krinsky believes firmly that the Rebbe will be revealed as the Messiah, though it is remotely possible that he considers this only a strong likelihood. It is an absolute certainty that he does not firmly reject the Rebbe's Messiahship."[36]

When the messianic upheaval began in the early 1990s, a number of Jewish intellectuals attacked the Lubavitch movement along Berger's lines. Conservative Rabbi Arthur Hertzberg told the *New York Times* that the Lubavitch obsession with their Rebbe reminded him of the incredibly destructive influence of Shabbetai Tzvi. Hertzberg was referring to the manic-depressive Jew from Izmir in the Ottoman Empire who was declared by Nathan of Gaza to be the messiah in the seventeenth century but then converted to Islam rather than be put to death. The majority of Jews in the world had believed in him, and his sudden apostasy plunged Judaism into crisis. The death of the Rebbe is significantly different in that, while the majority of the Jewish world believed that Shabbetai Tzvi was the messiah, only one grouping within contemporary Judaism and perhaps only a faction of that grouping believe that the Rebbe was the messiah. In a worst-case scenario, the Lubavitch movement might have been torn in two by an ideological war over belief. The implications of such a conflict and split, however damaging, would have been far more limited than the repercussions from the Shabbetai Tzvi episode.

Like many other early critics, Hertzberg later changed his mind about the Lubavitch. His daughter in Fresno, California sent Hertzberg's grandchildren to the local Chabad school and he was impressed with the education

FIGURE 7.4. Doorway in Crown Heights. The Hebrew on the sign at the top reads "Welcome the Messianic King." Photo Rabbi Ayla Grafstein. *Courtesy of Rabbi Ayla Grafstein*

they received. Perhaps because of his personal association with them through those grandchildren, he began to speak in a more positive vein. It is also possible that the fact that the Lubavitch messianic fervor appeared to die down made Hertzberg less antagonistic. In any case, he told Sue Fishkoff that "Chabad has the biggest army of people in the Jewish world ready to live on the edge of poverty [for the sake of Judaism]. Those thirty-five hundred shlichim are the most holy group in the Jewish world today. They are every day engaged in kiddush Hashem [sanctification of God's name]." Everywhere he went, Hertzberg gushed, "I bump into one of these young couples working their heads off. They live on nothing, and they stay with it. I can disagree with their theology, but I can only admire them."[37]

After the Rebbe died, many Chabadniks were plunged into crisis. They could not imagine how life could continue without the Rebbe. They certainly could not imagine how Chabad could continue to function. But Chabad-Lubavitch has done superbly. The movement has managed to thrive without any rebbe at all. The planning for the post-Rebbe period began on the afternoon after Schneerson's wife's death in 1988. The Rebbe called Krinsky, his driver, and one of his secretaries into his office to dictate his will. Krinsky was named executor of that will, and Rabbi Avraham Shemtov was the alternative. Later that year, the Rebbe told the executive board of the Agudas Chassidei Chabad that he wanted to give them much more decision-making power.

Over the next two years, he had the corporate papers for the three major Lubavitch organizations redrawn: Agudas Chassidei Chabad, the umbrella organization for the entire Lubavitch movement; Merkos L'Inyoney Chinuch, the educational organization; and Machne Israel, the social service organization. The Rebbe continued as president of all three institutions, Rabbi Chaim Mordechai Hodakov became vice president, Rabbi Nissan Mindel became treasurer, and Yehuda Krinsky became secretary. With the exception of Krinsky, they have all passed away, therefore leaving Krinsky in control.

Despite Krinsky's levelheadedness, others in the movement continued their messianic agitation. In January 1996, the International Campaign to Bring Moshiach put up a huge billboard near the George Washington Bridge in upper Manhattan proclaiming that the Rebbe was indeed the Messiah. The following month, the International Campaign to Bring Moshiach held a convention at the New York Hilton at which Rabbi Butman told reporters that they would be able to "cover the greatest event in the history of mankind."[38] The Chabad leadership felt that they had to distance themselves from this overt messianism. They placed full-page ads in the *New York Times* and elsewhere to make it clear that they did not endorse Rabbi Butman's messianic proclamations.

While most probably view this incipient messianism as psychologically unhealthy, religiously heretical, and potentially destructive, others consider this messianic fervor to be the central element in the success of Chabad. Samuel Heilman has argued that "the messianism drives the outreach effort." There is no doubt that the shluchim are intensely idealistic, and that idealism has to be based upon the belief that they are doing something that has the potential to change the world for the better. What could be more important than helping to bring (back) the messiah? On the other hand, in the very same sentence, Heilman explains that the outreach efforts force Lubavitchers to become "less enclavist and insular."[39] This has the effect of mainstreaming them, making them less obsessed by their original mission and more involved in local communal affairs. Whatever motivates the shluchim to go out into the field, once they become part of a local Jewish community they have to become immersed in the day-to-day needs of individual Jews.

The consequence of their success is that Lubavitch is being transformed. Spurred on by the death of the Rebbe, Chabad has continued its metamorphosis from a classic Hasidic group clustered around a charismatic rebbe living in isolation to an international synagogue-based movement with a distinctive theology and specific ritual practice, like many other American Jewish groups. This is a fascinating development because it is happening at exactly the same time that the denominations that emerged at the beginning of the twentieth century are losing their distinctiveness (discussed in chapter 3). Chabad-Lubavitch may, however, not be satisfied becoming only a part of the new Jewish denominational spectrum, but have much grander ambitions to influence all peoples and transform not just the Jewish community but the entire world.

Chabad is already searching for other ways to expand their reach. They have been successful at encouraging Jews of all backgrounds to perform individual mitzvot. They have cruised their "mitzvah tanks" around Jewish neighborhoods, college campuses, and established themselves as part of the urban landscape on street corners and bus and train stations. In recent years, they have come up with new marketing techniques to encourage the study of Judaism, including giving away free iPods to children who sign up for Hebrew classes or offering a "spa day for the soul" with pedicures, cooking lessons, and Torah study for women. Now, Chabad of San Francisco is offering a free cable car tour of the City by the Bay. Open to all, the fare is simply the promise to do one random act of kindness. The trolley bears a sign stating the program's slogan: "Mitzvos on the spot for people on the go." What is particularly interesting about this appeal is that it is not limited to or even directed specifically at Jews. This is deliberate because Chabad seeks to transform not just the Jewish community but the entire world. Rabbi Moshe Langer explains that he believes that "random acts of goodness and kindness will usher in world peace."[40]

8 Herculean Efforts at Synagogue Renewal

In 1985, Congregation B'nai Jeshurun (BJ) was a struggling historic Conservative congregation on the Upper West Side of Manhattan. Despite the fact that it was the original Ashkenazic synagogue in New York and indeed the entire United States, its membership had dwindled to less than eighty family units, and it had trouble forming a minyan, even on Shabbat. But then the congregation hired Rabbi Marshall T. Meyer, who had been the leader of the Conservative movement in Argentina, where he had built a rabbinical school, trained an entire generation of South American Conservative leaders, and fought against the political repression of the Argentine military government.

Setting up his office using a card table, a payphone, and a roll of quarters in an alcove of the synagogue building, Meyer began attracting people to congregational activities by emphasizing the Jewish obligation to engage in social activism, openly expressing compassion with the downtrodden. At a time when synagogues—and particularly Conservative synagogues—still tended to be formal and stuffy, Meyer insisted on being called by his first

name as part of a warmer and more informal approach to building relations with people. Later J. Rolando ("Roly") Matalon, a former student at
the Seminario Rabinico Latinamericana (which Meyer had founded) was
brought in to help. The crowds quickly grew, particularly on Friday nights,
with much singing and dancing and expressions of emotion rather than sed-
entary obligation. In 1989, Ari Priven, who had also been a student of Meyer's in Argentina, became the congregation's cantor.[1]

Over the next eight years, Meyer succeeded in rebuilding BJ, in the process creating the model for the revitalization of moribund synagogues. I use
the word *rebuilding* in a symbolic sense, but the congregation actually had
to physically rebuild. In May 1991, late on a Friday night, the roof of the
synagogue building collapsed, dropping a half ton of plaster onto the bimah
and throughout the sanctuary. The building was fortunately empty at the
time, and no one was hurt. The congregation was hosted at the Church of
St. Paul and St. Andrew, which was at the corner of 86th Street and West
End Avenue. The two congregations hung a large banner from the front of
the church with the words of Psalm 133: "How good it is when brothers
and sisters dwell together in harmony." The church sanctuary was considerably larger than the synagogue building. I was able to attend a service in the
church building on a Friday night during the summer and found virtually
every seat taken. A few years later, I attended another Friday night service,
this time in the synagogue building. The number of worshippers seemed
considerably smaller, but nevertheless the excitement was palpable. Even
though Rabbi Meyer had died of cancer in December 1993, congregants that
I spoke to continued to credit him with their success. While most rabbis are
quickly forgotten, Meyer's name has remained on people's lips as one of the
early pioneers of the current synagogue transformation efforts.

In contrast to the typical suburban congregation where people sat still
listening to a rabbi and an operatic-style cantor or choir, the BJ experience
emphasized participation and involvement. Worshippers join with the song
leaders in soulful yet upbeat nigunim, listening to the four-piece band, which
includes a mandolin player, a cellist, and two percussionists. They mix traditional Conservative liturgical music with neo-Hasidic melodies, some of
which were composed by Shlomo Carlebach. There are a number of other
musical influences, including folk music, Israeli pop songs, and even reggae.
During Kabbalat Shabbat, some of the regulars spontaneously leave their
seats and start dancing a hora (an Israeli folk dance) down the center aisle

and in the middle of the sanctuary on the bimah. The synagogue building is used for the smaller services and many of those who cannot fit into the lower floor look down from the balconies, singing and clapping just as enthusiastically. The prayers are led by a number of singers sitting toward the front. Everyone joins in with them immediately, giving the visitor the sense that this really is a congregation and not just a group of spectators watching as religious professionals preside. The service avoids responsive readings in English and the Hebrew prayers are sung rather than spoken. This creates an intensely spiritual and palpable atmosphere, with the mood swinging between calm meditation and rousing enthusiasm. One of the rabbis—Rabbis Marcelo Bronstein and Felicia Sol have joined Matalon—gives a short sermon, which they call a *dvar Torah*, a word of Torah. The message is short and direct—being Jewish is not only about ritual, but requires each person to try to make the world a better place. During one of my visits, a rabbi spoke about the ongoing slaughter of innocents in Darfur in Sudan, urging everyone to do something to help stop the humanitarian catastrophe.

Already in the spring of 1999, Synagogue 2000 (S2K, now Synagogue 3000), an organization created to help synagogues revitalize themselves, began to look at BJ as a possible model for synagogue renewal elsewhere. Many were skeptical, pointing out that BJ's success was built primarily on factors that could not be replicated elsewhere. It was on the Upper West Side of Manhattan, an area with the heaviest concentration of active young Jews in the country. Many were single, and BJ was one of the best places to meet a possible mate. While all of this was true, it was also correct to say that BJ was doing a number of things that could be useful for other synagogues, whether they were in New York City or Toledo, Ohio. Synagogue 2000 put together an advisory committee of successful congregational rabbis, cantors, and lay people. These advisers traveled around looking to gather models elsewhere, including the Saddleback Megachurch in Irvine County south of Los Angeles. As Rabbi Lawrence Hoffman, the codirector of Synagogue 2000, told me, "the goal was hardly to imitate what was obviously evangelical worship. But the S2K visitors walked away with a number of principles themselves, which BJ (and others) would use successfully in their already successful venture in synagogue renewal."[2]

The next step came with a grant from Steven Spielberg's Righteous Persons Foundation(RPF). The idea "bubbled up" during a brainstorming session between Hoffman and Ron Wolfson, the two codirectors of Synagogue

2000, and Marge Tabankin and Rachel Levin of RPF. Why not experiment with an ethnographic study of contemporary Jewish worship? They decided to hire cultural anthropologist Ayala Fader and ethnomusicologist Mark Kligman to do a study, which they conducted during the 2000–2001 academic year. Their goal was to try to discover what made the "BJ phenomenon" so popular. Fader and Kligman identified four core elements they felt made the congregation different: congregants felt that they experienced God in the services and through the community, they loved feeling engaged in what was an extremely participatory congregational experience, they appreciated the approach to Jewish practice that was both traditional and innovative, and they believed that the congregation had an extremely effective leadership structure. Suggesting that the congregation took advantage of postmodern understandings of culture, Fader and Kligman felt that the BJ experience was so powerful because it broke down distinctions that were usually regarded as impenetrable. BJ was a brand new synthesis of the old and the new, of the denominational and the postdenominational, of the impulse toward ritual as well as toward social justice. BJ strove to be both authentic and innovative, responsible but allowing for a great deal of choice, traditional but progressive, and democratic, but with a strong central authority.

The most important lesson that many drew from BJ's success was that vibrant music can bring in large crowds on Friday night. The old adage concerning real estate is that the three most important things are "location, location, location." When Ron Wolfson of the University of Judaism, the cofounder of Synagogue 2000 along with Rabbi Lawrence Hoffman, was asked, "is there any one thing that is essential to the creation of a spiritually moving prayer service?" he answered: "There are three things: music, music, music."[3] But was there more to the recipe than just vibrant music? Leaders from all sorts of congregations in different geographical regions of the country began visiting BJ, not only because they were curious, but also in order to see whether they could develop their own version of the BJ experience. A number of clones soon started popping up.

The most successful congregational startups were created in places where there was a similar convergence of fortuitous circumstances, such as IKAR in Los Angeles. BJ started a program to train rabbinic interns who could then go out and help other existing synagogues or start new congregations, utilizing the techniques that they had learned. The BJ rabbis emphasized that what visitors saw on Friday nights was possible only because of a complex and sophisticated approach to congregational life, and it was not just enough to observe a couple of Friday night services and think you could go and replicate the experience. Perhaps the best known BJ intern was Rabbi Sharon Brous, who had been a Marshall T. Meyer Rabbinic Fellow when she was a student at JTS. She created IKAR in Los Angeles in the spring of 2004, inspired by the spirit of B'nai Jeshurun. The name IKAR is the Hebrew word for "essential principle" or "most important thing" and comes from one of the most famous statements made by the Hasidic rebbe Nachman of Bratslav: "All the world is a very narrow bridge. But the IKAR is to fear nothing at all." Brous was named three years in a row to the Forward 50, a list of the most important American Jews of the year. "In the burgeoning world of unconventional young congregations, Sharon Brous, thirty-two, has taken on an unusual role, doubling as a youthful firecracker, storming the barricades, and a grand dame, dispensing wisdom."⁴

IKAR combined a traditional service with liberal politics. Brous explained that she modeled her congregational structure on the approach used by the liberal political organization MoveOn.org, doing much of her publicizing through e-mail and letting people know about upcoming programs primarily through the congregation's Web page. Like B'nai Jeshurun, IKAR stresses social justice advocacy. "We wanted to provoke a cultural shift."⁵ She explained that "we believe that serious, passionate, and authentic engagement with Torah is an enduring response to the deepest cry of the human heart. We believe that prayer and learning in a kehillah kedoshah, a holy community, can be soulful, inspiring, and profoundly impactful." Summing it all up, she wrote that "matters of the spirit are intimately linked to matters of the world, and that the Jewish community has a distinct responsibility to participate in social justice and tikkun, healing."⁶

The question was: could large mainstream congregations that were not being rebuilt from the bottom up benefit from the BJ model? It soon became clear that the answer was yes, at least in cases where there were many younger people looking to socialize. Already back in 1997, Sinai Temple in Los Angeles pioneered what they later called "Friday Night Live", a take-off on the name of the popular television show *Saturday Night Live*. Senior Rabbi David Wolpe had heard about the success B'nai Jeshurun had been enjoying in Manhattan and he visited to see what they were doing. Like BJ, Sinai Temple had a large cadre of twenty and thirty somethings, and Wolpe felt that a BJ-style service might work well for them. He asked Sinai Temple musical director Craig Taubman to compose melodies for a new type of Kabbalat Shabbat service that would create a euphoric spirit that could reach the alienated young adults whom Wolpe was hoping to attract.

Every second Friday evening of the month at 7:30, young Jews in the twenty-five to forty age bracket gather to join with Taubman and his band in the singing of traditional prayers with a new beat. Wolpe delivers short and upbeat sermons, sprinkled with references to pop culture, that are designed to relate to contemporary concerns. "I wanted to create a service that would engage and inspire young people, to bring them back to synagogue and make them realize that Judaism has a great deal to offer them," explained Wolpe.[7] Taubman adds that the effort to connect with worshippers begins as soon as they approach the building. "We greet people outside, make them feel welcome, and enter the sanctuary with them. There is music playing as we walk in. They can sing to it, hum to it, and, if they can't do that, we urge them to clap to it."

Taubman describes the music as "gentle," putting the volume at about half what it would be in a traditional Conservative service. This softness has led some of the congregations that have copied Sinai to call their version of the service "Friday Night Unplugged," based on MTV Unplugged, a concert series where artists perform without amplification. Despite the lower volume, the enthusiasm is definitely high voltage. "When I sing, people frequently get up and dance. It's spontaneous, it just happens." Their five-piece band is on one side of the bimah, playing soft music as the worshippers come into the sanctuary. Taubman plays guitar and other musicians handle piano, bass, saxophone, and percussion. Taubman comes down the stairs of the bimah and goes into the congregation, encouraging them to sing and clap frenetically. The music is simple and the words are easy to learn. In many cases, the crowd does not even need to know any of the words; they can just hum along. Clapping in rhythm is encouraged and brings people into the service. Wolpe wrote me that "Friday Night Live has moved far beyond Sinai Temple. In the last decade, it has spawned Friday Night Live Services all around the country, and in Europe." He is proud that they have successfully built a community through the service which extends to their ATID program (meaning future in Hebrew), in which young people study together, plan mitzvah projects, and engage in communal activities. Friday Night Live has attracted guests ranging from Elie Wiesel to Rick Warren, all of whom draw a great deal of attention and even larger attendances. "On Shabbat you will hear a Grammy-award-winning Jewish guitarist do a riff on *ein keloheinu,* and the next week a Gospel choir singing a Hebrew song. It is enlivening, uplifting, and embracing."[8] Following services, Sinai Temple is "transformed into a Friday night hot spot with an array of opportunities to meet new people, engage in stimulating discussion with one of our many featured speakers, dance, groove to a live band, or just schmooze with other young professionals."[9]

Others have applied a similar formula in more suburban environments. Rabbi Steven Lebow, nicknamed the "Rock 'n Roll Rabbi," has designed a Friday night service for his Atlanta-area congregation that draws between four and five hundred worshippers every week. "We always have guitar and drums, and sometimes we play Jewish songs to a rock 'n' roll beat, or include [melodies of] Bob Dylan and the Grateful Dead in the service." On Purim one year, Lebow and Cantor Steven Weiss impersonated the Beach Boys, chanting the Scroll of Esther to the tune of "California Girls." The next year, they dressed up like John Lennon and Paul McCartney and chanted the scroll to the tune of "Yesterday." "If you make people feel good, they'll come back."[10] When I asked Rob Weinberg of Experiment in Congregational Education to read an earlier draft of this chapter, he told me that the story just related contains the implicit assumption that the central goal of synagogue transformation is to get more people to come to shul. "Through both my work and my personal experience, I have come to believe that the goal is not to get people to come to the synagogue but, rather, for the synagogue to bring Judaism to people's lives in ways that matter and that enhance their lives." He worried that ending this opening section with a description of how rock music helped attendance would lead the reader to believe that "synagogue revitalization is just about turning Judaism into entertainment that makes people feel good. It's a lot deeper than that."[11]

The Need for Developing New Models for Successful Congregations

Synagogues were and are regarded as the spiritual cornerstones of the American Jewish community. While there are a plethora of Jewish organizations, the synagogue has always represented Judaism as opposed to Jewish political advocacy or Jewish leisure activities, which have their own organizations. The synagogue fulfilled a threefold function; it was traditionally a beit knesset, a house of assembly, a beit midrash, a house of study, and a beit tefillah, a house of prayer. During different periods of Jewish history, the synagogue may have served these functions in different proportions. Some scholars believe that the earliest synagogues were primarily places of assembly where the local community gathered to hear important pronouncements or discuss the issues of the day. More recently, many synagogues were primarily houses of prayer, where congregants would come to attend services, especially on Rosh Hashanah and Yom Kippur. The impression that the synagogue existed primarily to cater to the High Holy Day worshipper became stronger over the course of the last few decades, until the "worship crisis" became so severe that it could no longer be ignored.

Most synagogues provided the full spectrum of services and continued their regular practices for several decades with slowly diminishing results. What had once been relatively effective programming strategies no longer seemed to work. But there was a reluctance to change and most congregations continued with their routine. Attitudes changed suddenly after the 1990 National Jewish Population Survey (NJPS) found an intermarriage rate of 52 percent among those Jews who had married between 1985 and 1990. This got the communal leadership thinking about why that was occurring and what that meant for the existing communal consensus, labeled "the Jewish civil religion" by Jonathan Woocher in his book *Sacred Survival*. But if attachment to Israel and survivor guilt from the Holocaust was not enough to keep people Jewish, then what was? The answer was obvious—it was the same thing that had kept Jews Jewish for thousands of years: Judaism.

Judaism had historically been transmitted in a variety of ways, the synagogue being only one. The importance of the synagogue had actually increased in the post–World War II period. The Jewish neighborhood, which had formerly stood as the most important cultural transmitter of Jewish ethnic identity, was disappearing, as most Jews moved out of the inner city to the suburbs (see chapter 1). In addition, the Jewish home no longer played the central role it had once, as mothers were going back to school to train for the careers they had postponed. This was an irreparable loss, since the home had traditionally been the most important institution for the practice of Jewish ritual and transmission of Jewish values. Women in particular were in a tough bind. If they became active in their congregations, they were seen as contributing to the "feminization of American religion." If they took full-time jobs, they were accused of neglecting their children's religious education at home. The bottom line remained the same—the family was no longer capable of adequately transmitting Jewish identity and Jewish values to the next generation.

The 1990 NJPS indicated that American Jews were less likely to join synagogues than just a few decades earlier and, if they did join, were less likely to attend services. Many of the synagogues that existed had been built for a congregation that was now aging and seemed ill-equipped to serve the needs of the younger generation. Likewise, the programming had been designed for a generation who were now in their seventies and eighties, and it did not appeal to their children and grandchildren. There was the fear that a whole generation might walk away from Judaism, and, if that happened, subsequent generations would be lost as well. A number of approaches were tried to deal with this "continuity crisis," including synagogue renewal programs, which were created to address what New York philanthropist Michael Steinhardt called the "failed enterprise" of American synagogues. The problem was obvious, but the solution was not. Convincing people to immerse themselves in the tradition would open their eyes to the beauty and wisdom of the Jewish religion, but this was not going to happen for the vast majority. Most American Jews knew little about the liturgy, and they were unlikely to take the time necessary to learn sufficient amounts of Hebrew. Most were nonobservant and no longer felt the natural rhythms of the Jewish week, which led up to the Sabbath as a needed day of rest and rejuvenation.

Some of the synagogue renewal organizations that were created argued that congregations had to redefine themselves as spiritual communities. They needed to get away from the concept that congregants were consumers who were purchasing certain services by paying dues. This mindset prevented the emergence of an altruistic covenantal community focused on trust and warmth, rather than lifecycle events and High Holy Day services. Hoffman reported that a "mystery shopper" was sent to several synagogues to ask about the possibility of joining. "No synagogue discussed any responsibility other than dues. No one expected him to be anything other than a 'customer' balancing synagogue offerings against other demands of his time. No one engaged him in discussions of religious commitment, spiritual search, the gifts he had, or the passions that move him."[12]

Many synagogues seemed moribund, holding uninspired services that catered to small groups of habitual attendees, most of whom sat passively in the congregation looking bored. Many congregations were empty most of the week, filling up only for life cycle events and, of course, the High Holy Days. Other congregations had many activities during the week, but few of those programs focused on spirituality, which would presumably be of central importance for religious institutions. Spiritual seekers found little nourishment in the synagogue. Many stopped attending. Others defected completely, joining other religions or even "cults." Synagogue affiliation rates were disappointingly low, and many joined only for a few years in order to prepare their children for bar and bat mitzvahs. In my first rabbinic position in Cape Town, South Africa, a family sent in a resignation letter on the Monday following their youngest daughter's bat mitzvah. I called the father to ask if I or the congregation had offended his family in some way. "Of course not, Rabbi, you did a wonderful job, and the congregation has always been nice. It's just that we've been planning to resign for years, just as soon as our children finished their bar mitzvah training."

The synagogue appeared to be in desperate need of what was humorously called "rejewvenation." A number of private family foundations came forward with new and innovative ideas and a number of new organizations were created to try to build momentum toward synagogue renewal. These organizations developed programs that worked with lay leaders as well as rabbis and entire congregations. Some brought individuals to conference centers from various parts of the country, others sent consultants directly to the synagogues. A new strategy was necessary. The question was what aspect of congregational life was in need of being changed the most. Many congregations have been putting the priority on reworking their religious services, particularly their Friday night structure. They have placed particular emphasis on new, more exciting, and more participatory music, but there are synagogues that have gone far beyond that, experimenting with new approaches to liturgy and even the Torah reading. National programs have encouraged them to broaden their offerings, moving away from a "one size fits all" approach. Whatever the activity, the principle was the same—individuals can connect to their religious tradition through the creation of a warm and caring community in which the values of the tradition are not only taught but also embodied and emulated.

Despite the changing cultural environment described in chapter 2, most synagogues remained cold and bureaucratic. In chapter 3, I have argued that the American Jewish religious movements were slow in responding to the changing social trends and expectations. The leaders of the various denominations had historically avoided being too self-critical for fear of jeopardizing their positions and relationships with lay leaders as well as other professionals. This reluctance may once have been a positive attribute, but had become a severe impediment to institutional change. Synagogue leaders now became aware that they needed to adapt—and needed to do so urgently.

The new generation of denominational leaders were given greater freedom to examine the strengths and weaknesses of their movement and make bold recommendations for improvement. For example, just look at the Reform movement. Rabbi Alexander M. Schindler, president of the UAHC, was almost universally loved and attracted a great deal of attention through a series of bold policy pronouncements. His support for outreach and his inclusion of a radical proposal to proselytize unchurched gentiles was newsworthy enough to make the front page of the *New York Times*, as the reader learned in chapter 4. Yet he did little to make his organization function more effectively and did not pay attention to the dynamics within the individual congregations that comprised his movement. In contrast to Schindler's "big ideas" style of leadership, the new leader of the Reform movement has prioritized organizational restructuring and institutional revitalization. In December 1999, UAHC president Rabbi Eric H. Yoffie sent a letter to temple leaders noting that while some synagogues had been successful, "all too often, our services are tedious, predictable, and dull. Far too often, our members pray without fervor or concentration and feel religiously unsatisfied in our synagogues." Yoffie suggested that Reform Jews needed to rediscover the power of prayer. "We sense that our Judaism has been a bit too cold and a bit too domesticated. We yearn to sing to God, to let our souls fly free." At the UAHC Biennial in Orlando that same month, Yoffie proposed a "new Reform revolution" that would include five specific worship initiatives.

Yoffie argued that the revitalization of worship needed to start at the local level. He urged synagogue boards to devote two meetings to defining their congregation's worship agenda. Using guide books specially prepared for this task, the board could discuss "Why Worship Matters" and "Getting Unstuck." The congregation should then turn to the rebuilding of congregational worship committees, which in many cases had become no more than the technical apparatus for distributing High Holy Day tickets. "If we are to realize this revolution, the committee must become the primary venue for rethinking the congregation's worship agenda."[13] Worship committees needed to undertake an in-depth self-evaluation of congregational worship. They could utilize iWorship, an e-mail discussion list specifically created by the UAHC to address issues connected to creating meaningful Shabbat and daily worship experiences. Yoffie emphasized that the deadening prayer service that was unfortunately so typical around the country could destroy the movement and it was of the highest priority to figure out a way to bring new life into what was essentially the central "product" of the synagogue.

Revising the Liturgy and Rethinking the Worship Experience

Most American Jews have little interest in the historical development of the traditional liturgy, but they have a belief in God and an interest in spiritual concerns. The hope is that a contemporary approach to prayer can draw in spiritual seekers, as well as keep already committed synagogue goers engaged. The trend toward revising liturgy is strictly a non-Orthodox interest. The Orthodox recite the traditional Hebrew words exactly the way they were recited by their parents and grandparents. There has been interest in some Orthodox circles in the musical side—often traditional hazanut, and they have prepared new translations and commentaries, but no reputable Orthodox leader would consider changing any of the actual words of the prayers. There may be differences in the cosmetic aspects of how they pray, but many of these minor changes are unintentional and unnoticed, while others are strictly matters of convenience that have no religious meaning. While the non-Orthodox have likewise changed many cosmetic aspects of worship, they have also engaged in a fundamental reassessment of the purpose of prayer and the most effective means of ceremonial enactment.

The Reform movement has seen a particularly drastic liturgical transformation. *The Union Prayer Book* (UPB) was originally published in 1895, and was eventually adopted by virtually every Reform congregation in the country. Although it was revised a couple of times, it remained virtually unchanged throughout its eighty years of use. But then in 1975, the CCAR published *Gates of Prayer: The New Union Prayer Book* (GOP), which restored a great deal of the Hebrew that had been edited out of the original UPB. Entire prayers that had been deleted were now restored, at least in part. Phrasing that had been banned as representing antiquated beliefs was now rehabilitated, at least in certain cases. This reflected the "return to tradition" so much in evidence in the Reform movement by the 1970s.

In addition to restoring some of the original Hebrew liturgy, the new prayer book reflected the increasingly pluralistic nature of the movement. It was more than twice the size of the old UPB and had ten different Friday night services and six different Saturday morning services, most of which reflected alternative theological visions. In other words, the first Friday night service had a completely different conception of God than did the second Friday night service, which was just a few pages later in the same thick blue hard cover prayer book. In service 1, the English accompanying the Maariv Aravim prayer immediately before the Barchu states that God "is Creator of day and night, rolling light away from darkness, and darkness from light; He causes day to pass and brings on the night."[14] Yet, just a few pages later, in service 2, the English at the very same point in the service reads, "A vast universe: who can know it? What mind can fathom it? We look out to the endless suns and ask: What are we, what are our dreams and our hopes?"[15] The first service emphasized the belief in an all-powerful God who controls the world and must be worshipped for that reason. In contrast, the second service stressed the importance of the spiritual search, suggesting that God could be found in the inspiration drawn from the miracle of the universe. While they are not necessarily theologically contradictory, they are so radically different that it is hard to believe they come out of the very same prayer book.

This theological multiplicity was not seen as a problem by most Reform Jews. Indeed, many did not pay the slightest attention. As a new rabbi in the mid 1990s, I wanted to see which theology or theologies had the most meaning for my congregants. Every Friday night for a month, I chose one of the first eight Sabbath evening services. After four weeks of doing the same service, I then moved to the next. My hope was that those in attendance would notice the differing theologies and comment on those differences, but that did not happen. Only when one of the services did not include Lecha Dodi, a popular liturgical song, did I start to get any feedback at all. Even though service 1 spoke of an omnipotent, omniscient God and service 2 spoke of God as the still small voice within us, virtually no one in the congregation seemed to notice. I felt surprised that the words of the prayers—recited in large part in English—seemed to make so little difference to them.

This observation would not surprise Steven M. Cohen and Arnold M. Eisen, who together have studied "the moderately affiliated Jew." Eisen told an audience at the University of Michigan that "the words in the prayer book simply do not very much interest the Jews to whom we spoke."[16] He explained that "whether Orthodox, Reform, Conservative, or Reconstructionist, the liturgies describe a God in whom the Jews we met do not believe." I would put it a little differently. Rather than consciously rejecting the traditional conceptions of God, people focus only on spiritual experiences that touch them emotionally. In their search for individualistic fulfillment, the American Jew simply ignores anything that does not immediately resonate. It is not so much that they do not believe in the God described in the various Jewish liturgies, rather they found that the presentation did not move them.

If the goal was to translate the traditional liturgy correctly, then a single well-done volume would suffice for a generation or longer. But that was not the goal. Rather, each movement needed to publish a prayer book that would touch people's souls. Achieving such an amorphous goal was obviously challenging, and the denominations found themselves pressured into editing new prayer books with increasingly short intervals between editions. The Reform movement only used the *Gates of Prayer* for Shabbat and weekdays and the *Gates of Repentance* for High Holy Days for a few years when calls began being heard for a new prayer book. There were two specific omissions in the GOP that were regarded as particularly serious: the lack of gender-sensitive or gender-neutral language and the absence of transliterations on the pages next to the Hebrew words. The Reform movement published a series of temporary prayer books in the early 1990s and began working on a completely new book, *Mishkan T'filah: A Reform Siddur*, which was published after many delays in 2007. The Conservative and Reconstructionist movements likewise came out with a series of new prayer books for Shabbat, weekdays, the pilgrimage festivals, and High Holy Days.

One of the main purposes of all the new prayer books was to "empower" the congregation. The synagogue service that had been established as normative in the postwar period had been a spectator experience. While the styles differed substantially, both Reform and Conservative rabbis ran the service. They told the congregation what page to turn to and when to sit and stand. The congregants were expected to follow instructions and listen passively. The rabbi served as the authority figure and the entire structure of the worship experience was designed to reinforce rabbinic authority. The congregants lived their daily lives without much thought about religion, which was relegated to the handful of hours a month that they may have spent in the synagogue. The justification for change was that if individuals were allowed to be involved in the ritual rather than just observing it, they would be better equipped to derive spiritual benefit from synagogue services.

When they were in the sanctuary, the congregants abrogated their personal responsibility for religious consciousness to their rabbis, who drew ego gratification from the prestige that their status of symbolic exemplar bestowed upon them.[17] In a modern context, the rabbi served in a role similar to the one that had been played by the Kohen (priest) in the Temple in Jerusalem, performing the ritual on behalf of the people. Each denomination had their own customs, designed to emphasize the unique role played by the rabbi, customs that reinforced the congregants' feelings that they were religiously incompetent. Reform rabbis wore black robes and spoke in formal, almost Shakespearean-like English, while Conservative rabbis read extended paragraphs in Hebrew. But, whatever the language, the impact was similar—the synagogue was the place to passively absorb a little bit of Jewish religion.

Having been trained in an authoritarian era, some older rabbis either failed to understand or refused to adjust to the changing dynamics. This could and did lead to congregational meltdowns, one of which I witnessed firsthand at Congregation Emanu-El B'ne Jeshurun in Milwaukee, Wisconsin. The congregational board eventually began to realize the extent of the damage and had to repudiate promises that in turn caused tremendous anger and bitterness. The historic synagogue building located in the city of Milwaukee had to be sold, a reflection not only of the changing geographical patterns of Jewish settlement but also of the need for prayer spaces that are better suited for twenty-first-century spiritual exploration.

Like other Americans, Jews now wanted to participate actively. Chapter 2 showed how Jews began to develop new approaches to prayer during the 1960s. The havurah movement was particularly influential. But the impact of changing attitudes took a couple of decades to filter down to the mainstream. By the 1980s, the authoritative religious model was breaking down. Americans were no longer willing to be passive. In whatever they did, they wanted to be actively involved. They were more educated than their parents and certainly their grandparents had been, and they no longer saw the rabbi as someone with greater learning and sophistication. It is true that the rabbi still had a greater knowledge of Judaism, but that only heightened the feeling that changes needed to be made. People who are competent and well educated should be able to participate actively and broadly in ritual life, they argued, without needing to undergo extensive technical preparation.

The new synagogue architecture was designed to meet the more participatory needs of the changing synagogue. The bimah was built much lower, with broad carpeted steps allowing unfettered access from all directions. Congregants could thus easily ascend and descend from the bimah in order to lead a reading, open or close the ark, or help in some other part of the service. The rabbi was much closer to the congregation, which enabled her to interact more extensively with them. When Temple B'nai Israel, the congregation that I lead in Albany, Georgia, planned their new synagogue building in the late 1990s, architect David Maschke put in movable chairs that could be set up in an almost unlimited number of configurations. Some congregations preferred circular arrangements that made it possible for congregants to see each other rather than just looking at the rabbi and cantor (or choir). Many sermons were now discussions rather than lectures and the rabbi served as more of a facilitator rather than an authority figure. The rabbi no longer speaks down to the congregation—figuratively as well as literally—but rather engages in dialogue with them on an egalitarian basis.

Rabbi Jeffrey Summit, long-time Hillel director at Tufts University, points out that "there has been a real shift from performance to participation in worship. The concept of participation has changed to where the physical act of singing—being involved in body and breath and song—has become very important."[18] This shift frequently required altering the synagogue setting itself. Some congregations found that smaller chapels better served their worship needs than their massive, imposing sanctuaries. Other congregations found that the type and size of the building was not as important as having the flexibility to create different types of seating arrangements that could facilitate community interaction. Temple Israel in Boston, for example, began holding one of their Friday night services in an atrium where they could place movable folding chairs. This allowed them to create a seating structure where worshippers could see each other, and made it easier for everyone to participate.

This participatory model is also being applied to the Torah service. One of the many challenges facing the more traditional congregations was how to keep congregants interested during what could be a long and arduous Torah reading. Every Saturday morning, synagogues were supposed to read the weekly portion (the sidra) from the Torah. (They also read a shorter selection from the weekly portion on Monday and Thursday mornings). Since the Torah is divided into fifty-four sections (parshiot), the weekly Torah reading could take forty-five minutes or longer. For those who could follow the Hebrew and had studied parshat hashavua, this could be an exciting chance to follow the Torah reader's cantillation. But for those with less background and knowledge, the Saturday morning Torah reading became monotonous, with many of the congregants spending the time chatting freely with their pew mates. I remember going to services at an Orthodox synagogue in Binghamton, New York one Saturday morning, where the rabbi repeatedly stopped the Torah reading, banging his hand aggressively on the reader's table and insisting that the congregants stop their private conversations. They quieted down briefly, but soon resumed their talking, provoking the rabbi yet again. One solution was to shorten the Torah reading, but this was not in itself going to further the original goal of teaching the congregation about the Torah.

FIGURE 8.1. Completely unrolling a sefer torah on Simchat Torah at Temple B'nai Israel, Albany, Georgia. The chairs in the middle of the sanctuary were moved away to create space, something that would not have been possible with stationary pews. Photo Dana Evan Kaplan. *Courtesy of the author*

FIGURE 8.2. Peter Pitzele demonstrating the Mask of Joseph as part of Bibliodrama, a creative approach to experiencing the Bible. Also called Pop-Up Torah, Open-Bible Play, Experiential Bible, or Modern Midrash, this method has opened new insights into ancient sources. *Courtesy of Peter Pitzele*

One creative response to this problem was to dramaticize the Torah portion of the week. Peter Pitzele pioneered a methodology of psychodrama called Bibliodrama that draws on the individual's own experiences to act out family stories from the Bible. "The search for a credible spirituality began for me as a solitary quest. It began in response to a few scattered moments of transcendent, almost hallucinatory, insight that had moved and troubled me as a young man." Pitzele tried a variety of religious programs and disciplines, including both Christian and Eastern spiritual approaches. "I often sampled and studied these but found I could not stay. I seemed unable or unwilling to conform my ideas about God and the meaning of life to any existing tradition or school of thought." He composed his own private theology, which he describes as "an eclectic system of ideas, Eastern and Western, shamanic and poetic, classic and romantic." When he reached his midforties, however, he felt the need to reconnect with his Judaism and found that he could do this best by studying the book of Genesis. He didn't just study Genesis, he wanted to demonstrate the relationship between myth and experience through the imaginative retelling of a psychodramatist.[19]

Theoreticians have long spoken about the therapeutic culture of narcissism in the United States. Television talk show hosts such as Jerry Springer (the child of Holocaust survivors) had made fortunes bringing people onto a forum where they could express their innermost feelings and act out their strongest emotions. While much of the spectacle was a crass distraction from serious issues facing the country, the underlying psychological need was very real. Synagogues had historically done virtually nothing to tap into the enormous emotional need that Americans felt to talk about themselves and to relate their personal life stories to their religious tradition and community. Psychodrama was a way for the congregation to witness emotional scenes being acted out and make the ancient story of Judaism come alive for them. Pitzele and others were able to make the stories of the Torah contemporary and relevant by showing how they contained not only religious truths but also psychological tension that could be shown dramatically. This turned what might have been a long, boring reading of a text in a foreign language into an exciting reenactment full of human emotion and psychological nuance.

This drew in part from innovative programming being done in Christian congregations, but there were quite a few differences. For example, unlike many churches, these synagogues did not take psychodrama into the realm of public confession. Some churches had long featured testimonies from individuals who would stand up and tell the congregation how they had found Jesus after many years of hard drinking, constant womanizing, and what they saw in retrospect as their self-destructive patterns of behavior. For most American Jews, personal witnessing in front of everyone else in the synagogue would be taking emotional vulnerability several steps too far.

There was historically relatively little precedent for the public expression of personal feelings. The early Talmudic sages had included various private and personal prayers in the Amidah, the standing prayer also known as the Eighteen Benedictions (even though there were actually nineteen). The entire congregation collectively confessed their sins on the High Holy Days by reciting the Viddui, the Al Chet, and similar prayers. Modern synagogue ritual was tightly choreographed, and it would have been lacking decorum for an individual to abruptly stand up and start talking about the sins they had committed. Jews had no desire to start confessing their sins one at a time in public—they did not suddenly want to start copying Pentecostals. Yet they needed a way to make the worship experience more personal. The lack of opportunity for emotional expression contributed to the sense that services were cold, and Judaism—or at least institutional Judaism—had little to contribute to the individual's sense of psychological well-being.

One of the hottest Jewish educational programs that focuses on personal growth via the arts is Storahtelling, the storytelling of the Torah. What Storahtelling tries to do is mix translation of the parsha with a dramatic reenactment. There is considerable improvisation as the Storahtelling actors recount the theme of the Torah portion of the week, glossing it with a contemporary midrashic commentary. "Bridging myth and dogma, ancient words and contemporary needs, we boldly proclaim, restore and reinterpret Jewish rituals and stories for a modern age and an intellectual free market."[20] They have four program models: Shultime, synagogue-based ritual performances; Showtime, theatrical productions that adapt Jewish myths and rituals for a popular audience; Schooltime, training programs that familiarize artists and educators in local communities with the Storahtelling technique; and RituaLab, an experimental format that they call a reimagined worship arena for the twenty-first century.

Founder Amichai Lau-Lavie explains that it is part psychodrama and part psychotherapy, with the Storahtelling staff using the stories of the Torah to engage worshipers. "We use edu-tainment. We make them laugh. It's 95 percent humor, culture, radical fun, and 5 percent meaning. If they want more, they'll come back next time."[21] Storahtelling started out mostly being performed at Jewish conferences, but has now been invited to present at hundreds of synagogues, schools, seminaries, and camps worldwide. A smaller but growing number of congregations and Hebrew schools now use the Storahtelling method on a regular basis.

Some congregations began to experiment with special services that tried to address the emotional needs of an increasingly stressed population. Healing services devoted to the emotionally and physically damaged became particularly successful. There was certainly opposition to the insertion of a special prayer for those in need of healing when that might include oneself. The idea that Jews would pray to God for concrete personal benefit ran counter to many people's understanding of Judaism. It is true that there is a prayer for healing in the Amidah and that it is customary to pray for those who are ill during the Torah reading, but these were either prayers for all those who were ill or, at the very least, for someone else. Personal prayers for one's own healing were seen as excessively egotistical and therefore inappropriate.

FIGURE 8.3. Storahtelling troupe acting out the biblical story of the Tower of Babel. Through their theatrical performances, Storahtelling makes ancient traditions accessible to the new generation, advancing Jewish knowledge while raising social consciousness. Photo Benjamin Thomas. *Courtesy of Storahtelling*

Prayers should be altruistic, and the individual worshipper should never demand that God intercede for one's own personal gain. Doing so on Shabbat was seen by some as an even more egregious breach in tradition. Healing service advocates disputed this, arguing that synagogues could provide the religious knowledge that all human beings have a soul, which comes from God and can provide the capacity to heal. This healing could include physical diseases, but would also be broad enough to include emotional suffering— everything ranging from overcoming acne to dealing with terminal cancer.

New prayers were composed and new ceremonies created. Jewish folk music composer Debbie Friedman wrote "Mi Sheberach" (The one who blesses), for a simchat chochma, the joy of wisdom, a new ceremony that was invented to celebrate wisdom in honor of a friend on her sixtieth birthday. The prayer offers the hope of healing for those in suffering. "My friend was having a very difficult time in her life and a number of her friends were also struggling. Yet she had arrived at this age and was determined to embrace it." Introduced at the UAHC biennial in San Francisco in 1993, the tune has become the most popular adopted liturgical melody in recent decades. Part of its appeal is the integration of creative English phrases into a Hebrew prayer.[22]

> Mi she-bei-rach a-vo-tei-nu
> M'kor ha-bra-cha l'i-mo-tei-nu
> May the source of strength
> Who blessed the ones before us
> Help us find the courage
> To make our lives a blessing
> And let us say, Amen.

> Mi she-bei-rach i-mo-tei-nu
> M'kor ha-bra-cha l'a-vo-tei-nu
> Bless those in need of healing
> With r'fu-a sh'lei-ma
> The renewal of body
> The renewal of spirit
> And let us say, Amen.[23]

Friedman talked about offering worshippers a sense of "spiritual connectedness." The leaders of synagogue renewal considered this to be potentially powerful. Rabbi Lawrence Hoffman explained that he and his colleagues at Synagogue 3000 began to see healing "as embedded in a culture that honors the humanity of others; that looks for the best, not the worst in everyone; that helps people succeed, not fail; and that eliminates the cultural aggravations that drive up blood pressure, cause embarrassment, promote guilt, and chase people away."[24]

There are organizations that are specifically designed to help bring a new sense of spirituality to the synagogue. Other organizations have been created to encourage the development of spirituality that are not specifically devoted to synagogue renewal but nevertheless are directly involved in that process. The Institute for Jewish Spirituality sees its mandate as helping Jews "to find a deeper, more meaningful connection with the Spirit of the universe, with God." They organize long-term programs for rabbis and other synagogue leaders to help them nurture their own spirituality and bring a new sense of Judaic spirit to their congregations. Their programs are based on the premise that spiritual growth is a lifelong process that requires commitment, practice, and guidance. The institute teaches them, experientially, "the profound practices and exquisite texts of the Jewish religion." The goal is to help them to bring the sacred into the secular and thereby promote individual spiritual development and supportive communities. The IJS continues the spirit of Hasidism and therefore emphasizes the teachings of classical Hasidic thought as well as other types of mysticism and meditation. By studying the traditional sources as well as encouraging individuals to evaluate their own personal growth, they hope to encourage "a new creativity and practice, and in language" which is both innovative and rooted in the tradition.

Experiments in Congregational Transformation

Although this chapter is devoted to the topic of synagogue renewal, it is important to note that congregations can only revitalize themselves if they have enthusiastic individuals on whom they can rely. A great deal of research has been done in recent years on the nature of Jewish identity and the ways in which Jewish education can be made more effective. Social scientists have found that successful Jewish learning has to engage students in experiences that integrate all three dimensions of human psychology: the emotional, the cognitive, and the behavioral. Leonard Saxe and Fern Chertok call this "The 1, 2, 3 Principle," which they humorously suggest could stand for "kishkes, kortex, and kinesthetics." It is not enough to just teach facts, nor will it be sufficient to just do things. Rather, effective Jewish education needs to marshal the head, the heart, and the body.

As a direct result of the new individualistic ethos, people will become involved in the Jewish community if they feel a personal reason to do so. When they are children, they are sent to their synagogue religious school and undergo additional preparation for their bat or bar mitzvah. Some continue on to confirmation, but, for many, the bat or bar mitzvah ceremony marks the end of formal involvement in Judaism, except, perhaps, for certain family celebrations or commemorations. Saxe and Chertok explain that "these occasions serve as important soul-searching and family-bonding experiences, but are inadequate to make Judaism personally meaningful or help build a sense of Jewish peoplehood."[25] Programs that can engage young people on all three levels simultaneously are the most effective.

Although much work has been done to improve the quality of the afternoon religious school, a formal educational program that only meets a few hours a week cannot possibly accomplish the necessary objectives, no matter how dedicated the teachers or how effective the curriculum. Rather, Jewish synagogue and educational experiences have to be supplemented with Jewish camping, youth group, and Israel travel experiences. My congregation has two young members, siblings both in their twenties. Both were raised in the temple and are now married to non-Jewish spouses. Although both have become members of the temple, one shows greater interest than the other. Why? Part of the reason is that he went on the March of the Living, which was a program that sent young American Jewish youth to see the concentration camps in Poland. The group then concluded their trip with a short stopover in Israel. March of the Living provided him with the intense emotional experience that gave him the motivation to learn and do more.

Jewish education, to be most effective, needs to be a collaborative effort. For decades, each of the denominations worked in relative isolation. They certainly talked to each other informally and in particular synagogue organizations, but there was never any sustained effort to pool knowledge and insights to improve the quality of the Jewish religious experience and the effectiveness of their overall programming. This was, however, never true in the Jewish educational world. Although the different streams certainly did work separately, there were a number of frameworks that brought educators and lay leaders together across denominational lines, especially the bureaus of Jewish education and the Council for Jewish Education.[26] They were,

FIGURE 8.4. Reform youth celebrate Shabbat with song at a URJ-affiliated summer camp. The URJ camps translate religious concepts into real life experiences, developing positive personal character traits in consonance with the ideals of Reform Judaism. *Courtesy of the Union for Reform Judaism*

however, regarded as second- or third-tier organizations. The action was inside each of the religious movements.

As more programming began being done outside of the denominational framework, it became clear that a community-wide effort could be successful. The first major transdenominational event was a 1975 conference of Jewish educators put together by an organization that became known as the Coalition for the Advancement of Jewish Education(CAJE). This was a historic effort that was later copied elsewhere in the world, where similar educational conferences were likewise organized. While Orthodox groups were less inclined to participate, most other Jewish educators from across the denominational spectrum were excited by the opportunity to learn from teachers that they did not normally encounter. CAJE began as a countercultural force, but eventually became the predominant Jewish educational programming center. By the time that private foundations began funding new and innovative programming, CAJE was one of the few models of how transdenominational planning could lead to exciting results. In February 2009 CAJE announced that it was closing because of mounting debt.

While education was clearly a central element in any successful transformation process, it had to be seen as part of a holistic system. Synagogue leaders need to look carefully at the assumptions that have been made about what synagogues are and be willing to take bold steps to respond to the needs of people who may not be vocalizing those needs. Indeed, they may not be visible. But the hope is that making the right types of changes will make the synagogue a more attractive option. Congregations need to become warmer, more inviting. Over the course of the last forty or fifty years, synagogues have become known as cold, or at least indifferent, institutions that focus on raising funds and reflect the social and economic status of their members. This turns off many people, particularly in the younger age groups who are looking for something more intense, more personal, and more spiritual.

Ron Wolfson writes that, during the course of his research, he discovered there were two groups who had mastered the importance of what he calls "radical hospitality." One was the megachurches and the other was Chabad (discussed in chapter 7). "Walk into a Chabad House and you are immediately embraced by a warm and inviting culture. The Chabad rabbi will often offer visitors a meal on site or an invitation to someone's home for Shabbat lunch. The welcoming of guests is one of their highest priorities."[27] The enthusiastic outreach of Chabad is being accepted as a model for even relatively staid suburban congregations that just a few years ago would not have dreamed of proactively welcoming new people. Now they understand that potential members are looking for a community that they can call home and mean it. Synagogues first have to learn what it means to embrace the stranger and then need to market themselves to those not yet part of their community. The *New York Times* recently reported that several synagogues on Long Island, as well as in Seattle, Tucson, and elsewhere, are stationing volunteers in supermarket aisles near the kosher food section just before Passover. Reporter Michael Luo spoke with Rabbi Aaron Schonbrun of Congregation Beth David in Saratoga, California, where volunteers set up tables at two nearby supermarkets. "The idea is, 'Listen, everybody goes shopping.' Even your average Jewish person that may be vaguely aware that it's Passover, or may not be aware it's Passover, or is just in the supermarket."[28] As Chabad, the Kabbalah Centre, and other nonestablishment groups have attracted followers, even the most change-resistant of mainstream Jewish leaders have had to take note.

The question is: How does one adapt successful strategies of religious innovation without alienating the core group who were pleased with the status quo within existing congregations? The answer is that they must go beyond immediate needs and create sacred communities. This sacred community, called in Hebrew a *kehillah kedoshah*, stresses warm, personal relationships where caring is one of the paramount values. Worship is engaging, learning is central, and repairing the world, *tikkun olam*, is a moral imperative (see chapter 3). This may sound almost utopian, but a number of professionals working in the emerging field of synagogue transformation believed that they had strategies that could make a concrete difference. But turning fossilized institutions into vibrant spiritual communities requires a great deal of strategic thinking and a tremendous amount of transdenominational cooperation.

They shared the objective that Jews of all types could, and should, work together to develop strategies that might prove effective and that could be applied in a variety of settings. The first formal synagogue transformation initiative was the Experiment in Congregational Education (ECE), which was created in 1992, and run out of HUC-JIR in Los Angeles. Rabbi Rachel Cowan helped to promote the ECE through her work with the Nathan Cummings Foundation. Other foundations also contributed, including the Mandel Associated Foundations, the Covenant Foundation, and the UJA-Federation of New York. As is clear from its name, the ECE tries to build a culture of Jewish study and learning while simultaneously encouraging the congregation to begin a serious process of examining what they were doing in order to make fundamental, long-lasting changes. The ECE works to engage individual Jews in Jewish learning for Jewish living, a snappy phrase that basically means the congregation focuses on encouraging people of different ages and with different backgrounds to study. The main goal is to figure out ways in which the synagogue can embrace a "culture of learning" where it permeates all aspects of congregational life. Many of the private family foundations looking to fund innovative transdenominational projects ironically turn to denominational institutions. The fact that ECE was and is sponsored by HUC-JIR indicates the complex nature of both denominational and transdenominational trends. The denominational organizations are the best funded and are staffed by the most experienced professionals. Some—particularly those in California—are looking beyond the boundaries of their religious movement and already see themselves as transdenominational in certain ways. They believe that what benefits American Judaism as a whole will benefit their particular constituency and what benefits their particular constituency will benefit American Judaism as a whole.

Their fundamental belief is that Jewish learning is a primary pathway through which to initiate congregational transformation. The ECE seeks to strengthen synagogues as critical centers of Jewish life by helping congregations apply methods through which they become "self-renewing congregations of learners". They do not approach congregations with a recommended vision or a predetermined programmatic solution, but rather provide the advice for creating a mechanism so that the congregation can find their own answers. As the ECE mission statement phrases it, "With our tools, materials, and consultation, congregations take ownership of a process through which they arrive at—and realize—their own visions."

ECE teaches that learning is both *torah l'shma*, learning for its own sake, as well as a catalyst to transform the synagogue from a membership association into a "community of meaning." Members should feel that they want to actively practice what they have learned and what they are teaching. They feel connected to others through the giving and receiving of *gemilut hasadim*, acts of loving kindness. Through regular prayer, Sabbath, and holy day observance, they want to structure and sanctify time and they want to deepen their understanding of Judaism through substantive Jewish learning so as to ground ceremonial practice in Jewish traditional sources.

This could prove quite effective, but it is a lengthy process. Many were scared off by the difficulties of transforming an entire culture that had been in place for decades, but Rabbi Richard Jacobs of the Westchester Reform

Temple (WRT) in Scarsdale, New York felt that he had to take action. "To tell you the truth, the Judaism I had experienced as a youth growing up in a large suburban Reform synagogue seemed shallow and uninspiring. The dreary services lacked passion and relevance. Our religious education was woefully inadequate."[29] When he first became a rabbi, Jacobs believed that if he could just articulate a compelling vision of what the temple could become, then members would surely listen to him, and they could all work together to immediately transform the synagogue. But, to his immense disappointment, Jacobs found that, even though a few modest changes were implemented, the underlying pattern of congregational passivity remained untouched. So when Sara Lee, the director of the Hebrew Union College's Rhea Hirsch School of Education in Los Angeles, invited the WRT to be one of the pilot congregations in the ECE, Jacobs was enthusiastic.

At first, the temple's board was hesitant, concerned that the "experts" from Los Angeles were going to dictate how they should run their congregation. They slowly changed their mind as they saw that the purpose of the program was not to order board members around, but rather to give congregational leaders the tools they needed to make changes themselves. The congregation established a task force that began holding regular weekend conferences to lay the groundwork for permanent organizational change. Jacobs reported that this process was difficult. "If any of us thought the retreats would be a shopping trip for new programmatic ideas, we were wrong." The ECE staff encouraged the temple's leaders to develop a vision that would become the basis for systematic change. They spent many hours doing exercises designed to help them to better understand what their congregation stood for and how it should change in order to more effectively serve its members. "The visioning work frustrated some members of our task force, who wanted to solve problems and implement changes, not discuss the many limiting assumptions that inhibit real transformation."

The task force met to study new approaches to religious practice as well as to make field trips to "cutting-edge congregations." They spent a year studying and reflecting on what their temple might be "at its very best." They also visited other Jewish educational institutions such as summer camps, Hillel foundations, Jewish museums, and so forth in order to better envision what their congregation could potentially become. Over the same time period, a group of trustees began creating a new congregational mission statement that reflected their evolving conceptions of what Judaism could mean to them. After much discussion and debate, they wrote down what they believed were the five central pillars of their temple's sacred work: Talmud Torah, "lifelong and life enhancing Jewish learning"; Avodah, "personal and communal religious practices, including worship that fills our lives with spiritual depth"; Chavurah, "a welcoming, inclusive, and sacred community that embraces each of us with support, care, and wisdom"; Tikkun Olam, "ongoing involvement in bringing healing and justice to the brokenness in our world"; and Klal Yisrael, "strengthening our bonds to Israel and the Jewish people in all lands and building commonality among the various streams of Judaism."

After about a year of working with ECE, the task force prepared a series of "community conversations" to discuss the progress that the congregation had been making. Just under half of the one thousand member families participated, which was considered an impressive percentage. One of the ideas generated during these evenings was what became known as Sharing Shabbat. This full alternative educational program, intended for families with children in kindergarten through fifth grade, became a spirited participatory service that was designed to engage worshipers of all ages. Almost one-third of the eligible religious school families began coming to the program regularly on Saturday mornings. The ECE later developed the Online Learning Experience for other congregations to use to learn about and "experience" various alternative models and programs around the country, including Sharing Shabbat.

ECE stressed the centrality of Judaic study, and therefore incorporated that study into all activities undertaken by the group. As the WRT continued through the ECE process, they began to realize that the temple needed a different kind of space. Rather than just building another institutional structure filled with classrooms or offices, the congregation decided that they wanted smaller, more intimate "sacred spaces." The temple bought an old house that was adjacent to the synagogue building, renaming the renovated mansion the Center for Jewish Life. They began to offer "spiritual support groups," which ranged from a guitar-accompanied folk Shabbat prayer service to Alcoholics Anonymous. Host to a wide variety of more spiritually oriented congregational activities, it proved of tremendous value in creating an atmosphere of warmth and intimacy.

The WRT discovered the same thing that many others in the Jewish community have been observing—that informal Jewish experiences such as summer camp, youth group, and Israel trips are among the most powerful ways to connect young Jews to Judaism. The congregation hired a youth rabbi who devoted his time to children and especially to teenagers, a group that was being underserved. They expanded the standard youth group and confirmation offerings, creating a multiplicity of innovative programs designed for the modern teen, including a theater program and informal Torah study that focused on contemporary ethical dilemmas. The youth rabbi was charged with getting to know the young people on a personal level, while at the same time offering them Jewish spiritual alternatives. The goal was not only to provide varied programming but also to give the teenagers a positive Jewish role model that they could relate to and form a close relationship with.

Many of those involved in the strategic planning process wanted to re-align the temple's activity calendar to better reflect the synagogue's new core values and religious mission statement. They decided to move most of their committee meetings to Tuesday night so that everyone could be free to attend the Jewish arts programs on Mondays, adult learning programs on Wednesdays, and healing services and support group meetings on Thursdays. They were no longer willing to tolerate a situation where the board members ran the temple and did little or nothing else. After ECE, everyone concurred that the leaders of the temple had to agree with and feel strongly about their stated core values.

After four years of ECE-guided change, the task force felt ready to begin transforming the worship service, which Jacobs called the "most delicate area of synagogue life." The task force brought together about thirty-five people to study the prayer curriculum, which had been developed by Synagogue 2000. The working group was intended to develop into a spiritual gathering that would share their "spiritual journeys" through guided reflections as they studied the varied possibilities of the Jewish prayer experience. They experimented with different modalities of worship, including classical Reform, neo-Reform, meditation and guided imagery, and traditional davening.

They eventually decided to offer two separate Friday night services, a 6:15 Kabbalat Shabbat and an 8:15 classical Reform service. The early service, which was mostly Hebrew songs accompanied by a gentle guitar, met in the small chapel where the group could build an intimate prayer atmosphere. The classical Reform service retained most of the old-style worship characteristics, but even here the congregation decided to make some changes. The service began not in the sanctuary but in the social hall with everyone gathered around a large Shabbat table. The congregants were encouraged to join in an opening nigun followed by candle lighting and kiddush that everyone could do for themselves. They then were encouraged to greet each other warmly and move into the sanctuary to continue the service. This dramatically changed the atmosphere that had typified the formal, staid, classical Reform service.

The congregation found that allowing themselves the opportunity to experiment was the most important lesson they took out of the whole process. Jacobs is not sure whether the congregation made all the right decisions, but he is comfortable with the innovative steps taken. "The double Friday night services might turn out to have been a bad idea, or they may continue to grow in popularity. We won't know unless we are willing to experiment and then honestly assess our successes and failures. I am convinced that we are on the right path because we are not afraid to make mistakes as we slowly transform our synagogue." Jacobs is now confident that the members have learned to trust the process that leads to changes, which is the necessary basis for further evolution.

In recent years, the ECE has developed a program called the RE-IMAGINE Project, which focuses on reenvisioning children's Jewish education in the congregational setting. They are now conducting their third cohort for that project in the New York area with funding from UJA-Federation of New York. A total of thirty-two congregations have participated in this innovative program so far. They are also working with a cohort of seven congregations in The RE-IMAGINE Project of Los Angeles in partnership with the Bureau of Jewish Education of Greater Los Angeles, with funding through the Jewish Funders Network and the Jewish Federation of Greater Los Angeles. The RE-IMAGINE Project in Los Angeles follows on the heels of two precursor projects in California—the innovative Models of Religious School Project funded by the Koret Foundation, the Nathan Cummings Foundation and the Jewish Community Endowment in San Francisco and the DrEAMRS consortium with WRT and two other ECE alumni congregations. They are also conducting a follow-up pilot project in New York called RE-IMAGINE Professional Learning. Three alumni congregations of the original RE-IMAGINE Project are participating. The goal of this project is to equip a team from each congregation to develop professional learning for their teachers. They work to align the teaching being done with the congregation's vision for Jewish learning, which they developed as part of the original pilot project, as well as with the congregation's newly implemented alternative models of education.[30]

ECE has also engaged in a lower-intensity project called FOCUS: Teacher Recruitment, developed with funding from the Righteous Persons Foundation and funded in New York by UJA-Federation. The project gives congregations a taste of working with ECE while they take a systemic look at how they recruit teachers. The goal is to help them to devise strategies for getting the right teachers for their congregational religious schools. This is an essential task. I remember when I was a graduate student in Albany, New York. I wanted a part-time job in the Jewish community and I chose to take a Hebrew School teaching position at a local Conservative congregation because it met twice a week rather than the once a week that the Reform temple's Sunday School met. The principal was an Israeli woman who had fallen into the position and the congregation provided no training whatsoever. While some of the teachers may have been parents who had been teaching for years, those of us with little or no experience were left to sink or swim on our own. The senior rabbi met with us exactly once during the two years that I taught there. He spoke to the teachers for no more than three minutes, retelling the story of the little engine that could. That was it.

With the help of the ECE DrEAMRS process, congregations are now establishing task forces to figure out ways of making religious school a meaningful and educational experience. Temple Emanuel of Beverly Hills appointed a twenty-two member task force who worked over a ten-month period to design a flexible innovative educational experience that would be offered as an alternative to the additional program. Called KEF, meaning "fun" in Hebrew, the new religious school option emphasizes active experiences with the family as a whole rather than the traditional classroom learning. Sue Bruckner, chair of the task force at Temple Emanuel, said, "It's exciting to know that we can choose parts from a number of different approaches to design what is right for our community. Our group is energized by knowing that we are developing something that will be for the benefit of our synagogue for many years to come."[31]

Synagogue 3000 Reenvisions What Spiritual Engagement Can Mean

The best known synagogue transformation program is Synagogue 2000 (now called Synagogue 3000, S3K, which focuses primarily on research), which was started in 1995 by Rabbi Lawrence Hoffman of HUC-JIR in New York and Ron Wolfson of the American Jewish University (formerly the University of Judaism) in Los Angeles. They developed a wide-ranging curriculum that synagogues use to rethink their overall approach to their mission and goals in order to deepen the spiritual engagement of their congregants. Both Hoffman and Wolfson had long been involved in thinking about how synagogues could function more effectively, but they had never met each other in person. It was Cowan who introduced them and suggested they work together. Wolfson said that their goal is "to equip and inspire congregations to be the spiritual and educational centers for peoples' lives and not just a kind of fee for service, 'give me some tickets to the High Holidays and drop off my kids' kind of place." Hoffman wanted to use Synagogue 2000 as a vehicle for helping people to rethink what the synagogue stood for. He asked congregational leaders to "imagine our synagogues as places where eternal Jewish values such as caring for the stranger and believing in the power of human beings to change the world are represented in every temple board decision. Envision a spiritual home where every single congregant, not just the social action committee, is performing *ma'asim tovim* [good deeds] in the larger community." Imagine a congregation "where Shabbat services are so participatory and compelling that you cannot help but be moved by the reality of God's presence."[32]

Synagogue 2000's mission was to work collaboratively with congregations of all denominations to realize "the power of sacred community" through a transformative strategic planning process to blend authentic Jewish values with the best practices of modern organizational theory. They implemented their mission through the creation of cohorts of synagogues, each of which embarked on a three-year "journey of transformation," during which groups of lay leaders and synagogue professionals participated in conferences and mentoring to help them create positive change. Each group of congregations experimented with new models of synagogue life, studying Jewish text and engaging in provocative discussions and exercises in group dynamics. Synagogue 2000 worked with congregations from different cities and they would occasionally work with an entire Jewish community, with most of the funding usually coming from the local Jewish Federation. The congregations would go through an extensive process of trying to analyze their needs and slowly develop strategies for building more effective religious communities. As Rabbi Aryeh Azriel of Temple Israel of Omaha, Nebraska put it, "this is not something one just does for a short time."

Synagogue 3000 has tried to build on the successes of Synagogue 2000 while learning from its mistakes. Funded with a major gift from the Marcus Foundation, which was established by Home Depot's Bernie Marcus, the goal is to bring a more dynamic approach to congregational life throughout the country. The S3K offices in Los Angeles and New York now run two major programs: a leadership network and a synagogue studies research initiative. Their leadership network brings together rabbis, cantors, and artists from across the entire spectrum of Jewish religious life, including promising alternatives to traditional synagogue structures. The goal is to push experimental visions forward by showcasing their work to others who can apply the principles of what they do in their own congregations. They aim to support those who are developing new "emergent" spiritual communities in order to create new models for the transformation of American synagogue life. "We stand for spirituality beyond ethnicity, Judaism as a life-long journey beyond the pediatric and the geriatric; community beyond corporation; and commitment beyond consumerism. Success for us is when synagogues develop deeper relationships with their members rather than simply offering more programs."[33]

They have continued their community work as part of their synagogue studies research initiative, launching a pilot program in Atlanta, Marcus's home community. According to Wolfson, "it started with Bernie Marcus. He shared his ideas about how the Jewish community can do a better job of connecting to clients. He wanted to bring all of that to Atlanta in a focused project with clear goals, and that's exciting." Atlanta has one of the fastest-growing Jewish communities in the United States, drawing thousands of Jews from smaller towns and cities throughout the South as well as people from the North and abroad. Yet only one-third of Jewish households in Metro Atlanta belong to synagogues, and only 20 percent of those arrived in the last decade. Furthermore, while there is no quantitative evidence, observers believe that only a small percentage of synagogue members attend services regularly. Synagogue 3000 partnered with the Jewish Federation of Greater Atlanta, the Marcus Foundation, and twenty-one area synagogues to answer the questions why do people affiliate when their children are in religious school but then drop out? What does the synagogue need to do to create lifelong members?

Market research tended to be very limited; what little there was focused almost entirely on people who were already members. The problem was that instead of finding out what their potential "customers" wanted, synagogues only heard from their existing "clientele." That is obviously not the way to expand one's customer base. Jay Kaiman, the head of Jewish philanthropy at the Marcus Foundation, explained how a more business-based marketing approach could impact Jewish spirituality: "The Jewish community must continually look at how we touch lives. The synagogue is an important part of the fabric of Jewish life." Their hope is that "through dialogue, sharing of best practices and a focus on improvement, synagogues will be able to stimulate willing, learning and striving participants." To begin the strategic planning process, each of the twenty-one synagogues formed teams of five key leaders who agreed to attend monthly leadership training sessions. These leaders normally included rabbis, cantors, executive directors, presidents, and whoever else the congregation felt was a central leader. The synagogue leadership team had to be heavily invested in the idea that change needed to happen and that particular changes would be beneficial. If most of the congregation felt that way but one or more key leaders did not, Wolfson explained, nothing would happen. He told the *Atlanta Jewish Times* that "our focus in the Atlanta initiative is to ask the question: Not just how do we reach out to more members, but also how to deepen the relationships. It starts with a welcoming attitude, but it also probably requires a greater investment in synagogue staff and training. The quality is in the details. When we do our research, we talk to people who are shul shoppers. What's their impression?"[34]

One of the goals of Synagogue 3000 is to help revitalize the Jewish High Holy Days. Rosh Hashanah and Yom Kippur are the two or three days when many Jews who usually do not go to synagogue feel obligated to attend services, and so it is the best opportunity congregations have to show how they have changed and how friendly, welcoming, and exciting they can be. Yet there are serious security concerns. Even before September 11, synagogues had been aware that they were potential targets for terrorists. Since that time, it has become essential to take precautions to ensure the safety of those in attendance. Off-duty police officers are now routinely hired to guard synagogue buildings, and some congregations have even installed electronic scanners to check for weapons, just like in airports. This does not help to generate the warm and fuzzy feeling that congregations are looking to create. Some of those who understand the need to run the gauntlet of security find the obligatory High Holy Day tickets to be the most objectionable part of the experience. Many vociferously object to this practice, pointing out that it is likely to drive people away rather than draw them in. Those active on synagogue boards point out that congregations need income to meet their financial obligations and that it's not fair for members to pay thousands of dollars in dues while others saunter in and take what they want without contributing anything. There are clearly two conflicting interests at work, and the Jewish community as a whole must figure out ways to meet everyone's needs without embittering either the insiders or the outsiders.

Ron Wolfson and Shawn Landres explain the conundrum: "The very barriers that guard our gates can discourage those taking new and tentative steps toward affiliated synagogue life. What good is praying for the gates of Heaven to open when the gates of the shul are shut?"[35] They suggest that security personnel can easily be trained in the art of greeting. "You don't have to be fluent in Hebrew or even be Jewish to say 'Shanah tovah.'" They argue that "ultimately, all members of a sacred community have the responsibility of creating a culture of welcome and safety." Security experts recommend "hardening the target" by making it more difficult for a potential terrorist to infiltrate the airport, the office building, or the synagogue. Wolfson and Landres suggest that the best way to "harden the target" is to "soften our hearts. A synagogue whose members care enough to greet one another is a synagogue whose members are its first and most important line of defenses against the unusual, the people or vehicles that don't look quite right, the potential threat." This approach can not only alleviate security concerns, but can go a long way toward creating the warm and welcoming community that unaffiliated American Jews want.[36]

Once the unaffiliated are in the doors, what does the synagogue have to do to "turn them on"? Despite the fact that they are called the *yamim noraim*, the Days of Awe, many American Jews have found the long services to be deathly boring. S3K has identified congregations that are doing interesting things that deviate from the standard model. One year, Craig Taubman led a band for a Rosh Hashanah service at Sinai Temple, Rabbi Sharon Brous offered a mid-afternoon restorative yoga on Yom Kippur and, on another occasion, a disco breakfast, at IKAR, Liz Lerman presented a Yom Kippur creative dance celebration in conjunction with Rabbi Daniel Zemel themed after Daniel Pearl's "I am Jewish" statement at Temple Micah in Washington, D.C., and so forth.[37] The goal is to figure out ways to engage the young adults who will constitute the synagogue population of the coming generation.

Steven M. Cohen explains that younger Jews share an ethos that has four complementary components. In response to their feeling of alienation, they want to take ownership of their Jewish lives, "by constructing their own opportunities for Jewish engagement." In response to the bland communal establishment, they have created "nuanced niches" that provide "differentiated opportunities for expressing Judaism." In response to the coercion that they experienced, they "prize the work of individual initiators." And in response to the divisions that they felt, "they crossed boundaries."[38] One example is the recent surge in grassroots independent minyanim across the country.[39] These communities are spearheaded by "unaffiliated" but very engaged Jews in their twenties and thirties who were not being served by area synagogues. In many ways, they are a second wave of the havurah movement of the 1960s and 1970s, but with a renewed focus on traditional prayer and a focus on the quality of the worship experience. Their organizational model is very different from a synagogue: there is no paid staff, no rabbi, and no cantor. There is no sermon either, just a short (five-minute) dvar Torah during services, although Torah study during the week is often intense and traditional chavruta style. These communities are deeply committed to engaging in social action both locally and globally.

One of the early innovators of this type of community is Kehilat Hadar, a two-thousand-strong group on New York's Upper West Side started in April 2001 by Elie Kaunfer, Ethan Tucker, and Shai Held. Led by members, Hadar has galvanized a population that eluded the traditional synagogue, even among the varied options of New York City. Hadar is devoted to a full liturgy, egalitarian participation, and a spirited approach to services. In 2002, the *Forward* dubbed Hadar a "national model," and, indeed, similarly structured communities have begun in Boston, Washington, D.C., Los Angeles, San Francisco, New Haven, and elsewhere in New York. Already in 2002, the *Forward* named Elie Kaunfer, one of the original founders of Hadar, to their Forward Fifty list, writing that "eighteen months ago a group of three friends gathered in a bar on New York's Upper West Side to pull together what they thought the synagogue-saturated neighborhood lacked—a minyan that combined the traditions, commitment and spirituality of an Orthodox congregation with the egalitarianism of the Conservative movement's Camp Ramah." Almost immediately, Kehilat Hadar "was drawing crowds of more than 200 mostly-single, mostly under-35 Jews, successfully drawing in the demographic slice every Jewish group covets and making itself a national model."[40]

Linda Lantos, who worshipped with Hadar on Yom Kippur, explained why it resonated with her in a way that "normal" synagogues did not. "I didn't grow up in a religiously observant family. . . . In day school I soon made friends who introduced me to Shabbat, and I immediately knew that I wanted it to be a part of my life. It was the warmth and special serenity of the Shabbat atmosphere that I fell in love with in my friends' homes." However, when she began to attend synagogue, "I was surprised that I didn't find the same peace and welcoming warmth. . . . I found many places dishearteningly judgmental and pretentious and I began to wonder how Jews expected to develop a relationship with God when they forgot to treat the people sitting next to them in a synagogue with respect." It was only when she found Hadar that "I felt like I was embracing, and being embraced, by a community. At Hadar, the room is filled with a genuine honesty and sincerity that I had never before experienced. People are eager to learn and eager to teach and there seems to be no line drawn between the two." Lantos added, "I am grateful that there are people with vision, ideology, and unwavering commitment to creating a place like Hadar. It is not only a center for prayer, but a community of sharing and learning that fosters a profound opportunity for both spiritual and intellectual growth. From the first moment at Hadar I felt at home."[41]

In 2006, Kaunfer co-organized a national conference of eleven independent minyans less than five years old. The Nathan Cummings Foundation and Synagogue 3000 provided financial support for the conference. "People are looking for new ways to engage intensely with the substance of Judaism, and these minyanim are an example of that larger spiritual phenomenon. The minyan community allows people to take ownership of their Jewish experience by actively creating a world of prayer, study and social action."[42] In May 2008, Kaunfer received one of five Avi Chai Fellowships that grant $75,000 a year for three years to emerging Jewish leaders. Hadar will use the money to create the first year-round egalitarian yeshiva in North America, presumably similar in many ways to Machon Pardes, a coed yeshiva in Jerusalem that has been popular for the last couple of decades.

Synagogue 3000 looks at the many new sociological studies being done on Jewish young adults, and young adults generally, with a view to apply the lessons learned. For example, the Center for Religion and Civic Culture at the University of Southern California launched a "Congregations That Get It" project to study Christian, Jewish, and Muslim congregations that successfully engage young adults. Over the course of a year, the research team visited congregations in five major cities and held exploratory conversations with young adults, religious leaders, and others who could provide insight into what worked. They focused on fifteen congregations and attempted to figure out how young adults made religious choices and what might be the most effective approaches. Not surprisingly, they discovered that there was no single formula for success, but that there were numerous ways that congregations could engage members of this population.

The researchers found that most of these young adults who were interested in congregational life were not involved out of a sense of familial or religious obligation. This is a startling break with the past. Rather, "their active involvement is focused on their current realities and interests: what matters to them now."[43] They saw that affiliation is a conscience choice that young adults make continuously, based on how they feel at any given moment; they decide how often they want to attend synagogue functions and how actively they want to participate in various types of programs. This emphasis on choice extends to the religion's belief system as well. They may accept certain beliefs and doctrines and not others, or they may change certain religious concepts, either consciously or unconsciously.

But, whether the congregations are targeting young adults, those who are middle aged, or older people, the obstacles to meaningful synagogue renewal are formidable. Congregational leaders may expect to see a dramatic transformation overnight and can become frustrated when that does not happen. Programs that try to get large numbers of people to think long-term about their relationships with each other and with Judaism are fraught with difficulty. One of the biggest problems was and is providing enough help to make sure the congregations implement the program successfully. Temples need the right leadership and enough money to build and maintain momentum. As Rabbi Eric H. Yoffie, the president of the URJ, asked, "How many of these changes can you bring about in the absence of the resources and the personnel to help make it happen?"[44]

Even with enough resources and highly trained staff, change comes slowly and is not always easy to spot. Rabbi Jerome Epstein, the executive vice president of the United Synagogue of Conservative Judaism, summed up the challenge of successful implementation of synagogue transformation: "You've got to divide it between short-term and long-term impacts. There is definitely a culture change that I've seen in the congregations . . . in terms of reaching out to people, thinking about things differently. The big problem is sustaining those changes."[45]

Creating Multiple Opportunities for Pluralistic Forms of Worship

Seagrams business tycoon Edgar M. Bronfman Sr. has recently argued that "an ethos of experimentation is precisely what is needed in order to attract more people to Judaism and create a renaissance in Jewish life." Bronfman had been bored by the standard services being offered, and he set out to understand why congregations seemed to stick with such uninspiring religious programming. "Synagogues have long been bastions of the most conservative tendencies—lengthy, drawn-out services, geshrying over our historical grievances, and focused more on God's needs than on man's yearnings. Instead we should encourage synagogues to become places of joy where people find meaning and fulfillment."⁴⁶

One strategy was to focus on creating a variety of programs that were designed to start on the basis of what people wanted, rather than what rabbis thought they needed. Like Bronfman, the late Charles Schusterman, a Tulsa oilman, felt that something had to be done to revitalize synagogues. He had heard how many American Jews found their congregations uninteresting, and he could see why they might feel that way. Yet he knew that they were more likely to come in contact with a synagogue than with any other kind of Jewish institution. His widow, Lynn Schusterman, remembered: "My late husband Charles was concerned because he realized that people needed synagogue spirituality, but that synagogues were not welcoming. Jews would go twice a year for the High Holy Days, but that basically [ended] their synagogue-going. He wanted to see if there was an idea that would make synagogues more engaging." They knew what it felt like because the Schustermans themselves fell into that category. "We were those Jews who went twice a year."⁴⁷

In December 1999, Charles Schusterman told the *Jewish Telegraph Agency* that "the synagogue needs to serve the central role for Jewish renewal in the Diaspora." To instill Jewish identity in the next generation "we must focus on our religion. Being a cultural Jew is not adequate if we want to provide continuity to our children and grandchildren."⁴⁸ Schusterman started discussing his idea for a synagogue transformation project in late 1997 and began formulating specific plans for the Synagogue: Transformation and Renewal (STAR) foundation in late 1998. The following year, he asked his friends Edgar M. Bronfman Sr. and Michael Steinhardt, a hedge fund manager on Wall Street, to work with him to establish a program for "comprehensive synagogue transformation and renewal across the denominational spectrum."

STAR was funded by foundations established by the three friends—the Charles and Lynn Schusterman Family Foundation, the Jewish Life Network/Steinhardt Foundation, and the Samuel Bronfman Foundation. None of the three were particularly pious—Steinhardt declared himself to be an atheist. But all cared deeply about the quality of Jewish life in the country and were willing to donate substantial funds to help revitalize the synagogue. Schusterman said that he and his friends wanted STAR to go beyond just education and worship. "We may be interested in a bolder approach that would be supporting renewal activities that may be outside the activities of the established institutions. We may see something exciting and provide it funding, disseminate the information about what they're doing so that other synagogues can be stimulated by other ideas."

They spent the first eighteen months researching what could make synagogues work more effectively, identifying and studying congregations such as BJ that had successfully transformed themselves. They gave out challenge grants to already thriving congregations to see "what innovations would bubble up," as Rabbi Hayim Herring, the executive director of STAR, put it. From that process, thirty-six synagogues applied for $85,000 grants to be awarded over a three-year period and twelve were chosen to begin the program in the spring of 2003. They were selected in part because of their variety, including Reform, Conservative, Orthodox, and Reconstructionist congregations that ranged in size from small to large in different parts of the country. The STAR foundation copyrighted a concept that they call Synaplex—a play on cineplex, a multiple theater—to create worship services and educational, social, and cultural programs that all run concurrently on Shabbat. Herring said that the goal of Synaplex is "to have the congregation become the place to be, no matter who you are, what you believe. Our approach is, let's not just talk about a renewed vision of Jewish life; let's give people up front a different picture." Even though it takes four to six months to launch Synaplex, "once it launches you see the results right away. When suddenly you are seeing three, four, five times the number of people, you don't have to imagine how a synagogue can be different."[49]

STAR looks for ways to improve the transmission of Judaism and then seeks to develop programs that can help further that goal. For example, many organizational consultants have long believed that rabbinic education in seminary did not adequately prepare rabbis for their work in congregations, so STAR has launched a program to provide rabbis with new ideas on how to become dynamic organizational leaders. The problem, as Rabbi Matthew Kraus explains it, is that "seminaries are . . . not adequately fostering creative and innovative thinking, sometimes producing rabbis who combine an overdeveloped sense of their own authority coupled with limited ability in the critical reflection necessary for adapting to changing circumstances."[50] HUC-JIR, JTS, YU, and the newer rabbinical schools are all trying to reconceptualize their curriculums to produce more thoughtful and effective rabbis, but the process is a long one.

STAR saw an opportunity to create continuing education programs that could help pulpit rabbis become more effective. The result was the creation of PEER, an executive leadership program for young rabbis, and From Good to Great, a professional development program for rabbis who have been out of seminary for about fifteen years. (I was privileged to be part of the second cohort of the From Good to Great program, which began in June 2007.) Herring explained to me that "when you look at STAR's activities, it really spans a series of programmatic responses to key questions confronting the American Jewish community. So while program is our vehicle for expressing those responses, we're really much more in the co-invention and thinking business."[51]

STAR's best known innovation has been Synaplex, the idea of multiple Shabbat programming. The first congregation to use the word *Synaplex* appears to have been Congregation Emanu-El in San Francisco. In an article in the *Forward* in 1998, Senior Rabbi Stephen S. Pearce is quoted as referring to "Synaplex-multiple worship opportunities." Pearce said that historically his temple had had the attitude that "if you don't like the one service [that the temple offered on a Friday night], go elsewhere." Pearce felt that this narrow-minded thinking was not meeting the needs of the many unaffiliated Jews in San Francisco and was not doing anything for the congregation either. "There was the feeling that the shul was unresponsive [to the needs of the unaffiliated and even the younger members of Emanu-El]." Pearce believed that they needed to "move from the hierarchical/imperious rabbinate to the collaborative rabbinate," and that this has "propelled our growth." Similar congregations that have stuck with the "old model," Pearce explains, are "shriveling on the vine."[52] In addition to Synaplex, Pearce takes pride in Emanu-El's "easy entry Voluntary Dues," which he describes as another Emanu-El invention that has now been copied by forty-plus other congregations. In this system, new members are able to name their own dues commitment, including "nothing." Partially as a result of the voluntary dues concept, Emanu-El's membership has grown from fourteen hundred to twenty-five hundred households. Of course, it helps that Emanu-El has many wealthy members who are able and willing to contribute generously, making this program possible.

Shortly after Pearce arrived at Emanu-El in 1993, the congregation began offering multiple services, including a "traditional" Reform service led by the cantor in the main sanctuary following the classical Reform model; a service of "peace and comfort" that the congregation called "a healing, spiritual service for those in need of extra support at difficult times in their lives"; and a Shabbat La'am, which is "an informal worship experience with an emphasis on contemporary liturgy and music." Two small havurahs, informal social and worship groups that decided independently how they were going to pray, met at the congregation monthly. A "family-sharing Shabbat" featured birthday and family celebrations. A Tot Shabbat was organized for small children who could crawl around and make as much noise as they wanted.

A monthly Young Adult Shabbat was inaugurated in 1996 for those in their twenties and thirties with about forty worshippers. By 2002, they were getting more than one thousand people at each service, which featured a young assistant rabbi and a song leader. In addition to the monthly Friday night service, the young adult community sponsors all sorts of other activities, including "Spookot," a Sukkot celebration held on the site of one of the temple's original cemeteries that is now a park in the Mission Delores area. Working with Synagogue 2000, the congregation initiated a series of Jewish Journey groups that met not for worship, but for a wide variety of special interests ranging from yoga to cooking to walking tours of San Francisco.

Temple Beth Hillel–Beth El in Wynnewood, Pennsylvania has alternative Friday night and Saturday morning services using different liturgies. Rabbi Neil Cooper believes that multiple prayer groups on Shabbat can be extremely beneficial. "It may be stating the obvious, but different people have different spiritual needs. If I had more space to start more minyanim, I would start them. We could have five different davening groups going on here [simultaneously]."[53] His congregation is careful to reinforce the sense that everyone is part of the same congregation, even if they pray separately. All the worshippers from the different services come together after prayers for Kiddush, blessing the Sabbath together. In addition to their alternative adult services, the congregation also has Tot Shabbat, for small children ages two to four; youth services for children of all ages; family services; and a Gesher service for those who have "graduated" from Tot Shabbat. Several times a year, the congregation offers Shabbat Shalom Yeladim, a brief 6 PM service followed by a Shabbat meal and educational program geared for nursery school children. They have a Shabbat service and dinner twice a year for Magic Moments children and offer a Shabbat B'Yachad, which is popularly referred to as a Carlebach-style service because of the quality and quantity of singing.[54] Temple Judea of Palm Beach Gardens, Florida was one of the earliest congregations to work with STAR on Synaplex and has seen their membership increase from under 200 families in 2005 to 528 in 2007. There were other factors at work as well, including a new building, but Rabbi Joel Levine gives much of the credit for his congregation's success to Synaplex. The temple has used the ideas that they learned from Synaplex to organize specialty-themed Shabbat weekends focusing on topics that they think can appeal broadly to people who are not "too religious." They had a special Shavuot Synaplex service that included a guided meditation imagining the giving of the Ten Commandments on Mount Sinai. There was a dramatic reading of the Ten Commandments, a covenant affirmation by the congregation and the sounding of the shofar.

Another Synaplex Shabbat explored Jewish genealogy and Jewish museums around the world. An audiovisual presentation helped worshippers visualize the immigration of Jews to America and genealogical stations helped those interested to get a sense of where their families had come from. One of their most successful programs was on the spirituality of Jewish cuisine. Titled "From Your Mouth to God's Ear," the marketing—which STAR helped them with—focused on drawing in Jews who like to eat. This did not prove to be a very difficult task and they were able to bring in huge crowds for the events scheduled on that weekend. Four stations were set up, each of which dealt with a significant Jewish food: wine, challah, spices, and lamb. Participants spent fifteen minutes at each station learning about Judaism through taste testing and then rotated to the next station.

Levine also inaugurated a Bring Your Pets to Shabbat Synaplex program. This outdoor Kabbalat Shabbat service was held under the temple's large colonnade, where Levine and the temple musicians conducted an upbeat interactive service that focused on teaching the pet owners about Judaism's views on the dignity of animals. During the prayers, Levine stood in front of each pet and owner and read a two-sentence lesson from the Torah, Talmud, or midrash pertaining to respect for animals. Over eighty dogs came with their owners to the service, as well as many cats, birds, and a few more exotic pets. The *oneg* (refreshments after services) included special treats for pets as well as for people. Levine stressed that what was most important was to be open to "out-of-the-box thinking." The synagogue staff meets twice a month for "brainstorming sessions" to consider new programs that can be designed to appeal to those previously untouched and provide them with entertainment as well as spiritual nurturing.[55]

FIGURE 8.5. Rabbi Joel Levine with his wife Susan and Howard Gordon, executive producer of the television show *24*, at a Synaplex event at Temple Judea, Palm Beach Gardens, Florida. *Courtesy of Rabbi Joel Levine*

That is not to say that Synaplex did not have its critics. Rafi Rank, the rabbi of the Midway Jewish Center in Syosset, New York and vice president of the International Rabbinical Assembly, finds the idea excessively commercial. In his Cyber Rav column in the *Jewish Post of New York*, he answered a letter dealing with Synaplex. "Dear Cyber Rav," the person wrote him: "I recently came across an article about an organization, STAR. But the synagogue they are trying to create sounds Hollywoodish, and in some circles has been dubbed a "synaplex" (like cineplex). The synagogues would be offering services as usual, but on top of that, could also offer a variety of cultural events like storytelling, Torah yoga classes, cooking, classes on Israel or business ethics, etc. What's your thoughts about this?" He signed himself "Popcorn Lover While at the Movies, But in Shul?" Rank responded by saying that he was of course in favor of anything that would draw Jews to synagogues. Nevertheless, he was skeptical about whether Synaplex could transform American Jews, rather than just bring them to synagogue. "I think the project will ultimately draw Jews to the synagogues, but I just don't think it will result in creating the kind of Jews that we want—reverent, spiritual, and Jewishly involved. The program is aimed at secular Jews and seems to water down Jewishness with secular or new-age spiritual spins." Rank argues that "it is a project that asks Jews to come to synagogue not for transformation, but for confirmation of who they have become—assimilated, secular, and alienated." Citing the Synaplex Jewish cooking programs, he comments that "to have Jews cooking on Shabbat, even if it is a kosher recipe, is not my idea of success. In a traditional setting, cooking on Shabbat is forbidden. I love yoga too, but to have Jews in synagogue on Shabbat doing yoga is not my idea of success. I want Jews in synagogue who are as adept at davening as they are at flexing their bodies."[56] Rank may be expecting the impossible.

The emphasis in many congregations is on informal social activities that bring together groups with similar interests. The Temple in Atlanta promotes Synaplex as "a flexible format of cultural, educational, spiritual and social events offering expanded opportunities to learn, gather, pray and enjoy together." "Synaplex @ The Temple" featured all the following on a single Friday evening: a family camp-style service accompanied by three guitars at 6:15; "Jews for Cheeses for Twenties and Thirties" only at 6:45; a "Varsity Hamburger and Hot Dog Dinner", also at 6:45; "Tales of Jewish Horror and Suspense" at 7:30; a meditation service at 7:30; "Unwind with Wine for Forties and Older", also at 7:30; a book group at 8:00; "How to Make a Golem at 8:30"; and "Come to the Cabaret!" at 9:30.[57] These Synaplex events are obviously entertainment oriented and occur only periodically. The idea of Synaplex is that if people enjoy coming to temple on Shabbat, they will return, and if Shabbat programming is fun, people will be more open to learning.

There are no definitive answers to any of the issues relating to synagogue renewal, but there is a consensus that new approaches are needed. Even in a time of economic crisis, there are numerous philanthropists who are interested in helping Jewish institutions rethink how they can function more effectively. Things are changing quickly, and they feel that it is crucial to act decisively. Aryeh Rubin, a philanthropist who is active in Miami, New York, and Tel Aviv, stresses the urgency of the situation: "We are living in a unique time in the history of the Jewish people. We have the most prosperity, the most freedom, and the most power that we have had in 2,000 years." Yet at the same time, "we are at a most dangerous time; our physical enemies wish to destroy us, and the culture demon—the attraction of secular society—is leading a goodly number of us to assimilation, and more often than not, to a symptom that is deadly to us as a people, to apathy."[58] If the synagogue can become a spiritual center that both excites the imagination and touches the heart, the hope is that it can break the cycle of apathy and assimilation and create a new paradigm, one that can lead to a vibrant American Judaism in the twenty-first century.[59]

Conclusion

The Future of Judaism in America

In 1207 BCE, a stone column called the Merneptah Stela was commissioned by the pharaoh of Egypt. The text reads as follows:

The chiefs are thrown flat and say, "Peace!"
Not one of them lifts his head among the border enemies.
Libya is seized,
Hatti is pacified,
Gaza is plundered most grievously,
Ashkelon is brought in,
Gezer is captured,
Yanoam is made nonexistent,
Israel is stripped bare, wholly lacking seed,
Hurru has become a widow, due to Egypt.
All lands are together "at peace":
Anyone who stirs is cut down,
By the king of Upper and Lower Egypt, Merneptah.[1]

It is the first and only time that Israel is mentioned in an Egyptian document. What is so ironic is that Merneptah is boasting that Israel had come to the end of its history: "Israel is stripped bare, wholly lacking seed." This pharaoh was one in a long line of enemies who predicted the demise and destruction of the Jewish people.

Many Jews and non-Jews have predicted the demise of Judaism over the course of the last thirty-two hundred years, but the Jewish people—and the Jewish religion—have somehow managed to survive. In an often repeated formulation, Simon Rawidowicz spoke of Israel as "the ever-dying people." He wrote that the world has many different perceptions of the people of Israel, but the people of Israel see themselves in only one way: that of an entity that is constantly on the verge of disappearing: "He who studies Jewish history will readily discover that there was hardly a generation in the Diaspora that did not consider itself the final link in Israel's chain. Each always saw before it the abyss ready to swallow it up." During the course of the last two thousand years, "there was scarcely a generation that while toiling, falling, and rising, again being uprooted and striking new roots, was not filled with the deepest anxiety lest it be fated to stand at the grave of the nation, to be buried in it." Each generation "grieved not only for itself but also for the great past that was going to disappear forever, as well as for the future of unborn generations, who would never see the light of day."[2]

Rawidowicz's essay was originally published in Hebrew in 1948, the year that the State of Israel came into being, and was first translated into English in 1967, the year of the Six-Day War. Despite his extensive references to ancient and medieval pessimists, the author was surely influenced by the euphoria generated by the victory and expansion of the State of Israel. As a result of the miraculous creation of the third Jewish commonwealth, many modern Jews became optimists, believing that, even in the worst of times, they would eventually overcome their adversaries. That may explain why the Jewish holidays that celebrate the victory of the Jews over ancient enemies have become and remain so popular in contemporary America.

However, survival in the twenty-first century will be more difficult to sustain than it ever was before. In the United States, at least, there will need to be new justifications for preserving the Jewish people as a separate religious entity. Contemporary Jews are faced with the irony that Judaism has established itself as an important component of American culture, while Jews themselves are losing much of the distinctiveness that made them a historical people. Intellectual formulations—such as Emil Fackenheim's concept of the 614th mitzvah not to give Hitler a posthumous victory—that served as justifications for the preservation of Judaism in the past may not prove as convincing and effective in the coming decades.

The future of Judaism depends on many factors that are not determinable. First and foremost is the social, political, and religious course of the State of Israel. Despite the hope that Israel would find a way to live in peace with its neighbors, this has not happened, and it seems almost certain that there will be a great deal of conflict and possibly even warfare in the near future. The State of Israel faces an ongoing conflict with the Palestinians, but also has to plan for the possibility that more distant enemies, particularly Iran, might launch a preemptive attack using nonconventional weaponry. There is an even greater possibility that the Iranian government, or a faction within the leadership, might transfer nuclear material for a "dirty bomb" to Hezbollah, Hamas, or Al-Qaeda. While the thought is too horrible to contemplate, the destruction of the State of Israel would be a devastating blow to Judaism as a religion and the Jews as a people.

Barring any such catastrophe, there is still a great deal of uncertainty. Relations between Orthodox and non-Orthodox Jews have been steadily deteriorating. The two groups are rapidly moving toward nonrecognition of one another, and this is already leading to the creation of two separate Jewish peoples. Unfortunately, there is ample historical precedent for this sad state of disunity. There have been numerous schisms throughout the course of Jewish history, and the damage that they did is well documented. Unless there is some development that helps the parties to reconcile, there will be two or more groups of Jews with different basic beliefs and values, different normative practices, and different definitions of who is a member of their religious group.

Even though the danger of schism would seem to be serious enough to warrant an emergency response, it seems likely that the American Jewish community will continue to move apart. Despite efforts by the United Jewish Communities, private family foundations, and others to keep the entire Jewish community united, nothing substantive has been achieved. An era of dual denominationalism is developing, supplanting the tripartite division of American Judaism that emerged in the early years of the twentieth century. While it seems likely that each of the existing movements will continue to maintain their partisan institutions in the short term, Rabbi Paul Menitoff's thesis that the religious middle will collapse over the next two decades will likely turn out to be largely true.

In Israel, the stark division between the Orthodox and the secular is likely to continue, despite the best efforts of the non-Orthodox denominations and new indigenous expressions of Judaism among Israel's "secular" population. Should the Orthodox rabbinate be able to establish even greater control over religious life in the State of Israel, the possibility exists for an open Kulturkampf. Hundreds of thousands of Soviet Jews immigrated to Israel with non-Jewish family members, and they deeply resent the Orthodox chief rabbinate's restrictive policies on marriage, divorce, and burial. American Jews are increasingly angry that their non-Orthodox religious movements are not recognized in the State of Israel. Their response has so far been to increase fund-raising efforts and build educational institutions and synagogues around the country, but they may become far more belligerent if the Israeli response continues to be arrogant and condescending.

A hint of this possibility emerged recently when Israeli president Moshe Katzav refused to address Eric H. Yoffie, the leader of the URJ, with the title *rabbi*. While this may seem like a trivial slight, the symbolic importance of the president of the State of Israel refusing to implicitly recognize the legitimacy of Reform Judaism is disturbing at best. Since an emotional connection with Israel is one of the basic building blocks of American Jewish identity, an open ideological battle between the Orthodox establishment of Israel and the non-Orthodox religious denominations of the Diaspora would have a devastating impact on the American Jewish community. This scenario is unlikely, however, if only because of the high number of intermarried immigrants from the former Soviet Union. The power of these former Soviet immigrants is likely to force a greater separation between religion and personal life in Israel.

The good news is that Jewish religious life continues to demonstrate signs of vitality and effervescence, both in the State of Israel and in the Diaspora. There are numerous yeshivas in which Orthodox men (and now a few women as well) are studying advanced Talmud. In fact, it is frequently stated that there are more full-time yeshiva students in the State of Israel today than there ever were in Eastern Europe. Likewise, there are thousands of full-time Talmud students in the United States. The Lakewood Yeshiva in New Jersey alone has over one thousand full-time advanced students. The non-Orthodox have likewise shown a renewed commitment to serious Jewish study, and several innovative programs such as the Melton Program, Me'ah, and the Skirball Center for Adult Jewish Learning have shown positive educational results. I taught a course this past fall at the Siegal College of Judaic Studies via video cam, allowing students from all over North America to come together in a virtual classroom every Tuesday night. This would have been technologically impossible just a couple of years ago. There has been a proliferation of independent minyanim (prayer groups), an explosion of Jewish studies courses and programs on university campuses, and the development of all sorts of cutting-edge cultural activities. While many Jews lose interest in Judaism, others deepen their ongoing involvement, and some find their way back to the faith that their parents or grandparents abandoned.

But, if some are returning to Judaism, it is not the exact same religion their grandparents knew. American Jews today see their Judaism very differently than did earlier generations. If most Jews in the 1940s and 1950s saw being Jewish and being American as separate components of their identity, that is no longer the case. American and Jewish values are increasingly seen as indistinguishable, a process Sylvia Barack Fishman calls coalescence. It is not just that the authority of historical Judaism has been diminished, but the distinction between what is Jewish and what is American has been effectively eliminated. "The boundaries have disappeared and the two belief systems have merged into one coalesced whole widely known as 'Judaism.'"[3] American and Jewish principles have become "hybridized." Liberal American values such as pluralism, democracy, inclusivity, and so forth are now seen as Jewish values. Likewise, elements of Judaism are now seen as part of American culture and society.

Many of the X, Y, and millennial generations embrace panculturalism, the desire to integrate various aspects of multiple cultures. They have an interest in dibs and dabs of Jewish culture, but they don't want to be defined by that interest. In many cases, they actually reject the very idea of Jewish peoplehood upon which Judaism was historically based. Joey Kurtzman, the senior editor of Jewcy.com, recently engaged in an interesting conversation with Professor Jack Wertheimer on Jewcy's Web site. Kurtzman was responding to the question "Is it true that American life has annihilated Jewish peoplehood?" He answers that it seems plain to him that the answer is yes. "Modern American life is the most corrosive acid ever to hit the ghetto walls. Young American Jews are whoring after Moab so fervently that the boundaries between Israel and Moab are being washed away. We're not merely influenced by the non-Jewish world—we're inseparable from it." After the exchange of a couple of letters, Kurtzman tells Wertheimer that "the Jewish-American leadership must eventually confront the reality that Judaism cannot thrive amongst a significant proportion of young American Jews unless we jettison the language and ideology of peoplehood."[4]

With this sort of broad universalistic attitude, it is going to be hard for synagogues—which historically have stressed the ethnic component of the Jewish religion—to attract and retain the new generation. Aware of this, some of the more forward-thinking Jewish philanthropies have created sophisticated cultural centers to draw in Jewish panculturalists. But it is difficult to hold their interest and nearly impossible to convince them to make a serious commitment. They are attracted to the latest trend and may move on before even the most adroit organization can begin programming for it. These Jewish hipsters may love Jon Stewart's comedy and Matisyahu's reggae, but they are not interested in Jewish institutions that are based on a long-term commitment to community. They "resent" lectures about not "marrying out" and are "offended" by pressure to conform to traditional Jewish norms. Many are so far removed from any normative Judaism that they do not even understand why their more traditional peers are surprised by their attitudes and behaviors.

Optimists are hopeful that the Jewish community can find ways to engage the as yet not committed; maybe they can. Any Judaism that the iPod or digital generation creates will almost by definition be constantly evolving and probably transitory. Some of the more creative ones will certainly use Jewish themes in their novels, films, and plays, and Americans will continue to hear about Jewish neuroses and how Jews deal with their identity issues. The question that I implicitly try to raise in this book is how that might affect the future contours of American Jewish religious belief and practice. The answer to that is unknown. What is known is that increasing numbers of American Jews no longer make a direct connection between their Jewish ethnic background and Judaism as a religion. Further, they feel that they can embrace a number of different identities that either may emerge naturally from their family and educational background or may be self-selected.

Historian David Biale suggests that "instead of bemoaning these multiple identities, Jews need to begin to analyze what it means to negotiate them and, by so doing, perhaps even learn to embrace them." It is necessary to regard intermarriage and other developing trends as "creating new forms of identity, including multiple identities, that will reshape what it means to be Jewish in ways we can only begin to imagine." Biale asks what these multiple identities may mean for the future of American Judaism: "Whether these new forms of identity spell the end of the Jewish people or its continuation in some new guise cannot be easily predicted because there is no true historical precedent for this development."

There are certainly a number of historical epochs that do have the potential to teach us valuable lessons. The current shift in self-identification could be compared to the tremendous religious changes that took place after the Roman destruction of the Second Temple. At the end of the first century CE, Rabban Yochanan Ben Zakkai assembled a small group of sages in Yavneh and created new ways to remember traditional practices. With the Temple gone, there was no way to provide the ritual setting for the kohanim (priests) to perform their rituals. With the Temple gone, there was no way to offer the sacrifices. With the Temple gone, much of what had been known as Judaism up until that time was obsolete. The sages needed to respond to a radical new reality and they did so.

The sages of the classical rabbinic tradition reinterpreted biblical commandments and reinvented contemporary Judaism for their times. Biale suggests that American Jews are faced with just such a moment right now and that creative leaders can respond with an equal amount of transformative zeal. "Such moments of revolutionary transformation are always fraught with peril, but whatever one's view of it, the task for those concerned with the place of Jews in America is not to condemn or condone but rather to respond creatively to what is now an inevitable social process."[5]

Afterword

Rabbi Zalman Schachter-Shalomi

With great pleasure I write this afterword to Dana Evan Kaplan's *Contemporary American Judaism: Transformation and Renewal.* The book is a masterful and sympathetic portrayal of American Judaism in the early years of the twenty-first century. Kaplan understands the difference between what is important and what is not and is able to paint a detailed picture of the Judaism of the future without apologetics but with a lot of color. Kaplan touches on the right points in just the right way. He draws on his exhaustive knowledge as both a scholar and a pulpit rabbi. One of the things that I liked most was that Kaplan stresses that *American* Judaism is not just Judaism in the United States but rather is Judaism that has been deeply influenced by America (just as other Judaisms have been influenced by and in turn have internalized the landscape and culture they lived in).

Kaplan adeptly describes how American Judaism developed since World War II and then presents his thesis that the preexisting status quo has been shattered. American Jews are now insisting that their Judaism needs to be spiritual, something that was foreign to them until recently. It is important that we become aware that what goes on in the name of spirituality today is different than what people have subsumed under that word before. In the past, spirituality was connected with a body-hating asceticism that saw in the sensual life that evil which it wanted to purge from itself. This is no longer the primary meaning of the word. With our seeing the image of earth from outer space for the first time, a new awareness came to us; we are intrinsic to the life of earth. The words in the second portion of the Sh'ma' "that you may live heavenly days right here on this earth" had taken on a new sheen. The new scientific cosmology freed many Jews from a literal reading of the Bible, and, because they've gotten to know our neighbors and their religions and seen the values they aspire to live, we abandoned the triumphalism of our European tradition. This was a gradual process that began with the onset of the Second World War, the Holocaust, and the immigration of the survivors.

Ram Dass has said that, from an economic point of view, India is certainly a developing country, but, from a spiritual perspective, the United States is the country that is just now developing. Western society has invested heavily in intellect but unfortunately less so in emotions and very little in spirituality. In recent years, Americans have begun embracing spiritual approaches to life, and this has now begun to transform American Judaism. Kaplan's book does a terrific job in chronicling this dramatic shift, including the impact of the Jewish Renewal movement. The assumptions that guided American Jews have lost their power and new approaches are just now developing.

Every group has a mythology of its own, and, as Kaplan describes in chapter 1, the mythologies that were working up to the Holocaust have collapsed. The mythology that had to do with "God is always going to protect us" collapsed on the one hand. On the other hand, the idealistic Zionist dreams of the early twentieth century have also now collapsed in Israel, indicated, for example, by everything that has happened with the kibbutzim. So now we are in a situation where we are looking at a quality arising that is happening everywhere in the world. New forces have emerged that are responding to the spiritual needs of the Jewish people. For example, in Russia and the former Soviet republics, you can see where Chabad has done a fantastic job in reestablishing a wide net of Jewish bases there. However, this creates a problem because liberal Jews have also tried to set something up in those places and they have encountered a great deal of turf conflict. And they haven't been able to do what they needed to do. We will see what happens in the coming years there.

Kaplan's book provoked me to think back on the past. When I go back to 1968–69, it was a time of a great awakening. Most of the things that had to do with reestablishing the infrastructure for Jewish Life—to have yeshivas there and to have kosher slaughterhouses and mikveh and all the other necessities for a halachic life—had been already set up. As soon as they could, traditional Jews who had recently arrived in the United States created an enclave for themselves to keep goyish America out of their circle and protect their children. But the young people who did not belong to the immigrant population were those who broke away from it because they were looking at something else. They were looking at something much more universal. At that time, the *Whole Earth Catalog* came out, and I looked at the *Whole Earth Catalog* with envy. I felt that this was a wonderful model for us and that we need to do something like this for Jews. That year I was teaching and studying at Brandeis. In appreciation for their hospitality, I undertook to teach a course in psychology of religion. The people who were the first editors of the Jewish catalog, the Strassfelds and Richard Siegel, were among my students, and some of the term papers that were submitted for the work they did with me began the *Jewish Catalog*. This was simultaneous with the beginning of the havurah movement in which I participated. How were we to create a fusion of the burgeoning aquarian culture with the Judaism that we wanted to experience with intensity?

And, in fact, the retooling that was necessary was very hard because there was a deep ambivalence. On the one hand, Chabad people were saying, "America is not our friend; we must beware that it will not corrode our values and culture—and we have to do it exactly as we did in Europe" and, at the same time, they got very quickly media-happy, as you can see when you look on the Web and see the presence of Chabad all over the place. Then there was the other issue too: the rebbe, who was a charismatic, made a very important and risky and yet valuable shift. He moved from charisma to institution and therefore created a franchise of Chabad Houses all over the world that fit with the current communication possibilities that we have. If you follow Teilhard de Chardin, you realize that we are moving to a place that he called the "noosphere"—that is to say, how information moves from one place to another very quickly, and the more we are connected, the more we become one. Then came the moonwalk, and with it the pictures that came from outer space—seeing earth from outer space, and along with it came Gaia consciousness, as if to say, "earth is alive." If earth is alive, how are we to look at the religions? It became pretty clear that every religion is a vital organ of the planet—that you cannot play triumphalism as we used to play before.

This made a great deal of difference, and so while all the institutions that we have in the United States are based on what the emerging industrial age/machine age of that time—I am thinking of Benjamin Franklin, for example—and from then on, they were thinking in those terms of building machinery. So they built the Congress like this machinery, and our entire government is built on this machinery, and the banking business is built on the machinery, and none of the people have yet seen what they needed to see—that we are organically connected and that machines do not offer the best cosmology and ethical action directives, but a cosmology that is organismic does offer that. And this is what came through as I was working on my book *The Paradigm Shift* and showing that Judaism has to go through a paradigm shift from its now obsolete point of view. We have to abandon the Deuteronomic point of view of Jewish triumphalism that *mashiach* is coming and then all the goyim finding out they were wrong to knowing that we are looking at something that is a lot more organismic.

When I published my book *Jewish with Feeling*, the title I wanted to give it was *If You Are So Universal Why Be Jewish?* and this is the big question that still remains, so as you watch American Judaism grow it is trying to let go of its triumphalism. It is having trouble making a shift in its new system, to find out how can we keep our integrity without being destroyed ourselves and yet say that other religions are legit too. That's the reason why I use the organismic view that every religion is a vital organ, and you can't expect that the whole body should be liver or the whole body should be bone or heart or brain. They all have to collaborate with each other in keeping the world alive. In fact, the big issue today is how to heal the planet, and on this we see the shift going very very strongly on the part of Judaism too. Eco-kosher—which Kaplan discusses in chapter 2—and all kinds of other things that have to do with service and with recognition of other religions as also ways in which God communicates with us.

Kaplan's book will take us into the historical panorama, and we will now begin to understand the continuity that shaped us. The more we know how we came to be, the better we know how to steer. We cannot steer just by the rearview mirror, and you're asking me the question what do I see through the windshield now about the future, and about this I have to say two things. One, most of my life I was sort of thirty years ahead of the pack because I had a wider event horizon to see things and other people were looking through the rearview mirror, but now that I am coming toward the close of my life, I don't see so far ahead. But one thing I do see, that the question of how to reformat halacha so that it should fit into the current emerging technology—not the old technology, but the emerging technology—in which we have to start rethinking what do we mean by work that is forbidden on Shabbos and that is not, and to go with the old agricultural hunter/gatherer system of handicraft is not the only way in which we could define work as forbidden. On the other hand, the issue of hobby has to be opened up to people. Is a hobby work when I'm not interested in selling? So Shabbos is going to be reunderstood. What will be reunderstood about kashrut will depend on our understanding of recycling because even the most observantly created matzah will have molecules in it that in the recycling spaceship earth belonged to something that wasn't kosher at one time, and, the more people are going to start looking into these things, halacha will change.

The other thing that is definitely going to change is the input of women. This will happen with the next pope in some way and it will happen with Jews too. Right now we're trying very very hard to maintain the understanding of the rabbinic hegemony and say that that came down from Moses at Sinai and cannot be changed. There is an emerging movement to start saying Torah not only comes from Sinai but it also comes Min HaShamayim, from God and in the present. And some people are even speaking of Torah coming from earth, what we can learn from Gaia from our planet in which the divine voice speaks to us. So all these things I foresee for the future. The interesting thing is how God stirs the genetic pot so that in twenty years we will find—or even before that, fifteen years—we will find many brides and grooms under the huppah that did not come from Jewish ethnic stock. And that is also part of the adoption thing and so on, so forth. So there is a mixing going on that we cannot predict at this point where it is going to go.

There are two things happening. One is that there are a large number of people who Judaism likes to call psycho-Semitic souls. That's to say, people who feel an affinity for Judaism, and if I go mystical I would say that those people were recycled souls from the Holocaust who this time decided not to be born as Jews. But we need to make special space for them and treat them in such a way that they will be happy to be with us. Furthermore, at one point we used to always think that the fence of halachah has to be firm so people shouldn't be able to slip out. And that a loophole has to be closed up. But, on the other hand, I find that right now we have to make loopholes for people to come in. There's a great deal of immigration going on in these intermarriages, and the way in which we can bring them in clearly and with guidance and not only let it happen by happenstance—this is going to be very important in the future. Kaplan spends much of the second half of his book describing the new manifestations of Jewish spirituality, in particular the baal teshuvah movement, Chabad, and Jewish Renewal. These groups have become immensely influential. So how did this happen? In the beginning, people would go to shul for their Judaism, and then they would go to the growth center or to the zendo for their spirituality, and more and more it has happened that these things became joined together. And so the issue . . . people don't want to spin their wheels when they come to shul. They have become more and more aware through psychotherapy and spiritual work that their Judaism has to deliver some transforming. It has to give them transformation, as Kaplan describes in his book. If I want to live better and be more conscious and so on, I must have a Judaism that allows me to do that.

There's another issue that has to do with energy. The shuls where energy is low have become "mazel tov facilities," what Kaplan calls "bar mitzvah factories." In each case, we are clear what is happening. These are facilities that help people celebrate life cycle events, but they don't create any shift and change in them. There were new models budding up in different places that the average synagoguegoer was not aware of for a long time. But once you attended something, you saw something. Look what Shlomo Carlebach did. I call him the *genius of virtuous reality* because when he told you stories he would want you to get into a virtuous feeling or a virtuous behavior and then it was also important that that person would then start to thinking, "Oy, if only I could live that way. That would be so wonderful." And that yearning remained and that music—take a look—it's become public domain, and hardly anybody knows where it's from. You look at my tallit, the one with the rainbow colors, and nobody knows where it's from, but people are buying it because it corresponds. You know once you go from black and white to color on the television you want the same thing about your religion too. And once you allow for color then it's not black and white, I am right and you are wrong, you have a blue Judaism and I have a green Judaism, and if you go to spiral dynamics then it begins to make a whole lot of sense.

Kaplan asks me if I am optimistic about the future of American Judaism. That's the reason why I speak about a vital organ. The earth cannot sustain itself without having vital organs, and Judaism is a vital organ. Right now Judaism is, on the one hand, anemic. On the other hand, Islam is, at this point, high fevered and has an inflammation. Christianity has got its schizophrenia between the fundamentalists and the others. But, you know, these changes are going to take place, as somebody said, "one funeral at a time." If you ask will the seminaries continue as they were in the past, at least for another fifty to sixty years, but by and large we see the people coming out of the other seminaries join groups like ours because the *haverschaft*, the relationship, the spiritual intimacy that's available—this is what the people are looking for. And if you see what the rabbis preach about these days, they are not making big pilpul, they are not doing a lot of midrash that doesn't have anything to do with life. They're trying to give people notions about life. One of the best mirrors that I can find today of American Jewish emotional and spiritual expression is in Jack Riemer's sermons. Did you ever hear them? Read through them and you can see that they all deal with American issues.

As Kaplan accurately quotes me at the end of chapter 6, I believe that Judaism is like an ancient tree, and the core of any mature tree is old wood. The old wood is crucial to maintaining the tree's structure, its ability to withstand the changing winds, but no growth is going on there. The living processes that are the growth of the tree, its message to the future, take place only in the tree's newest and outermost ring. We today are that outermost ring, and the growing is up to us. Of course we need to remember and understand our past as we grow into the future. Any new growth must spring from the DNA that created, and continues to create, the Jewish organism. Our texts, our history, our stories, our traditions, are all part of the fundamental blueprint of our faith. The better we learn to listen to the voices of the past, the more we can learn of ancient wisdom that, with a little imagination, is still precious and applicable today. But religion becomes oppressive when we have too much preservation and not enough innovation. Some things the past cannot teach us. These things we must learn from the present—our present—and our future. Our task as new cells is not to respond to the weather of yesteryear; we have to deal with the challenges of today. And so when I'm saying I'm optimistic, I'm optimistic that something will emerge, you know. I'm as optimistic as I am when I see a newborn baby.

Notes

Preface

1. Louis Jacobs, "Judaism: The Religion, Philosophy, and Way of Life for the Jews," *Encyclopedia Judaica* (Jerusalem: Keter, 1972), 10:383–397. See also Jacob Neusner, "Defining Judaism," in Jacob Neusner and Alan J. Avery-Peck, eds., *The Blackwell Companion to Judaism* (Oxford: Blackwell, 2000), 3–19; the Jacobs essay has been reprinted in Neusner and Avery-Peck, *The Blackwell Reader in Judaism*, 3–8.

2. Gershom Scholem, *On Jews and Judaism in Crisis* (New York: Schocken, 1980).

3. Jacob Neusner, *Between Time and Eternity: The Essentials of Judaism* (Belmont, CA: Wadsworth, 1975), 6.

4. Correspondence with Alan Avery-Peck, June 29, 2007.

5. Jonathan Z. Smith, *Imagining Religion: From Babylon to Jonestown* (Chicago: University of Chicago Press 1982), 1–18.

6. Michael L. Satlow, *Creating Judaism: History, Tradition, Practice* (New York: Columbia University Press, 2006).

7. Michael L. Satlow, "Defining Judaism: Accounting for 'Religions' in the Study of Religion," *Journal of the American Academy of Religion* 74.4 (December 2006): 839.

8. Martin Buber, *On Judaism*, ed. Nahum N. Glatzer (New York: Schocken, 1967), 16.

Introduction

1. George Gallup, Jr., and Jim Castelli, *The People's Religion: American Faith in the Nineties* (New York: Macmillan, 1989), xv.

2. Robert N. Bellah, Richard Madsen, William M. Sullivan, Ann Swidler, and Steven M. Tipton, *Habits of the Heart: Individualism and Commitment in American Life* (New York: Harper and Row, 1985), 221.

3. Ibid., 235.

4. Michael Luo, "With Yoga, Comedy, and Parties, Synagogues Entice Newcomers," *New York Times*, April 4, 2006, www.nytimes.com/2006/04/04/nyregion/04synagogue.html.

5. Dana Evan Kaplan, *American Reform Judaism: An Introduction* (New Brunswick, NJ: Rutgers University Press, 2003).

1. A Historical Overview from 1945

1. Jessica Branch, "A Smart Beauty Who Claimed the Throne," *Forward*, http://www.forward.com/issues/1998/98.12.04/fastforward.html.

2. Salo Wittmayer Baron, "The Second World War and Jewish Community Life," *Steeled by Adversity: Essays and Addresses on American Jewish Life* (Philadelphia: Jewish Publication Society of America, 1971), 454.

3. Correspondence with Jonathan D. Sarna, May 12, 2007.

4. Nathan Glazer and Daniel Patrick Moynihan, *Beyond the Melting Pot: The Negroes, Puerto Ricans, Jews, Italians, and Irish of New York City* (Cambridge: Harvard University Press, 1963), 290–291.

5. Robert N. Bellah, "Civil Religion in America," in Bellah, *Beyond Belief: Essays on Religion in a Post-traditional World* (New York: Harper and Row, 1970), 170.

6. Correspondence with Nathan Glazer, April 23, 2007.

7. Will Herberg, *Protestant, Catholic, Jew: An Essay in Religious Sociology* (Garden City, NY: Anchor/Doubleday, 1955), 46.

8. Ibid., 23.

9. Ruby Jo Reeves Kennedy, "Single or Triple Melting Pot? Intermarriage Trends in New Haven, 1870–1940," *American Journal of Sociology* 49.4 (January 1944), cited in Herberg, *Protestant, Catholic, Jew*, 33.

10. Herberg, *Protestant, Catholic, Jew*, 260.

11. Byron L. Sherwin, "Thinking Judaism Through: Jewish Theology in America," in ana Evan Kaplan, ed., *The Cambridge Companion to American Judaism* (New York: Cambridge University Press, 2005), 117–132.

12. Joshua Loth Liebman, *Peace of Mind* (New York: Simon and Schuster, 1946).

13. Statement of Purpose, *Judaism*, inside front cover.

14. Abraham Joshua Heschel, *God in Search of Man: A Philosophy of Judaism* (New York: Farrar, Straus, and Giroux, 1955), 3.

15. Nahum N. Glatzer, *Franz Rosenzweig: His Life and Thought* (New York: Schocken, 1953); "'I Am a Memory Come Alive': Nahum Glatzer and the Legacy of German-Jewish Thought in America." *Jewish Quarterly Review* 94.1 (Winter 2004): 123–148.

16. Abba Hillel Silver, *Where Judaism Differs* (New York: Collier, 1989), vii. The original text was entitled *Where Judaism Differed* and was published by Macmillan in 1956.

17. Nathan Glazer, *American Judaism* (Chicago: University of Chicago Press, 1957, 1972, 1988), 132; correspondence with Nathan Glazer, March 12, 2007.

18. Marshall Sklare and Joseph Greenblum, *Jewish Identity on the Suburban Frontier*, 2d ed. (Chicago: University of Chicago Press, 1979), 57.

19. Jenna Weissman Joselit, "Lighting the Way," *Forward*, December 1, 2006, http://www.forward.com/articles/lighting-the-way/.

20. Elizabeth Ehrlich, *Miriam's Kitchen* (New York: Penguin, 1997), 179.

21. Herberg, *Protestant, Catholic, Jew*, 260.

22. Barbara Ward, "Report to Europe on America," *New York Times Magazine*, June 20, 1954, cited in Herberg, *Protestant, Catholic, Jew*, 1.

23. Jonathan Sarna, *American Judaism* (New Haven: Yale University Press, 2004), 291.

24. George Goodwin, "Wright's Beth Sholom Synagogue," *American Jewish Journal* 86 (September 1998): 325–348.

25. Percival Goodman and Paul Goodman, "Modern Artist as Synagogue Builder," *Commentary* 7 (January 1949): 52.

26. Eugene B. Borowitz, *A New Jewish Theology in the Making* (Philadelphia: Westminster, 1968), 33; Eugene B. Borowitz, *The Mask Jews Wear: The Self-Deceptions of American Jewry* (New York: Simon and Schuster, 1973).

27. Andrew Greeley, *The Denominational Society* (Glenview, IL: Scott, Foresman, 1972), 137–139.

28. Eli Lederhendler, *New York Jews and the Decline of Urban Ethnicity, 1950–1970* (Syracuse: Syracuse University Press, 2001), 67.

29. Susannah Heschel, "Following in My Father's Footsteps: Selma Forty Years Later," *Vox of Dartmouth* 23.4 (April 4, 2005), http://www.dartmouth.edu/˜vox/0405/0404/heschel.html.

30. Arthur Hertzberg, *A Jew in America: My Life and a People's Struggle for Identity* (San Francisco: Harper San Francisco, 2002), 403.

31. Glazer, *American Judaism*, 114.

32. Peter Novick, *The Holocaust in American Life* (Boston: Houghton Mifflin, 1993), 133.

33. Emil Fackenheim, *To Mend the World: Foundations of Future Jewish Thought* (New York: Schocken, 1982), 308.

34. Emil Fackenheim, *The Jewish Return Into History: Reflections in the Age of Auschwitz and a New Jerusalem* (New York: Schocken, 1978), 19–24.

35. Fackenheim, *To Mend the World*, 295.

36. Irving Greenberg, *Voluntary Covenant* (New York: National Jewish Resource Center, 1982), 17.

37. Melvin Urofsky, *We Are One: American Jewry and Israel* (Garden City, NY: Doubleday, 1978), 31.

38. Arthur Hertzberg, "Israel and American Jewry," *Commentary* 44 (August 1967): 69–73.

39. Jack Wertheimer, *A People Divided: Judaism in Contemporary America* (Hanover, NH: Brandeis University Press, 1997), 30.

40. Jacob Neusner, *Death and Birth of Judaism: The Impact of Christianity, Secularism, and the Holocaust on Jewish Faith* (New York: Basic Books, 1987), 279.

41. Steven T. Rosenthal, *Irreconcilable Differences? The Waning of the American Jewish Love Affair with Israel* (Hanover, NH: Brandeis University Press, 2001); Steven T. Rosenthal, "Long-Distance Nationalism: American Jews, Zionism, and Israel," in Dana Evan Kaplan, ed., *The Cambridge Companion to American Judaism* (New York: Cambridge University Press, 2005), 209–224.

42. Michael E. Staub, *Torn at the Roots: The Crisis of Jewish Liberalism in Postwar America* (New York: Columbia University Press, 2002), 280–308.

43. Paul Wilkes, *And They Shall Be My People* (New York: Grove-Atlantic Monthly, 1994–1995), 224.

44. Michael Strassfeld, Sharon Strassfeld, and Richard Siegel, *The First Jewish Catalog: A Do-It-Yourself Kit* (Philadelphia: Jewish Publication Society, 1974).

45. Rodger Kamenetz, "Has the Jewish Renewal Movement Made It Into the Mainstream?" *Moment* (December 1994): 42.

46. Marshall Sklare, "The Greening of Judaism," *Observing America's Jews* (Hanover: Brandeis University Press, 1993), 75–86.

47. Rodger Kamenetz, *Stalking Elijah: Adventures with Today's Jewish Mystical Masters* (San Francisco: HarperSanFrancisco, 1997), 247.

48. Harold S. Kushner, *When Bad Things Happen to Good People* (New York: Avon, 1981), 10.

49. Abraham Cohen, "Theology and Theodicy: On Reading Harold Kushner," *Modern Judaism* 16 (1996): 229–261.

50. Calvin Goldscheider, "Demography and Jewish Survival," in M. Himmelfarb and V. Baras, eds., *Zero Population Growth: For Whom?* (Westport, CT: Greenwood, 1978), 128, proceedings of the American Jewish Committee Conference on Population and Intergroup Relations, New York, 1975.

51. Jack Wertheimer, "Recent Trends in American Judaism," *American Jewish Year Book* 89 (1989): 162.

52. Samuel C. Heilman, *Portrait of American Jews: The Last Half of the Twentieth Century* (Seattle: University of Washington Press, 1995), 74.

53. Laurie Goodstein, "Democrats: The Observances; Lieberman Balances Private Faith with Life in the Public Eye," *New York Times*, August 18, 2000, A:19.

2. The Reengagement with Spirituality

1. Arthur Green, *Restoring the Aleph: Judaism for the Contemporary Seeker: A Study Guide* (Aventura, FL: Targum Shlishi, 1998).

2. Debra Nussbaum Cohen, "From 'Om to 'Shema,'" *Jewish Week*, February 2, 2001, 18.

3. Lawrence A. Hoffman, *The Journey Home: Discovering the Deep Spiritual Wisdom of the Jewish Tradition* (Boston: Beacon, 2002), 1.

4. J. J. Goldberg, "The Lure of the East," *Jerusalem Report*, November 7, 1991, 30.

5. Wade Clark Roof, *A Generation of Seekers: The Spiritual Journeys of the Baby Boom Generation* (San Francisco: HarperSanFrancisco, 1993), 70.

6. Jeffrey K. Salkin, "How to Be a Truly Spiritual Jew and Avoid the Pitfalls of Quick-Fix Religious Consumerism," in Allan L. Smith, ed., *Where We Stand: Jewish Consciousness on Campus* (New York: UAHC, 1997), 120.

7. Wendy Kaminer, "Why We Love Gurus," *Newsweek*, October 20, 1997, 60.

8. The Spirituality Institute at Metivta, brochure, 2000.

9. Interview with Gail Greenfield, March 14, 2006.

10. Arthur A. Goren, "A 'Golden Decade' for American Jews: 1945–1955," *Studies in Contemporary Jewry* 8:9.

11. Correspondence with Steven M. Cohen, March 5, 2007.

12. Charles S. Liebman and Steven M. Cohen, *Two World of Judaism: The Israeli and American Experiences* (New Haven: Yale University Press, 1990), 13–34.

13. Helen Fremont, *After Long Silence* (New York: Dell, 1999), back cover.

14. Sanhedrin 44a; *Shulchan Aruch*, Even Ha-Ezer 4:5,19.

15. Sara Bershtel and Allen Graubard, *Saving Remnants: Feeling Jewish in America* (New York: Free Press, 1992), 42.

16. Lawrence Kushner, "The Tent Peg Business: Some Truths About Synagogues," *New Traditions: Explorations in Judaism* (Spring 1988), http://urj.org/worship/letuslearn/sl17tentpeg/.

17. Hoffman, *The Journey Home*, 214.

18. Wade Clark Roof, *Spiritual Marketplace: Baby Boomers and the Remaking of American Religion* (Princeton: Princeton University Press, 1999), 4.

19. Zalman Schachter-Shalomi, with Joel Segel, *Jewish with Feeling: A Guide to Meaningful Jewish Practice* (New York: Riverhead, 2005), 81.

20. Ibid., 116.

21. Ibid., 86.

22. Ibid., 82.

23. Correspondence with Jack Steinhorn, November 26, 2007.

24. Alan Wolfe, *The Transformation of American Religion: How We Actually Live Our Faith* (Chicago: University of Chicago Press, 2003), 183.

25. Richard H. Schwartz, "Vegetarianism: A Global and Spiritual Imperative?" in Michael Lerner, ed., *Best Jewish Writing 2002* (San Francisco: Jossey-Bass, 2002), 132.

26. Schachter-Shalomi, *Jewish with Feeling*, 152.

27. Arthur Waskow, "Eco-Kashrut: Environmental Standards for What and How We Eat," http://www.MyJewishLearning.com.

28. Arthur Waskow, *Down-to-Earth Judaism: Food, Money, Sex, and the Rest of Life* (New York: Morrow, 1995), 129.

29. Interview with David Hershcopf, March 18, 2007.

30. Avi Shafran, "Cremation Is Growing in Popularity, But It Runs Counter to Jewish Beliefs," *JTA*, February 7, 2007, http://www.jta.org/page_view_story .asp?intarticleid = 17557&intcategoryid = 5.html.

31. Correspondence with Neil Gillman, March 5, 2007.

32. "Going Green to the Grave," *Time*, February 26, 2007, 13.

33. Correspondence with Avi Shafran, March 5, 2007.

34. Interview with David Hershcopf, March 16, 2007.

35. Joe Eskenazi, "Many Opt for Cremation, Despite Jewish Law," *J.*, May 13, 2005, http://www.jewishsf.com/content/2–0–/module/displaystory/story_id/25831/edition _id/501/format/html/displaystory.html.

36. Terry Bookman, *God 101: Jewish Ideals, Beliefs, and Practices for Renewing Your Faith* (New York: Perigee, 2000), 132.

37. Yitzchok Adlerstein, "The Hijacking of Tikkum Olam," http://www.cross -currents.com/archives/2007/05/04/the-hijacking-of-tikkun-olam/.

38. Religious Action Center of Reform Judaism, promotional literature.

39. Interview with Kathy Butt, April 1998.

40. Leonard Fein, "These Statistics Don't Lie," *Forward*, April 20, 2001, 13.

41. Correspondence with Jeremy Deutchman, May 7, 2007.

42. Pamphlet from Jewish Fund for Justice: Faith-Based Community Organizing: A Unique Social Justice Approach to Revitalizing Synagogue Life, 2003, 1.

43. Gary Rosenblatt, "Gleaning the Good News," *Jewish Week*, February 9, 2007.

44. Adlerstein, "The Hijacking of Tikkum Olam."

45. Michael Lerner, *Jewish Renewal: A Path to Healing and Transformation* (New York: Putnam's, 1994), xvii.

46. Ibid., xvii.

47. Peter Byrne, "The Rabbi Who Would Save the World," *SF Weekly*, March 20, 2002, 21–25.

48. Beyt Tikkun Charter, January 12, 2007, http://www.beyttikkun.org.

49. Correspondence with Nan Fink Gefen, March 19, 2007.

50. Debra Nussbaum Cohen, "From 'Om' to 'Shema,'" *Jewish Week*, February 2, 2001, 16, 18.

51. Stephen Mitchell, foreword, Sylvia Boorstein, *That's Funny, You Don't Look Buddhist: On Being a Faithful Jew and a Passionate Buddhist* (San Francisco: HarperSanFrancisco, 1997), xii–xiii.

52. Rodger Kamenetz, *The Jew in the Lotus: A Poet's·Rediscovery of Jewish Identity in Buddhist India* (New York: HarperSanFrancisco, 1995), 8.

53. Insight Meditation Society and the Barre Center for Buddhist Studies, http://www.dharma.org.

54. Interview with John Brim, March 19, 2007.

55. Rodger Kamenetz, *The Jew in the Lotus* (San Francisco: HarperSanFrancisco, 1994), 7.

56. Louis Sahagun, "At One With Dual Devotion," *Los Angeles Times*, May 2, 2006, http://articles.latimes.com/2006/may/02/local/me-jubus2.

57. Goldberg, "The Lure of the East," 29–30.

58. Sahagun, "At One with Dual Devotion."

59. Ibid.

60. Sara Yoheved Rigler, "Conflicts of a Buddhist Jew," *AISH*, May 15, 2005, http://www.aish.com/spirituality/odysseys/Conflicts_of_a_Buddhist_Jew.asp.

61. Emanuel Feldman, "The Editor's Notebook: 'Buddha Is Not as Bad . . .' the Floundering of American Judaism," *Tradition* 32.1 (Fall 1997): 2.

62. Sylvia Boorstein, *That's Funny, You Don't Look Buddhist: On Being A Faithful Jew and a Passionate Buddhist* (San Francisco: HarperSanFrancisco, 1997), 21–22.

63. Ibid., 7.

64. Ibid., 25.

65. Ibid., 161.

66. Cohen, "From 'Om to 'Shema,'" 18.

67. Ibid., 18.

68. Ibid.

69. Melinda Ribner, *New Age Judaism: Ancient Wisdom for the Modern World* (Deerfield Beach, FL: Simcha, 2000), 10.

70. Aryeh Kaplan, *Meditation and Kabbalah* (Boston: Weiser, 1982).

71. Aryeh Kaplan, *Jewish Meditation* (New York: Schocken, 1985), vii.

72. Ibid., viii.

73. Alan Brill, Introduction to "Kabbalistic Visionary Prayer," MS; correspondence with Alan Brill, March 25, 2007.

74. Vision Statement, Kavvanah.org.

75. Ellen Bernstein, "How Wilderness Forms a Jew," *The Jewish Lights Spirituality Handbook: A Guide to Understanding, Exploring and Living a Spiritual Life* (Woodstock, VT: Jewish Lights, 2001), 121–128.

76. Niles Elliot Goldstein, *Gonzo Judaism: A Bold Path for Renewing an Ancient Faith* (New York: St. Martin's, 2006), 24.

77. Correspondence with Jamie Korngold, November 26, 2006.

78. Jamie Korngold, *God in the Wilderness: Rediscovering the Spirituality of the Great Outdoors with the Adventure Rabbi* (New York: Random House, 2007), http://www.adventurerabbi.com/jamie-personal-statement.htm.

79. Rachel Silverman, "Judaism Finds Its Niche in Great Outdoors," *JTA*, July 7, 2006, http://www.jewishjournal.com/home/searchview.php?id = 16111.

80. Goldstein,, *Gonzo Judaism*, 21–23.

81. Ibid., 36.

82. The Walking Stick Foundation, http://www.walkingstick.org.

83. Gershon Winkler, with Lakme Batya Elior, *The Place Where You Are Standing Is Holy: A Jewish Theology on Human Relations* (Northvale, NJ: Aronson, 1994), xxi.

84. Ibid., xv.

85. Ibid., xvi.

86. Ibid., xviii.

87. Ibid., xx.

88. Correspondence with Julius Ciss, June 22, 2007, http://www.jewsforjudaism.org.

3. *The Rise and Fall of the American Jewish Denominational Structure*

1. Andrew M. Greeley, *The Denominational Society: A Sociological Approach to Religion in America* (Glenview, IL: Scott, Foresman, 1972).

2. Robert Wuthnow, *The Restructuring of American Religion: Society and Faith Since World War II* (Princeton: Princeton University Press, 1988), 97.

3. Denise Eger, "Can Judaism Survive?" Congregation Kol Ami Sermons from Web site, March 29, 2004, http://www.kol-ami.org/sermons/archive/2004/03/index.html.

4. Paul Menitoff, "Are Jews Entering A Post-Denominational Era?" *CCAR Newsletter* (February 2004): 1–10.

5. Joe Berkofsky, "Reform Leader's Swipe Sparks Angry Rebuttals from Conservatives," *JTA*, March 2, 2004, http://www.jta.org.

6. Debra Nussbaum Cohen, "Reform Leader Predicts Demise of Conservatives: CCAR Head Gives Ailing 'Bridge' Movement Two Decades," *Jewish Week*, March 5, 2004, http://www.thejewishweek.com.

7. Maurice Eisendrath, *Can Faith Survive? The Thoughts and Afterthoughts of an American Rabbi* (New York: McGraw-Hill, 1964), 243–244.

8. Michael A. Meyer, *Response to Modernity: A History of the Reform Movement in Judaism* (New York: Oxford University Press, 1988), 358.

9. Jerome D. Folkman, *Design for Jewish Living: A Guide for the Bride and Groom* (New York: Union of American Hebrew Congregations, 1955); Abraham J. Feldman, *Reform Judaism: A Guide for Reform Jews* (New York: Behrman House, 1956); Frederic A. Dopplet and David Polish, *A Guide for Reform Jews* (New York: Bloch, 1957).

10. Meyer, *Response to Modernity*, 369.

11. Eugene B. Borowitz, *Reform Judaism Today: Reform in the Process of Change*, vol. 1 (New York: Behrman House, 1983), xii, 52.

12. Reform Judaism—A Centenary Perspective, Central Conference of American Rabbis, http://ccarnet.org/Articles/index.cfm?id =41&pge_prg_id =3032&pge_id =1656.

13. Correspondence with Richard Levy, May 31, 2007.

14. Robert Gordis, *Understanding Conservative Judaism* (New York: Rabbinical Assembly, 1978), 216.

15. Meyer, *Response to Modernity*, 137.

16. Correspondence with Michael A. Meyer, May 24, 2007.

17. Neil Gillman, *Conservative Judaism: The New Century* (West Orange, NJ: Behrman House, 1993), 48.

18. Ibid., 61.

19. Morris Adler, "New Goals for Conservative Judaism—An Address [1948]," in Mordechai Waxman, ed., *Tradition and Change: The Development of Conservative Judaism* (New York: Burning Bush, 1958), 280.

20. Abraham J. Karp, "The Conservative Rabbi—'Dissatisfied But Not Unhappy,'" *American Jewish Archives: The American Rabbinate, a Centennial View* 35 (Cincinnati: American Jewish Archives, 1983): 188–262.

21. Marshall Sklare, *Conservative Judaism: An American Religious Movement* (Glencoe, IL: Free Press, 1972 [1955]), 88.

22. Jonathan D. Sarna, "The Debate Over Mixed Seating in the American Synagogue," in Jack Wertheimer, ed., *The American Synagogue: A Sanctuary Transformed* (New York: Cambridge University Press, 1987), 363–393.

23. David Golinkin, ed., *Proceedings of the Committee on Jewish Law and Standards of the Conservative Movement, 1927–1970*, vol. 3 (Jerusalem: Rabbinical Assembly and Institute of Applied Halakhah, 1997), 1118–1120.

24. Joe Berkofsky, "As Schorsch Marks Eighteen Years at JTS, Some Say Movement Lacks Leadership," *JTA*, May 19, 2004.

25. Daniel J. Elazar and Rela Mintz Geffen, *The Conservative Movement in Judaism: Dilemmas and Opportunities* (Albany: State University of the New York Press, 2000), 45.

26. Interview with Joel Meyers, May 29, 2007.

27. Sklare, *Conservative Judaism*.

28. Correspondence with Bob Carroll, May 13, 2007.

29. Ibid.

30. In Our Community, JTS mass e-mail, Ben Harris, "New JTS Chancellor Energizes Conservative Rabbis, Movement," May 1, 2007.

31. Reena Sigman Freedman, "The Emergence of Reconstructionism: An Evolving American Judaism, 1922–1945," *American Jewish Archives* 48 (Cincinnati: American Jewish Archives, 1996): 1–22.

32. Mordecai M. Kaplan, "Preface," *The Jewish Reconstructionist Papers* (New York: Behrman's Jewish Book House, 1936), v.

33. "Resolution Regarding Children of Mixed Marriages," May 5, 1968, *The Reconstructionist* 34.8 (May 31, 1968): 30; correspondence with Richard Hirsh, May 28, 2007.

34. David Polish, ed., *Rabbi's Manual* (New York: Central Conference of American Rabbis, 1961), 112; Solomon Freehof, *Recent Reform Responsa* (New York: Central Conference of American Rabbis, 1963), 76.

35. Julie Wiener, "Are the Reconstructionists Becoming More Mainstream?" *JTA*, November 7, 2000, htttp://www.jta.org/page_print_story.asp?inarticleid = 6500 &intcategoryid = 4.

36. Debra Nussbaum Cohen, Focus on Issues: Reconstructionist Movement," *JTA*, http://www.jta.org/page_print_story.asp?intarticleid = 4948&intcategoryid = 6.

37. Ben Harris, "For Reconstructionists, Growth Proves to Be a Two-Edged Sword," http://www.jta.org/page_print_story.asp?intarticleid = 17294&intcategoryid = 4.

38. Jonathan D. Sarna, *American Judaism: A History* (New Haven: Yale University Press, 2004), 87; correspondence with Jonathan D. Sarna, May 8, 2007.

39. Sklare, *Conservative Judaism*, 43.

40. Jacob J. Schacter, "The Sea Change in American Orthodox Judaism: A Symposium," *Tradition* 32.4 (1998): 93.

41. Aryeh Spero, "Orthodoxy Confronts Reform: The Two Hundred Years' War," Dana Evan Kaplan, ed., *Contemporary Debates in American Reform Judaism: Conflicting Visions* (New York: Routledge, 2001), 120.

42. Correspondence with Lawrence Grossman, April 30, 2007.

43. William B. Helmreich and Reuel Shinnar, "Modern Orthodoxy in America: Possibilities for the Movement Under Siege," Jerusalem Letters, Jerusalem Center for Public Affairs, no. 383, June 1, 1998, http://www.jcpa.org/cjc/jl-383-helmreich.htm.

44. Gary Rosenblatt, "Modern Orthodox Outnumber Haredim Here," *Jewish Week*, February 25, 2005.

45. Julie Gruenbaum Fax, "New Face of Study: Yeshivat Chovevei Torah Offers Students Alternative Views with Its 'Open Orthodoxy' Policy," *Jewish Journal*, December 27, 2002.

46. Saul J. Berman, "Edah to Close—Programs to Continue," press release from Edah, July 3, 2006, http://www.edah.org/edah-to-close.htm.

47. Adam Dickter, "Modern Orthodox Think Tank to Fold," *Jewish Week*, June 30, 2006; correspondence with Jonathan D. Sarna, October 16, 2008.

48. Jonathan D. Sarna, *American Judaism: A History* (New Haven: Yale University Press, 2004), 237; Dickter, "Modern Orthodox Think Tank To Fold."

49. Interview with Norman Lamm, May 14, 2007; correspondence with Norman Lamm, May 21, 2007.

50. Correspondence with Lawrence Grossman, April 30, 2007.

51. Reuven Bulka, *The Coming Cataclysm: The Orthodox-Reform Rift and the Future of the Jewish People* (New York: Mosaic, 1989).

52. Jack Wertheimer, *All Quiet on the Religious Front? Jewish Unity, Denominationalism, Postdenominationalism in the United States* (New York: American Jewish Committee, 2005).

53. Correspondence with Bradley Artson, June 27, 2007.

54. "Statement of Purpose," *Journal of the Academy for Jewish Religion* 3.1 (May 2007/5767): p. 87.

55. Correspondence with David Greenstein, August 22, 2007.

56. Arthur Green, "Rabbis Beyond Denomination," *Contact: The Journal of Jewish Life Network/Steinhardt Foundation* 7.4 (Summer 2005): 3.

57. Michael H. Steinhardt, "My Challenge: Towards a Post-Denominational Common Judaism," *Contact: The Journal of Jewish Life Network/Steinhardt Foundation* 7.4 (Summer 2005): 15.

4. Facing the Collapse of the Intermarriage Stigma

1. *The O.C.*: "The Best Chrismukkah Ever," season 1, episode 13, "The Chrismukkah That Almost Wasn't," season 2, episode 6, and "The Chrismukkah Bar Mitz-vahkkah," season 3, episode 10, Fox Broadcasting Company, December 3, 2003.

2. Michael McCarthy, "Have a Merry Little Chrismukkah," *USA Today*, http://www.usatoday.com/money/industries/retail/2004–12–15-chrismukkah_x.htm.

3. Correspondence with Ron Gompertz, September 19, 2007.

4. Ibid.

5. Emma Zayer, "Chrismakkuh Takes Root," *Daily Colonial*, February 7, 2007, http://www.dailycolonial.com/go.dc?p = 3&s = 317.

6. Kristin Reichardt, "Chrismakkuh: Redefining Tradition," *Independent Collegian*, December 6, 2004, http://media.www.independentcollegian.com/media/storage/paper678/news/2004/12/06/ArtsLife/Chrismakkuh.Redefining.Tradition-822217.shtml.

7. McCarthy, "Have a Merry Little Chrismukkah."

8. Jane Ulman, "A Recipe for Kris Kringle Kugel?" *JTA*, December 18, 2005, http://www.jta.org/page_view_story.asp?strwebhead = Chrismukkah+time+is+here+again&intcategoryid = 5.

9. Elihu Bergman, "The American Jewish Population Erosion," *Midstream* 23 (October 1977): 9–19.

10. Samuel S. Lieberman and Morton Weinfeld, "Demographic Trends and Jewish Survival," *Midstream* 24 (November 1978): 9–19.

11. Steven Cohen, "The Self–Defeating Surplus," *Moment* (June 1987): 31.

12. Avi Shafran, "Reinforce Halachic Tradition," *Forward*, October 25, 2002, 13.

13. J. J. Goldberg, *Jewish Power: Inside the American Jewish Establishment* (Reading, MA: Addison-Wesley, 1996), 66.

14. Ibid., 67.

15. Debra Nussbaum Cohen, "Leader of Agudath Israel, Moshe Sherer, Dies at 76," May 22, 1998, JTA.org.

16. Alice Goldstein and Sidney Goldstein, *Jews on the Move: Implications for Jewish Identity* (Albany: State University of New York Press, 1995).

17. Daniel J. Elazar and Morton Weinfeld Elazar, *Still Moving: Recent Jewish Migration in Comparative Perspective* (New Brunswick, NJ: Transaction, 2000).

18. Ephraim Z. Buchwald, "Stop the Silent Holocaust," letter, *Moment* 17 (December 1992): 4–5.

19. Ephraim Buchwald, "Conversion and the American Jewish Agenda," *Judaism* 48.191 (Summer 1999): 274.

20. Steven M. Cohen, "A Tale of Two Jewries: The 'Inconvenient Truth' for American Jews," Jewish Life Network/Steinhardt Foundation, 2006.

21. Larry Tye, *Home Lands: Portraits of the New Jewish Diaspora* (New York: Holt, 2001), 254–255.

22. Paul Golin, "Intermarriage Tipping Point Long Past, But Institutions Must Now Catch Up," *JTA*, November 22, 2006, http://jta.org/page_view_story.asp?intacticleid = 17311&intcategoryid = 4.

23. Eric H. Yoffie, "The Importance of Outreach in Maintaining Reform's Autonomy, Diversity, and Pluralism," in Dana Evan Kaplan, *Contemporary Debates in American Reform Judaism: Conflicting Visions* (New York: Routledge, 2001), 150.

24. Charles DeLaFuente, "The Call to the Torah, Now Heeded Online," *New York Times*, July 1, 2004, C3.

25. Interview with Celso Cukierkorn, February 8, 2007.

26. Interview with Peggy Posnick, February 9, 2007.

27. Correspondence with Peggy Posnick, October 1, 2008.

28. Carolyn Slutsky, "Converting, on Their Own Terms," *Jewish Week*, February 2, 2007, http://www.thejewishweek.com/news/newscontent.php3?artid = 13613.

29. Alexander M. Schindler, "The Case for a Missionary Judaism," in Steve Israel and Seth Forman, eds., *Great Jewish Speeches Throughout History* (Northvale, NJ: Aronson, 1994), 244–248.

30. Numbers 25:6–8.

31. Peter L. Berger, *The Sacred Canopy: Elements of a Sociological Theory of Religion* (Garden City, New York: Doubleday, 1967), 170–171.

32. David Polish, ed., *Rabbi's Manual* (New York: Central Conference of American Rabbis, 1961), 112.

33. "The Status of Children of Mixed Marriages," Report of the Committee on Patrilineal Descent, March 15, 1983, http://data.ccarnet.org/cgi-bin-resodisp.pl?file = mm&year = 1983/.

34. Debra Nussbaum Cohen, "Reform Conference to Re-examine Controversial 'Patrilineal' Policy," *Jewish Telegraphic Agency*, June 16, 1998, http://www.jta.org/cgi-bin/iowa/news/article/19990212Reformrabbistore.html.

35. Sue Fishkoff, "New Conservative Initiative Reaches Out to the Intermarried," *JTA*, December 7, 2006, http://www.jta.org/page_print_story.asp?intarticleid = 16101&intcategoryid = 4.

36. David Ellenson and Kerry Olitzky, "Conversion Is Not an Outreach Strategy," *Forward*, May 12, 2006, http://www.forward.com/articles/1396/.

37. Ibid.

38. Sue Fishkoff, "Conservative Day Schools to Debate Admitting Children of Non-Jewish Moms," *JTA*, December 12, 2007, http://joi.org/bloglinks/JTA%20NEWS%20Conservative%20Day%20Schools.htm.

39. Irving Greenberg, "Will There Be One Jewish People By the Year 2000?" *Perspectives*, CLAL: The National Jewish Center for Learning and Leadership, (June 1985, revised February 1986).

40. Reuven Bulka, *The Coming Cataclysm: The Orthodox-Reform Rift and the Future of the Jewish People* (Oakville, Ontario: Mosaic, 1984).

41. Irving Greenberg, "A Lag B'Omer Legacy: Judaism Heading for Tragedy," *J.*, May 23, 1997, http://www.jewishsf.com/content/2-0-/module/displaystory/story_id/6260/edition_id/116/format/html/displaystory.html.

42. Interview with Norman Lamm, May 14, 2007.

43. Ibid.

44. Ibid.

45. David Landau, *Piety and Power* (New York: Hill and Wang, 1993), 292.

46. Interview with Lamm, May 14, 2007.

47. Interview with Shlomo Amar, Israeli Sephardic chief rabbi, Israeli Broadcasting Authority, Reshet Bet Radio, 6:45 AM, November 21, 2006.

48. Interview with Irving "Yitz" Greenberg, March 30, 2007.

49. Samuel Freedman, *Jew Versus Jew* (New York: Simon and Schuster, 2000), 94.

50. Correspondence with Stanley Wagner, June 19, 2007.

51. Hillel Goldberg, "Fifth Anniversary of the Mikveh of East Denver," *Dei'ah ve Dibur*, August 20, 2003, http://chareidi.shemayisrael.com/archives5763/REI63amoed .htm.

52. Bulka, *The Coming Cataclysm*.

53. Lawrence Grossman, "Jewish Communal Affairs," *Amercan Jewish Yearbook* 91 (1991): 200.

54. Ibid.

55. Tom Tugend, "In L.A., Promise to Dying Wife Leads to Unified Conversion Court," *JTA*, April 14, 2003, http://www.jta.org/page_print_story.asp?intarticleid = 12656&intcategoryid = 4.

56. Interview with Mayer Selekman, February 1999.

57. Sue Fishkoff, "To Officiate or Not? Mixed Marriage Source of Debate at Reform Rabbis' Parley," *JTA*, July 2, 2006, http://www.jta.org/page_print_story .asp?intarticleid = 16775&intcategoryid = 4.

58. Ibid.

59. The Rabbinic Center for Research and Counseling's Web site is www .rcrconline.org.

60. Debra Nussbaum Cohen, "Forty-Seven Percent of Rabbis in Two Movements Conducting Intermarriages," *Jewish Bulletin of Northern California*, March 22, 1996, http://www.jewishsf.com/bk960322/usrabbis.html; Irwin Fishbein, Rabbinic Participation in Intermarriage Ceremonies: Summary of Rabbinic Center for Research and Counseling 1990 Survey; Irwin Fishbein, Rabbinic Participation in Intermarriage Ceremonies; Summary of Rabbinic Center for Research and Counseling 1994–95 Survey; correspondence with Irwin Fishbein, June 21, 2007.

61. Interview with Jacques Cukierkorn, May 2, 2002.

62. Bruce Phillips, "American Judaism in the Twenty-First Century," in Dana Evan Kaplan, ed., *The Cambridge Companion to American Judaism* (Cambridge: Cambridge University Press, 2005), 397–415.

63. Marshall Sklare, *America's Jews* (New York: Random House, 1971).

64. Sue Fishkoff, "Keeping the Faiths: Intermarried Parents Teach Two Religions at Bay Area Sunday School," *J.*, December 24, 2004, http://www.jewishsf.com/ content/2–0–/module/displaystory/story_id/24510/edition_id/482/format/html/ displaystory.html.

65. Anna Rachael Marx, "Dovetail Only Encourages the 'Inter' Among Interfaith Families," *J.*, August 13, 2004, 18–20.

66. Correspondence with Edmund C. Case, July 23, 2007.

67. Correspondence with Mary Rosenbaum, May 30, 2007.

68. Sue Fishkoff, "Raising Jewish-Christian Children: Some Interfaith Families Opt for Both," *JTA*, August 10, 2004, http://www.jta.org/page_view_story.asp? intarticleid = 14368&intcategoryid = 4.

69. *Dovetail: A Journal by and for Jewish/Christian Families* 6.6:3; correspondence with Rosenbaum, May 30, 2007.

70. Dan Cohn-Sherbok, *Messianic Judaism* (New York: Continuum International, 2000); Dan Cohn-Sherbok, ed., *Voices of Messianic Judaism: Confronting Critical Issues Facing a Modern Movement* (Clarksville, MD: Messianic Jewish Resources International, 2001); Carol Harris-Shapiro, *Messianic Judaism: A Rabbi's Journey Through Religious Change in America* (Boston: Beacon, 1999).

71. Correspondence with Carol Harris-Shapiro, July 25, 2007.

72. Correspondence with Eric H. Yoffie, March 22, 2007.

73. Jack Wertheimer, "Judaism Without Limits," *Commentary* 104.1 (July 1997): 26–27.

74. Correspondence with Alan Laufer, November 2, 2007.

5. Inclusivity as a Social Value

1. Interview with Hinda Langer, March 1, 2007.

2. Rebecca Alpert, *Like Bread on the Seder Plate: Jewish Lesbians and the Transformation of Tradition* (New York: Columbia University Press, 1997), 2.

3. Susannah Heschel, "Orange on the Seder Plate," in Catherine Spector, Sharon Cohen Anisfeld, and Tara Mohr, eds., *The Women's Passover Companion: Women's Reflections on the Festival of Freedom* (Woodstock, VT: Jewish Lights, 2003), 70–77; "The Orange on the Seder Plate," in Catherine Spector, Sharon Cohen Anisfeld, and Tara Mohr, eds., *The Women's Seder Sourcebook* (Woodstock, VT: Jewish Lights, 2003), 208–213.

4. Susannah Heschel, lecture in South Florida, April 5, 2001; correspondence with Susannah Heschel, March 21, 2007, May 7, 2007, and June 3, 2007.

5. Anita Diamant, *Pitching My Tent* (New York: Scribner, 2003), 148–150.

6. Rachel Adler, paper delivered at Brandeis-Bardin Institute, California, June 1983.

7. Blu Greenberg, "Orthodox Feminism and the Next Century," *Sh'ma*, January 2000, http://www.shma.com/janoo/feminism.htm.

8. Abigail Pogrebin, *Stars of David: Prominent Jews Talk About Being Jewish* (New York: Broadway, 2005), 311.

9. Judith Plaskow, *Standing Again at Sinai: Judaism from a Feminist Perspective* (San Francisco: HarperSanFrancisco, 1990), 67.

10. Sue Fishkoff, "Judaic Texts, Individual Precedent May Leave Room for Female Mohels," *Jewish Telegraphic Agency*, January 17, 2006, http://www.highbeam.com/doc/1P1-117742967.html.

11. Plaskow, *Standing Again at Sinai*.

12. Ibid., 3.

13. Ibid., 75.

14. Correspondence with Judith Plaskow, October 30, 2006, and November 9, 2006.

15. Correspondence with Rachel Adler, May 1, 2007.

16. Rachel Adler, "The Jew Who Wasn't There: Halakha and the Jewish Woman," in Suzanna Heschel, ed., *On Being a Jewish Feminist: A Reader* (New York: Schocken, 1983).

17. Correspondence with Adler, May 1, 2007.

18. Rachel Adler, *Engendering Judaism: An Inclusive Theology and Ethics* (Boston: Beacon, 1998).

19. Rachel Adler, "In Your Blood, Live: Revisions of a Theology of Purity," *Tikkun* 8.1 (January/February 1993), reprinted in Jacob Neusner, ed., *Signposts on the Way of Torah* (Belmont, CA: Wadsworth, 1998), 218.

20. Elizabeth Koltun, ed., *The Jewish Woman: New Perspectives* (New York: Schocken, 1975).

21. Adler, "In Your Blood, Live," 38–41.

22. Chaim Stern, ed., *The Gates of Prayer for Shabbat and Weekdays: A Gender-Sensitive Prayer Book* (New York: CCAR, 1994).

23. Marcia Falk, *The Book of Blessings: New Jewish Prayers for Daily Life, the Sabbath, and the Moon Festival* (Boston: Beacon, 1996).

24. Marcia Falk, "What About God? New Blessings for Old Wine" *Moment* 10.3 (March 1985): 32–36.

25. Falk, *The Book of Blessings*, xvii.

26. Ibid., 18.

27. Ibid., xvii.

28. Ibid., 429.

29. Ibid., xvii.

30. Jill Huber, "Pioneering Female Rabbi Readies for Retirement," *Deep South Jewish Voice*, June 2006, 51–52, reprinted from the *New Jersey Jewish News*.

31. Paul Zakrzewski, "Pioneering Rabbi Who Softly Made Her Way," *New York Times*, May 20, 2006.

32. Pamela S Nadell, *Women Who Would Be Rabbis: A History of Women's Ordination 1889–1985* (Boston: Beacon, 1998), 188.

33. Sandy Eisenberg Sasso, "Celebrating Thirty Years of Women as Rabbis," speech delivered on the occasion of the thirtieth anniversary of women as rabbis, Toronto, Canada, June 10, 2002.

34. Ibid.

35. Nadell, *Women Who Would Be Rabbis*, 189.

36. Ibid.

37. Vicki Cabot, "On Shabbos the Rabbis Wear Skirts," *Greater Phoenix Jewish News*, September 11, 1992, 10–11.

38. Janet Marder, "How Women Are Changing the Rabbinate," *Reform Judaism* 19.5 (Summer 1991): 5.

39. Lisa Keys, "Feting a Feminist Rabbi Who Broke 'Stained-Glass Ceiling,'" *Forward*, May 18, 2001.

40. Interview with Michael and Linda Lieberman, April 5, 2002.

41. Aaron Blumenthal, "An Aliyah for Women," *Proceedings of Rabbinical Assembly*, 55:168–181, repr. Seymour Siegel, ed., *Conservative Judaism and Jewish Law* (New York: Ktav, 1977), 275.

42. Elliot N. Dorff, "Custom Drives Jewish Law on Women," in Walter Jacob and Moshe Zemer, eds., *Gender Issues in Jewish Law: Essays and Responsa* (New York: Berghahn, 2001), 82.

43. Kenneth A. Briggs, "Only Female Presiding Rabbi in U.S. Begins Her Work in a Small Town," *New York Times*, August 16, 1979, A20; correspondence with Rebecca Alpert, May 28, 2007.

44. Correspondence with Amy Eilberg, May 5, 2007.

45. Correspondence with Joel Roth, May 10, 2007; interview with Joel Roth, May 16, 2007.

46. Beth S. Wenger, "The Politics of Women's Ordination: Jewish Law, Institutional Power and the Debate Over Women in the Rabbinate," in Jack Wertheimer, ed., *Tradition Renewed: A History of the Jewish Theological Seminary* (New York: JTS, 1997), 485–523.

47. Advertisement, Agudath ha-Rabbanim, *Jewish Press*, December 10, 1982.

48. Blu Greenberg, "Judaism and Feminism," from Elizabeth Koltun, ed., *The Jewish Woman: New Perspectives* (New York: Schocken, 1976).

49. Blu Greenberg, *On Women and Judaism: A View from Tradition* (Philadelphia: Publication Society of America, 1981), 6.

50. Greenberg, "Orthodox Feminism and the Next Century."

51. Chana Henkin, "New Conditions and New Models of Authority—the Yoatzot Halachah," *Nishmat*, http://www.nishmat.net/article.php?id = 160&heading = 0.

52. Haviva Ner-David, *Life on the Fringes: A Feminist Journey Toward Traditional Rabbinic Ordination* (Needham, MA: JFL, 2000).

53. Steven I. Weiss, "The Orthodox Jewess Rabbi Who Wasn't," *Canonist*, May 2006, http://www.canonist.com/?p = 752.

54. Interview with Sharon Liberman Mintz, December 8, 2006.

55. Marilyn Henry, "Orthodox Women Crossing Threshold Into Synagogue," *Jerusalem Post*, May 15, 1998.

56. Interview with Sara Hurwitz, December 12, 2006.

57. Elicia Brown, "Women to Lead Halachic N.Y. Shul: Move by Upper West Side Congregation Pushes Gender Boundaries," *Jewish Week*, August 18, 1997.

58. Michael Luo, "An Orthodox Jewish Woman, and Soon, a Spiritual Leader," *New York Times*, August 21, 2006, http://www.nytimes.com/2006/08/21/nyregion/21rabbi,html?pagewanted =2&_r =2.

59. Tzipporah Heller, "Feminism and Judaism," aish.com, January 9, 2000, http://www.aish.com/societywork/women/Feminism_and_Judaism.asp.

60. Greenberg, "Orthodox Feminism and the Next Century."

61. Steven Greenberg, *Wrestling with God and Men: Homosexuality in the Jewish Tradition Updated* (Madison: University of Wisconsin Press, 2004), 74.

62. Leviticus 18:22 and Leviticus 20:13.

63. Greenberg, *Wrestling with God and Men*, 75–76.

64. Yaakov Levado, "Gayness and God," *Tikkun* 8.5 (October 1993): 54–60.

65. Greenberg, *Wrestling with God and Men*, 6.

66. Interviews with Allen B. Bennett, July 3, 2002, May 30, 2007.

67. Correspondence with Stacy Offner, May 10, 2007.

68. Correspondence with Rebecca Alpert, May 31, 2007.

69. Denise L. Eger, "Embracing Lesbians and Gay Men: A Reform Jewish Innovation," in Dana Evan Kaplan, ed., *Contemporary Debates in American Reform Judasim: Conflicting Visions* (New York: Routledge, 2001), 180.

70. Sue Levi Elwell, with Rebecca T. Alpert, "Introduction: Why a Book on Lesbian Rabbis?" in Rebecca T. Alpert, Sue Levi Elwell, and Shirley Idelson, eds., *Lesbian Rabbis: The First Generation* (New Brunswick, NJ: Rutgers University Press, 2001), 1.

71. Plaskow, *Standing Again at Sinai*, 238.

6. Radical Responses to the Suburban Experience

1. Jennifer Bleyer, "Rabbi's Journey Leads to 'Ecstatic' Minyan," *Forward*, May 12, 2006.

2. Zalman Schachter-Shalomi and Joel Segel, *Jewish with Feeling: A Guide to Meaningful Jewish Practice* (New York: Penguin, 2005), 20.

3. Correspondence with David Ingber, May 4, 2007, May 15, 2007, June, 7, 2007, July, 6, 2007, and July 17, 2007.

4. Bleyer, "Rabbi's Journey."

5. Correspondence with Shaul Magid, July 17, 2007.

6. Correspondence with Michael Lerner, June 24, 2007.

7. Michael Lerner, *Jewish Renewal: A Path to Healing and Transformation* (New York: Putnam, 1994), 1.

8. Ibid., 1–2.

9. Correspondence with Lerner, June 24, 2007.

10. Shaul Magid, "Jewish Renewal: Toward a 'New' American Judaism," *Tikkun* 21 (2006): 57.

11. Correspondence with Lerner, June 24, 2007.

12. Shaul Magid, "The De-Centering of American Judaism," *Tikkun* 21 (September/October 2006): 56.

13. Magid, "Jewish Renewal."

14. Correspondence with Mitchell Chefitz, November 27, 2006.

15. Correspondence with Susan Saxe, May 7, 2007.

16. J. J. Goldberg, "Seasons of Reinterpretation: How a Radical Demonstration Thirty-two Years Ago Changed the Culture of Passover," *Jewish Journal*, April 21, 2000, http://www.jewishjournal.com/old/jjgoldberg.4.21.0.htm.

17. Interview with Zalman Schacter Shalomi, May 1, 2008.

18. Susan Goldstein, "Interview with Rabbi Zalman Schachter-Shalomi," *Religion and Ethics Newsweekly*, September 30, 2005.

19. Shohama Harris Wiener and Jonathan Omer-Man, ed., *Worlds of Jewish Prayer: A Festschrift in Honor of Rabbi Zalman M. Schachter-Shalomi* (Northvale, NJ: Aronson, 1993), inside front cover.

20. "Zalman Schachter-Shalomi," *Havurah Shir Hadash*, Ashland, Oregon, http://www.havurahshirhadash.org/rebzalman.html.

21. Yonassan Gershom, "What B'nai Or Was Like in the Old Days . . ." from the introduction to *Forty-nine Gates of Light: Kabbalistic Meditations for Counting the Omer* (self-published, 1987).

22. Correspondence with Phyllis Berman, September 11, 2007.

23. Tirzah Firestone, *With Roots in Heaven: One Woman's Passionate Journey Into the Heart of Her Faith* (New York: Dutton, 1998), 225.

24. Correspondence from Arthur Waskow, September 11, 2007.

25. Correspondence from Phyllis Berman, September 11, 2007.

26. Avraham Arieh Trugman, "Probing the Carlebach Phenomenon," *Jewish Action* 63 (Winter 2002): 2.

27. Mark Kligman, "Recent Trends in New American Jewish Music," from Dana Evan Kaplan, ed., *The Cambridge Companion to American Judaism* (New York: Cambridge University Press, 2005), 364.

28. Elli Wohlgelernter, "Simply Shlomo," *Jerusalem Post Magazine*, April 20, 1995, 9.

29. Adam Dickter, "Facing a Mixed Legacy: First Carlebach Conference to Grapple with Issue of Abuse Head On; Opposition to Street Naming," *Jewish Week*, September 9, 2004.

30. Shlomo Carlebach, "Yedid Nefesh," radio show interview with Robert L. Cohen, November 1979.

31. "Practical Wisdom from Shlomo Carlebach," *Tikkun* 12.5: 53, http://www.havurahshirhadash.org/shlomoarticle15.html.

32. Dickter, "Facing a Mixed Legacy."

33. Ibid.

34. "Practical Wisdom from Shlomo Carlebach."

35. Ibid.

36. Gabrielle Birkner, "When Children Go Frum," *Moment* (December 2001), http://www.momentmag.com/archive/deco1/feat1.html.

37. Ibid.

38. Ibid.; also see M. Herbert Danzger, *Returning to Tradition: The Contemporary Revival of Orthodox Judaism* (New Haven: Yale University Press, 1989).

39. Interview with Phillip Slepian, November 6, 2006.

40. David Klinghoffer, "Sympathy for the Devil: The Strange Case of Sinner-mensch Jack Abramoff and the Jewish Community That Abandoned Him." *Jewish Journal*, January 27, 2006.

41. Yitzchok Adlerstein, http://www.cross-currents.com.

42. Joshua Hammer, *Chosen by God: A Brother's Journey* (New York: Hyperion, 1999), 2.

43. Debra Nussbaum Cohen, "Matisyahu's New Spiritual Groove," *Jewish Week*, November 28, 2007.

44. Interview with Esther Jungreis, December 8, 2006.

45. Tina Levitan, "Rebbetzin Esther Jungreis: The Big Apple Rebbetzin Enthralls Audiences Worldwide," *Jewish Post*, http://www.jewishpost.com/jp1003/jpn1003e.htm.

46. Interview with Barbara Janov, November 8, 2006.

47. http://www.hineni.org.

48. "A Tribute to Rabbi Aryeh Kaplan ZT"L (1934–1983)," http://www.teshuva.bravehost.com/a_tribute.htm.

49. Correspondence with Alan Brill, March 28, 2007.

50. William Helmreich and Reuel Shinnar, "Modern Orthodox in America: Possibilities for a Movement Under Siege," Jerusalem Center for Public Affairs, no. 383, June 1, 1998, http://www.jcpa.org/cjc/jl-383-helmreich.htm.

51. Interview with Yitzchak Rosenbaum, November 7, 2006.

52. Schachter-Shalomi with Segel, *Jewish with Feeling*, 149.

7. The Popularization of Jewish Mystical Outreach

1. Robert Wuthnow, *After Heaven: Spirituality in America Since the 1950s* (Berkeley: University of California Press, 1998), 114–149.

2. Jay Michaelson, "It's the Deity, Stupid: Young Jews Come to Judaism Seeking the Divine," *Jerusalem Post*, October 11, 2005, http://www.jpost.com/servlet/Satellite?cid = 1128955358613&pagename = JPost%2FJPArticle%2FShowFull.

3. Correspondence with Peter E. Nussbaum, July 9, 2007, July 14, 2007, and July 16, 2007.

4. Correspondence between Peter E. Nussbaum and Bob Stein, forwarded to me by Bob Stein, December 24, 2007.

5. Nathaniel Popper, "'Boom Burbs' Filling Up on People, But Jewish Life Is Slow to Follow," *Forward*, August 25, 2006.

6. Eric H. Yoffie, "Reform Reflections: The Good and Bad of Chabad," July 12, 2007, http://blogcentral.jpost.com/index.php?cat_id = 8&blog_id = 72&blog_post _id = 1303.

7. Alan Brill, "The Essence of Commitment: The Philosophy of Rabbi Menachem Mendel Schneerson," unpublished paper, May 28, 2002.

8. Chanan Tigay, "Public Menorah Displays Testament to the Growing Acceptance of Chabad," *JTA*, December 13, 2005, http://joi.org/bloglinks/Public%20Menorah%2 0displays%20-%20Chabad%20-%20JTA.htm.

9. Interview with David Eliezrie, August 10, 2007.

10. "Chabad's Global Warming," *New York Jewish Week*, http://www.shabboshouse .com/CampusChabad/QQ/Dershowitz.htm.

11. Correspondence with Aryeh Rubin, October 19, 2007.

12. Correspondence with David Berger, June 28, 2007.

13. Neal Karlen, *Shanda: The Making and Breaking of a Self-Loathing Jew* (New York: Touchstone, 2004), 28.

14. Jon Pareles, "Album Review: A Wiser Voice Blowin' in the Autumn Wind," *New York Times*, September 28, 1997.

15. David Gates, "Dylan Revisited," *Newsweek*, October 6, 1997, http://www .newsweek.com/id/97107?tid = relatedcl.

16. "Still on the Road: 1980 Second Gospel Tour," item 5410, Orpheum Theater, Omaha, Nebraska, January 25, 1980, http://www.bjorner.com/DSN05347%201980%2 0Second%20Gospel%20Tour.htm#DSN05410.

17. "Dylan's Hebrew Verse," *Forward*, September 26, 2007, http://www.forward .com/articles/11699.

18. "Singer/Songwriter Bob Dylan Joins Yom Kippur Services in Atlanta," September 24, 2007, http://www.chabad.org/news/article_cdo/aid/573406/jewish/Singer Songwriter-Bob-Dylan-Joins-Yom-Kippur-Services-in-Atlanta.htm.

19. Reb Yudel, "Bob Dylan Yom Kippur Sighting, 2007," September 24, 2007, http://www.shmoozenet.com/yudel/mtarchives/001839.html.

20. Brill, "The Essence of Commitment."

21. Tigay, "Public Menorah Displays."

22. Ibid.

23. Ibid.

24. Mike Kamber, "Ban the Web? Not Lubavitch Jews," *Wired*, January 19, 2000, http://www.wired.com/news/culture/1,33626-0.html.

25. Ibid.

26. Sue Fishkoff, *The Rebbe's Army: Inside the World of Chabad-Lubavitch* (New York: Schocken, 2003), 282.

27. Kamber, "Ban the Web?"

28. Simon Jacobson, ed., *Toward a Meaningful Life: The Wisdom of the Rebbe* (New York: Morrow, 1995).

29. Jonathan Mark, "Chabad's Global Warming: Outsiders Praise 'The Most Effective Jewish Organization,'" *New York Jewish Week*, December 2, 2005, www.the jewishweek.com/news/newscontent.php3?artid = 11742.

30. David Klinghoffer, "One Love, One Chabad Heart," *Forward*, March 31, 2006, http://www.forward.com/articles/one-love-one-chabad-heart/.

31. Correspondence with David Berger, June 28, 2007, July 3, 2007.

32. David Berger, *The Rebbe, the Messiah, and the Scandal of Orthodox Indifference* (Oxford: Littman Library of Jewish Civilization, 2001).

33. Correspondence with David Berger, June 28, 2007.

34. Correspondence with Immanuel Schochet, October 21, 2007.

35. Steven Weiss, "Conference Weighs Rebbe's Legacy," *Forward*, November 11, 2005, http://forward.com/articles/6877.

36. David Berger, "David Berger Comments on Yehuda Krinsky Letter," February 4, 2007, www.lukeford.net/blog/? = 101#more-101.

37. Fishkoff, *The Rebbe's Army*, 15–16.

38. Ibid., 267.

39. Ibid., 270.

40. Josh Richman, "A 'Cable Car' Tour of San Francisco, for the Price of a Mitzvah," *Forward*, June 27, 2007, www.forward.com/articles/11054.

8. Herculean Efforts at Synagogue Renewal

1. Sandee Brawarsky, *A History of Congregation B'nai Jeshurun, 1825–2005*, 180th anniversary benefit program book, May 24, 2005, 5.

2. Correspondence with Lawrence Hoffman, July 5, 2007.

3. Ron Wolfson, *The Spirituality of Welcoming: How to Transform Your Congregation Into a Sacred Community* (Woodstock, VT: Jewish Lights, 2006), 96.

4. "Forward 50," http://www.forward.com/forward-50/.

5. "Hipster Jews: Helping or Hurting?" *Jewsweek*, November 14, 2005, http://www.jewsweek.com/bin/en.jsp?enDispWho = Article%5Eli1905&enPage = BlankPage &enDisplay = view&enDispWhat = object&enVersion = o&enZone = Stories&.

6. IKAR Web site, http://www.ikar-la.org/index.html.

7. Michael Aushenker, "Will Friday Nights Ever Be the Same?" *Jewish Journal of Los Angeles*, May 7, 1999, http://www.jewishjournal.com/old/fnl.5.7.9.htm.

8. Sinai Temple—Evening Services, http://www.sinaitemple.org/religious/FNL. php.

9. Correspondence with David Wolpe, April 12, 2007.

10. Heather Robinson, "Profile: Meet the Rock 'n' Roll Rabbi," *Reform Judaism* 31.1 (Fall 2002): 79.

11. Correspondence with Rob Weinberg, July 27, 2007.

12. Wolfson, *The Spirituality of Welcoming*, 88.

13. Eric H. Yoffie, "Iv'du B'Simchah: Worship with Joy," *UAHC Worship Initiatives* (New York: Union of American Hebrew Congregations, 1999).

14. Chaim Stern, ed., *Gates of Prayer: The New Union Prayerbook* (New York: Central Conference of American Rabbis, 1975), 129.

15. Ibid., 147.

16. Arnold M. Eisen, "Rethinking American Judaism," David W. Belin Lecture in American Jewish Affairs, presented March 24, 1999, at the Jean and Samuel Frankel Center for Judaic Studies, University of Michigan.

17. Jack Bloom, *The Rabbi as Symbolic Exemplar: By the Power Vested in Me* (Binghamton, NY: Haworth, 2002).

18. Michael Endelman, "Turning to the Spiritual Sounds of Synagogue Life: A Book Examines the Relationship Between Ritual Music and American Jewish Identity," *Forward*, April 13, 2001, http://www.forward.com/issues/2001/01.04.13; Jeffrey A. Summit, *The Lord's Song in a Strange Land: Music and Identity in Contemporary Jewish Worship* (New York: Oxford University Press, 2000).

19. Peter Pitzele, *Our Father's Wells: A Personal Encounter with the Myths of Genesis* (San Francisco: HarperSanFrancisco, 1995).

20. "Storahtelling: Jewish Ritual Theater Revived," brochure, 2005–2006; correspondence with Amichai Lau-Lavie, March 29, 2007.

21. Jewsweek Staff, "Hipster Jews: Helping or Hurting?"

22. Hank Bordowitz, "Singing Unto God," *Reform Judaism* 30.4 (Summer 2002): 65.

23. Debbie Friedman, "Mi Sheberach," http://www.debbiefriedman.com/Mi _Shebeirach.mp3.

24. Lawrence Hoffman, *Rethinking Synagogues: A New Vocabulary for Congregational Life* (Woodstock, VT: Jewish Lights, 2006), 103.

25. Leonard Saxe and Fern Chertok, "The Kishkes, Kortex, and Kinesthetics (1, 2, 3) Principle," *Reform Judaism* 35.3 (Spring 2007): 64.

26. Correspondence with Jonathan Woocher, July 6, 2007.

27. Wolfson, *The Spirituality of Welcoming*, 52.

28. Michael Luo, "With Yoga, Comedy and Parties, Synagogues Entice Newcomers," *New York Times*, April 4, 2006, http://www.nytimes.com/2006/04/04/nyregion/ 04synagogue.html?ex = 1301803200&en = 250107fb4c3e876e&ei = 5088&partner = rssnyt&emc = rss.

29. Richard Jacobs, "Forsaking the Status Quo in Scarsdale: How We Transformed Westchester Reform Temple," *Reform Judaism* 28.47 (Summer 2000): 51–59.

30. Correspondence with Rob Weinberg, June 1, 2007.

31. "DrEAMRS Consortium Explores Alternatives in Supplementary Education," Experiment in Congregational Education Web site, http://www.eceonline.org/templates/nu.php?content=nu/dream.txt.

32. Lawrence Hoffman, "Why Congregations Need to Change," *Reform Judaism* 28.4 (Summer 2000): 49, http://reformjudaismmag.net/cgi-bin/jsearch.pl.

33. "Synagogue 3000's Purpose," http://www.synagogue3000.org/purpose.html.

34. Michael Jacobs, "Packing the Pews: Synagogue 3000 Pilots Effort to Restore Shuls to the Center of Jewish Life," *Atlanta Jewish Times*, March 9, 2007, http://jtonline.us/main.asp?SectionID = 23&SubSectionID = 58&ArticleID = 2499.

35. Ron Wolfson and Shawn Landres, "Greet and Guard on Rosh Hashanah," *Jewish Week*, September 30, 2005, www.thejewishweek.com/top/editletcontent.php3?artid = 451.

36. Ibid.

37. Sue Fishkoff, "Field of Synagogue Studies Emerges," *JTA*, November 5, 2006, www.jta.org/cgi-bin/iowa/news/article/Newfieldofsynago.html.

38. Steven M. Cohen, "Continuity Beyond Communal Walls," *Forward*, May 25, 2007, www.forward.com/articles/continuity-beyond-communal-walls/.

39. Sue Fishkoff, "Turned Off by Traditional Services, Young Jews Form New Prayer Groups," September 11, 2006, http://www.uricohen.net/aperture/Minyans_spring.pdf.

40. "The Forward 50," *Forward*, November 15, 2002, http://www.pjalliance.org/article.aspx?ID = 176&CID = 20.

41. Correspondence with Linda Lantos, August 20, 2007.

42. Correspondence with Elie Kaunfer, August 14, 2007.

43. Tobin Belzer and Donald E. Miller, "Synagogues That Get It: How Jewish Congregations Are Engaging Young Adults," *S3K Report*, number 2 (Spring 2007): 1.

44. Jennifer Siegel, "Synagogue Renewal Efforts Earn Mixed Results," *Forward*, May 13, 2005, http://www.forward.com/articles/3475/.

45. Ibid.

46. Edgar M. Bronfman, "Synagogues Must Experiment to Remain Vital in Jewish Life," *JTA*, May 8, 2007, http://jta.org/cgi-bin/iowa/news/article/20070508bronfmanoped.html.

47. Deborah Netburn, "Ticket to Shabbat: U.S. Synagogues Are Selling Sabbath Services with a Brand New Name: Synaplex," *World Jewish Digest* 3.5 (January 2006): 35.

48. Debra Nussbaum Cohen, "'Transforming' the Synagogue", *JTA*, December 28, 1999.

49. Netburn, "Ticket to Shabbat," 35–37.

50. Correspondence with Matthew Kraus, June 18, 2007.

51. Interview with Hayim Herring, April 11, 2007.

52. Correspondence with Stephen Pearce, July 7, 2002, April 22, 2007.

53. E. J. Kessler, "Rabbis Bucking for Friday Nights at the 'Synaplex': Trend Sees Practice of Holding Several Smaller Minyans Within a Synagogue," *Forward*, June 5, 1998, 2.

54. Correspondence with Neil Cooper, April 12, 2007.

55. Correspondence with Joel Levine, April 12, 2007.

56. Rafi Rank, "Rabbi's Message—Shabbat Goes Hollywood?" *Jewish Post of New York*, http://www.jewishpost.com/jp0903/jprabbi0903a.htm.

57. Synaplex @ The Temple promotional flyer, August 18, 2006.

58. Correspondence with Aryeh Rubin, October 19, 2007; www.targumshlishi.org.

59. Sidney Schwarz, *Finding a Spiritual Home: How a New Generation of Jews Can Transform the American Synagogue* (San Francisco: Jossey-Bass, 2000), 46, 233, 243, 250; correspondence with Sidney Schwarz, May 21, 2007.

Conclusion

1. Robert B. Coote, *Early Israel: A New Horizon*, (Minneapolis: Fortress, 1990), 73.

2. Simon Rawidowicz and Benjamin C.I. Ravid, eds., "Israel: The Ever-Dying People," in *State of Israel, Diaspora, and Jewish Continuity* (Hanover, VT: Brandeis University Press, 1986), 54.

3. Sylvia Barack Fishman, *Negotiating Both Sides of the Hyphen: Coalescence, Compartmentalization, and American-Jewish Values* (Cincinnati: University of Cincinnati, 1996); *Jewish Life and American Culture* (Albany: State University of New York Press, 2000).

4. Joey Kurtzman, "The End of the Jewish People," June 11, 2007, http://www.jewcy.com/dialogue/2007–06–11/joey1; "The Coming Jewish Schism" 19 June 2007, http://www.jewcy.com/dialogue/2007–06–11/joey3.

5. David Biale, "The Melting Pot and Beyond: Jews and the Politics of American Identity," in David Biale, Michael Galchinsky, and Susan Heschel, eds., *Insider/Outsider: American Jews and Multiculturalism* (Berkeley: University of California Press, 1998), 31–32.

Glossary

Agudath ha-Rabbanim: Union of Orthodox Rabbis.

Agunah: A woman whose husband cannot or will not grant her a divorce.

Al Chet: A High Holy Day prayer asking God to forgive the congregation for their sins.

Aliyah: Being called up to bless the Torah before and after each reading; alternatively, to move to Israel.

Amidah: The standing prayer which forms one of the central components of a Jewish religious service. Also called the Tefilah, the Prayer, or the Shmoneh Esreh, the eighteen benedictions.

Aramaic: A Semitic language that was spoken widely in the early centuries of the common era and was used as the primary language in the Talmud and other rabbinic texts.

Ark: The sacred space where the Torah scrolls are kept in the synagogue, usually at the front of the sanctuary. It is called aron hakodesh in Hebrew.

Ashkenazi (Ashkenazim, pl.): Those Jews who settled in Central Europe in the Middle Ages. The word Ashkenaz, which came to mean Germany in medieval Hebrew, appears in Genesis 10:3.

Atid: Meaning the future in Hebrew.

Avodah: the spiritual service of God. Originally referring to one of the sacrifices in the Temple.

Avodah zarah: Idolatry. The term literally means "foreign worship."

Baal teshuva (baalei teshuva, pl., baalot teshuva, pl. fem.): a Jewish person from a non-Orthodox background who embraces Orthodox Judaism.

Bagel: Round bread product with a hole in the middle that became known as a traditional American Jewish food item.

Barchu: The call to prayer preceding the Shema and its blessings.

Bar mitzvah: Coming of age ceremony for boys at age thirteen at which the young man is called up to read from the Torah.

Bat mitzvah: Coming of age ceremony for girls at age twelve or thirteen. The ceremony itself varies depending upon the denomination. It usually includes the reading of the Torah.

Beit din (batei din, pl.): A rabbinical court consisting of three rabbis that is required to perform conversions, divorces, and other Jewish legal processes.

Beit knesset: A house of assembly.

Beit midrash: A house of study.

Beit tefilah: A house of prayer.

Ben or shalom zachor: The ceremony held on a Friday night after the birth of a baby boy.

Bench: To pray after completing a meal.

Bimah: The pulpit or raised platform in the synagogue.

Brit: The covenant between God and Israel. The term is frequently used to refer to the circumcision ceremony. The word is pronounced, and sometimes spelled, "bris" in Ashkenazic Hebrew.

Brit bat: The covenant of a daughter ceremony. Also called Simchat Bat, Shalom Bat, and others. Brit bat or britah is an alternative version of the ceremony, which includes a physical act such as washing the baby's feet as a concrete representation of the establishment of the covenant.

Brit goral: The covenant of fate. This term was used by Rabbi Joseph B. Soloveitchik.

Brit milah: The covenant of circumcision, which is performed on all Jewish males at eight days of age.

Chabad: The Hebrew acronym for *Chochmah, Binah,* and *Da'at* meaning Wisdom, Understanding, and Knowledge. Alternatively called Lubavitch Hasidism, Chabad believes in intensive religious outreach to Jews of all backgrounds.

Challah: Braided loaf baked in preparation for the Sabbath and holy days.

Chametz: Leavened bread and other food products that are prohibited during the eight days of Passover.

Charoset: A mixture of apples, nuts, and wine that is eaten during the Passover seder as part of the evening ritual.

Chavruta: A study partner, usually for the study of Talmud.

Chavruta study: The educational methodology in a yeshiva in which two students study a text together by reading it out loud and debating each point back and forth.

Cheder: An afternoon religious school, usually referring to one established by Eastern European Jewish immigrants in the first half of the twentieth century

Cherem: A form of excommunication from the Jewish community.

Chevra Kadisha: A burial society.

Chutzpah: A Yiddish word meaning a lot of nerve.

Daf: A page of Talmud

Daven: The act of praying, usually referring to traditional prayer.

Diaspora: The dispersion of the Jews.

Dvar Torah: A brief comment on the weekly Torah portion, which is replacing formal sermons in many synagogues.

Emet Ve-Emunah: A statement of principles issued by the Conservative movement in 1988.

Etrog: A citron that is one of the four species waved on Sukkot.

Ezrat Nashim: A woman's gallery, particularly as it relates to a synagogue. The term originally referred to the courtyard of the Temple, an area where women congregated. The name was adopted by the Jewish feminist movement that emerged out of the Conservative movement in the early 1970s.

Gabai: A lay person who volunteers to perform various duties in connection with Torah reading.

Galut: Exile.

Gemara: Extensive legal debates on the contents of the Mishnah, brief rabbinic legal statements. The Mishnah and the Gemara together form the Talmud.

Gemilut hesed (gemilut hasadim, pl.): Acts of loving-kindness, social welfare.

Gelt: Money.

Gesher: Literally a bridge, this Hebrew word is frequently used as the name of an educational or religious program that attempts to bridge differences of various types.

Get (gittin, pl.): A religious document of divorce.

Haftorah: A reading chanted from one of the books of the prophets following the Torah reading in traditional synagogues.

Haggadah: The liturgy for the Passover seder.

Haimish: In Yiddish, warm and comfortable.

Hakafot: Literally meaning "going around in circles," it is the sevenfold dancing procession made with the Torah scrolls on the holiday of Simchat Torah.

Hanukkah: Eight-day festival of lights celebrating the victory of the Maccabees over the Hellenizers in the second century BCE.

Haredi: In this book, used to refer to all ultra-Orthodox Jews, as distinct from the Modern Orthodox. Technically, it refers to either "Lithuanian," non-Hasidic Jews of Ashkenazic descent, Hasidic Haredim of Ashkenazic descent, or Sephardic Haredim.

Hashkamah: An early morning worship service, usually in traditional congregations.

Hasid: A type of ultra-Orthodox Jew who follows a rebbe.

Hatafat dam brit: the drawing of a drop of blood to symbolically indicate that a circumcision is being performed to bring the man into the covenant.

Havurah (havurot, pl.): A small group of like-minded Jews, usually young and liberal leaning, who assemble for the purpose of facilitating Shabbat and holiday prayer services.

Hazan (hazanim, pl.): A cantor who chants and sings Hebrew prayers during services in the synagogue. Hazanut refers to the art of cantorial music.

Hechsher (hechsherim, pl.): A rabbinical stamp or sign indicating that food or other products have been certified as kosher by a rabbinical authority.

Heter: Rabbinic dispensation.

Hevra: Group, usually implying a close group of likeminded individuals.

Hillul Hashem: Literally the desecration of God's name. Referring to any act that brings dishonor to the name of God.

Hiloni (hilonim, pl.): Secular Jew in Israel.

Hora, or horah: Israeli folk dance.

Hoshanah Rabbah: The seventh day of the Jewish holiday of Sukkot on which worshippers circle around the sanctuary with their lulavs and etrogs while reciting hoshanahs.

Ikar: The essence, the core meaning.

Kabbalah: A form of Jewish mysticism.

Kabbalat mitzvot: Accepting the yoke of the commandments.

Kabbalat Shabbat: Service for welcoming the Sabbath.

Kaddish: Mourner's prayer for the dead.

Karaites: A medieval Jewish sect that rejected the Oral Law. A small number exist today, most of whom live in Israel. There are, however, some Karaites in California and elsewhere in the United States.

Kashrut: The Jewish dietary laws.

Kavanah (kavanot, pl.): Having intent; concentrating on a religious thought or act.

Kehillot/kehillah: Community.

Kehillah kedoshah: A holy community.

Ketubah (ketubot, pl.): A Jewish marriage contract.

Kiddush: The prayer chanted over wine to consecrate the Sabbath.

Kippah: A head covering worn by men (and now some women) to show respect for God during worship. Also called a yarmulke or skullcap.

Kittel: White ceremonial robe worn by groom or by a worshipper on the High Holy Days.

Kiruv: The bringing of people closer to Torah. The term refers to outreach efforts undertaken by Orthodox baal teshuva organizations.

Klal Yisrael: The community of Israel

Kohen (Kohanim, pl.): A priest who served in the Temple in Jerusalem.

Kollel: A yeshiva program for married men in which they receive a stipend.

Kol Nidre: The prayer annulling all vows that opens the Yom Kippur evening service.

Kosher: Ritually "fit," usually used to refer to food.

Latkes: Fried potato pancakes that are eaten on Hanukkah to remember the miracle of the oil which burned for eight days instead of one in the Temple in Jerusalem.

L'chaim: Is a toast meaning "to life" in Hebrew.

Lecha Dodi: A popular liturgical song sung as part of the Kabbalat Shabbat service recited on Friday night. The words literally mean "come my beloved," a reference to the mystical concept of the Sabbath as a bride.

Maariv Aravim: An evening blessing recited after the Shema.

Macher: Yiddish meaning "big shot," one of many words that have migrated from Yiddish into English.

Machon gevohah (mechonim gevohim, pl.): An institute for advanced Orthodox Jewish studies, frequently for women, in which the students receive a monthly stipend.

Machzor: A High Holy Day prayer book.

Madricha ruchanit: Female religious mentor in a liberal Orthodox synagogue.

Magid: a preacher or storyteller.

Mah nishtanah: the four questions traditionally asked by the youngest child present at the Passover seder.

Mamzer (mamzerim, pl.): a child born of an adulterous or incestuous union.

Mashgiach: The supervisor over Kosher food production.

Masorti: Traditional. The term is used in a general sense in Israel to refer to those Jews who are traditional-minded but not strictly observant. It has also been taken as the official Hebrew name of the Conservative movement in Israel and other countries outside the United States.

Matzah: Unleavened bread eaten during Passover.

Matzah ball: A matzah meal ball eaten in chicken soup.

Mechitza (mechitzot, pl.): The physical barrier between the men's and women's sections in Orthodox synagogues.

Melacha: Thirty-nine categories of forbidden work on the Sabbath.

Menorah: Candelabra that is lit one candle per night during Hannukah to represent the one cruse of oil left in the Temple.

Mezuzah (mezuzot, pl.): Scroll with a decorative casing placed on the door post of Jewish homes.

Midrash (midrashim, pl.): Classical rabbinic biblical interpretations dating from second to fifth centuries CE.

Midrashah (midrashot, pl.): An institute of advanced Orthodox Jewish studies for women.

Mi Sheberach: A blessing recited for the health and welfare of specific individuals. In traditional synagogues, it is read after each aliyah to the Torah, whereas in more liberal congregations Debbie Friedman's creative rendition is usually sung.

Mikveh (mikveot, pl.): A body of running water in which one is immersed or immerses in order to achieve ritual purity.

Minhag (minhagim, pl.): An accepted tradition or group of traditions.

Minyan (minyanim, pl.): A quorum of ten adult Jewish males (and now females in all non-Orthodox streams) required for public worship.

Mishnah: A compilation of brief rabbinic legal statements edited by Rabbi Judah the Prince around the year 200 CE.

Mitzvah: A commandment (in religious terms) or a good deed (in popular terminology).

Mohel (mohelim, pl.): A ritual functionary who performs circumcisions.

Neshama: The soul, or alternatively, an animating spirit.

Niddah: a Hebrew term, which literally means separation, generally considered to refer to separation from ritual impurity. In traditional Judaism, the term usually refers specifically to the regulations governing female impurity resulting from menstruation.

Nigun (nigunim, pl.): a wordless melody.

Oneg Shabbat: Literally meaning joy of Shabbat, this usually refers to the gathering after services during which refreshments are served. It can sometimes be a more extensive program including music, dance and other means of celebrating the Sabbath experience.

Oy vay: Yiddish for "Woe to me!"

Parsha, Parshat hashavua: The portion of the week, the section of the Torah read in synagogues on Saturday morning and in some congregations on Monday and Thursday mornings as well. Also called sidra.

Posek (poskim, pl.): rabbinic legal scholar with sufficient halachic expertise to make policy decisions.

Rebbe: Charismatic Hasidic rabbi.

Rebbetzin: A rabbi's wife.

Responsa (responsum, sing.): Jewish legal responses to halachic questions.

Rosh Hashanah: The Jewish New Year, which is observed by Jews around the world by attending synagogue services and undergoing a process of repentance and forgiveness.

Rosh kehila: head of community.

Seder: The ritual meal conducted on the first (and in traditional homes on the second) night of Passover.

Sephardi (Sephardim, pl.): Jews who descended from the Spanish exile of 1492.

Shalom bat: Also called simchat bat. Ceremony for welcoming a newborn female baby into the covenant.

Shammes: Ritual director.

Shealot u-teshuvot: Responsa literature.

Shechina: The dwelling presence of God, especially in the Temple in Jerusalem. It represents the feminine attributes of the presence of God.

Shechitah: The ritual of slaughtering a kosher animal for the purpose of eating.

Shema: The Shema Yisrael is the central prayer of Judaism encapsulating the religious concept of ethical monotheism. The text, which begins with the words "Hear, O Israel, Adonai is our God, Adonai is One!" is taken from Deuteronomy 6:4.

Shiksa: A derogatory Yiddish term for a female non-Jew.

Shirah b'tzibbur: Group sing-alongs.

Shiur: A Talmud lecture or lesson.

Shiva: A seven-day period of mourning following the death of a close relative.

Shlichut: Religious or national service.

Shluchim (shaliach, sing.): Religious emissaries sent by the Chabad-Lubavitch Hasidic movement around the world.

Shofar: A ram's horn that is blown one hundred times as part of the Rosh Hashanah liturgy and at the conclusion of Yom Kippur.

Shtetl: A small Jewish village in Eastern Europe.

Shul: A Yiddish term for a synagogue, almost always used to refer to a traditional congregation.

Shulchan Aruch: An authoritative code of Jewish law.

Siddur (siddurim, pl.): The Jewish prayer book.

Sidra: See parsha.

Simcha chochma: Literally the joy of wisdom, this is a new ceremony conducted for those who reach a certain age.

Smicha: Rabbinic ordination.

Sofek mamzerim: Under the presumption of being bastards because their parents did not get a kosher get before remarrying.

Taharah: The ritual of purification; the process of preparing and purifying the deceased for burial.

Taharat hamishpachah: Family purity, a euphemistic expression referring to the laws governing sexual relations between husbands and wives.

Takanah: A rabbinic enactment.

Tallit: A rectangular, fringed prayer shawl.

Talmud: The oral law that consists of the Mishnah and the Gemara. It is a vast compilation of legal discussions divided into six orders and sixty-three tractates.

Tanach: the three parts of the Hebrew Bible, including the Torah, the Prophets, and the Writings.

Tefillah: One of the central prayers of every religious service. Literally, the prayer. Also called the Shmonah Esrei, The Eighteen Benedictions, or the Amidah, the standing prayer.

Tefillin: Phylacteries. Leather boxes containing biblical verses that are worn on one's body while praying. Used primarily by Orthodox men.

Teshuvah: Repentance.

Tikkun olam: A Hebrew phrase meaning "repairing the world" or "perfecting the world," usually referring to the Jewish imperative to work for social justice.

Tisch: The table where a Hasidic rebbe ate with his disciples.

Toanot: legal advocates for women dealing with divorce cases.

Torah: The first five books of the Bible.

Torah l'shma: Jewish religious learning for its own sake, rather than for any perceived benefit.

Treif, trefe: Unkosher food.

Tsuris: Worry or sorrow.

Tum'ah: Ritual impurity

Tzaddik: A title given to those who are considered particularly righteous, specifically a spiritual master. The root of the word *tzaddik,* is *tzedek,* meaning justice or righteousness, and the term therefore refers to one who acts righteously.

Tzitzit: Ritual fringes worn by observant Jews on the corners of four-cornered garments, including the tallit (prayer shawl). In Orthodox Judaism, only men wear them, whereas in the more liberal movements they can be worn by anyone choosing to observe the mitzvah.

Tzedakah: A Hebrew word meaning charity, based on a root meaning justice.

Viddui: A High Holy Day prayer in which the congregation confesses their sins.

Wissenschaft des Judentums: The nineteenth-century German intellectual movement committed to studying Judaism scientifically.

Yamim noraim: The High Holy Days, literally the days of awe.

Yarmulke: Skull cap for men and, in the liberal movements, for women too. The yarmulke traditionally indicated humility before God. Also called kippah.

Yichus: Ancestry, family prestige.

Yiddish: A Jewish language based on German written with the Hebrew alphabet.

Yiddishkeit: Eastern European Jewish atmosphere; also used by Orthodox Jews to refer to a commitment to strict Orthodox Judaism.

Yoetzet halacha (yoatzot halacha, pl.): Female experts in Jewish law in areas directly pertinent to women.

Yom Kippur: The Day of Atonement. The central themes of this High Holy Day are atonement and repentance. Jews pray and fast from one evening to the following nightfall before the gates of heaven close and their destiny is determined.

Zionism: The political movement to establish and support a Jewish country in the historic land of Israel.

Zohar: A mystical commentary on the Torah which was attributed to Rabbi Shimon bar Yohai but actually was written by Moses de Leon and others in thirteenth-century Spain.

Index